OUTLAW TALES

of the

OLD WEST

Fifty True Stories of Desperados, Crooks, Criminals, and Bandits

EDITED BY

ERIN H. TURNER

T W O D O T ®

GUILFORD, CONNECTICUT
HELENA, MONTANA

A · T W O D O T® · B O O K

An imprint and registered trademark of Rowman & Littlefield

Distributed by NATIONAL BOOK NETWORK

Copyright © 2016 by Rowman & Littlefield

British Library Cataloguing-in-Publication Information Available

Library of Congress Cataloging-in-Publication Data Available

ISBN 978-1-4930-2328-8 (paperback)
ISBN 978-1-4930-2329-5 (e-book)

∞™ The paper used in this publication meets the minimum requirements of American National Standard for Information Sciences—Permanence of Paper for Printed Library Materials, ANSI/NISO Z39.48-1992.

Contents

MONTANA OUTLAWS

NEBRASKA OUTLAWS

NEVADA OUTLAWS

NEW MEXICO OUTLAWS

OKLAHOMA OUTLAWS

OREGON OUTLAWS

SOUTH DAKOTA OUTLAWS

TEXAS OUTLAWS

UTAH OUTLAWS

Preface

For more than twenty years, TwoDot Books has been telling the stories of the outlaws and bad guys who shaped the myth and history of the West. This collection of fifty outlaw tales includes well-knowns such as Butch Cassidy and the Sundance Kid, Frank and Jesse James, Belle Starr (and her dad), and Pancho Villa, along with a fair smattering of women, organized crime bosses, smugglers, and of course the usual suspects: highwaymen, bank and train robbers, cattle rustlers, snake-oil salesmen, and horse thieves. Men like Henry Brown and Burt Alvord worked on both sides of the law either at different times of their lives or simultaneously. Clever shyster Soapy Smith and murderer Martin Couk survived by their wits, while the outlaw careers of the dimwitted DeAutremont brothers and bigmouthed Diamondfield Jack were severely limited by their intellect, or lack thereof. Nearly everyone in these pages was motivated by greed, revenge, or a lethal mixture of the two. The most bloodthirsty of the bunch, such as the heartless (and, some might argue, soulless) Annie Cook and trigger-happy Augustine Chacón, surely had evil written into their very DNA.

In most of these stories, the bad man or woman finally gets his or her just desserts—either through due process or at the hands of their friends turned enemies—but a few were too slippery to ever get caught. Many times their comeuppance was long past due, but for some vigilante justice may have been a bit too hasty—we'll never really know, since they didn't get their day in court. There are plenty of sad endings, but these tales of lawmen and citizens who combined forces to fight crime and their wily opponents are part of our American story and well worth exploration.

ALASKA OUTLAWS

KLUTUK

The Man from the Mountain

The newspapers called him Klutuk, after the creek by which his cabin was located, up the Nushagak River near the Tikchik Lakes country. But he went by many different names. Eskimos called him "the giant" or the "man of the mountains." White trappers called him a "crazed Indian," the "mad trapper," the "wild man," or the "murderous monster." According to the *Cordova Daily Times,* Klutuk, a fur trapper of Yupik Eskimo heritage, killed as many as twenty people with an ax and a gun during a murderous career on the early twentieth-century Alaskan frontier. His death has remained shrouded in ambiguity. Various people say he eventually died of natural causes, that he finally received frontier justice, or even that he would never die. Many Eskimos believe that he is a phantom lurking in the ice fog on the frozen upper Nushagak region of southwestern Alaska. There he skulks in the moon shadows of the scraggy black spruce, waiting to pounce on the unsuspecting who stray into the territory he so jealously guards against trespass.

Territorial authorities looked for Klutuk for years. Beginning in 1919, he haunted white and Native trappers alike in the region between Cook Inlet and the Kuskokwim River. In that year he reportedly killed two Natives and then boasted he would kill more people if he wanted. "It was no different than killing a moose," Klutuk was supposedly heard to say. Natives avoided speaking of him, and whites tried to downplay what they viewed as primitive superstitions. Nevertheless, fear of Klutuk spread far and wide throughout the isolated Kuskokwim country. It crept into the minds of even the heartiest frontiersmen like the icy breath of the north wind penetrating the chinking of a log cabin. Few people, Native or white, ventured into his rugged domain. In the summer, the vast and empty land patrolled by the phantom Klutuk was full of swampy muskeg and thick with mosquitoes. Natives utilized a few seasonal fish camps along the Kuskokwim and its tributaries. White fur trappers stayed away until freeze-up. Only after the ice formed on the rivers would they enter the region in the fall. They made arrangements for pilots to fly them out, or they packed out their cache of furs before spring breakup made traveling impossible.

By 1927 rumors of Klutuk's murderous deeds had spread widely through the camps and villages along the rivers and on the coast. Trappers reported sightings and told stories of feeling hunted like an animal while working their winter traplines. At five foot four and 140 pounds, Klutuk, a man in his mid-thirties during the height of his baneful reign, was not physically intimidating in the usual sense. But as the legend grew, so too did exaggerations of his cunning, wilderness prowess, and skill in the deadly sport of hunting man. He had, after all, dispatched Andrew Kallenvik near the little fishing village of Dillingham earlier that year. This murder was no small accomplishment, for Kallenvik was no tenderfoot, but a seasoned outdoorsman with a keen eye for trouble. He was also a large and powerful man, given to legendary bouts of bad temper and fits of violence when he drank. Once, in a drunken rage, Kallenvik broke into a home and severely beat a man and woman living there.

Kallenvik was camped with his trapper partner F. F. Peterson and their guide Butch Smith, waiting for the freeze-up of the Nushagak River that fall so they could head up to their winter traplines. The men planned to trap near Klutuk's lines that season, and Klutuk was not happy about their encroachment. He came into their camp with his famous black dog. Smith had heard the stories of a lone Eskimo trapper with a black dog who had recently killed trappers Charles Anderson and Arvid Sackarson for getting too close to his territory. He warily allowed Klutuk to remain in the camp, and when the opportunity arose, he warned his partners about the nature of their fireside guest. The three hatched a plan to send word to the authorities that Klutuk was in their camp. Smith and Peterson left the next day. They told Klutuk that they had to pack supplies over to the riverbank a few miles away. The sturdy Kallenvik stayed to keep an eye on Klutuk, but he started to drink to pass the time, and perhaps to calm his nerves. What exactly happened next is difficult to say, since Klutuk allegedly was the only surviving witness.

Somehow, he got the drop on the larger Kallenvik. Perhaps the burly trapper drank too much, and with his senses dulled and his guard down, Kallenvik allowed the cunning Klutuk to make his move. Regardless, when the partners returned to camp, they found Kallenvik's lifeless body lying facedown in a coagulated pool of blood. A bloody ax that lay nearby, the large gash in the back of Kallenvik's skull, and the bullet hole in his arm told the story plainly enough. The two men needed no other details. They buried Kallenvik where he fell. Then they tracked Klutuk to a nearby slough, but there the trail turned into swamp. With few options, Smith and Peterson ended their pursuit and reported the incident to the Territorial authorities.

Tracking a man in a trackless wilderness is a thankless task. Just getting to the Kuskokwim Delta took Territorial deputy Frank Wiseman several months. He had to wait for freeze-up, for stormy seas to subside, and for a boat heading to Dillingham to pick him up. By then the trail was long cold. Finally, in January 1928, Wiseman heard rumors of a Klutuk sighting near Togiak. He caught a boat and trekked 50 hard winter miles by dogsled on what turned out to be a false trail. Territorial authorities were not pleased, but there was little the exhausted and exasperated Wiseman or anyone else could do at the time.

Gold panners and fur trappers provide Alaskan history with its most colorful and celebrated figures of the frontier era. The truth of the matter, however, is that capital investment and industrial exploitation fueled Alaskan development in the decades prior to World War II. Investment in large-scale mining was just beginning in the Kuskokwim region when Klutuk began his murderous reign. News spread by spooked trappers and Natives about the phantom of the frozen wastes threatened investor profits and slowed down the development of mineral resources in the region. Local lawmen groaned whenever rumors of Klutuk sightings materialized. Territorial officials, moved by the pressure of corporate interests, grew increasingly desperate to turn the phantom Klutuk into just another dead outlaw. The men who had to track Klutuk knew they would again be heading into a vast and empty land, chasing shadows and fighting bogs and mosquitoes or bone-chilling temperatures. No one relished the thought of hunting down the man from the mountain.

In the spring of 1928, however, Jack Aho was missing—another white trapper who had failed to show up to meet his friends at breakup. There were numerous things that could have gone wrong for Aho, but most everyone blamed Klutuk. Once again, duty called. Wiseman was soon back on the trail.

By June, Wiseman had little information to give to his superiors about the shadow he chased. He finally caught a cutter to Dillingham. On August 3, he made his way in two boats with a posse of six men. They went up the Nushagak River for 155 miles. The posse did not see a single human along the way until they made Koliganek, a small Native fish camp. At that location, Wiseman split up his party, sending one boat up the Tikchik River, while he continued up the Nushagak another 120 miles to the Chichitnok River. He went up this small tributary stream for another 30 miles. At that point, Wiseman called a halt to the pointless chase. All along their journey into the Interior they had investigated the cabins used by trappers and prospectors, including one Klutuk lived in. They found all of them abandoned, with no sign of recent human activity. In fact, with the exception of a few seasonal fish camps on the Nushagak, they saw no other sign that anyone had been in the region lately. With good reason, too; people stayed out of this boggy country in the summer months. The rivers offered the only means of travel and country subsistence, but they also teemed with grizzly bears. It was too rough to travel off the rivers and lakes, and darn scary to spend much time on the riverbanks in the brush.

After seventeen fruitless days of searching, Wiseman's posse returned to Dillingham to make a report. Territorial authorities and interested parties could do little other than accept the news that Klutuk remained on the loose and could be anywhere. Wiseman was a good lawman and tracker, and he had done his best. But how, he must have wondered, could one small search party hope to find a man who wanted to remain hidden in a trackless wilderness the size of the state of Oregon? No constituted authorities welcomed this manhunt; they all knew the hardships and the minimal expectations for success.

Nonetheless, Wiseman did not give up. Late the following winter, Wiseman found himself in the fishing village of Bethel, located at the mouth of the Kuskokwim River. There had been new sightings, mainly Eskimos reporting instances where community members said that someone had shot at them out in the bush. When something unexplained happened, increasingly, Eskimos blamed Klutuk. He began to take on a legendary status among villagers on the Kuskokwim River drainage. Klutuk was now big medicine in their worldview, a sorcerer with great powers to be respected, even feared. Although Klutuk stood no more than five foot four, the Natives began to speak of him as a giant. To this day, there are some who believe he is still alive and dangerous. He can control events and wield power over those who enter his territory.

Wiseman placed little stock in such talk. Moreover, the few credible reports that came in, Wiseman soon found out, turned out to be Native hunters mistaking villagers for animals they were hunting. Wiseman was willing to head upriver anyway to make a reconnaissance, but breakup had come early. Consequently, he found no one willing to guide him into the upper Kuskokwim wilderness at that time of the season. Wiseman returned to file another report about his failure to find the elusive Klutuk.

A federal official with the US Geological Survey, B. D. Stewart, complained publicly that Klutuk's reign of terror was now negatively impacting the development of mining in the district. This complaint came at a crucial time in the Territory's history. The Great Depression had ravaged the Territory's fragile extractive economy. Officials wanted to exploit any opportunity for development—but the phantom Klutuk discouraged their efforts to develop the mining potential on the Kuskokwim.

More men were put on the case in the early summer of 1931. One of these men, a US deputy marshal called Stanley Nichols, ventured all the way up to the headwaters of the Mulchatna River, a small tributary of the Nushagak. In a cabin there, he found the body of a man who, Nichols reported, had apparently died of natural causes. The newspaper report simply stated that Nichols identified the dead man as Klutuk. Officially, Klutuk was dead. Territorial authorities closed the Klutuk case; problem solved. Many old-timers, however, have raised questions over the years. Some believe that Klutuk's death was not natural; rather, it represented an example of frontier justice meted out by some individual or group of vigilantes. Others do not believe that the body found by Nichols was Klutuk.

Fred Hatfield was one of the nonbelievers. He told an alternate version of the demise of Klutuk based on an eyewitness account. His own, published in two different venues, created a minor literary controversy in the early 1990s. Back in the early 1930s, Hatfield had moved into the Kuskokwim region to run traplines in the winter and to fish out of Dillingham in the summer. He ended up spending some twenty years trapping in Alaska and, over time, became an old-timer. One of the early pioneers that Hatfield befriended was Butch Smith, the man hired to guide Peterson and the unfortunate Kallenvik up the Nushagak in 1928. One day in 1934, Smith took the young Hatfield under his wing and began to ask about where he planned to set his traps during the coming winter. He told Hatfield that he knew of an exceptional region that was largely untapped by trappers far up the Nushagak in the Tikchik Lakes country. Smith, an occasional prospector in the region, had built a cabin several years earlier. It was far upriver in an isolated area that teemed with fur-bearing critters. Smith painted an alluring picture for the cocky young Hatfield. Like most greenhorns, Hatfield desperately sought approval from hardened wilderness-savvy veterans. Smith appeared to be according him some respect for his frontier skills and strength. He was finally being recognized by the old-timers. He had made it; he was a heroic last frontiersman!

There was one catch, Old Butch warned: Klutuk. Not many true Alaskans were unaware of the tales of the old Eskimo phantom, but few had heard them from somebody who had direct knowledge. Smith told Hatfield about the death of Kallenvik. It would be dangerous to trap that far up the Nushagak, he warned, but then again, he must have thought the young Hatfield was ready for the challenge. Klutuk's cabin was a good 40 miles away from Smith's. The chances were good that Klutuk would never even know that Hatfield was there if he was smart and he played it safe. Hatfield boasted that he could handle Klutuk, phantom or man. That was the kind of talk that Smith expected to hear. While Hatfield was upriver, he could also check in on Smith's friend Jake Savolly, who had failed to come downriver after breakup. The tenderfoot Hatfield took Old Butch's bait. He did not seem to realize his new confidant did not want to personally go up the Nushagak to look for his lost friend. Too dangerous up there with a crazy murderer on the loose! Smith had simply played on the young Hatfield's youthful pride.

Hatfield flew in to the upper Nushagak in the fall on Matt Flensburg's plane. He dutifully checked in at the cabin of Smith's friend Jake and found that it had been abandoned for some time. There was hardly anything there at all. Tired from his travels, Hatfield lay down on Jake's cot to get some rest. Not long after, he awoke to find himself covered in shrews nibbling at his clothes and skin. He jumped off the cot in horror, brushed the little critters off, and ran outside to calm down. As his head cleared from the sleep and the fright, he caught sight of something in the brush to the backside of the cabin. It was the remains of Butch's friend, Jake Savolly. Jake's bones had been picked clean by the shrews so that they looked, Hatfield later wrote, to have been polished. The way Jake's remains were placed, with arms outstretched, gave the appearance that his body had been dragged by someone to where it lay. That someone could only have been Klutuk, Hatfield quickly concluded. That explained why there was nothing useful left at the cabin. Klutuk had killed Jake and cleaned out his cabin. Hatfield knew that Jake represented Klutuk's fifth victim, and he wisely concluded that he did not want to be number six. He made up his mind right there to hunt Klutuk down and kill him.

Hatfield's self-serving story, told more than fifty years after the fact, had the makings of a John Wayne or Clint Eastwood movie script. He ratcheted up the bravado and inflated the lead character with an epic heroism grounded firmly on frontier common sense. He became, he wrote, a hunter of man. "If you know the habits of any animal, he's easy to trap," Hatfield boldly stated; "A man isn't [any] different." Hatfield's protagonist, the young Hatfield, just had to learn the habits of his prey. It was a simple, almost natural thing for a hunter to do. Study the prey and then trap it using the knowledge gleaned from observation.

Hatfield buried Jake and then went off to find Klutuk's trapline. In the first printed version of the story, he pulled up about thirteen traps, set them off, and threw them in the snow. In the second, that number increased to twenty. He then circled all the way around Klutuk's trapline and doubled back in several places. Hatfield intended to throw Klutuk off, make him feel hunted, force him to stay put for the winter, or risk ambush anywhere at anytime. He believed that he had tied Klutuk up for the winter.

Hatfield traveled by snowshoe, a quiet and stealthier mode of travel than a noisy and unpredictable dogsled team, Klutuk's mode of travel. Hatfield surmised that Klutuk would not risk being discovered snooping around his cabin. Of course, that did not take into account the possibility that Klutuk, a man who lived off the land for extended periods, might have a pair of snowshoes somewhere!

When April came, Hatfield hopped on the plane owned by Matt Flensburg to head for Dillingham. He intentionally left behind everything except his fur pack. He was implementing a grand strategy—one that would take more than a year to accomplish. He expected Klutuk to see the plane, head for Hatfield's cabin, clean out the gear and supplies, and then lay in ambush for him upon his return the following season. Hatfield chuckled when he told his plan to Old Butch Smith in a Dillingham watering hole. Smith was upset to learn about the death of his friend Jake, and he seemed to be increasingly concerned for the safety of the cocky young greenhorn.

"Fred," Smith said, "Klutuk knows that you were there, and he is darn sure to be waiting for you to return since you left all your gear. What are you going to do?" Hatfield enjoyed hearing the frontiersman's concern. He told Smith not to worry, that he had thought everything through. He would not return to Smith's cabin, but would instead go to Harry's cabin on Rat Creek, a little stream that connected Tikchik Lake to the river bearing the same name. Klutuk would see him fly in and know that he had been had. He would have to wait cautiously another year before he could lay another trap for Hatfield. But by this time, Hatfield would finally spring his own trap on Klutuk. Hatfield asked Smith if he could get his hands on some strychnine. Just a small dose of that would be enough to put down a grizzly bear.

Matt flew Hatfield in to Rat Creek and left him at the cabin with assurances that he would return in March. This would be early enough that Klutuk would have plenty of snow on the ground to get his dog team up to Rat Creek after he saw Hatfield fly out for the summer. Hatfield did not trap much that winter; he was too scared to get out much. When he did, he constantly looked over his shoulder. Being hunted frayed his nerves some. The cold, dark, and quiet of winter close to the Arctic Circle was tough enough to bear all alone. It became another thing altogether when you knew there was a phantom nearby waiting for the chance to kill you.

Hatfield passed a long and cold trapping season, staying close to his cabin in a constant state of alert. He even brought a Swede saw, a thin-bladed implement that made virtually no noise. While cutting wood he listened for dogs that would signal the presence of Klutuk. He lived with the feeling of constantly being watched. His mind played tricks on him. One evening Hatfield heard a strange tapping at the window of the cabin. He cautiously looked in the direction of the window so as not to give notice, but nothing was there. Then, there it was again. What was that tapping? Edgar Allen Poe would know. Was he beginning to hear things? He heard the noise again. He finally discovered a mink stabbed in the head deeply by two porcupine quills. Crisis averted, he took stock of the state of his nerves.

Seven months of this torture and it was finally March. It was time to set the trap for Klutuk. Matt would fly in soon to pick up Hatfield, so everything needed to be ready. Hatfield pulled out the leather bag containing his tins of tea and sugar—a staple item that could make any bad situation in the bush seem better. He knew that Klutuk would take them if left behind. That was his plan. He pulled out the strychnine package and carefully measured out two tablespoons of sugar to every quarter-size portion of the poison. Hatfield filled up his sugar tin in this manner, carefully packed everything away in the carry bag, and hung it from a nail on the log wall.

Not long after he readied the trap, Hatfield heard Matt's plane come in. He knew Klutuk heard it too, so he wasted no time gathering up the few items that he did not plan to leave behind. It would be darn good to see another human being after that long and lonely winter. He said hello to Matt and climbed aboard. Within hours they were back in Dillingham, and soon Hatfield was out in the bay on a fishing boat to earn a grubstake for next winter on the trapline. It was odd; Hatfield had been anxious to get back to Dillingham, but now found himself impatient to get back up to the Rat Creek cabin.

After an interminably long season of fishing, it was finally time to head back to the wilderness trapline. Hatfield flew back in with Matt, said his good-byes, and then cautiously headed to the cabin. He was not sure what to expect or what he might find. The tea and sugar, along with the traps, were gone, but everything else was just as he left it! Hatfield grew more confident—he began to think that he had won. He started to scout around the cabin looking for signs, and then started on down the trail Klutuk would have taken on his dogsled. Two miles away he found Klutuk's camp. Cautiously, he crept up close, until he saw that there were no dogs. More observation revealed that the camp had been mauled by grizzly bears. They had scattered gear everywhere and ripped the tent to shreds. Still no sign of Klutuk. Where was the phantom?

Finally, he saw what was left of a human skeleton covered in torn-up shreds of winter travel clothing. "My two years of feeling hunted," Hatfield wrote, "were over." He found Klutuk's .30-30 rifle and removed the custom-made ivory sight. A trophy to be sure, but not for himself! He packed it away, buried the bones he had found, and left everything else behind. For the rest of the winter season, he trapped where he pleased and went about his days and nights without a care. When he got back to Dillingham, he proudly gave Old Butch the ivory sight. Klutuk was dead, he told the old-timer. He told no one else for fifty years, and trusted that Smith would remain true to the code of the frontier and say nothing to anyone.

Had justice been served? In the eyes of Territorial officials and the law, Klutuk had already been dead for several years before Hatfield made his first trip up the Nushagak River. When his story came out in the 1980s, it gained Hatfield quite a bit of notoriety back east, where he had gone to retire from his life on the Last Frontier. When old-timers in Alaska heard about it, they too became interested, but mainly because they did not believe Hatfield's tale. If he did poison someone, then it was an innocent man, some said. Hatfield should be arrested, they argued, because there is no statute of limitations in Alaska for murder. Others were infuriated with Hatfield because it was a commonly recognized right on the frozen Alaska frontier to make use of shelter and food when one got into trouble. Many speculated that the man Hatfield claimed to have poisoned was not Klutuk, but some poor, unsuspecting traveler who needed shelter and food.

Nothing ultimately came of these debates, but the controversy surely helped sales of Hatfield's published memoir.

Who was Klutuk? Did he really kill a score of people? How did he die? No one can answer these questions today with any certainty, and we will probably never know. But the story of Klutuk reveals elements of a way of life that has long since disappeared, along with the values and beliefs held by people on that long-ago northern frontier.

NELLIE "BLACK BEAR" BATES AND WILLIAM SCHERMEYER

It was May 1923 in Iditarod, Alaska, the time of breakup when the snow melts and the ice goes out of the rivers. It is a time of great promise and relief for the people of the Far North. Alaskans don't get too excited about spring. The famous Johnny Horton song reveals the reason for this northern indifference to the third week of March. The chorus says it all: "When it's springtime in Alaska, it's forty below." Breakup, usually in May, is the important sign of warmth that the sourdoughs wait for. After eight months of winter, the warmth of the sun returns and the trees and plants once again turn green.

For Nellie "Black Bear" Bates and her partner in crime, Bill Schermeyer, it was an especially memorable breakup season. The two stood in the empty parlor of his locked and boarded-up Iditarod Roadhouse. Schermeyer smiled nervously as he alternately peered out the window and then glanced at Black Bear. At first glance one might have thought that the leaves were popping from their buds right there in front of the two criminals, inside the roadhouse. A more thorough examination, however, would have revealed the true explanation for the apparent indoor foliage.

Black Bear was furiously working with a hot iron with an intensity one does not usually bring to such a chore. Schermeyer knew that he should stay focused on his watch, but he could not help himself; he just had to watch Black Bear. Who could resist such a view? Here was one of the most famous prostitutes of the Far Northern mining frontier standing in his roadhouse at the ironing table. There was a damp canvas sack on the floor by her side. Black Bear kept reaching down to put her hand in the sack in an intense effort to dry thousands of dollars in damp currency. The bills were hanging on the furniture and shelves and some had fallen like leaves on the floor around Black Bear. Yes, it was hard for Schermeyer to remain focused on his watch. The spring-like view inside captivated him in a way that springtime in Alaska never had.

The canvas sack had contained thirty thousand dollars in cash and had been buried in the snow some distance from the roadhouse for much of the winter. Now, with the bills dried, it was time to divide the loot, find safer and longer-term hiding places, and wait until things cooled down and it was safe to begin to use the money. Black Bear chose to use mason jars, while her accomplice went with hollowed-out batteries that he placed in flashlights. They each chose a secure and private location and then buried their shares once more.

By September, Schermeyer had grown impatient. He dug up his stashed money, pulled out a few small bills, and made some purchases of mundane supplies for the roadhouse. Then he waited to see if his actions generated any suspicion or investigation. If they did, he was prepared to claim that he had merely used some bills that recent lodgers at his roadhouse had left to pay their bill for a night's stay. When nothing came of it, he gained confidence and decided that his stay in Alaska had gone on long enough. It was time to head outside to kick up his heels while he still could.

In the fall of 1924, Schermeyer was almost seventy years old. He had never broken the law before—that is, if you don't count selling bootlegged whiskey to his roadhouse customers. But all the roadhouse operators did that; it was just a part of running that kind of establishment. It was good business. No, he had been a law-abiding Territorial citizen since his first days in the North Country in 1900, when he had arrived in Alaska to search for gold. He had moved on from the Klondike to the Fairbanks rush in 1904, and then sometime later to Kantishna, in the present-day Denali backcountry, to try his luck as a miner there. He eventually ended up in Iditarod by 1912.

Schermeyer was beginning to feel the pinch of age; hard winters put the hurt on many people's joints, causing aches and pains. He gave up on mining for gold and got into the roadhouse business during the winter months to serve dogsledders and other hearty, cold-weather travelers in need of a hot fire, a meal, and a warm bed. In the summer months he fared well growing vegetables in his greenhouse. Schermeyer was not poor by any means, but he was not getting rich either. By 1924 he felt it was time to sell out, take his legal and illegal gains, and head for warmer climes on the West Coast. He was tired of work and wanted a few years of fun before the end came.

Black Bear looked at the future differently. Although not yet a full-fledged legend of the Far North, many people in the Alaskan gold rush communities knew her personally, or had heard of her. Nellie Bates was one of thousands of women who either alone, with a spouse, or with a partner had traveled north to find fortune, to accompany men, to escape an unsatisfying existence in the States, or to take advantage of perceived opportunities.

In the traditional narratives of the gold rush era, men have dominated the focus of historians. In the popular myth, rugged male individualists confronted natural and man-made dangers in an epic quest for gold and furthering America's progress. Women, if they entered into this pageant, served mainly as exotic, or even erotic, accessories to the main storyline of hardship and struggle that came to symbolize Western American expansion. Certainly the rugged, individualistic men of the Far North lived lives worthy of note, but women represented only 10 percent of the "stampeders" who made their way to the gold fields of Alaska. Still, they took their place alongside the men and faced the same hardships and obstacles, such as the journey over the mountains to the Klondike, or the brutal reality of travel by dogsled through the Alaskan Interior at 50 below.

Contrary to the general view, not all of these women were prostitutes. Most of them found that the gold was not easy to come by, and they had to rely on their wits and work ethic to get by. Women of all ages, single or divorced, married or widowed—all those willing to meet the challenges and to work hard—often found excellent opportunities to not only get by, but to get ahead.

Experienced in cooking, sewing and washing clothing, and cleaning, women found their skills in high demand in the gold camps and towns of Alaska. Men were willing to pay top dollar for these services. Many women got their start in a restaurant or laundry and soon found themselves in a position to hang out a shingle as proprietors of their own establishments. Professional women also came north to work in offices, public and private, for newspapers, and as teachers and nurses. Women also staked claims to their own mines, bought and sold claims and real estate, and ran larger-scaled mining operations that hired laborers to do the work.

Of course, times were tough for many men and women who were lured north by the hope and promise of a better life. Oftentimes, those down on their luck found that life did not get any easier for them in the North. The popular view of fallen women, or "soiled doves," in Alaska's gold rush history seems rather romantic. In local days of commemoration in the early twenty-first century, gold rush–era prostitutes are always portrayed as good-time women, the prostitutes with hearts of gold, living a free and fun-loving life, providing companionship and love, for a price, to the lonely prospectors. In this wildly unrealistic image, the oldest profession looks innocent, fun, and lucrative. Fabulously attired women spent their time having rich and boisterous gold seekers buy them drinks in crowded bars, fight over them, and queue up to have earthy fun with them.

More recently, historians have questioned this popular view to remind us that the American frontier always comprised a complex and often tangled mix of attitudes and values. On the one hand, gold rush prostitutes are viewed with fascination, and with a tendency to emphasize the sensational and the erotic. Yet, on the other hand, modern-day prostitutes who ply their trade on the streets don't receive anywhere near the positive associations. Perhaps that is because people today can see the physical and psychological effects of this precarious existence on the faces of modern prostitutes, and in the grim statistics that underscore the reality of life on the streets: the drug and alcohol use, the violence, and the diseases, to mention a few.

Life was similar for many of the prostitutes of the gold rush era. They faced some of the grim realities of street workers in modern American cities. Prostitution was a vocation for many, but one that often encumbered their lives in ways that they neither controlled nor expected. Wide social acceptance on the frontiers of America for these women or their profession remained elusive. It certainly was not a glamorous lifestyle. Working day in and day out in a canvas tent with one dirty miner after another tended to be tedious, even monotonous, rather than fun and adventurous. Prostitutes tended to come from the poorest of frontier families; they turned to the profession at an early age and lacked educational and vocational skills. These roots in poverty and ignorance were rarely transcended by such a vocation. Prostitutes often suffered economic and social deprivation for their entire lives. Most of them earned little money, in part because they earned their living by selling services to poor working-class men. Those who did secure decent financial windfalls often lacked the knowledge or ability to successfully manage such resources. It must be remembered that these women lived on the fringes of frontier society, and often experienced violence and the capricious nature of local legal authority. In sum, the legal system tolerated them as criminals working an illegal, if "necessary," vocation.

Nellie "Black Bear" Bates was the exception to the rule, however, and her remarkable story suggests that some women *did* build lives for themselves that transcended the pit of prostitution on the frontier. Forty-year-old Nellie Bates was an old hand at the world's oldest profession in 1922. She had worked mining camps and communities in Alaska since 1901. After two decades, Black Bear, as she was affectionately known by the miners, actually accumulated some capital to show for her hard work. She also proved herself a savvy businessperson over the years and earned a reputation for grubstaking miners at fair interest rates. Black Bear also invested her earnings in profitable mining ventures. The men who knew her liked her and respected her business acumen.

Unfortunately for Black Bear, one investment in a mine on Chicken Creek had recently lost seventeen thousand dollars, a tidy sum in the early 1920s. So she was hard at work at her trade, providing "company" for the lonely miners of a little town called Flat. She hoped to raise more money to invest, or perhaps to purchase a ticket on the next steamship down the Yukon and back to the lower forty-eight states. The losses took a toll on her psychologically, and she remained unsure about whether she could muster the stamina to continue on. She realized that her youth and vitality were rapidly fading. The "sporting life" remained a young woman's game, especially on the Last Frontier, a place so primitive and rugged that just getting through a winter day could exhaust the heartiest men and women.

One day in late November 1922, the mail carrier, Bill Duffy, arrived in Flat to make his delivery and rest his dogs for the return trip to McGrath and Nenana. He visited Black Bear and the other working girls for a few days. After thinking the matter through, Black Bear asked Bill if she could ride with him on his trip. She had decided that Seattle would be a welcome relief after twenty years of darkness, cold temperatures, and hard work on the Alaskan frontier. Another working girl, Nadine Saum, took a ride as well, hoping to get to Iditarod to try her luck there for a time. When the mail-sled dog team had rested up, the three packed their things and loaded onto the sled. Nadine bundled up to ride in the sled, Nellie rode the runners, and Bill ran by their side with the gee pole to direct the dog team.

Mushing on winter trails can be a bonding experience. Temperatures often drop to 50 below. In such conditions, small groups remain dependent on each other to survive the challenges of the weather, to note the changing trail conditions, and to guard the health of the dogs. Everyone had to work together to ensure the safety of the group. This trip went off without anything unusual happening. They camped a few nights out as they made their way toward Iditarod. At night around the fire, Bill told stories. The one that Black Bear liked the most was the one that revealed the contents of the canvas mail pouch tucked away on the sled. Bill could not resist that one!

A few months earlier, Dexter Horton Bank, a Seattle concern, had mailed thirty thousand dollars in currency to a McGrath man called Thomas Atkins. The money shipped out on a steamer in early October to Seward, Alaska. From there it was placed on a steam engine and rode the rails to Nenana. Once it arrived in Nenana, postal workers placed it on the mail sled. After a few weeks spent waiting for proper trail conditions, the dog team finally mushed off to make the 250-mile trek to McGrath. While the trails were finally ready for travel in late November, the mail team—a relay team of two sets of sleds, dogs, and drivers—was delayed twenty days when an inexperienced musher lost his way and had to backtrack to find the right trail.

The mail finally got through, but once it arrived in McGrath, a new problem arose. The postmaster in McGrath did not have a key to open the mail bag. Bill Duffy, the experienced mail carrier of the relay team, found himself carrying the McGrath mail pouch with him all the way to the end of his line: Flat. Postal authorities told Duffy to hold on to the pouch until he found a postmaster with the right key to open it. The postmistress of Flat possessed the right key and opened the bag. This gave Duffy an opportunity to satisfy his curiosity about the contents of the troublesome mail bag. The Flat postmistress then instructed Duffy to drop the pouch off in McGrath on his return trip.

Imagine trying to keep that secret to yourself in the presence of two women on a lonely, frozen, and dark Alaskan trail. Duffy could not resist the temptation. So, he told Black Bear and Nadine about the saga of the canvas mail pouch, right up to the point where they entered into the story. Here he was, Duffy told them, on his way back to McGrath with a whole lot of cash.

Black Bear liked the story. In fact, she could not stop thinking about it on the trail. Maybe her efforts to escape the Far North had been a little too hasty after all?

The trio kept working the dogs and the sled on the trail, finally making Iditarod after several more days of hard work. Once there, Nadine said good-bye to them. Now it was only Nellie and Bill on the sled. They stopped 16 miles out of Iditarod at a roadhouse operated by Bill Schermeyer. Weeks earlier, Black Bear had invited friends from the surrounding districts to come wish her bon voyage on her trip to Seattle. There was a good crowd of well-wishers there to greet her, and soon the bootlegged booze began to flow and spirits began to soar.

Bill Duffy joined in on the merriment. He left the mail pouch on the sled without any concern for the large stacks of cash on board. Everyone knew each other at the party, so Duffy believed there was no need to distrust them.

The party inside Schermeyer's roadhouse raged into the long Alaskan winter night. Nellie had not been drinking as much as her friends, but kept up appearances nonetheless. She finally cornered the proprietor of the roadhouse in a quiet nook and popped a question to him. By this time, word of Bill Duffy's cargo had spread far and wide. He had told the story to several people in Flat before he'd left that community, and they had done the rest.

Indeed, Schermeyer knew what Duffy carried on his sled even before Black Bear brought it up. She simply asked Schermeyer if he was game to make some money that night. It was a vague comment, but he got the point. He smiled and answered affirmatively. That was all the two new partners in crime needed to say to each other.

The guests continued with their libations and card games into the night. Nellie used their distractions to slip away from the party for a few moments. She went outside to the barn where the dog team slept. Her heart was racing, and she looked about repeatedly to ensure that no one witnessed her actions. She quietly patted the exhausted dogs to keep them quiet. She need not have worried. After days spent with her on the trail, her presence was not enough to stir the exhausted animals from their blissful slumber.

Nellie grabbed the canvas money bag from the McGrath mail pouch and stashed it under her dress. She walked back toward the main building, but stopped at Schermeyer's fish cache, a small shed-like structure suspended by four large poles about fifteen feet off the ground. Alaskans used these structures to store food in a manner that made it accessible only to humans by a pole ladder. It was the best way to keep bears and other camp robbers out of the smoked and frozen meats.

Nellie climbed up the ladder and opened up the cache. She barely noticed the strong fish smell that wafted lazily out of the structure in the frozen air. She shoved the bag in under some fish, carefully made her way down the ladder, and went back to the roadhouse to mingle with her well-wishers. When she got inside, her heart was pounding. She was exhilarated by the ease with which she had carried out her act of theft. She made eye contact with Schermeyer. He made no response, but understood the signal.

The rest was left to him. Schermeyer's role in this heist was to take the pouch and hide it in a secure spot until the heat of the thievery died down and it was safe to use the money. Schermeyer went out to the cache after the last of the revelers had finally passed out. It was morning, but still dark near the Arctic Circle. He harnessed his dogs to a sled, grabbed the bag, and mushed his team down the trail from his roadhouse out into the frozen bush. He found a good location up on a little knoll with good drainage and buried the sack in the snow. Then he drove his dog team over the site repeatedly to remove all signs of his burial activities.

Satisfied with his work, Schermeyer noticed for the first time that day the stirrings of hunger. He got his dog team back on the trail home and then mushed them back to the roadhouse to get breakfast on the griddle before his hungover guests woke up.

That spring, at breakup, Schermeyer retrieved the money bag and stashed it close to his greenhouse operation in Iditarod. The postal investigation remained ongoing. Consequently, neither he nor Black Bear felt comfortable using any of the currency. On one occasion, Black Bear somehow discovered that a postal inspector was headed out to Schermeyer's place for an interview with the man who ran the roadhouse where the money had been lost.

Black Bear descended into a state of panic and raced out to warn her accomplice and to make sure that the money was well hidden. Schermeyer felt uneasy about the burial spot and decided that the inspector would look all over his grounds if he became the least bit suspicious. So, he moved the hiding place again, this time to his garden, where he dug a hole deep enough, he felt, to prevent discovery.

Later that September, Schermeyer dug up the money again, just in case. He was concerned that he had buried the bag too deep. If they needed to move out in a hurry during the winter, they might run into trouble breaking through the rock-hard frozen ground. This time he stuck the bag of money under a few tons of carrots in his root house. There it stayed until the next spring, when the two coconspirators decided to check on it once more.

It took them several days to find it again, but once they did, they discovered that all the bills were now wet. They spent several nerve-racking days locked in his house, ironing the bills and hanging them out to dry. All the while, Schermeyer stood guard. When that task was finally completed, the two carefully placed the bills into mason jars and dug a hole out in the field. After the thaw, Schermeyer dug up the loot one more time and buried it in the ground under his barn. The stress had finally caught up to them both. They agreed to just lay low, but that was a sentiment easier said than done for the two jumpy novice criminals. They knew in their rational minds that a little investment in time would pay great dividends later, and potentially keep them out of trouble with the law. But fear and panic kept creeping in from the more primitive parts of their brains. Somehow they remained patient for another year, until 1924.

By the summer of that year, they both felt that things had quieted down with the investigation. Schermeyer dug up the money for the last time—he had hidden it in so many different locations over the last year that he had lost count! When nothing more was heard from investigators, he grew more confident. He and Black Bear met to dry the money and divide up the spoils of their heist. Schermeyer used a few of the bills in town on some minor purchases, and then sat back for several weeks to see what, if anything, would come of it.

Nothing! Schermeyer started to make some plans. He was no longer a young man. It seemed that now was as good a time as any to finally make the great trek south to retire in the States. It seemed to him that he had spent a lifetime at heavy work in Alaska. He liquidated his assets in Iditarod and prepared to head Outside.

Right before Schermeyer took passage, Black Bear came to him once again in a fit of fear. She informed him that Bill Duffy, the mail-team driver, had become suspicious of them and had accused them of the theft. He wanted to cut a deal with them in exchange for his silence. Black Bear pleaded with the old man to cooperate with her on the deal. By this time, old Schermeyer wanted no trouble. He just wanted to get out of Alaska and live out the rest of his days in relative leisure. He agreed to give Duffy a portion of his share of the loot to keep him quiet. It was four thousand dollars' worth of insurance!

Schermeyer first traveled to Eugene, Oregon. While he resided in that small city, he ran into hard luck. An illness incapacitated him for some time. Perhaps all of the stress from the heist and trying to lie low had taken a toll on him. It had been difficult for him to sleep on many nights as his imagination and fear of discovery repeatedly got the best of him. His nerves had been about shot before he finally made his escape from the Last Frontier.

Things got so bad for him that he rented a room in Eugene and hired a private nurse. Alas, it appeared that the woman was not much of a nurse after all, but had used all her womanly charms to gain his confidence. He did regain his health, but the nurse decided to help herself to one thousand dollars in diamonds that Schermeyer had purchased with his stolen money. He took her to court and charged her with theft, but she was able to beat the charge and keep the diamonds. Easy come, easy go.

Schermeyer took the geographic cure and kept heading south all the way to San Diego, hoping to escape from his troubles, and perhaps a guilty conscience as well. There he took up with a prostitute and her friend. The three spent a great deal of time together, often crossing into Mexico to go to the track to watch the horse races on a daily basis. Before long, he discovered that those two wenches had taken money from him too.

Schermeyer decided it was time to take stock. His leisurely retirement plan had not panned out as he had expected. Indeed, he discovered that he was nearly broke. What to do, he thought, until he finally hit upon an idea. It was a long shot, but he had nothing to lose. He wrote to his former partner in crime, Black Bear, and told her of his run of bad luck with the dishonest women of the Outside World. Could she find it in her heart to take pity on an old friend and fellow Alaskan and send him a little spending money? Perhaps enough to get back on his feet, he pleaded. It would be just a loan, he added. Maybe five hundred dollars?

Black Bear had been experiencing a run of bad luck of her own. She responded to three plaintive inquiries from Schermeyer. Each time, she told him that she could not help out. Seeking to place the blame on others, Schermeyer told himself that he should have known better than to have trusted prostitutes!

Schermeyer was grieved to discover that his old accomplice had become so cold. But there was little he could do, so he decided to head for Los Angeles for a visit and to see if he could change his luck for the better. Again, things didn't work out the way he had hoped. While he was there, postal inspectors caught up with him. It would seem that he had attracted their attention when he took his former nurse to court in Oregon to try to get his diamonds back.

The story had made the local papers. The inspectors caught wind of it and began to put two and two together. They had been trying to track him down ever since. They asked him if he would speak to them and answer a few of their questions. The old man could hardly say no under the circumstances. In fact, he had grown tired of running and decided that it was time to face the consequences of his actions, own up to his part of the caper, and seek some kind of redemption and peace in his last years. More to the point, he was angry at Black Bear and agreed to testify against her!

US Marshal Lynn Smith of Fairbanks traveled to Los Angeles at government expense to accept Schermeyer's confession to the crime, arrest him, and personally supervise his return to Alaska. Smith was the marshal at Flat at the time of the heist in January 1923 and had a personal stake in the outcome of the trial against Black Bear. He also knew the Territory's star witness on a personal level. He actually liked Schermeyer and thought that it was best for him to turn Territorial witness because he would get a better deal from the government on his own charge.

Smith felt bad for the old man. Sure, he had sold bootlegged booze at his roadhouse, but he was essentially an honest businessman. The fact that Smith blamed the entire incident on Black Bear and viewed the prostitute as having coerced the old-timer into doing something he would not have ordinarily done suggested that he embraced the double standard held against women in the North, especially those involved in prostitution. Black Bear had caught Schermeyer at a weak moment, Smith believed, after she had already launched her plan, and then she kept the pressure on him. Before he knew what had really happened, the poor old guy found himself already implicated in the crime. Had he had time to sleep on her offer to be an accomplice, Smith assured himself, the old-timer surely would have steered clear of getting himself involved in such a dirty deed. Such was the view of constituted authorities in Alaska. Justice was blind, indeed!

Black Bear was put on trial in Fairbanks in early 1926. She flatly denied having anything to do with the theft. With the help of Tom Marquam, who served as legal council for the defense, Black Bear poked holes in Schermeyer's testimony, pointing out that there was absolutely no direct evidence that tied her to the crime outside of the Territorial witness, who claimed to be merely her accomplice. There was only Schermeyer's word and anecdotal evidence that Black Bear was spending more money than she earned. Just how the prosecution determined the income of a prostitute who was working in a black-market economy and illegal industry was not explained.

The toughest obstacle that the prosecution had to overcome was the statute of limitations on prosecuting theft. It was too late to do anything about Black Bear's possible connection to the initial crime of stealing the money. The only thing that the Territory could hope to get her on was taking a share of the ill-gotten loot. On that line they had no hard evidence.

It was a poorly conceived, even desperate case brought by the government. The jury was hung. But that did not stop the prosecution from bringing a new case against the defendant a few weeks later. The second time was not a charm for the government, and the jury brought back a verdict of not guilty. Officials at the Postal Service complained that the jury, comprised as it was of Alaskans, was not fit, and had allowed the defendant to get away with the crime because they did not like the government and she had not hurt anyone.

There may have been something to these suspicions. The defense attorney, Marquam, had emphasized the strength, power, and monetary resources brought to bear by the government in their case against his client. Indeed, it was an almost brutal array against Black Bear that included three Justice Department attorneys, several inspectors connected to the US Postal Service, and a small army of government agents, all carrying boxes of official documents that they claimed implicated the defendant.

Of course, it was still not a fair fight. Despite the image he created of a poor defenseless woman, the fact of the matter was that Nellie "Black Bear" Bates had many friends in Fairbanks and throughout the mining communities of the Interior. She was now living with Bill Duffy, the man who had run the postal dogsled team at the time of the theft. The two of them had been tipped off that Black Bear was going to be charged with the crime. They quickly went from Flat to Fairbanks ahead of the grand jury indictment, which would lead to her arrest and being held in jail for the duration of the trial. The two of them looked up all their old friends from her gambling and prostitution days. They reminded their friends and acquaintances that Black Bear had been a prostitute with a heart of gold who had helped out many miners who were broke or otherwise down on their luck. She had loaned money and grubstaked many of them. This little public relations campaign probably helped, given the fact that the jury would comprise people that either knew Black Bear personally or knew of her and her story.

Hers was a story that the old-timers were proud to tell. It was a story of the rugged Far Northern Frontier. And around these parts, by God, Black Bear was a true sourdough heroine. She took on a large federal bureaucracy and won fair and square in their eyes!

In the end, Schermeyer was the only one who ever served time for the crime: a year in jail. He died shortly after his sentence was over. Black Bear married Bill Duffy to become an honest woman. Many thought that he had probably been involved in the crime all along, but there was nothing to do but smile about it at that point. In the end, the government had spent several times more money than had been stolen trying to investigate the crime and then prosecute the alleged perpetrator. That thought must have stirred the heart of Black Bear as she contemplated her luck and her pluck!

JEFFERSON RANDOLPH "SOAPY" SMITH

Dictator of Skagway

An icy cold winter day on the White Pass trail could leave a man curiously thirsty for a stiff drink. And so it was for Andy McGrath, a toll road employee on the White Pass, who made his way down the trail to Skagway for some weekend fun in January 1898. He stepped up to the bar, slapped his bill down, and called for a drink. The saloon keeper, John Fay, brought him a libation and took the money. Fay, however, did not return with any change. McGrath confronted Fay about the matter, whereupon Fay unceremoniously threw him out of the saloon. Not only did he not get his due change, but McGrath also lost the drink he had ordered. A man should not receive such treatment, he told the local deputy marshal, a man called Rowan.

After Rowan heard the complaint, he told McGrath that he needed to find the doctor for his wife, who had just gone into labor. The deputy walked with McGrath to the saloon, hoping to quickly resolve the dispute, and perhaps find a doctor at the same time. This was Skagway, after all. As the two men walked into the saloon, Fay met them with a hail of gunfire, cutting them down. Rowan and McGrath fell dying to the floor.

Skagway residents soon heard the news. Townsmen responded with an uproar. Fay felt the heat immediately and sought refuge with his gambling friends. These men claimed ties to the leader of the organized criminal underworld of Skagway, a man called "Soapy" Smith. As mobs looked for Fay in the alleys, on the streets, and in the brothels and saloons, Smith put the word out on the streets that he commanded 200 gunmen in town. Anyone who tried to put a rope around Fay's neck would be shot, Smith warned.

Soapy Smith was no ordinary two-bit crime boss. He quickly moved to not only protect Fay, but also to enhance his personal reputation in town. He convinced Fay to surrender to the authorities, and then used his influence network to control the meeting called to administer justice. The men selected to guard, investigate, and serve as jurors were all Smith's men. Their names had been put forward by the editor of the local paper, the Skagway *Alaskan,* who also worked for Smith. Territorial officials eventually tried Fay in Sitka. He received a light sentence. Meanwhile, Smith milked the incident for all it was worth. He raised money to give to Rowan's widow and fatherless child, listing himself as the first contributor. Smith used the tragedy to appear as a defender of law and order, an enemy of mob justice, a benefactor to widows, a charitable businessman, and a man who could offer protection to criminals. Smith was at the top of his game, and he knew it; he was the self-proclaimed "Dictator of Skagway."

Jefferson Randolph Smith hailed from Georgia. Although no documentation exists to prove it, he claimed to be a member of a prominent Southern family. He had the ability to turn on the Southern charm and genteel behavior. Smith used these attributes to con people everywhere he set up shop. His smooth Southern drawl, highbrow turn of phrase, and calls to honor and chivalrous behavior proved irresistible. Perhaps his powers of persuasion were honed when he studied to be a Baptist preacher.

Smith left his wife and six children in St. Louis to embark on a famously checkered career. He soon achieved success as a crime boss through hard work and determination. Who knows what heights Smith might have scaled in the legitimate business world had he only loosed his endless energy and talent on legal pursuits. Smith traveled in powerful circles and knew many connected people. He carried on a substantial correspondence with many politicians, civic leaders, and powerful citizens in both North and South America.

Smith began his career as an underworld figure in Leadville, Colorado. He first arrived in that town from Texas, where he hired on to herd cattle on the famous Chisholm Trail. While in Leadville, a man called Taylor befriended him and taught him most of the tricks of the bunko trade, including the shell game and how to make a deck of cards work for you. He took these lessons and mastered them, even adding a few phrases to the American lexicon, including the "sure-thing game." Smith eventually ended up in Denver, where he exerted an extensive influence on organized criminal activity. He had his hands in all types of con and bunko operations and became known as "Soapy." (In his early con man years, he would set up a table with soap bars on it. He would then wrap bills of various denominations around the soap, followed by a white wrapper. He'd mix the bars up and offer to sell them for one dollar. He had a shill in the crowd who bought the bar containing the hundred dollar bill, at which point this whipped up the interest of the onlookers who would then buy the soap bars. Smith knew which bars had bills and which did not, and it subsequently became a famous con game and earned him the name "Soapy.") Even local barbers were in on his network. They customarily nicked the necks of wealthy men to signal Soapy's associates that they were good marks for a fleecing.

From Denver, Smith moved on to a silver-mining camp called Creede, also in Colorado. He moved his entire operation there and pushed out other small-time con men who refused to function under his control. After the silver boom died out in Creede, Smith returned to Denver until 1897. In that year the first news about the Klondike strike in Canada hit the presses. The entrepreneurial Smith knew that this gold strike presented unique opportunities, but they would only last for a short time. He needed to act before the early birds and law-and-order types established control of the region. Smith wanted to be in on the ground floor to take full advantage of the opportunities presented by the disorder of a gold rush.

This operation was to be the crown jewel of his outlaw career. Smith wanted to gain control over a boomtown—not just its underworld, but the entire town. This plan called for accomplices, and he handpicked associates based on their years of service, loyalty, and skill sets. There was the "Reverend" Charles Bowers, a longtime associate who possessed a voice like a preacher and an appearance of calm and piety that allowed him to pull off his deceptions with a flawless panache. But this peaceful facade hid a ruthless reality. Bowers had committed cold-blooded murders, including the time that he had shot and killed a policeman. Smith wanted Bowers because of his solid ability to steer new suckers to the phony businesses run by associates where they would be quickly separated from their money. Smith also respected his knowledge of secret handshakes and signals used by fraternal societies. Use of these coded communications allowed him to disarm even the most cautious victims.

Then there was Syd Dixon, the son of an extremely wealthy family who had been raised in exclusive social circles. Well educated and sophisticated, Dixon carried himself with an aristocratic air so convincing that he was able to gain the confidence of men of means and distinction. He resorted to a life of crime because he had squandered his portion of the family fortune on an opium addiction and was desperate to maintain his drug habit and playboy lifestyle.

George Wilder served the Smith gang as its advance man. He played the role of a successful businessman with an insider's knowledge of a sure-thing deal. He could quickly gain the confidence of strangers and convince them that he had a great investment opportunity.

A few other men who served as muscle and intelligence gatherers rounded out the well-seasoned company of scoundrels. They invaded Southeast Alaska as if engaged in a military operation. First, they scouted out potential sites to locate their base of operations. Skagway eventually emerged as the chosen site; it was perfect in Smith's view because it would be the main point of entry into the Klondike. And, there was almost no law and order present in the entire region. Territorial officials commissioned only a US marshal and one deputy to serve the entire Alaskan panhandle.

The Soapy Smith gang hit Skagway in 1897 like a tidal wave. By October, a matter of weeks after arrival, the gang took over control of the town's underworld. They ran con games, illegitimate business establishments, rigged gambling tables, shell games, and street thefts. Meanwhile, the leader of the gang maintained the aura of upstanding citizen and supporter of law and order. Smith never missed an opportunity to appear on the side of legal authorities. He wore conservative business attire, spoke in a soft and educated manner, and established a social network of legitimate town leaders that included journalists, clergy, and businessmen. He was known to attend Bible classes, even occasionally teaching a session. Smith even raised funds for the church and for the indigent, and he passed out twenty-dollar bills to the widowed and homeless at Christmastime.

On a voyage from Seattle to Skagway aboard the steamship *City of Seattle,* Smith saw an accident occur that killed a passenger. The drunk victim had been swinging from a hanging light fixture that broke loose from the ceiling and crashed down onto his head, crushing his skull. The vessel was overcrowded and passengers were already predisposed against the ship's captain for the unpleasant conditions. They decided to make an issue of the accident and called a meeting that resulted in a resolution to sue the shipping company for fifty thousand dollars in damages.

Smith saw his chance and took it. He rifled through the pockets of the dead man and produced an item that he claimed was his. He accused the deceased of being a thief and challenged the leaders of the meeting to continue to press their case against the shipping company in the name of the dead man, whom Smith described as a "cheat" and a "bum." This had the desired effect, cementing his reputation among the passengers as a man who championed law and order. The incident also prevented the passengers from taking over the vessel and demanding its return to Seattle, where they wanted to press their case. In short order, the ship disgorged its angry but subdued passengers in Skagway. There, Smith and his men set about to fleece as many of them as they could get their hooks into.

By early spring, a conflict for the heart and soul of Skagway raged. It pitted law-abiding folk against the operators of saloons and gambling houses and con games. Smith emerged as the leading figure of the latter. Another early arrival to the Skagway scene, a man called Frank Reid, spoke on behalf of the former. The middle-aged Reid had been one of the first men to arrive on the beach at Skagway. He had helped to lay out the town site and possessed impeccable credentials as a Western pioneer. Reid hailed from Illinois and had received a degree from the University of Michigan. He had trekked across the plains, fought Indians in Oregon, become a schoolteacher in the Willamette Valley, and then had headed to the Far North to seek his fortune in the Klondike rush. He earned a reputation as a fearless man, a good engineer and surveyor, and a dead aim with a gun. Even Soapy Smith begrudgingly respected and, some said, feared Reid.

Along with two former policemen friends, Reid organized a vigilance committee in the wake of the crime spree touched off by Smith's gang and associated outlaws. The committee called on the federal government to send troops and place the town under martial law. The troops arrived on February 8, 1898. With this backing, the vigilantes made a move to clean out Skagway of its undesirable elements. Most of the underworld figures either left town on their own to ply their schemes in other Alaskan locations (at least until the heat died down), or the committee drove them out. Most, that is, except for Soapy Smith himself. So successful had he been at cultivating a reputation of supporting law and order that many members of the vigilance committee believed he was a good and public-spirited man.

The accomplishments of the vigilantes proved to be fleeting. Smith sent most of his gang and associates away until the storm unleashed by the vigilantes had passed. They continued to rob and con stampeders on the trails and in other camps and gold towns. Soapy Smith continued to get his cut from these activities. Holdups and shootings became more frequent outside of town, and within a matter of weeks, the lawless element began to drift back into Skagway. By this time, Smith was in full control of the criminal element in the community.

By early March, it seemed that the situation had grown worse than ever. The vigilance committee met again and posted a warning:

> *WARNING*
> *A Word to the Wise should be sufficient. All con men, bunco*
> *and sure-thing men and all other objectionable characters*
> *are notified to leave Skagway and the White Pass Road*
> *immediately and remain away. Failure to comply with this*
> *warning will be followed by prompt action.*
> *Signed: The Committee of 101 [term used to demonstrate*
> *the strength in numbers of the committee]*

Rather than allow such an announcement to scare him, Smith calmly responded with subterfuge to confuse the situation. He formed his own vigilance committee, called the Committee of Law and Order. Smith moved to win over the legitimate business community to his side by presenting himself as the rightful representative of the law in Skagway. He divided the town into newcomers and established commercial interests, and warned the latter that the former had created the current troubles in order to gain economic control of the town. This charge stretched the bounds of credulity. Frank Reid, after all, had been in Skagway almost from the day it was founded, and his friends ran the initial businesses in the community. But, it was a credit to Smith's abilities of persuasion that he successfully implemented this bit of propaganda.

Smith put up posters all over town with a warning of his own:

> *The business interests of Skagway propose to put a stop to the*
> *lawless acts of many newcomers. We hereby summon all good*

citizens to a meeting at which these matters will be discussed.
Come one, come all! Immediate action will be taken for relief.
Let this be a warning to those cheechakos [newcomers to
Alaska] who are disgracing our city. The meeting will be held at
Sylvester Hall at 8 p.m. sharp.

Signed: Jefferson R. Smith, Chairman

Smith led a rousing meeting that night, pledging to devote his life to the protection of the residents of Skagway. The crowd greeted the speech enthusiastically. Strategically placed members of the Smith gang helped to whip up the frenzy of support for their leader. Smith's committee posted another proclamation stating that 317 men stood ready to respond to any action that they believed smacked of vigilantism or blackmail.

The strategy worked. Smith successfully divided and confused Skagway residents. He further complicated matters when some of his men infiltrated the rival Committee of 101. Gang members disrupted these meetings and created an air of fear, doubt, and disorder. The effort to clean up Skagway died out and the troops returned to their post at Dyea. A triumphant Smith reassumed control of the town.

By April 1898, the Smith gang included in its ranks a motley crew of thugs, thieves, con men, prostitutes, gamblers, pimps, and so on. Many were closely tied to Smith, while others simply sought out his protection and a little turf to operate their own illegal activities in exchange for a percentage. Above them all, Smith continued to portray himself as an upstanding and law-abiding town booster and father.

Smith lived by and enforced a rule within his network to never go after a full-time resident of Skagway. He even went so far as to return money to a young chief of the Skagway fire department after members of his organization robbed him. He returned the money and then trashed the men responsible for the deed. Smith occasionally staged events in which he prevented minor larcenies in public to bolster his image. These were so successful that even worried parents sought Smith's help to track down their wayward daughters. Smith also took the part of the local stevedores when they went on strike. This stance earned him the support of organized labor in Skagway. He also endeared himself to local church ministers by leading donation drives. Smith even curried public favor by leading a well-publicized campaign to adopt the stray dogs of Skagway.

While these activities appeared to be self-serving, the kingpin of Skagway developed into a complex figure that used much of his ill-gotten gains for philanthropic purposes. Indeed, despite the vast and profitable crime network that he ran, he possessed almost no personal capital or assets. For example, Smith set up a widows' fund. Oftentimes the women who received money from Smith had been made widows by Smith's own men. He provided support for men who had become paupers while in the Klondike, including men who had lost everything to Smith's crime network. Smith paid for the funerals of people who died with no money and no friends.

Such generosity paid dividends, of course. It seemed that Smith had all the major community institutions under his sway in one way or another. He had a tough group of skilled men plying their nefarious trades and bringing him his 50 percent cut. He had a broad spy network within Skagway and along the trails, sending in intelligence regarding potential victims to be fleeced and the disposition of community members and authorities. He had a team of men organizing and analyzing the data that his spies sent in. Finally, he possessed an uncanny ability to influence public perception.

By the summer of 1898, Soapy Smith appeared to reach the pinnacle of his power. He presided over a well-oiled criminal machine that reached into the Pacific Northwest states and beyond, into Central America. The criminal mastermind even led the Fourth of July parade through town and then sat next to the Territorial governor on a rostrum draped with flags. In public he appeared as the fair-minded proprietor of the best restaurant in Skagway, an oyster bar that served up the most sumptuous meals available in town. It was located in the center of Skagway's business district and had a beautiful bar made of imported mahogany. This facade, like the owner's public image, served as a screen to hide a dark underside. Behind the mahogany bar, there was a smaller parlor where Smith's nefarious associates bilked many a bright-eyed and trusting cheechako of all their money. Outside of the small parlor was a high-fenced outside yard fitted with a secret passage that allowed Smith's associates to flee without a trace. Then, once the victim realized the game that he had fallen for and gave chase, he would be dumbfounded by the empty fenced yard.

All of the ill-gotten gains for this plot went into Smith's safe, but he always stayed out of it personally. Occasionally he tried to help out a poor wayfaring victim and adopted the pretense of a great persuader of the outlaw element. He appeared to use his benevolent influence to get the thieves to return at least a portion of the loot to the victim. Smith, however, always got his 50 percent cut. He could legitimately claim that he had high expenses and took a big risk. There were bribes to dole out, attorneys to pay, and the need to silence the occasionally loud complaints from some who protested the treatment that they received in the parlor. The musclemen needed to eat too.

It was an incredible organization—or so it seemed. And yet the whole thing came crashing down after one man challenged Smith and refused to be cowed. J. D. Stewart prospected on the Yukon near Dawson in the Canadian Territory. He was not an especially bright man; in fact, to Smith's gang, he appeared ripe for the taking. Stewart came down from Dawson across the White Pass early that season to make his way back to British Columbia, where he intended to spend some of his hard-earned twenty-eight hundred dollars in gold dust. His arrival signaled good things to come for many permanent residents in Skagway. Every year Skagway commercial interests eagerly awaited the exodus of gold-laden prospectors from the Klondike. Anxious to return home, many of these prospectors took the all-river route down the Yukon and out of Alaska by steamer through St. Michael. Although it was a much easier route, it took longer. Many chose to hike out in the mid- to late summer, down to either Skagway or Dyea. The business owners of both towns looked forward to the money that would be made from these men.

In the summer of 1898, Stewart made it to Skagway, where residents warned him to steer clear of Soapy Smith's oyster bar and saloon. Smith's men nevertheless talked him into entering the back parlor to weigh his gold for exchange by an assaying company. Sure enough, Stewart handed over the gold. Before he knew what had happened, it was on its way into the backyard. He tried to give chase, but Smith's men grabbed him and pretended that he was an out-of-control drunk. They pushed him through the saloon and out the front door onto the boardwalk. When he freed himself, he tried to find the man who had run off with his poke, but found nothing.

Stewart was fleeced and angry. He went straight to the local deputy marshal and demanded the return of his gold. The marshal, under the pay of Smith, told him that he could do nothing to help Stewart. He told Stewart that he should go back to the Klondike if wanted to get more gold.

This treatment did not sit well with Stewart, and he made his way through the community spreading news of what had happened. The town quickly was in an uproar. What would happen if news got out on the trail about this incident? Would all of the prospectors choose to take the Yukon route and avoid Skagway? This was a serious situation indeed.

By mid-day on July 8, Frank Reid and his two friends had re-formed the Committee of 101 to address the situation. Stewart's fleecing had become the only topic in town, and longtime residents had taken to the streets. The situation in Skagway grew tense as rumors circulated that Dawson's gold miners were all choosing to take the Yukon River route out of the Klondike. The townspeople, who had cheered Soapy Smith at the Fourth of July festivities just a few days before, now cursed his name.

Smith's spies worked overtime to gather information about the tenor of the community. They told him that a crowd had gathered outside the storefront of a local outfitter. Smith donned his mackinaw coat, shoved his revolvers into the large front pockets, and walked down to confront them. When he arrived, he castigated them for cowardice and dared them to challenge him. They could see the outlines of the handguns in his coat. The crowd melted away and Smith returned to his restaurant.

Soon afterward, Judge Sehlbrede from Dyea arrived. He met with Smith and suggested that it might be wise to assist in the return of Stewart's gold. It would go a long way toward resolving the situation and defusing the tension. Smith angrily retorted that Stewart had lost his money fair and square through gambling, but that he would see what he could do. The judge told Smith that he would give him until four o'clock that afternoon to facilitate the return of the gold, or else . . .

The entire town had turned against Smith. None of his gang or associates had ever experienced anything quite like this turn of events. Fear gripped them. Some of his confidants saw the writing on the wall and urged him to cooperate. Many others in the crime syndicate lost their composure. A good many quietly slipped out of town.

The combination of the townsfolk and his own gang turning against him made Smith stubbornly dig in his heels. To back down now would ruin everything he had worked so hard to build. He would suffer a loss of face publicly. It would end his ability to run the town and his illicit operation. Soapy Smith had become egomaniacal. Who were these people to tell him what to do or to make threats and demands? He started to drink that afternoon. Soapy rarely touched the stuff. This resort to the bottle suggested that the stress of the situation was playing heavily on his nerves. The booze also dulled his ability to think rationally.

As the afternoon wore on and the deadline came and went, Smith continued to hit the bottle. It sustained his cocksure attitude, but something was different about the source of his courage and bluster. Before it had been genuine, but now, in the face of this, his most intense crisis, it seemed to his close associates that for the first time Soapy did not know what to do. Smith had taken to the street outside his restaurant, where he paced back and forth with a rifle in his hand. He swore out oaths of vengeance to those that sought to harm him. The man who had ruled Skagway with the velvet glove covering the iron fist stood exposed for what he was: a violent thug and criminal.

By nine o'clock that evening, the drink and strain finally got to Smith. He started to walk alone down the deserted streets of Skagway, still with his rifle in hand. Twilight descended on the quiet town as Smith made his way down to the docks. A small crowd began to gather behind him, keeping a wary distance. Smith noticed the men following him and derided them as cowards. He dared them to come closer and then demanded that they go home. None accepted his challenges, but none of them went home, either.

At the docks, Frank Reid stood with three other men. They guarded the gangway that led to the location of a vigilance committee meeting. As Smith turned a corner near the docks, about twelve of his men fell into formation behind him. It was a scene meant for Hollywood. The gang continued relentlessly toward certain trouble.

As they drew near the docks, Smith and his entourage by chance ran into John Clancy, one of Smith's partners in the restaurant. Clancy warned Smith that if he wanted to stay alive, he better turn around. Smith brushed him aside with a wave of his Colt .45 revolver. Clancy told Smith to suit himself and walked back into town.

As Smith neared the ramp to the dock, Reid spotted him. He told Smith that he would not be allowed to disrupt the meeting, and to back off. "Damn you, Reid," Smith retorted. "You're at the bottom of all my troubles. I should have got rid of you three months ago." Smith continued until the two adversaries stood face to face, neither willing to back down from the challenger. It was a moment that would have inspired a filmmaker such as Sergio Leone, who famously dramatized his spaghetti Westerns with extreme close-ups of gunfighters about to swing into action.

The two men continued to stare each other down. Suddenly, Smith raised his Winchester lever-action rifle and pointed the barrel at Reid's head. Reid responded instantly by grabbing the muzzle and forcing it down toward the ground, while at the same time reaching for his holstered revolver with the other hand. Reid now had the drop on Smith, who, panic-stricken, pleaded with Reid not to shoot. But it was too late. Reid pulled the trigger. Misfire! At that moment, Smith's rifle went off and a bullet shattered Reid's hip. Reid fell to the ground, but kept his wits about him and squeezed the trigger again just as Smith fired a second time. This time Reid's gun fired. Although Smith's second shot tore into Reid's leg, Reid's aim was true. His second shot tore through Smith's heart. The dictator of Skagway fell, dying. Reid fired a third round and hit Smith in the knee as he crumpled to the ground.

The two men lay in a pool of blood. Smith gasped once more for air and then became motionless. Reid was writhing in agony, mortally wounded. A woman screamed nearby. Reid's compatriots rushed to his assistance and raised their guns menacingly at the Smith gang. Smith's men looked at their fallen leader and then at each other. Slowly they started to back away from the scene as a mob of vigilantes began to make haste in an effort to support their wounded hero.

As they reached Reid, the bleeding man, in agony, managed to say, "I'm badly hurt, boys, but I got him first." The vigilantes gave Reid three cheers as they placed him on a stretcher. Then they followed him as he was whisked off to see a doctor. Smith's body lay all night where it fell.

In the aftermath, Reid died of his wounds. The good people of Skagway buried both Reid and Smith in the community cemetery. Reid's funeral was the largest in Skagway history, and the town placed a large monument at his grave that attested to his bravery. It read: HE GAVE HIS LIFE FOR THE HONOR OF SKAGWAY.

US and Canadian officials tracked down members of Smith's gang. There was no escape from Skagway. The authorities closed down the dock with a dragnet. The Canadian Mounties guarded the passes into the Klondike. There was nowhere to run and no place to hide. One by one, the gang members were either captured or turned themselves in. Law and order finally came to Skagway.

ARIZONA OUTLAWS

AUGUSTINE CHACÓN

Hombre Muy Malo

On the evening of December 18, 1895, Paul Becker, a clerk tending Mrs. McCormack's store in southern Arizona's Morenci Canyon, locked up and headed for the local saloon to grab a bite to eat. Three men watched him leave. Augustine Chacón, Pilar Franco, and Leonardo Morales climbed through a transom at the rear of the store looking for money, guns, food—anything they could steal.

After Becker had his fill at the saloon, he headed back to McCormack's and walked in on the bandits. They ordered him to open the store safe. Becker lunged at the trio, knocking the gun out of one man's hand and grabbing for a knife held by another. The knife sliced across Becker's hand. They again demanded he open the safe and again Becker refused. According to Becker's later statement, Augustine Chacón then plunged a knife into the clerk's side and left him for dead. The three men departed the way they came, richer by a mere twenty-five dollars and two watches. Becker staggered back to the saloon where Constable Alex Davis removed the six-inch knife still stuck in his side.

Augustine Chacón, a man who admitted to killing over fifty men during his lifetime, had struck fear around Morenci and across most of southern Arizona long before he entered McCormack's store that night. And while his life did not start out on the wrong side of the law, he ended up on the wrong end of a hangman's noose.

Born in Sonora, Mexico, around 1856, Chacón claimed he worked as a farmhand and *vaquero* (cowboy), even hiring on for a while with the Mexican border patrol. Around 1888 he arrived in Morenci and was employed as a cowboy on Ben Ollney's ranch. Over six feet tall with a mass of black hair covering his body, including a voluminous beard and mustache, he aptly fit his nickname *El Peludo* or "The Hairy One."

Chacón earned the respect of his *compadres* on the ranch and his boss found no fault with his work until the day Chacón disputed the size of his paycheck. Chacón and Ollney exchanged heated words, and at one point Ollney purportedly laughed in Chacón's face. Ollney drew his gun but was no match for the wily cowboy. When the smoke cleared, the rancher lay dying in the dust. Ranch hands raced to his rescue, but five cowboys also met their fate at the end of Chacón's gun.

Chacón hightailed it into the hills with a posse in hot pursuit. They quickly caught up with him but Chacón knew if he could not outrun a posse, he could certainly outshoot them. He killed four before a bullet smacked into his arm, yet he still managed to escape.

Chacón eluded the law for several months until someone recognized him one night near Fort Apache. Although he argued his innocence, a vigilante group threw him in jail with the promise of a sunrise hanging.

When the first streaks of dawn peered between the barred windows of Chacón's cell, only a pile of hacksaw blades and a few sawed-off bars lay where the outlaw should have been sleeping. Some said Nelly Ollney, the rancher's daughter, who never believed Chacón murdered her father, provided the tools for his escape.

For the next few years, Chacón roamed back and forth across the Mexican border, earning his living by smuggling cattle and horses from one country to the other. He was back in Morenci by early 1894.

One cold winter morning, two clerks who worked at the nearby Detroit Copper Company made camp at Eagle Creek to enjoy a few days of hunting and fishing. When a band of outlaws came upon them, the naïve young men stood no chance. The bandits were after guns and ammunition and lost little time eliminating the campers to acquire their goods. No one witnessed the killings, but Chacón was the name Morenci citizens put to the merciless slayings.

For a while Chacón hung around the town of Tombstone, where outlaws and lawmen were often one and the same. It was not long before Cochise County Sheriff John Slaughter caught wind of Chacón's presence. Determined to bring him in, Slaughter and his deputy, Burt Alvord, found their man visiting friends in a large tent just outside of town. Alvord covered the front of the canvas building, Slaughter the back.

As Chacón fled out the back way, Slaughter fired, certain he had hit his man even though the night was as black as *El Peludo*'s heart. Slaughter noticed one of the tent's guy ropes had broken and assumed Chacón had tripped over it, dying as he rolled down a ravine running behind the tent.

With lanterns lighting the way, the lawmen headed down the abyss. But the ditch gave up no body. Chacón had apparently tethered his horse below for a quick getaway. Unscathed, he probably tripped over the rope just as Slaughter fired.

By now Chacón had few places he felt safe, but for some reason he kept returning to Morenci. Then came the break-in at McCormack's store.

The day after the robbery, Constable Davis, who was also a Graham County deputy sheriff, gathered a posse and followed the bandits' trail up a steep hill to a lowly cabin. From inside Chacón watched the posse approach. Suddenly, he bolted out the door, quickly followed by Franco and Morales. Gunfire exploded across the hillside as the bandits took refuge behind a barrier of huge boulders.

Eventually, Franco and Morales got to their horses and headed down the hill. Several of the posse followed, killing both men as they fled.

The war continued at the cabin. One member of the posse, Pablo Salcido, was a friend of Chacón's from their days as cowboys. Salcido convinced Davis he could talk the bandit into surrendering. He called to Chacón, and Chacón invited him to come ahead. As Salcido advanced, Chacón stepped into the open and fired one shot, felling his friend with a bullet through the head.

A hail of gunfire rained down upon the killer. Spent shells outnumbered the scraggly wildflowers scattered across the barren hillside in the bloodiest gunfight in Morenci history.

Suddenly, an eerie silence greeted the posse. Cautiously, they approached the boulder and found Chacón dazed with a bullet in his shoulder and a streak across his chest where another bullet had grazed him. Once again, *El Peludo* would be behind bars. But for how long?

Chacón recuperated in the tiny Solomonville jail, a facility the *Arizona Republican* ridiculed as "the most insecure in the Territory." Charged with the murder of Pablo Salcido, he wasted no time proving the newspaper article correct when he casually walked out of his cell one evening. Crouching in a nearby ditch, he waited for a chance to flee out of town. His freedom was short-lived when one of the men looking for him tripped and fell into the ditch on top of him.

On May 26, 1896, Chacón appeared before the Solomonville court and pled innocent to the killing of Pablo Salcido, claiming he would never shoot his friend. Despite his plea, he was convicted of murder with the hanging set for July 24, 1896. To ensure he would still be around, he was sent to a more secure jail in Tucson until the date of his execution.

Although Chacón appealed his case to the Supreme Court of Arizona Territory, the initial verdict was upheld. A group of citizens opposing the death penalty petitioned he serve life in the Yuma Territorial Prison, but they were also turned down. One newspaper claimed there was "a sentiment in Graham County amounting almost to a religious fervour [*sic*] against hanging [Chacón]." The delays extended his execution date to June 18, 1897. As he was being escorted back to Solomonville, he managed to saw off his shackles. This escape attempt was quickly thwarted.

With only nine days to go before he faced the gallows, Chacón seemed destined, finally, to die. But The Hairy One had other ideas.

No one knew where he acquired his supply of tools. Visiting friends probably brought them in piece by piece. A band of sympathetic Mexican prisoners supposedly played guitars and sang a selection of loud, lively songs as he cut his shackles, burrowed into the thick adobe wall of his cell, and sawed through broad beams embedded in the stone walls. When he finally broke through, he tumbled into the sheriff's office and sailed out the window, once again a free man.

For the next five years, Chacón hid out on both sides of the border. More than one unsolved crime was blamed on him, and he probably did commit his share, such as the 1899 murders of two men found in their home near New River, their house ransacked and robbed by a group of marauders. The posse that trailed the culprits through Pinal County into Globe, then along the Black River, garnered a description of the men from ranchers they passed. One of the desperados certainly fit Chacón's hairy countenance, but the killers were never caught.

In the late 1800s as the country expanded westward and territories attained statehood, Arizona Territory was repeatedly rejected in its bid for sovereignty. A major detriment facing Arizona was its reputation as a place where outlaws could still find refuge. In 1901 Territorial Governor Nathan Oakes Murphy organized the Arizona Rangers to enforce territorial law. Range boss Burton C. Mossman became the first captain of this new breed of lawmen; and during his one-year term, he and his men eliminated some of the most notorious outlaw gangs in the territory. Mossman was determined to bring in Augustine Chacón before his term was up. By now Chacón only came into Arizona when he needed to sell off rustled Mexican cattle or horses.

In April 1902 Mossman recruited two lawmen-turned-outlaws to help him capture Chacón—ex-deputy constable Billy Stiles and Burt Alvord, the man who had once tried to capture Chacón with Sheriff Slaughter. Mossman promised leniency for the two scoundrels if they helped with his plot. They were to contact Chacón at his Mexican hideout and entice him to cross the border into Arizona. Since Arizona Rangers had no authority in Mexico, he needed to get Chacón into the United States before he could arrest him. Mossman posed as an escaped horse thief who desired some of rancher Colonel Bill Green's fine racehorses located just this side of the US-Mexico border, and he wanted Chacón to sell the herd in Mexico. After sending the two reprobates into Mexico to contact Chacón, Mossman waited to see if the killer would take the bait. It was four months before he heard from his accomplices.

On August 31 Stiles met Mossman in the border town of Naco and handed the ranger a note from Alvord saying Chacón agreed to a meeting, "twenty-five miles within the Mexican line at the Socorro Mountain spring."

Mossman was not eager to cross into Mexico, well aware that if a Mexican patrol caught him arresting one of its citizens within its borders, he would be in deep trouble. But he was determined to get his man, so he and Stiles headed south. Three days later they met up with Chacón and Alvord.

Chacón was a reluctant host. His eyes never left the stranger who promised him good horseflesh. As Mossman, Alvord, and Stiles drank whiskey and exchanged small talk during the night, Chacón remained sober and silent. A drizzling rain left the men cold and uncomfortable, although Mossman had the protection of his yellow rain slicker. Beneath it, his hand never left the hilt of his gun.

The next morning Mossman warmed himself by the fire. He pulled out a smoldering twig, bowed his head against the morning breeze, and breathed deeply to ignite his tightly rolled cigarette. He glanced over at Chacón, and there was no question in Mossman's mind who was in charge around this campfire. He willed himself to make no suspect moves that would anger his smoking partner. He had one chance to get the drop on Chacón. If he faltered, he would be dead before his cigarette hit the ground.

Alvord saddled his horse saying he would bring back fresh water. He had no intention of returning.

Wiping his brow, Mossman realized it was not the morning rain drizzling down his face but his own sweat. He knew he had to act now. In one swift motion, he dropped the burning twig into the fire, reached beneath his slicker, drew out his gun, and arrested one of the most notorious murderers in southern Arizona. The fact that the capture was illegal made no difference to Mossman at the moment. He ordered Stiles to disarm Chacón and handcuff him.

The three men rode out of camp with Stiles in the lead, holding the reins of Chacón's horse. Chacón traveled with a rope around his neck and his hands cuffed behind his back. Mossman brought up the rear as the outlaw parade made its way back into US territory. Mossman watched his back for any signs of a Mexican patrol. His one-year commission as an Arizona Ranger had just expired.

Once in the United States, Mossman flagged down a train heading into Benson for the final leg of the trip. Graham County Sheriff Jim Parks met the entourage with a new pair of handcuffs for Chacón and a set of leg irons.

A reporter on the train noted the haggard face of the forty-six-year-old bandit. "His form is bent and his beard is tinged with gray. To be hunted like a wild animal for five years has left its mark on the outlaw." When asked where he was going, Chacón remarked, "I suppose they are taking me to Solomonville, and I want them to kill me this time. I prefer death to a term in the penitentiary."

When the reporter asked Mossman where he had captured Chacón, Mossman replied, "On a horse pasture located about seven miles this side of the Mexican line." Mossman and Sheriff Parks must have had a few moments to get their story straight because Parks backed up the lie.

Guards were posted outside the Solomonville jail, which had undergone a few changes since Chacón's last visit, including a new steel cage made just for him. However, the same gallows built in 1897 still waited, ensconced behind a fourteen-foot adobe wall to keep out the curious. Only those with invitations would be allowed to view the hanging.

The execution was scheduled for November 14, 1902, but once again, a citizens group petitioned to commute the sentence to life imprisonment, and once again, the argument was defeated. The date of the hanging was changed to November 21—Black Friday.

Chacón ate a hearty breakfast the morning of his execution, then visited with friends Sixto Molina and Jesus Bustos. He talked to the local Catholic priest several times during the day and finished off a big lunch. He put on a new black suit and shaved off his scraggly beard, leaving his drooping mustache intact. At 2:00 p.m. he headed toward the gallows.

As he entered the courtyard, about fifty people greeted him. Even more climbed nearby trees for a glimpse of *El Peludo*. He made his way up the steps of the gallows, passing the coffin that awaited him.

Chacón asked if he could have a cup of coffee and a cigarette before dying. He turned to the crowd and spoke to them in Spanish with an interpreter repeating his words. "It is nothing but right that when one is going to die that he be given a few moments of time to quietly smoke a cigarette," he said.

For thirty minutes he rambled on, once again swearing his innocence in the shooting of Pablo Salcido. "I have a clean conscience," he said. Raising his hand, he swore, "I am sure that this hand has never been guilty of murder. I may have stolen and done a good many other things, but I am innocent of this crime."

He asked for another cup of coffee, then sat down on the gallows steps to roll another cigarette and continue his conversation with the crowd. Finally, he was silent. "Is that all?" asked the interpreter. "*Si, es todo* [Yes, that's all]," Chacón replied.

Friends climbed the gallows steps to shake his hand. He asked to be allowed to live until 3:00 p.m., but his request was denied. "It's too late now," he said. "Time to hang." He was pronounced dead sixteen minutes later. Molina and Bustos carted off the body of their friend and buried him a few miles from Solomonville in San Jose.

The *Arizona Bulletin* reported the next day, "A nervier man than Augustine Chacón never walked to the gallows, and his hanging was a melodramatic spectacle that will never be forgotten by those who witnessed it."

Many years after Chacón's hanging, historian Ryder Ridgeway claimed he was giving a speech on outlaws in Oakland, California, when he noticed a stoic-looking man in the front row. The stranger showed little emotion as Ridgeway talked until he mentioned the name Augustine Chacón. Suddenly, the man was consumed with grief, tears streaming down his face. As Ridgeway concluded his speech, the man approached and bombarded him with questions about Chacón. Ridgeway asked what interest the stranger had in the old outlaw, and the man said he was Chacón's son. His mother had kept the facts of his father's reputation from him, saying he had died in Solomonville during a smallpox epidemic. Now he knew the truth.

In 1980 some of Chacón's family members dedicated a marble gravestone to the outlaw in the San Jose cemetery. On the marker, they inscribed the following words:

AUGUSTINE CHACÓN
1861 — 1902
he lived life without fear,
he faced death without fear.
HOMBRE MUY BRAVO

Maybe he was *muy bravo* to some, but to most he was the *hombre muy malo* (very bad man).

JAMES FLEMING PARKER

"I died game and like a man."

In the dwindling twilight, James Fleming Parker stumbled along the snow-slick trail of Diamond Creek Canyon near the foot of the majestic Grand Canyon. The chasm held nothing but a deep abyss from which he would never return if his foot slipped on the treacherous path. The small caves that dotted the sheer walls held other terrors. Mountain lions and black bears made their homes along these steep parapets, and Parker certainly did not want to spoil their sleep as he balanced gingerly on the precipice.

But what lay behind him was even more worrisome. A posse had been on his trail for days; he was exhausted and hungry. Traveling by foot since no horse could keep its footing on the rugged prominences, he had even walked through ice-encrusted waters to elude the persistent lawmen. As he crawled beneath a sheltering boulder, he dared not light a fire to warm his shivering, starving body. He found a flat stone and laid his head on the makeshift pillow. Parker knew he had made this cold, hard bed himself, and now he had to lie in it.

That snowy night in February 1897 was not the first time Parker had run afoul of the law. From his first breath in 1865, he was doomed to a life of hardship and trouble. At the age of fifteen, after his mother had died in childbirth and his father committed suicide, he was sentenced to California's San Quentin Penitentiary for stealing a steer.

Upon his release the teenager drifted into Arizona Territory and worked as a cowboy in the Prescott area. He became close friends with another ranch hand, George Ruffner, who would figure prominently in Parker's life and death.

Parker was an excellent wrangler. He and Ruffner participated in the July 4, 1888, Prescott rodeo, an event the town claims to be the first rodeo in history.

Parker never stayed in one place long. He returned to California and once again landed in San Quentin for stealing a farmer's wheat supply. Originally sentenced to five years, he was released on a technicality after serving only nine months. By 1895 he was back in Arizona working for Charlie "Hog-Eye" Miller at the Hat Ranch near Williams, Arizona, a town made up of lean-to shacks, one church, and about thirty saloons.

Parker had been at the Hat Ranch just a few months when horses and cattle began disappearing around northern Arizona at an alarming rate. A breeder who hired Parker to break a band of wild horses soon discovered several of his herd missing, but he did not initially suspect the good-looking, personable young man. However, after Parker started hanging out with Abe Thompson and his gang, known cattle and horse rustlers, the breeder suspected his hired hand of instigating the theft.

Abe Thompson and his men roamed northern Arizona pilfering cattle and horses, then driving them to market in southern Nevada. When more than forty horses turned up missing from a loading pen near Seligman, Thompson's gang was immediately suspected of the heist. Although a posse caught two of the rustlers, the rest of the gang escaped, riding into their almost unapproachable hideout in Robber's Roost, a canyon surrounded by towering walls and treacherous trails that lay near the confluence of Diamond Creek with the Colorado River.

Parker continued to remain relatively free of the law even though his name was often associated with missing livestock. In 1896 he went to work for Tom Wagner on the Bar Cross Ranch, near Williams, and had an opportunity to show his more compassionate side when Wagner got caught between a calf he had roped to brand and its irate mother. As the bovine took off after him and with only one direction to run, Wagner was heading straight toward a cliff when Parker rode up and lassoed the cow, saving Wagner from certain death.

Parker eventually became the undisputed leader of the Thompson gang. He preferred rustling horses over cattle, as they were easier to move about and did not complain as loudly. Yet he was looking for even more excitement and much more money.

Trains had been running through Prescott since 1887 carrying gold bullion out of California to wealthy eastern investors. Parker had no love of locomotion, particularly after a train hit two of his own horses and he received a mere pittance from the railroad for his loss. He decided to hit up one of the trains to get his fair settlement. He was not at all concerned about an 1888 law that made train robbery a capital offense punishable by hanging.

He set about determining when gold was scheduled to be shipped through Arizona on the Atlantic & Pacific Railroad and soon learned a healthy amount of bullion would be transported on the eastbound train February 8, 1897. The train would have to slow almost to a crawl as it struggled up a steep grade and maneuvered a sharp curve at Rock Cut, about halfway between Peach Springs and Nelson, small whistle stops along Arizona's northern frontier.

Parker rode into Peach Springs, sold his horse, and bought a one-way ticket to Barstow, telling everyone he had obtained work in California. When he climbed aboard the westbound train, he carried only his saddle, a bedroll, and his guns.

As the train pulled into Barstow, Parker got off, turned around, and boarded an eastbound commuter for southern Nevada. From there he acquired a horse and made his way back into Arizona. He took only one accomplice with him as he headed for Rock Cut, a man named Williams or Wilson whose true identity was never known.

On the night of February 8, the two men tethered their horses behind a small thicket along the tracks, the fire from copious cigarettes their only warmth. As the train slowed at the curve, Parker grabbed the ladder, jumped aboard the locomotive, leveled his gun on the engineer and fireman, and ordered them to stop the train. His partner was to uncouple the engine and express car, then fire two shots alerting Parker to move the two cars away from the rest of the train. They would unload the gold from the express car and be on their way. When Parker heard the signal, he commanded the engineer to move the locomotive and second car a few miles down the tracks.

He tied up the engineer and fireman and climbed into what he thought was the express car. On this train, however, the mail car had been coupled to the locomotive instead of the expected express car loaded with gold. Parker made the best of the situation and rifled through the mail looking for anything of value. He got away with about five dollars.

When the train made its unexpected stop, both the Wells Fargo agent and mail clerk knew something was up. With guns drawn they cautiously made their way to the front of the train where they spotted the second outlaw uncoupling the cars. The two shots Parker heard were those that killed his accomplice.

After his colleague failed to appear, Parker untied the engineer and fireman and instructed them to take the locomotive back down the track, couple the cars together, and get out of there. He watched as the train passed by and stayed nearby until morning. At dawn's light the only sign of his partner was blood on the tracks. Parker took off for Robber's Roost.

When the robbery was reported in Peach Springs, George Ruffner, who was now the Yavapai County sheriff, along with Coconino County Sheriff Ralph Cameron and Mohave County Sheriff Bill Lake, plus a handful of deputies and Indian trackers, took up the search for the lone train robber.

For days the posse stayed close on Parker's trail, even following the circles he rode in to confuse them. Eventually the path became more rigorous and the temperature soon dropped below freezing. When fresh snow eliminated all traces of Parker's whereabouts, the posse finally quit. Parker watched the men ride out of the canyon toward town.

The outlaw was also suffering from the elements, however. To keep his feet from freezing, he walked rather than rode his horse. At some point he removed his boots and wrapped clothing around his feet, maybe after fording Diamond

Creek. He slept in caves with a rock for his pillow. Yet as cold as he was, he believed he had escaped unscathed.

On February 22, back on the trail with fresh horses, the posse camped in a side canyon that emptied into Diamond Creek. A couple of deputies scouring for firewood came upon a tethered horse, its hoof prints matching those they had been following. One of the men stayed behind while the other reported back to camp. Soon a whistling Parker came strolling up the creek bed, his Winchester rifle casually draped across his shoulder. The deputy wasted no time making his presence, and his gun, known to the train robber. The outlaw gave up without incident.

Parker was incarcerated in Prescott and charged with train robbery. He shared a cell with accused forger Lewis C. Miller and Cornelia Sarata (sometimes spelled Asarta), arrested for assault. As always, Parker soon tired of his surroundings and desired a new location. On May 9, 1897, he escaped along with Miller and Sarata. If he had stayed in jail, he might have received a fairly light sentence since his bounty from the train robbery was so small. But when he made his bid for freedom, things did not go well.

The warm spring day afforded no breeze through the stifling jail. The prisoners demanded water. Jailer Robert Meador allowed Sarata, a trustee, to fetch a couple of buckets to quench their thirsts. Returning with full water buckets, Sarata stood behind Meador as the jailer unlocked the cell door. Parker rammed the door into Meador's face. Sarata wrestled him to the ground as Parker grabbed the heavy ring of jail keys and slugged Meador over the head.

Parker ran into the next room and grabbed a handful of weapons. He was almost to the front door when Assistant County Attorney Lee Norris, hearing Meador's cries, dashed down the stairs to see what the ruckus was about. As soon as he saw Parker, Norris turned in retreat, but Parker had no intention of letting the attorney sound an alarm. The bullet hit Norris square in the back. He lingered through the night but died before dawn. Norris had just asked his sweetheart to marry him.

Parker, Sarata, and Miller raced to a livery stable across from the jail. Parker was a connoisseur of good horseflesh, having once asserted, "They'll hang you just as high for stealin' a sorry hoss as for the best." He needed only an instant to spot the finest horse in the stable, a pure white beauty considered the fastest steed in the territory. Sure-Shot belonged to his old pal Sheriff Ruffner. Parker jumped aboard Sure-Shot while Miller and Sarata grabbed another horse and rode double as the trio hightailed it out of town.

About 150 men set out after the escaped prisoners. Ruffner, who was out of town when the jailbreak occurred, caught up with the posse at Lynx Creek, where they had cornered the three desperados. Shots rang out as the two sides squared off. Miller suddenly fell from the horse he shared with Sarata. Parker plucked Miller from the ground and onto Sure-Shot as he fled from the battle.

Some sources claim Jailer Meador fired three shots as the men fled their cells, one bullet hitting Sarata. Others believe Sarata was wounded at Lynx Creek. Whatever shape he was in, as Miller climbed aboard Sure-Shot, Sarata rode off, never to be seen again.

Parker and Miller raced across the valley with the posse and a team of bloodhounds in hot pursuit. Eventually, the two men parted ways with Miller heading toward Jerome on foot and nursing a wound he received either at the hands of Jailer Meador or at the Lynx Creek skirmish. Nine days later he gave himself up. Parker, however, was in no mood to return to the Prescott jail.

"Parker, the train robber and murderer, with a pack of bloodhounds and officers of the law on his trail, has baffled his pursuers and no doubt is safe from pursuit in the wilds of a country no one is more familiar with than he," bemoaned one May 16 newspaper article. "The fox is smarter than the hounds."

Parker made good time heading back to Robber's Roost, his old haunt. But Sheriff Ruffner was determined not to let the murderer and horse thief get away, particularly on his prize mount. He put up one thousand dollars of his own money for Parker's capture, bringing the total on the outlaw's head to four thousand dollars. The two men, who knew each other so well from their days as cowboys, stayed almost within shooting distance of each other, but Parker knew the terrain better and continually eluded his adversary.

He even had time for a little tomfoolery. Ruffner came across a piece of paper Parker had placed conspicuously on the trail. "A reward of $1,000 is offered by the undersigned for Sheriff Ruffner dead or alive," the note read, "— dead preferred."

Parker hid out with a band of sheepmen who obliterated his tracks by herding their flock across his path. The sheepmen had no use for lawmen, who often gave them trouble.

As he made his way toward Robber's Roost, Parker happened upon an empty ranch house. He took time to reshod Sure-Shot, putting the horse's shoes on backwards and riding along the river bottom for several miles to confuse the posse before properly replacing the horse's shoes.

Tom Wagner, the man who owed his life to Parker, found one of his best horses missing one day. In its place stood a very tuckered-out Sure-Shot. With his proclivity for good horseflesh, Parker soon abandoned Wagner's horse and acquired another from a livery stable in Williams.

Parker's trail eventually led to Hog-Eye Miller's Ranch, a place he was still welcome. When the bloodhounds picked up his scent, he headed into the Bill Williams Mountains, a tough ride for any man, horse, or dog over jagged granite rocks and loose shale. As the posse followed, the hounds' paws were soon torn and bleeding as they scrambled through the rough terrain, forcing the posse to return to town.

The next morning, sporting booties on their feet, the dogs picked up the scent again, but within a short time they began sneezing and howling. Parker had sprinkled pepper along the trail.

On May 23 two Navajos spotted Parker camping near the Little Colorado River and reported their discovery to Samuel S. Preston, proprietor of a local trading post. Preston notified Sheriff Cameron in Flagstaff, who immediately telegraphed Sheriff Ruffner in Prescott.

Not waiting for Ruffner to join them, Preston, Cameron, and about ten Navajo trackers headed out to find their prey. Just before daylight on May 26, the posse crept into Parker's camp as his fire smoldered and his horse snorted nervously in the predawn air. When one of the Indians fired a shot, Parker awoke with a start, a dozen guns aimed at his head.

With the outlaw in tow, the men started for Flagstaff, camping for the night near the Little Colorado River. Never one to give up when the odds looked decidedly against him, Parker strategized he would grab one of the tracker's guns and escape into the surrounding heavy brush. He was just about to make his move when Ruffner rode into camp to join the posse. Parker knew he stood no chance of eluding his old buddy.

He was placed in the Flagstaff jail where Lewis Miller was already occupying a cell. Not willing to take his eyes off his nemesis, Ruffner spent the night on a cot outside Parker's cell.

The next morning, with shackles on their feet, Parker and Miller hobbled their way to the train station for the ride into Prescott.

Just outside the tiny town of Whipple, the train made an unscheduled stop and Ruffner hustled the two outlaws off the train and into a waiting wagon. He had been warned that a lynch mob was forming at the Prescott depot so he ordered his prisoners be taken directly to the courthouse, determined they would arrive with their heads intact.

Ruffner's information was not quite accurate. About two hundred men were waiting in Prescott, but they were at the courthouse, not the train station. When Ruffner pulled up, Miller panicked. "My God, they're coming to hang us," he cried. Parker was more philosophical. "Try to have a little courage," he told Miller. "They can only hang you once." Ruffner, with his twin-barreled shotgun loaded and aimed, stoically told the crowd to go home.

On June 15, 1897, Parker was tried for the murder of Lee Norris. It took only three days to find him guilty. He was never charged with the train robbery.

Miller was given a life sentence as an accessory in Norris's murder. He served ten years in Yuma Territorial Prison and was released.

Parker's hanging was scheduled for Friday, August 13, but legal delays and appeals postponed the execution until June 3, 1898.

Supposedly acquiring religion while awaiting his fate, Parker was baptized into the Catholic faith just days before his hanging. On the eve of his last day on earth, however, when Ruffner asked if he had any last requests, the condemned man purportedly requested a visit from Flossie, one of the girls on Whiskey Row.

The morning of the hanging, Ruffner read Parker the death warrant and escorted him to the scaffold. Given the chance to speak, Parker replied, "I claim that I am getting something that ain't due me, but I guess every man who is about to be hanged says the same thing, so that don't cut no figure; whenever the people says I must go, I am one who can go and make no kick."

As the black hood was placed over his head, he asked it be removed so he could shake hands with everyone on the scaffold. When he got to the jailer, he gave him a message for the other prisoners. "[T]ell the boys that I died game and like a man," he said.

He requested his old friend, George Ruffner, replace the hood. As he did so, Ruffner sprang the trap that sent Parker to his death.

James Fleming Parker was taken to potter's field for burial. Sheriff George Ruffner drove the hearse.

ALBERT WRIGHT "BURT" ALVORD

Bandit with a Badge

On the evening of September 9, 1899, Willcox, Arizona, Constable Burt Alvord, who was also a deputy sheriff for Cochise County, surveyed the poker hand in front of him and ordered another round of drinks at Schwertner's Saloon. He enjoyed hanging out with Willcox's local boys, even if the cards in front of him were not profitable tonight. His pleasant evening was suddenly disrupted when a messenger burst through the saloon door—bandits had robbed the Southern Pacific train at Cochise Station! Alvord jumped up, his six-foot frame towering above the gathering crowd. Visibly upset that someone had moved in on his territory, he immediately rounded up a posse and headed to the crime scene.

His two deputies, Billy Stiles and Bill Downing, joined the posse at Cochise Station. He ordered Stiles to take some men and head north, and Downing to take the southern route. Alvord led a third group toward the Chiricahua Mountains. The bandits had been clever though. They had followed a rock-hard riverbed, exhausted of rain for months, leaving few hoof prints to follow. Alvord finally ordered the men back to town without finding any trace of the robbers.

Speculation grew as to who could have masterminded such a successful robbery. Almost a year passed before Willcox's own constable, the tall, sometimes ruthless but fun-loving Albert Wright "Burt" Alvord was fingered as ringleader of a group of men who straddled both sides of the law.

Alvord certainly started out on the right side of justice. His father, after bringing the family from California to Tombstone in 1880, often served as the town's justice of the peace. Born Albert Wright Alvord in Susanville, California, on September 11, 1867, Alvord was a young teen when he arrived in Tombstone. He may have witnessed the O. K. Corral gunfight on October 26, 1881, as he sometimes worked at the corral, sweeping out stables, tending horses, and making repairs.

Alvord received most of his education on the streets of Tombstone. He could shoot billiards with the best of the cowboys, and his whittling was of expert quality. He loved to play practical jokes and often resolved differences from his pranks with his fists, sometimes a gun. He particularly enjoyed a good bar fight.

In 1886 Cochise County Sheriff John H. Slaughter enlisted Alvord as deputy sheriff. Slaughter knew the twenty-year-old could handle himself with a gun and often acted on instinct. Frequently, the two lawmen surprised sleeping bandits by shucking their boots before sneaking into enemy camps. Although careful to note that they warned suspected culprits to surrender before firing, and insisting the men almost always reached for their guns, Slaughter and Alvord brought in few live prisoners.

Alvord earned a reputation as a hard-riding, quick-shooting lawman. He took part in such notable events as the search for suspects in the 1889 Wham Paymaster Robbery and the attempted capture of notorious killer Augustine Chacón, one of the most feared desperados in Arizona Territory.

Alvord discovered that hunting down outlaws sometimes brought lucrative profits. After killing a horse thief, he confiscated the bandit's cartridge/money belt, including five hundred dollars in gold. Sometimes he rode with another illegal equine collector, Eduardo Lopez, stealing Papago ponies and selling them for about ten dollars each. Sheriff Slaughter usually ignored his deputy's indiscretions.

Alvord served as deputy to several sheriffs after John Slaughter. "He was not one to mess with," according to historian Don Chaput, "but good to have around if force was a consideration." He knew the surrounding terrain as well as he knew how much whiskey was behind the bar. If things got out of hand during one of his practical jokes, the sheriff at the time was inclined to look the other way and let him have his fun.

He almost got himself killed in 1890 when he and Biddy Doyle played one prank too close to the vest. After fixing a wrestling match, the two men high-tailed it out of Bisbee with the money purse and an angry mob close behind. Another time he and Max Marks, after enjoying a lengthy session in a Bisbee saloon, telegraphed the *Tombstone Epitaph* that the "bodies of Marks and Alvord will arrive this afternoon." Two coffins waited in somber silence outside the O. K. Corral stage stop. As passengers departed the stage, so did Alvord and Marks. "Sure our bodies arrived," they said. "We never go out without 'em."

In 1894 gold was discovered in the tiny town of Pearce, about twenty miles east of Tombstone. With the mines came saloons, dance halls, and unruly miners hell-bent on having a good time. In 1896 Alvord became deputy constable of Pearce, and before long the little community was as peaceful as a cow pasture. He married Lola Ochoa and bought a house in town and a ranch in the Dragoon Mountains. For a while his days straddling both sides of the law lay behind him.

Alvord's reputation for cleaning up towns spread. In June 1897 he was asked to take on the job of deputy constable at Willcox. A month later Willcox's constable resigned, and Alvord took over the position.

While Pearce's problems stemmed from celebrating miners, Willcox entertained tough-riding cowboys. On one occasion a bunch of Friday-night buckaroos caught Alvord and his deputies off guard at Kasper Hauser's saloon. As they locked the lawmen in the basement for the night, the entertainment escalated upstairs.

The next morning cowboy Billy King let Alvord out and apologized for his part in the prank. King even offered to buy Alvord a new hat since his was demolished in the night's revelry. Alvord rubbed his shiny bald head, and, although somewhat aggravated the joke was on him this time, he slapped King on the back and escorted him out the saloon door. Shots rang out. Alvord returned to the saloon alone, gun in hand, claiming he killed King in self-defense. No charges were filed against Willcox's tough new constable.

In early 1899 Cochise County Sheriff Scott White again made Alvord a deputy. Between his constable job in Willcox and his job as Cochise County deputy sheriff, Alvord enjoyed authority across most of southeastern Arizona and acquired as many enemies as he did friends. To protect his back, he made Billy Stiles his deputy in Willcox, and sometimes enlisted the help of Bill Downing, a man of questionable background, and Matt Burts, a barfly.

Alvord managed Willcox so well, he was spending more of his time in local saloons rather than hunting down outlaws. With little money to spend (lawmen made paltry salaries), he devised a scheme to rob the Southern Pacific train at Cochise Station.

Alvord figured the payroll for the Pearce mines should be on board the westbound Southern Pacific train the night of September 9, 1899. He knew the engine had to slow to a crawl as it climbed the steep grade outside Cochise Station, just a few miles from Willcox. It was the perfect spot for a holdup. He had no trouble convincing his three deputies—Stiles, Downing, and Burts—to perform the heist.

Alvord and his deputies broke into a local mercantile to obtain the dynamite they needed. They struck a nearby mining camp to stock up on explosive caps and fuses. Downing supplied the horses. They were ready.

The train ascended the hill and let out one final exhaustive sigh of steam as it came to a stop beneath the water tank. As engineer C. A. Richardson readied the powerful machine to take on nourishment, he was suddenly facing the wrong end of a six-gun. Burts ordered Richardson and the fireman to uncouple the engine and move the mail and express cars away from the rest of the train toward a cluster of desert brush. Stiles disarmed the mail clerk and Wells Fargo agent.

Down the track Downing emerged from the bushes and ordered Richardson to take the engine several hundred yards away from the mail and express cars. The men placed a thundering amount of dynamite in the two cars, set the charge, and ducked for cover. The cars exploded hundreds of feet in the air with cash, gold coins, and jewelry blowing across the desert, creating a bountiful rainfall of wealth. The bandits quickly gathered the loot, jumped on horses secreted in the brush, and rode hard for parts unknown.

Meanwhile, Burt Alvord played poker in a Willcox saloon.

Even today, no one agrees how much money and gold was on the train; some figures ran as high as eighty thousand dollars. Since the Pearce payroll was on an earlier train, chances are the men realized much less than they anticipated. It was later determined that Alvord distributed a small portion of the loot to his accomplices, but most of it was never found.

Feeling flush after his first victory at robbing trains, Alvord struck again. This time, the scheme was a little more complicated, but the stakes just as lucrative. As before, he would take no role in the actual robbery, showing himself around town while the action happened far from his presence.

Alvord enlisted Stiles to waylay Wells Fargo agent Jeff Milton in Nogales. He did not want Milton on board the targeted train out of Nogales to Benson. Milton was a crack shot, and no savvy outlaw dared challenge him. At the last minute, however, Milton was called to replace the scheduled agent. He forgot to tell Stiles, who was waiting for him in Nogales.

The night of February 14, 1900, was as dark as a gunslinger's soul. Five men huddled against the cold deep in the Dragoon Mountains. Three of them, Bob Brown and brothers George and Lewis Owens, were ranch hands. Bravo Juan Yoas and Three-Fingered Jack Dunlap already had accumulated criminal records. Only the promise of a train full of gold kept the men warm.

Burt Alvord was at his usual post—lining up drinks at a Benson saloon.

On the morning of February 15, the New Mexico & Arizona train left Nogales as scheduled, except for the presence of Jeff Milton instead of the regular Wells Fargo agent. It made one scheduled stop in Fairbank, about twenty miles south of Benson, arriving near sundown. As passengers filled the platform, no one paid attention to the five men mingling with the crowd.

Bob Brown and Lewis Owens entered the engine's cab without incident, disarming the engineer and fireman.

When Jeff Milton opened the express car doors, no one was more surprised to see him than the three desperados who had made their way to the front of the crowd. But with little hesitation, they demanded Milton drop his weapon. Milton hesitated to shoot into the crowd until one of the bandits fired a shot through the agent's hat. In one quick move, Milton grabbed his rifle and opened fire.

The bandits blasted the rail car, wounding Milton as they boarded. They searched frantically for the keys to the safe. Milton, barely conscious, managed to grab his shotgun and hit Dunlap full force; some of the buckshot ended up in Yoas's rump.

Aware the gunfight had aroused more attention than they could handle and with no luck finding the keys to the safe, the men dragged the mortally wounded Dunlap off the train, grabbed their horses, and fled, richer by less than fifty dollars. They split up as they ran, abandoning Dunlap by the side of the road.

The next day the posse found Dunlap next to a blackened cactus. He had tried to start a fire but only succeeded in burning the plant as well as himself. The dying man survived the trip to Tombstone and lived a few more days, plenty of time to finger the culprits in the Fairbank heist, including the two who were nowhere near the robbery site—Burt Alvord and Billy Stiles. Dunlap also told all he knew about the Cochise Station robbery, again naming Alvord as the leader and implicating Stiles, Matt Burts, and Bill Downing.

The suspects were rounded up and jailed in Tombstone's tiny facility. Only Stiles remained free after he sang loud and fast to authorities about his part in the two robberies and named Alvord as ringleader. Alvord vehemently denied his involvement in both incidents. He did not relish sitting in a lockup with criminals he had arrested, and he had no intention of staying there.

On April 8 Stiles walked into the jailhouse and asked to speak to Alvord. Afterward, as the jailer led Alvord back to his cell, Stiles stuck a gun in the officer's side and relieved him of the jail keys. Alvord unlocked the cell doors, but only Bravo Juan Yoas walked out—the rest chose to take their chances at trial. Grabbing guns and rifles, the trio headed for the door, but the jailer made one last attempt to stop them, receiving a bullet in the leg as the trio fled.

About a week later Sheriff Scott White received a package in the mail. In it were the keys to the Tombstone jail and a note from the three escapees: "Tell the boys we are all well and eating regular." Alvord treated the whole episode as another of his pranks.

For three months the men were on the run. Stiles finally headed to his home in Casa Grande, leaving the other two riding toward Mexico. During their stay south of the border, Alvord and Yoas may have worked as armed guards in Mexican mines, since both were fluent in Spanish.

In 1902 Arizona Ranger Captain Burton C. Mossman set out to capture the killer Augustine Chacón and needed Alvord's help to bring in the desperado. Alvord may have ridden with Chacón at one time and the killer trusted him. When Alvord met up with Mossman in Mexico, he had been on the run for two years and was nursing a broken wrist. Mossman promised to recommend a lighter sentence for Alvord if he helped capture Chacón.

Alvord was ready to return to the states, and once he put Mossman in touch with Chacón, he fled north. A week later Alvord surrendered to Sheriff Del Lewis in the border town of Naco.

On December 1, 1902, Alvord appeared before a Tombstone judge. His attorney argued that Bill Downing had been found not guilty of the train heist because a jury thought the mandatory death penalty too harsh a judgment for robbing a train. The court agreed and ordered charges against Alvord dismissed.

Other allegations still loomed, however—the jailbreak and wounding of the Tombstone jailer, plus far more serious federal charges of tampering with the US mail during the Cochise Station robbery. By December 8 Alvord was back in jail, but paid his bail and walked out after serving eight days.

In July 1903 a grand jury indicted Alvord on six counts of tampering with the US mail. Bail was set at nine thousand dollars. This time the man who had initiated the robbery of two money-laden trains offered up no hard cash to pay for his release.

Stiles fled rather than testify against Alvord, but was recaptured. Not wanting the two desperados in the same jail, authorities sent Alvord to Phoenix to await trial while Stiles hung out in the Tucson facility. Both men were transported to Tombstone a few days before their December 10 trial date.

Unexpectedly, Alvord withdrew his not guilty plea and pled guilty to robbing the US mail. The court dismissed five additional charges against him, reducing his sentence to two years in Yuma Territorial Prison.

While Alvord waited to be transported to Yuma, he languished in the aging Tombstone jail with his old pal Stiles. The men wasted no time letting themselves out. On the evening of December 15, Alvord and Stiles slithered through a hole they had dug in the jail's adobe wall and walked away.

After stealing a couple of horses, they made one stop before heading toward the border. With their horses hidden behind a dry goods store and their guns drawn, the two escapees rapped on the shop's back door. Young Percy Bowden, who would later become a lawman, "opened the door to find two men with guns drawn and pointing in my direction." The men ordered Bowden to bring them warm clothes and supplies. After hearing the list of chores the boy did each day—milking sixteen cows and delivering milk before school, sweeping the store, and cleaning windows—they suggested their line of work was more lucrative but "might not last as long if the law caught up with them." They handed the boy two twenty-dollar gold pieces and disappeared into the night.

By January 1904 a five-hundred-dollar reward hung over each man's head. Accused of several robberies in the Sonora area, Alvord later claimed he had nothing to do with any of them. One of these thefts included eight thousand dollars in gold bullion that was never recovered.

On February 19 Alvord and Stiles were spotted hanging out at a ranch west of Naco, Sonora. Arizona Rangers surprised the two outlaws, severely wounding Alvord. Stiles escaped.

On March 3 Alvord entered Yuma Territorial Prison. He was released sometime in early October 1905. For a while he lived with a sister in Los Angeles, and then disappeared. Many believe he ended up on the Caribbean island of

Barbados, changed his name to Tom Wright, and died of fever in 1910. At the time he had in his possession about eight hundred dollars in gold, which was released to his sister.

In 1938 two of Alvord's nieces filed a note with the Arizona Historical Society stating their uncle had died on a small island off the Atlantic coast of Panama, "about the Fall of 1910."

Burt Alvord turned his back on justice, discarding his badge for a robber's six-gun. As one of Arizona Territory's most notorious bad men, he is remembered more for his lawlessness than his success in bringing justice to a handful of unruly western towns.

CALIFORNIA OUTLAWS

TIBURCIO VASQUEZ

A Spirit of Revenge

A light, frigid rain tapped the dirty windows of a small store located along the banks of the San Joaquin River near the town of Millerton, California. A half-dozen ferryboat operators were inside soaking up the warmth emanating from a fireplace. Four of them were huddled around a table playing cards, the other two were enjoying a drink at a makeshift bar, while an unkempt clerk arranged a row of canned goods across a warped shelf.

The clerk was entertaining the preoccupied men in the room with a song when the shop door swung open. He was the last to notice the figures standing in the entranceway. He looked up from his work after becoming conscious of his own loud voice in the sudden silence. He slowly turned to see what everyone else was staring at.

The outlaw Tiburcio Vasquez entered the store with his pistol drawn. Three other desperados, all brandishing weapons, followed closely behind. Vasquez, a handsome man of medium height with large, light-grey eyes, surveyed the terrified faces of the patrons as he smoothed down his brown mustache and goatee. "Put up your hands," he ordered the men. The clerk quickly complied and the others reluctantly did the same.

Two more of Vasquez's men burst into the store through the back entrance and leveled their guns on the strangers before them. "You don't need a gun here," the clerk tried to reason with the bandits. Vasquez grinned as he walked over to the man. "Yes, I do," he said as he placed his gun against the clerk's temple. "It helps quiet my nerves." Vasquez demanded that the men drop to the floor, facedown. After they had complied, their hands and feet were tied behind them. One of the men cursed the desperados as he struggled to free himself. "You damned bastard," he shouted at Vasquez. "If I had my six-shooter, I'd show you whether I'd lie down or not."

The bandits laughed at the outburst and proceeded to rob the store and its occupants of twenty-three hundred dollars. The November 10, 1873, holdup was one of more than one hundred such raids perpetrated by the thirty-eight-year-old Mexican and his band of cutthroat thieves and murderers in their violent careers. The desperados escaped the scene of the crime, eluding authorities for a full year before they were caught.

Prior to the gold rush, California's population was composed primarily of the original Spanish and Mexican settlers and indigenous Native Americans. News of the riches found in the foothills of the territory loosed a flood of white settlers into the area. In the pioneers' quest to tame the Wild West and transform the fertile California frontier into a "civilized" state, native Californians were forced into a new way of life. Families like Tiburcio Vasquez's harbored a great deal of animosity toward the white miners and businessmen who demanded that the original residents conform to their laws and way of living. Vasquez resented such treatment and from an early age began rebelling against what he called the "gringo's" influence.

Born in Monterey County, California, on August 11, 1837, Tiburcio was one of six children. His mother, Maria, was the daughter of explorer José Guadalupe Contua. His father, José, was a farmer who struggled to provide for his wife and family. Homesteaders from the East encroached on his land, making it difficult for him to compete for a share of the agricultural market. When Tiburcio was old enough to contribute financially, he took the only job he believed he could find, that of a cattle rustler and horse thief. He justified his outlawry by blaming the "Americans" for his lack of employment opportunity.

At the age of seventeen, Vasquez went into business with a friend, using his ill-gotten gains to become the co-owner of a dance hall. The fandango proved to be profitable, but was not without its share of problems. The white settlers who frequented the place treated the Mexican women who worked there badly, calling them names and insulting their ethnicity. Their actions further fueled the hatred Vasquez had for them.

Many wealthy Mexicans did not share Vasquez's opinion of the Americans. They disapproved of his criminal activities and refused to associate with him. One particular rancher, aware that his only daughter was romantically involved with the teenage bandit, forbade him from seeing her. When Vasquez disobeyed the order and kidnapped the man's daughter, the outraged rancher pursued the pair. The defiant young man refused to give up the girl, her father pulled a gun on him, and a gunfight broke out. Vasquez turned his paramour over only after he was shot in the arm.

Shortly after Vasquez's arm had mended, he was involved in another confrontation, this time with a constable. The dispute resulted in the death of the lawman.

At eighteen Vasquez was a fugitive on the run and he would remain so for two years. The ambitious criminal's natural leadership qualities attracted many like-minded desperados who joined forces with him. Together they robbed numerous stores and lone travelers in Northern California.

The authorities apprehended the outlaw in 1857. He was tried for his crimes and sentenced to five years in San Quentin. Vasquez escaped after ten months behind bars and was recaptured in 1859. After serving his time he was released, but within six months was charged with another robbery and sent back to jail. On August 3, 1870, he left prison again. He was a free, but not reformed, man.

Vasquez gathered together another group of bandits and started robbing stagecoaches traveling between San Francisco and Los Angeles, in rapid succession. He and his fellow desperados murdered numerous men during their hold-ups and gunned down any posse that tried to stop them.

One of the most heinous crimes committed by Vasquez and his men occurred in August 1873. The band of outlaws overtook a shop owner in the village of Tres Pinos in Monterey County and stole money from his register and the safe. Then they proceeded to make their way through the town, looting and vandalizing businesses.

Vasquez shot three innocent men. One of the members of his gang struck down a young boy, rendering him unconscious. After taking everything of value, the bandits rode off into the night. The terrorized community was outraged by Vasquez's savagery, a posse was formed, and an eight-thousand-dollar reward was offered for his capture.

Undeterred by the swarm of lawmen on their trail, Vasquez and his cohorts continued their crime spree, holding up a number of stores and stages in the San Joaquin Valley. One of the most ruthless of those robberies occurred in the town of Kingston. Vasquez attacked the hamlet in the dead of night and ordered his gang to tie up all the male citizens. One by one he stripped them of their personal possessions and money and then cleaned out the stores and hotel.

California citizens were furious over the outlaw's violent raids and at the inability of law enforcement officers to stop him. Governor Newton Booth responded to his constituents' cry for justice and appointed tough, respected Alameda County Sheriff Harry Morse to recruit a band of deputies to bring down Vasquez. Booth appropriated five thousand dollars to get the job done.

When word reached Vasquez that a highly trained posse had been formed, he decided the outlaws should disband for a while. Vasquez retreated to the Valley of the Cahuengas near Los Angeles and hid out at a friend's cabin.

Heavy rains in the area hampered Sheriff Morse's hunt for the desperado. His posse spent two months and traveled some 2,700 miles before getting a lead on where Vasquez was staying. In April 1874 the posse received a telegram that told them of a robbery at the San Gabriel Mission, nine miles outside of Los Angeles. Vasquez had been the culprit, and after the attack he had retreated into the Soledad Mountains.

A woman who lived in the vicinity of the desperado's hideout offered to escort the authorities to him. In exchange for the information, the woman, who was rumored to be the expectant mother of Vasquez's child, wanted a portion of the reward. Sheriff Morse was too far away from the scene to respond in a timely fashion, and a San Diego sheriff was asked to attend to the matter. The sheriff heard what the woman had to say, but he felt she was lying about what she knew and refused to investigate the tip.

The search for Vasquez continued for another month. Morse combed the terrain in the north and Los Angeles Sheriff William Rowland covered the southern portion of the state.

On May 13, 1874, Sheriff Rowland and his posse, which included George A. Beers, a sharp-shooting reporter from the *San Francisco Chronicle,* tracked the criminal down. Vasquez was exactly where the woman had told authorities he was four weeks before. When the bandit was alerted that the posse was closing in, he tried to make a run for it. Beers took aim with his shotgun and sent a volley of pellets into the bandit. Vasquez survived his injuries and was transported to Los Angeles to stand trial.

The news that the savage gunmen had been taken into custody spread quickly across the state. Curious citizens congregated at the jail to get a look at the notorious outlaw. An article in the *Los Angeles Star* on May 16, 1874, described the commotion surrounding Vasquez's arrival into the area.

> As the clerk of the City Council was about to read the last communication to that body yesterday, about 4:30 p.m., an unusual stir about the front attracted some attention, and in a moment more, City Fathers, City Clerks, City Surveyors, City Reporters and everybody else in the room, were making for the front door. Instinctively, we supposed Vasquez had something to do with the fuss. We were right. Vasquez was lying pale and bloody in a light wagon, in front of the entrance to the city jail.
>
> A surging crowd was gathering around. Two men who were taken in his company, at the time of the capture, were taken into the jail and locked up. In a moment after Vasquez himself was lifted from the wagon and was brought into the city prison.
>
> Dr. Wise presented himself; and assisted by several medical gentlemen of this city, rendered the wounded robber such surgical services he was required. . . . The bullets were extracted, the wounds pronounced not dangerous and opinion expressed that he would be well in a few days.

J. M. Bassett, the editor of the *Los Angeles Herald,* was later granted an interview with Vasquez. According to Bassett, although the outlaw was weak and recovering from his wounds, he held a long conversation with him. "His general demeanor is that of a quiet, inoffensive man," Bassett later wrote. "And but for his calm, steady eye, which stamps him as a man of great determination and firmness, no one would take him for the terrible Tiburcio Vasquez."

After Vasquez showed Bassett his leg where the buckshot had been removed, the journalist began asking him questions. The following is part of the conversation that took place:

"Where are they going to take you now, Vasquez?"

"I don't know," was the reply.

"And I suppose you don't care much now, do you?"

"Oh, well, that is not for me to say. I am not my own master now," he said with a shrug of the shoulders.

"Perhaps they will try you on account of your connection with the Tres Pinos affair. How do you think you would get through that?"

"Well, all I know is that I never shot a man in my life. I have had plenty of chances when I have had over five, ten, or twenty men tied hand and foot, but I never wanted to shoot anybody."

"Now, Vasquez, you don't really mean to say that you never shot a man in your life?"

"Yes, I do; I never shot a man."

"Do you like your robber life?"

"No, not at all . . ."

"Why did you live such a life, then? Wasn't it your own choice?"

"No, I was obliged to."

"What do you mean by that?"

"I mean that when I tried to settle down anywhere and tried to get a living, they came and drove me out. They wouldn't give me any peace."

"Who are they?"

"Why, the Americans—the officers."

"If you behave yourself they wouldn't meddle with you, would they?"

"Oh yes, they would; that didn't make any difference."

As soon as he was able to travel, the authorities loaded Vasquez aboard a steamer and escorted him to San Francisco. From there he would be moved to San Jose where his trial would be held. Hundreds of people flocked to get a glimpse of the outlaw. They stood outside the jails where he was housed, shouting his name. Some of the crowd was made up of Mexicans who believed Vasquez was a hero; others called him a "miserable, lying murderer," and demanded swift justice.

On January 6, 1875, Tiburcio Vasquez was tried in San Jose for the Tres Pinos murders. The galley was filled with local residents, many of whom visited the criminal in his cell when the hearing concluded each day. In one evening Vasquez received 673 visitors, the majority of them being women who saw the bandit as a folk hero.

Vasquez's trial ended two months after it began. After deliberating for two hours, the jury found him guilty and he was sentenced to hang on March 19, 1875.

As he was being led to the gallows, which had been imported from Sacramento, he offered an explanation for his actions to onlookers. "A spirit of hatred and revenge took possession of me," he said. "I had numerous fights in defense of what I believed to be my rights and those of my countrymen. I believed we were unjustly deprived of the social rights that belonged to us."

Just before he was executed, Vasquez turned to the lawman adjusting the noose around his neck and spoke one last word: "Pronto!" With that the trap door dropped out from under the outlaw and he fell to his death.

JOHN ALLEN

The Singing Barber

John Allen's mare slowly carried him through a dense grove of trees lining an overgrown trail in Tehama County, California. The sturdy rider sang to himself as he and his horse drifted in and out of the sunlight filtering through a canopy of massive pine and oak trees. If not for the pair of loaded pistols strapped to his waist and the shotgun cradled in his arms, one would have thought he was a traveling musician on his way to entertain prospectors at a mining camp.

Allen was a highwayman and horse thief who sometimes relied on his gifted singing voice to gain the trust of his unsuspecting victims. If his charm and talent as a performer could not separate his victims from the livestock and gold he wanted, he used his ability with a gun to take their possessions.

Born in approximately 1844 in New York, Allen never fit into the mold of the other bandits that roamed the California territory. The five-foot-six, twenty-five-year-old man had the face of an innocent boy, gray eyes, and reddish-brown hair. The unclad ladies and colorful flag tattoos that covered his forearms were as distinctive as was his manner of speech. He was a highly educated individual and spoke with the eloquence of a learned man.

Allen was a barber who decided to seek his fortune beyond the Mississippi. After settling in Shasta County in 1866, he opened a shop to practice his trade. He was personable, witty, and loved to talk. He became increasingly dissatisfied, however, with his modest income and decided to venture into the horse-stealing business.

His customers slowly began to notice that his extravagant lifestyle did not fit the earnings of a simple barber. He spent a great deal of money on prostitutes, alcohol, and celebrating at local saloons. He splurged on the barmaids attracted to his charismatic style and gift for waltzing. Women claimed he "danced like an angel." When he wasn't taking the ladies for a turn on the dance floor, he was playing the guitar and singing. His crisp baritone voice made women swoon.

Although residents in the various mining towns in Shasta County where Allen worked and played suspected the "singing barber" of criminal activities, no one could be sure. It wasn't until a rancher caught Allen stealing three of his best horses that their suspicions were confirmed. Five ranch hands pursued the thief through the local rocky terrain. Allen swore at them as he made his getaway. They fired a volley of shots that ricocheted off the trees and rocks. One of the men let loose a shotgun blast he was sure struck the outlaw. "I heard the bullets strike hard," he told local authorities, "but it didn't stop Allen. It sounded as though I shot at a bird on a tin roof." It was that incident that prompted sheriffs and deputies to begin referring to the desperado as Sheet-Iron Jack.

Undeterred by the possibility of getting caught, Allen roamed the territory stealing more horses from farmers and ranchers and selling them to desperados, often unscrupulous buyers. The more time that passed without his being caught, the more daring Allen became. His criminal activities grew to include robbing lone travelers he came across in the northern valleys. But in May 1871 Sheet-Iron Jack deviated from his outlaw ways to help a lost sojourner he had met while riding through Tehama County.

Digging his heels into the sides of the horse he was riding, Allen emerged from under the trees covering the rocky trail he'd been on and eyed the clearing ahead. Off in the distance he spotted a young man sitting alone on a boulder. He carefully scanned the area to see if there were any other people around, and when it appeared the young man was by himself, Allen trotted his horse over to him.

The man was frightened and a bit disoriented. He had no gear, horse, weapon, or shoes. When he saw Allen, he jumped behind the rock. Allen cautiously dismounted and just as cautiously approached the loner. "What are you doing afoot all the way out here, boy?" the bandit asked. The young man slowly stepped out from his temporary hiding place and flopped down on the ground, tired and embarrassed. Through a thick German accent, he explained to Allen that he was an immigrant on his way to the gold fields. His horse had suffered an injured hoof and he had stopped to contemplate how to proceed when a mountaineer happened along.

The mountaineer inspected the horse's hurt hoof and determined the animal was lame. He told the naïve prospector that it would take a year before the horse was fully healed. He offered to take the animal off the prospector's hands for thirty dollars. The young man decided to accept the offer and trek to the nearest town to get a new horse. He had woefully underestimated the distance to the next stage stop and had been walking so long that his shoes had given out.

As the conversation between the greenhorn and the outlaw continued, Allen learned that he had had his horse shod the day he began his journey. Allen surmised that his horse had gone lame because it had been improperly shod. He'd seen the scam played out on many unsuspecting settlers. A less than honest blacksmith does a poor job on the animal, and his partner in the field then rides out to take the injured horse away for a bargain price.

"You've been swindled," Allen told the lad. "I'm not opposed to it myself, but this is my beat, and nobody has any business doing any swindling here but me!"

Allen turned over a spare pair of boots to the young man and a canteen of water. He instructed him to stay at that spot until he returned. The irritated horse thief hurried off to find the lawbreaker.

Sheet-Iron Jack tracked the opportunistic mountaineer to an isolated canyon and snuck into his camp where his horses were tied to a row of sagebrush. The man had no idea that Allen was anywhere near until he heard him pull the hammer back on his pistol. The mountaineer put his hands up and slowly turned to face the gunman.

"Which one of those ponies belonged to the German boy you robbed?" he demanded. The man motioned to the animal with his head. "I bought that horse, mister," the man snapped back. "That's right," Allen replied. "For thirty dollars. Let's have it," he ordered, taking from the mountaineer the same amount that he'd offered the greenhorn. The frustrated mountaineer reluctantly surrendered his cash.

Allen pocketed the money, and with his gun still leveled at the man's head, he untied the stolen horse and hopped aboard his own ride. "I'm going to keep that thirty bucks as a lawyer's fee," Allen announced. The man was furious and began cursing and yelling. Allen jumped off his horse and hurried over to the impertinent man and stuck his gun in his stomach. "If you'd kept your mouth shut you'd have been better off," he told him through gritted teeth. "I should have remembered that a lawyer always takes all his client has got."

Allen forced the mountaineer to turn over his weapons and give him all the money he had, which amounted to more than six hundred dollars. Sheet-Iron Jack rode off warning the swindler to get out of the territory. He escorted the greenhorn's ride back to him and returned it and an additional thirty dollars. After advising the prospector to make sure his horses were properly shod in the future, Jack sent him on his way.

While making his way to the town of Redding, the German traveler met up with a posse tracking Sheet-Iron Jack. He told them about his encounter with the bandit and that Allen was a good man and his friend and couldn't be the hardened criminal they claimed.

For five years Allen ventured in and out of various Northern California counties stealing horses and robbing solitary riders. Thomas Godwin, the sheriff of Tehama County, made it his personal mission to apprehend repeat offenders like Allen. When Sheet-Iron Jack made off with several thoroughbreds within Godwin's jurisdiction, the relentless sheriff vowed to hunt him down and bring him to justice.

Godwin and his deputies had never laid eyes on Allen, but that did not dissuade them from forming a posse to track the horse thief. Armed with sufficient firearms and ammunition, and a description of the outlaw, the sheriff led his men through the countryside to look for Allen.

Like any competent desperado, Allen knew his way around the terrain and was keenly aware of when he was being followed. He spotted the posse from a bluff and decided to investigate. When the group of men bunked down for the night, the bold outlaw sauntered into their camp. He told the lawmen that he was a concerned landowner who wanted to help stop the criminal element that was roaming the area.

Allen was incredibly personable and a persuasive talker; no one suspected he wasn't being honest. He spent the next day with the posse advising them on the best route to take and speculating on the hideout of the thief. The following evening he led the men to a roadhouse where they decided to stay for the night. Over dinner Allen entertained the men with songs and comical stories. Sheriff Godwin was so impressed with Allen's positive influence over his deputies that he invited him to share his cabin with him.

Before dawn broke Allen slinked out of the inn, taking with him three of the deputies' best horses. When Godwin and the other law enforcement agents awoke and realized Allen had taken off with their rides, they quickly loaded their gear and hurried after him. The posse picked up his trail a few miles south of the roadhouse and followed it to a settler's cabin. The owner of the homestead told the men that Allen had stopped at his place just two hours prior to their arrival. He had watered the horses in his possession and before riding out had asked the man to give the sheriff a letter he had written. The letter thanked Godwin for the company, grub, and the horses.

The posse pursued Sheet-Iron Jack into the wilds of the Trinity Mountains where they lost his trail, never to find it again.

Ranchers in the area would occasionally band together and pick up where the posse left off to try to locate Allen and the livestock he stole from them. Because he rode alone, he was able to lose himself in narrow canyon passages and dense brush where large groups of men could not follow. Even with this advantage, the brazen bandit could not resist tempting fate. It was not unusual for him to linger a bit at any of the towns he was passing through while on the run. On one instance he attended a Saturday night social and danced with a half-dozen women before hurrying off into the night.

In mid-1876 Allen's luck finally ran out. He stopped at a saloon in Shasta and ordered too much to drink. The inebriated renegade started a fight with another patron and shot him during the altercation. Allen was arrested and thrown in jail. His trial was quick, but his charm prevailed. The judge sentenced the likeable outlaw to two years in prison.

Within a week after the hearing, Allen was transported to San Quentin. The stage he was riding in was held up just outside of town. The two robbers escaped after exchanging several bullets with the deputies onboard the coach. Appalled by their actions, the handcuffed Allen stuck his upper body out of the window of the stage and began shouting at the criminals. The figure of the restrained passenger caught their attention; they reconsidered their actions and retreated.

An article about the incident appeared in the next day's edition of the *Shasta Courier*. The editor wrote that "Sheet-Iron Jack cussed the robbers until the very air smelled of brimstone, and small streaks of lightening flashed from his mouth and played in fiery circles around his head. He said that it was an unmitigated outrage that a man could not be permitted to travel over Shasta County territory, especially when he was on his way to work for the interest of the state, without having his life endangered by shots fired by murderous highwaymen."

The robbery attempt did not stop authorities from taking Allen on to San Quentin. His stay at the prison was short-lived, however, because a gifted attorney found a problem in the sentencing. The technicality made it possible for Allen to be released after only five months of incarceration. The thief was retried, errors were corrected, and he was sentenced for a second time.

Allen escaped a week after his second appearance at San Quentin. The failed stagecoach robbery he had witnessed prompted the outlaw to attempt his own stage holdup. Instead of taking on such a job alone, Allen recruited the help of two other escaped convicts. From November 6 to November 11, 1876, the three men robbed five stages. Allen's cohorts did not lie low after the crime the way he did. They were careless and were quickly caught drinking the night away at a saloon in Shasta County.

The unscrupulous outlaws confessed their crime to the sheriff and led the lawmen and his deputies to the place where Allen was hiding out. Sheet-Iron Jack was captured and the three men were tried and convicted. By December 1876 Allen was on his way back to San Quentin to spend the next twenty-four years of his life at the facility.

In 1882 California Governor George Perkins was prevailed upon by Allen to review his case. The good argument he made for such a request, combined with his exceptional behavior behind bars, encouraged the governor to consider the matter. Perkins looked over the case against Allen and concluded that he had been convicted on insufficient evidence. On June 25, 1883, his sentence was commuted, but he was ordered to leave California and never return.

Sheet-Iron Jack did not leave the state. He returned to his old haunts and way of living. He was arrested again in the summer of 1884 for stealing horses and robbing a stage stop. He served his lengthy term in Folsom Prison, and when he was released in 1895, he moved to Oregon and lived out the rest of his days on a Modoc Indian reservation.

JUAN FLORES

He Took a Short Fall

Four teams of tired, uninspired horses pulled a line of buckboards filled with coffins over the dry, dusty terrain twelve miles outside of the village of San Juan Capistrano. The wagon drivers and a dozen other men riding with them stared soberly out at the land. Ahead in the near distance, they could see a smattering of dead bodies strewn across the semidesert floor. Misshapen dead horses, bloating in the heat, lay beside their lifeless owners.

As the buckboards inched closer to the carnage, the wheels of the vehicles cut through pools of clotted blood spread over the ground. The drivers slowed the teams to a halt, and without speaking, the men on board the wagons began unloading the wooden crates. Their busy hands then lifted the bodies off the hard earth and placed them in the coffins.

All of the corpses were wearing badges; five of the men were deputies and one was Los Angeles Sheriff James R. Barton. Each of the lawmen was riddled with bullets; they had been stripped of their belongings and their right eyes had been shot out.

The objective of the slain posse, dispatched on January 22, 1857, was to track down a cattle rustler and horse thief named Juan Flores. Flores's criminal activities began in 1855. He had run roughshod over a stretch of Southern California that extended from Sacramento to the San Joaquin Valley. Along the way he recruited more than fifty outlaws to assist him in the looting and killing of ranchers and their families.

When Sheriff Barton learned of Flores's hideout, he wasted no time organizing volunteers. The experienced lawman believed he could apprehend the murderous bandit. He had no idea when he was riding hard toward the area where Flores was last seen that he was riding into an ambush.

Once the sheriff's body and those of his deputies were secured in the coffins, the boxes were stacked inside the buckboards. Another posse was sent out to find Flores and bring him to justice, now not only for his existing sins, but also for the brutal slaying of Barton and his men. The search for Flores was one of the largest manhunts in Old West history.

Juan Flores was born in 1835 in Santa Barbara, California. His parents were well-respected members of the community and proud of the handsome son they believed would grow up to be an exceptional man. It is not known what prompted Flores to abandon the high hopes his mother and father had for him and embark on a life of crime. Historians suggest that the Flores family was a struggling family of farmers and that Juan aspired to a more affluent lifestyle. He was not opposed to achieving his goal illegally either. He left home at seventeen and joined a gang of ruthless cattle rustlers made up of American drifters, Mexican bandits, ex-convicts, fugitives, and army deserters.

Cattle were a critical element of the economy of the West. California-grown beef was used to supply the growing population of prospectors and immigrant families with meat and it increased in price daily. Because of the rising price of beef—and the profits to be made—the territory was infested with bands of cattle thieves committing depredations upon the ranges. Ranchers not only had to worry about bandits stealing from them, but hungry and desperate Native Americans as well. Some cattle owners lost entire herds to either Indians or rustlers.

Flores rode with a bandito bunch that raided cattle farms around the area of Rancho Santa Margarita. He primarily focused on stealing horses and was eventually arrested for the offense in 1856. He was tried and convicted and was ordered to serve his time in the jail at San Quentin. Flores was bitter over his circumstances and restless while confined inside a cell. Anxious to be free, he teamed up with a hundred other inmates in a massive jailbreak. The plans were thwarted before the prisoners were able to flee the premises, however.

Flores was discouraged, but he was not defeated. With the help of several fellow outlaws, his second attempt to break out of prison was a success. The elaborate escape involved overtaking the crew onboard a ship docked at the wharf at Point San Quentin. The inexperienced bandit sailors managed to steer the vessel out of the harbor amidst a barrage of gunfire from prison guards and law enforcement officers. The lawless crew navigated the ship through the open waters, making it to the Contra Costa shoreline where they docked. The men then split up and went their separate ways.

Law enforcement combed the hills around Santa Barbara looking for Flores and the others, but the felons could not be found. Flores had managed to elude the lawmen, making his way to San Luis Obispo. Once he reached the picturesque town, the ambitious renegade immediately began enlisting a host of like-minded criminals to join him in his illegal ventures.

The most savage of all of Flores's recruits was twenty-year-old Andres Fontes. Fontes claimed he was driven to a life of crime by Sheriff James Barton. The two had been in love with the same woman when Barton accused Fontes of stealing a horse to get rid of him. Fontes spent two years in prison for the alleged theft and vowed to kill Barton when he was released. His hatred for law enforcement and bent toward lawbreaking made him a natural to team up with Flores.

Bandits were drawn to Flores's charm and criminal vision. He organized and led more than fifty men on numerous cattle-rustling raids. It was an easy transition from cattle rustling to robbery for Flores. He organized the looting of small towns, stage holdups, and the ransacking of prospectors' camps. He and his men also kidnapped lone travelers and held them for ransom. Dead bodies were often left in the wake of the mayhem. Residents in mining communities throughout the state were petrified of the fugitive and his gang.

Flores fueled the fear with bold, public acts of violence. In late 1856 the bandit and his gang snatched a German settler off a trail outside of San Diego. They demanded the victim pay a hefty sum for his release, but the settler refused. Flores made an example of the man in the town square. With hundreds looking on, he shot the stubborn immigrant to death.

With the help of his love interest Chola Martina, Flores and his desperados invaded the homes and businesses of two well-known mercantile owners in San Juan Capistrano. One of the men was murdered trying to protect his property.

News of the gang's continual vicious attacks prompted Los Angeles Sheriff Barton to form a posse and set out after the murderers and thieves. Barton had been informed that Flores's band was some fifty men strong, but he believed that the number had been exaggerated by hysterical crime victims. The sheriff's underestimation of the strength of Flores's gang resulted in his death. One of the men who gunned down Barton was Andres Fontes. At last he had his revenge.

General Don Andres Pico, a prominent Los Angeles land owner and the brother of the last Mexican governor of California, took charge of forming a posse after the slaughter of Barton and his deputies. Pico pulled together a fifty-one-man army of Mexicans and Americans to go after Flores. Pauma Indian leader Manuelito Cota, in Temecula, joined the general in his efforts. Manuelito recruited forty-three Indians for the task. A group of enraged citizens in the San Diego area made up a third posse out to track Flores down.

Pauma scouts ventured ahead of the posses to look for clues as to where the bandit might have fled. The location of Flores's camp was finally narrowed down to the mountains around El Cariso. With the assistance of one of Flores's former gang members, Pico's Californians, as they were known, were able to find the exact location of Flores's cabin hideout. The Californians attacked the shelter under the light of a full moon. The desperados inside fired on the posse, killing or wounding many of their pursuers. Some of the bandits were shot while trying to make a run for their horses, others were captured unharmed, and some managed to get away. Juan Flores and Andres Fontes were two who escaped.

Flores and Fontes were lost in the smoke of gunfire and vanished into the tangled mountain thicket. General Pico sent for reinforcements, and shortly after his supplies of guns, ammunition, and men were replenished, he continued the pursuit of the outlaws. On February 1, 1857, a faction of the posse, headed by

Dr. J. Gentry from Los Angeles, cornered Flores and two of his companions near Santiago Mountain.

The bandits shot it out with the posse members, but realizing they were out-numbered, they surrendered. Flores and his diminished band of followers were escorted to a nearby ranch where they were placed under guard in a weathered adobe building. The prisoners' stay was meant to be temporary. Given Flores's previous success at escaping from his captors, the authorities wanted more law enforcement on hand to escort the criminal to the Los Angeles jail. But in spite of the precautions taken, Flores wriggled out of his cuffs and broke out of the crumbling, clay holding cell.

Posse members' tempers flared at the news that Flores had gotten away. General Pico ordered his deputies to immediately put to death the members of Flores's gang that were arrested with him. Pico then helped enlist more than 120 men to join the manhunt to find Juan Flores. For eleven days one of the largest posses ever assembled in the Old West searched the territory along the Los Angeles River between San Juan Capistrano and Temecula.

Almost twenty-four hours after Flores had escaped, he was stopped by two armed sentinels patrolling the grounds at a Simi Valley ranch. He lied about his identity, but his suspicious behavior led the guards to take him to the ranch owner to be questioned further. The land baron recognized the bandit and informed his men that the scoundrel in custody was none other than Juan Flores.

Flores was taken to Los Angeles, where he was tried and sentenced to death. After his trial ended on February 14, 1857, a hostile crowd surrounded the jail demanding the notorious outlaw be turned over to them. They wanted Flores hanged at that moment. On February 21 the criminal was turned over to the enraged mob and they led him to the gallows.

Before the noose was placed around his neck, the twenty-two-year-old Flores's arms and legs were bound and his eyes were covered with a white hand-kerchief. He whispered a few last words and then the trap door was sprung. He did not die instantly. The fall was shorter than planned and the rope was a bit too long. After a gruesome six-minute struggle, it was over.

COLORADO OUTLAWS

THE MUSGROVE GANG

Horse Thieves

The *Rocky Mountain News* reported in 1868 that "Musgrove was an outlaw who had made society his prey for several years, successively defying by boldness, when he could not outwit by cunning, the officers of justice. . . . He soon became the recognized chief of a band of land pirates, who lived by running off government stock, effacing the brand and then disposing of it."

Lee Musgrove was born in Como, Mississippi, probably sometime in the early 1830s. He had little education, but was said to be very bright and a natural leader. By 1849 he had grown into a tall, physically imposing young man. The California goldfields were ripe with the promise of adventure and wealth, so Musgrove decided to go there to begin his adult life. He left home and traveled to the Napa Valley, where he joined the search for gold. Soon though, he realized the odds were not in his favor for striking it rich.

As the Civil War was brewing in the East, he stayed in California and worked at temporary jobs. Being a Southerner, he might have gone back home and joined the Confederacy. Instead, he chose to remain in the West, but couldn't restrain himself from fighting his own "war" there. In 1861 he was involved in a heated argument, in which he sided in favor of the South's secession. The argument ended when Musgrove killed his defenseless rival.

Musgrove left the Napa Valley to avoid retaliation and headed to Nevada Territory. His defense of the South continued as a personal vendetta when he killed two more men in arguments there. He moved on to Cheyenne, Wyoming Territory, where yet another man's derision of the South inflamed him so much that he killed this adversary as well.

Musgrove had to flee again, and this time he went to Denver. By now the Civil War was coming to an end, and Musgrove maintained a low-key lifestyle while working in the area for about a year. He ranged as far as Fort Halleck, in Wyoming Territory, which was a center for Indian trade. Musgrove was involved in business dealings there. All went peacefully for him until an Indian called him a liar, which triggered Musgrove's short temper. He calmly drew his gun and shot the Indian in the head.

On the run again, Musgrove soon disappeared into the unknown. His name would not be heard again until 1868.

Marshal Dave Cook had been installed to clean up the lawless and wild activities pervading the young city of Denver. After his arrival in 1863 as a military detective, Cook had quickly established himself as the veritable force that would wipe out crime in Denver. His success in ferreting out criminals and bringing them to justice for the US Army led to his election as city marshal. Denver was able to enjoy an unusual period of peace from the hoodlums who were moving into towns all over the West.

In late 1867, the first report of a potential new threat came to Cook in a message from Kansas. Thirty horses had been stolen from a rural ranch. A week later, a report from New Mexico Territory informed him of a small community where homes and stores had been burglarized and the stagecoach had been held up. Next he heard from Wyoming Territory that fifty horses had gone missing. Utah Territory reported a raid by a gang. Nebraska, Texas, and Arizona Territory all reported that small settlements had been targeted.

The striking thing about all these reports was that the criminals and their booty all seemed to disappear into oblivion. Each crime was expertly planned and timed to maximize the greatest take. And the outlaws, as well as whole herds of horses, were not traceable.

By early 1868, every region bordering Colorado Territory had been hit by the raids. Finally, it would be included when forty horses were stolen from one horse breeder in the southeastern part of the territory. When these events first began, the local authorities in each location were unaware that the other crimes were occurring. They had no way of knowing of the similarities in all these offenses across the eight-territory swath.

Marshal Cook, however, had organized an association of his cohorts in law enforcement during the previous few years. He had seen the need to establish better interaction among crime fighters in the region. The old method for chasing down wanted criminals was for the local sheriff to follow the clues by himself, even if they led him across several territories. Cook suggested that lawmen work together and help one another in making arrests in other jurisdictions. His group was called the Rocky Mountain Detective Association. It was through this group that one of his associates first alerted him to widespread gang activity in the other territories. Soon all of the affected territories' law officers were notified of the extent of the crimes.

It was obvious to Cook that the raids had similar planning, suggesting they were somehow connected. He suspected the gangs' activities were masterminded by an individual, someone who was capable of outsmarting him and the other law enforcement officials in several regions. The question was, who was this person? And where was this leader headquartered?

Cook reasoned that there could be only one place for the gang leader to hide himself, and it was right under his nose. It had to be Denver. It was geographically located in the center of all the raid activity. Messengers could easily ride in and out carrying instructions. It was the region's largest city, which made it easy for someone to remain concealed. And since Cook had quieted the outlaw faction, no one would suspect that any desperado would choose to live there.

By involving his extensive association in the matter, Cook began to piece the information together. Local association affiliates were asked to look for signs of stock for sale and to trace the sellers. Every detail of the raids was studied. Denver's underworld was infiltrated for clues to anyone connected to the gang. A vague trail of information gradually began to form.

These efforts finally led to one man. The prime suspect was Lee Musgrove, the notorious criminal wanted for murder in nearly every territory of the region. His partners were also revealed to be two other killers named Ed Franklin and Jack Willetson.

Musgrove had been busy since he had gone underground three years before. Being a wanted man, he had to stay concealed. For income he began stealing horses, which led to larger-scale raids using recruited men. He began to plan a regional operation running up and down the Rocky Mountains. Musgrove could mastermind the operation while other outlaws would complete the missions. Estimates suggest that as many as two hundred men were part of Musgrove's scheme. They included hardened horse thieves, highwaymen, and murderers. It was the largest outlaw syndicate of the Old West.

This lawless group was divided into factions throughout the Rockies and some bordering territories. Musgrove placed the outlaw gangs in mountain and plains areas. He oversaw the planning and coordinated every detail of the raids, appointing various experienced hoodlums to lead each operation. The gangs struck with precision and always seemed to know when their victims were in the most vulnerable position. His plans always included ways to escape that would thwart pursuers.

Raids were only made out on the open prairie or at isolated locations. Rural ranches were favorite targets since they allowed stolen horse herds to be driven out into the desolate countryside. By the time posses could be formed to chase them, the gangs and their stolen herds had already disappeared into hundreds of miles of backcountry. They could ride for days, unseen by another human. The horses would be moved as far as 250 to 500 miles away.

These bands had been operating, unhindered by the law, for three months. Their methods were so simple and effective that the outlaws were able to carry out the disposal of their stolen horses in the midst of the public. Once the herd arrived in a chosen town, it was shipped by railroad to a more financially advantageous market. Moved rapidly and across huge distances, the horses arrived in the destination city, and local officials were completely unaware that they had been stolen. Pursuing law enforcement officials were left far behind.

It was not unusual for horses stolen in Colorado Territory to end up in Texas, while those stolen in Utah Territory might end up in Arizona Territory. The horses were then placed for public sale in the new market without arousing any suspicion.

With the horses sold, the gang was free to commit another raid near where they had unloaded their last herd. Musgrove had the next victim already targeted, and the outlaws moved into action again, carrying out the same maneuver of moving a stolen herd to a distant locale. This efficiency in planning resulted in a string of thefts that occurred with great regularity.

Marshal Cook was highly frustrated with his inability to locate Musgrove. If the leader could be found, the rest of the scheme could be broken. Although it was certain that Musgrove and his assistants operated out of Denver, they were often out of town overseeing various raids and attending to business. Each gang leader had to turn over the profits from their thefts to Musgrove, so rendezvous points had been set up in isolated locations. Payoffs were made first to the leader, and then distributed to his men.

Cook was soon notified by one of the association members that men on horseback had been seen about thirty miles from Denver near the Elmore Ranch. The men appeared to be scouting the ranch, which fit the profile of a Musgrove raid. Marshal Cook figured this might be his opportunity to stop a raid, so he left immediately for the ranch. Local guards were set up that night in case the men returned. About 2:00 a.m., four men swooped down upon the ranch and rallied its herd of horses. In the midst of this activity, the guards ran out and fired on the horse thieves, who returned gunfire and ran off, leaving the horses behind.

Marshal Cook arrived shortly after the attempted theft and pursued the outlaws into the mountains. When they circled back on their way to Denver, Cook cut them off and fired his gun at them. The men fled to a cabin, but gave up when one of them was wounded by Cook. After they were arrested, one of the arrogant outlaws said that Musgrove would come and rescue them. When Cook said he didn't think Musgrove was in town, the outlaw said Musgrove had left for a while to avoid some guy named Cook.

Because of the arrest of these four men, word was out to Musgrove that returning to Denver would be dangerous. The organization began to fold from that moment.

With Musgrove in hiding, messages to his gangs were disrupted. By now, other gangs were being traced using the information Cook had sent through the association. Six gang members were apprehended in Wyoming Territory as they tried to sell horses from Nebraska. Four more were arrested in what is now Arizona. Kansas citizens captured three gang members and lynched them on the spot. One of Musgrove's messengers was found at Georgetown, in Colorado Territory, and brought to Denver's jail.

Although some members of the gang were arrested, the rest of the outlaws remained unaware of these events. Over the next four months, the gang continued raids, but gradually lost communication with Musgrove. Messengers continued to try to get through and were arrested one by one as Cook intercepted them. Reports of continued roundups of gang members came in from several territories. One of Musgrove's top aides, Jack Willetson, and two of his men were captured and lynched in New Mexico Territory. Five arrests in Texas, ten in southern Colorado Territory, and two more in Wyoming Territory hailed the demise of Musgrove's syndicate.

Musgrove's whereabouts, however, were still unknown. Some theorized that he had left the region entirely. Cook wasn't convinced of that. Then a report came in that several holdups had occurred in northern Colorado Territory. Each had been perpetrated by a lone man. The descriptions of the bandit seemed to fit all accounts of Musgrove's appearance. Cook speculated that Musgrove had run out of money.

Soon Musgrove went back to horse stealing. He had crossed into Wyoming Territory for a night of several raids on small ranches. Musgrove then fled back into Colorado Territory. US Marshal H. D. Haskell had been alerted by Cook to be on the lookout. Almost immediately, Haskell and his posse were in pursuit of Musgrove. Haskell's posse finally had Musgrove cornered in a rocky gulch along the Cache la Poudre River near Fort Collins.

After Haskell kept Musgrove pinned down for twenty-four hours, Musgrove requested a truce to talk to the marshal. Haskell agreed and was allowed to walk into the hiding place, where he discovered that Musgrove had enough provisions to hold out for weeks. Haskell also noticed the stolen horses were hidden in a place where it was unlikely he could rescue them.

Musgrove offered to make a deal. He said Haskell could take back any stock he could identify on the condition that the posse would then leave. Haskell accepted and was able to verify ownership on most of the horses. Then he and the posse escorted the herd home. However, Haskell was not content to return without Musgrove. He sent most of the horses home with the posse, but separated some of them into a smaller herd. Hoping to draw Musgrove out, Haskell slowly meandered north pushing his part of the herd by himself. Sure enough, Musgrove followed and attempted to steal the horses at night when he thought Haskell was sleeping. Haskell was awake and waiting, and he easily captured Musgrove.

Another account of Musgrove's capture states that Abner Loomis of Fort Collins lived near the Cache la Poudre River at a place called Pleasant Valley. Loomis had known Musgrove lived in the area for years and also knew of his horse stealing. A deal had been struck between the two men, whereby Musgrove would not steal horses from the local farmers. If he did, they would come after him and kill him. Supposedly Musgrove kept this agreement, but Loomis had a change of heart when he later learned that the whole region was after Musgrove. Loomis is said to have entrapped Musgrove and led him right into the hands of US Marshal Haskell.

Though accounts of his capture may vary, it was Haskell who brought Musgrove into Denver and turned him over to Marshal Cook. After almost a year of work at putting an end to Musgrove and his gangs, Cook should have been overjoyed at the current situation. However, the date was early November and the courts did not reconvene until January. Cook knew he would have to hold Musgrove in jail until then, while many of Musgrove's gang were still at large. He believed it would be only a matter of time before a jailbreak would be attempted.

Sure enough, many of the old Musgrove gang began to filter into Denver. Ed Franklin headed for the city when he heard of Musgrove's arrest. Franklin had been the assistant to Musgrove throughout the gang's successful raids earlier in the year. He met up with Sanford Duggan, another outlaw, and they both rode into Denver together. One of their first acts was to rob a man of one hundred thirty-five dollars. That man turned out to be Judge Brooks.

Judge Brooks informed Marshal Cook immediately. Cook put out the alert and was soon notified that the hoodlums had gone on to neighboring Golden. Cook set out for Golden immediately, and in a confrontation designed to arrest the men, an innocent man was killed, as well as Franklin. Duggan escaped.

In Denver the next day, mob justice was underway. Word of Judge Brooks's holdup and the influx of Musgrove's gang members had alarmed and frightened the citizens. Adding this to the events that transpired in Golden the night before, the populace filled Denver streets and demanded the bandits leave town. Reports say that the huge crowds in the streets unnerved the Musgrove followers, who were holed up in the Holladay Street saloons and bordellos. Panicking, they retreated from the city in thirty minutes.

The crowd then headed for the county jail. The *Rocky Mountain News* reported that among the throng were doctors, merchants, professional people, and other prominent citizens. Amazingly, the mob moved along quietly with no shouting. It was orderly and determined. They held Musgrove responsible for all of the recent troubles.

Since the crowd was also well armed, their arrival was not met with resistance from the officers guarding the jail. By overwhelming agreement, the people removed Musgrove from his cell. He was then marched to the Larimer Street Bridge over Cherry Creek. Musgrove, observing the crowd around him, hoped for a last-ditch attempt to free him. But his cronies were nowhere to be seen.

A hangman's noose was suspended from the bridge. He only asked to have paper and pencil to write farewell notes to his wife in Cheyenne, and to his brother in Mississippi. He was given the materials and a few minutes to complete the letters. As he wrote, his legs were tied together. He was then hoisted into a wagon, which was positioned on the dry bed of Cherry Creek below the noose. Musgrove was defiant to the last as he supposedly smoked a cigarette, and then said: "Go on with your work." The noose was placed around his neck, and the wagon was pulled from under him. It was November 24, 1868, and Musgrove was dead.

Ten days later, Sanford Duggan was finally captured in Cheyenne and brought back to Denver. Marshal Cook knew the mood of Denverites had not changed with the death of Musgrove. Duggan was considered part of the same problem. Although Cook tried to protect Duggan so he could stand trial, it is suspected the marshal's own men betrayed him. A lynching party learned of Cook's plan to move Duggan to an unknown location. Before the transfer could take place, Duggan was seized and hung from the limb of a nearby cottonwood tree.

Lee Musgrove's legacy was a death trail—including those he killed, the scores who died following him, and his own violent end.

PUG RYAN

Robber & Murderer

*On Monday afternoon, a bunch of Kokomo children held a
luncheon on the summit of Jacque Mountain.*

*There on the mountainside the Carlson children picked
up an old watch and chain. Directly another gold watch was
found. Of course the children were excited and naturally ran
home with their treasure. [Their father] found the first clue to
ownership of one of the watches in the monogram, R.W.F. which
it bore.*

*. . . Mr. Robert W. Foote was apprised of the recovery of the
forgotten time piece. He took in the situation at once and said,
"My diamond is on that hill too; it will be found where the
watches were picked up, and I shall take the morning train to
Kokomo."*

*Sunrise next morning found Mr. Foote and Chet Acton
knocking on the door of the Carlson home in Kokomo. The
children were aroused and they led the way to the lone treasure
spot. Acton scratched in the dirt at the spot pointed out by the
children and in an instant uncovered the big diamond, to the
great joy of him who was ruthlessly deprived of it ten long years
before. The second watch proved to be the property of Ed Brewer
then residing in Glenwood Springs.*

—SUMMIT COUNTY JOURNAL, 1908

This incredible discovery had been the first reminder in ten years of outlaw "Pug"
Ryan, who had been wanted in Breckenridge (Summit County), Colorado, for
robbery and murder in 1898. Victims were relieved of gold watches, a diamond
pin, and cash, but worse were the devastating murders during the manhunt that
followed the brazen robbery.

Pug Ryan had been picked up in Seattle four years after the heinous crime.
He was five feet six and three-quarter inches tall, had a pug nose, gray eyes, light
hair, a scarred face and head, and the letters *P-U-G* tattooed on his arm. That
arrest spelled the beginning of the end for Ryan.

Breckenridge, Colorado, was a mining town on the verge of change by 1898. Ores were mostly played out, and miners were becoming a shrinking vestige of the era. The town had its share of rough-and-tumble transients, but it also boasted the elegant Denver Hotel and a strong citizenry portending a solid future. Runaway slaves Barney and Julia Lancelot Ford had been just one success story among many of migrants who had escaped one way of life to find a better one in Breckenridge.

Still, daily life in the mountain town was far from tame. Gambling was an accepted and legal form of entertainment everywhere in the state of Colorado in 1898. And on the Saturday night of August 11, the Denver Hotel was filled with patrons optimistically pitting their paychecks against the odds.

Around midnight the regular games of poker, faro, and roulette were in full swing in the game room, while the bartender filled and refilled the player's glasses. A loud boom was the first signal of anything unusual, from a sawed-off shotgun accidentally going off and putting a hole into the ceiling.

It turned out to be the bungled beginning of a robbery. Four hoodlums had stumbled in the back door and were intent on stealing the contents of the safe and possibly the bankroll of Charles Levy, who usually sat by the stove in the evenings. A local businessman and prosperous clothier, Levy was known to carry six to eight hundred dollars with him and thus was a prime target.

But when that shotgun went off, the robbers were exposed. Although the safe was full of cash and valuables, they now opted to bypass it in favor of more immediate loot. The gunmen quickly turned their guns on the patrons and robbed them instead. A small fortune in jewelry and gold pocket watches was gathered hastily from the vests of the victims. They also stole money lying on the tables from the faro games and from the bar collections. The pockets of the patrons were full of cash, but it was ignored by the thieves.

Each gold watch they took was said to have been an individual treasure in itself. George Ralston was one of the victims, and he later said that his was a family heirloom worth five hundred dollars. Other gold watches were taken from hotel owner Robert Foote and bartender Ed Brewer. Foote was also wearing a diamond stickpin that he had borrowed from a friend, who said it was worth two hundred fifty dollars.

One of the robbers was Pug Ryan, also known by several aliases: "Pug" Scott, J. C. Moore, L. A. Scott, and Lewis A. Scott. Another robber was Dick Manley, the third was Dick Bryant, and the fourth man was never identified.

The cash that was taken was minimal compared to the thousands of dollars left in the untouched safe. Altogether, though, the gang had rounded up a goodly sum for just a few minutes of thievery.

But it is what transpired next that not only made the incident far more significant to the citizens of Breckenridge, but also put Pug Ryan on the state's most-wanted list.

The ruffians fled on foot into the darkness, while the victims and law officers convened to figure out who had perpetrated the robbery and what to do next. It wasn't long before news of a suspicious bunch of newcomers was reported in Kokomo, a little settlement up over the steep Ten Mile Range from Breckenridge. The men had found a cabin, where they were spending the night.

Breckenridge Sheriff Jerry Detwiler sent his deputy Ernest Conrad to investigate. When Conrad arrived in Kokomo, he kept a low profile, but a local newspaperman had already gotten wind of the Denver Hotel burglary. He asked Conrad if he was there to capture the outlaws.

Conrad decided to deputize a local saloon owner and school board president, Sumner Whitney. Together they set out for the cabin. Once there they decided to go inside, but were completely unprepared for Ryan's defiance over their coming into "his" cabin. The deputies backed off and left the cabin, unsure of how to proceed. This time they decided to go back in and demand to search the premises. This demand pushed Ryan too far, and he opened fire on the deputies. He killed Conrad and mortally wounded Whitney. Just before Whitney was hit, he was able to fatally wound Dick Manley and kill Dick Bryant. Ryan was left standing and unhurt.

Before Ryan fled the cabin, he is said to have robbed his own partners, who lay bleeding. Then he escaped.

A Leadville man named John Barret heard shots ring out from the cabin, which was located not far from the platform of the train station where he was waiting for the Denver & Rio Grande train to arrive. He alerted local Kokomo residents, and they all ran to the cabin. A man named George Steve had gotten there first and later said he saw Ryan robbing Manley. But Ryan had jumped up and run off before Steve could stop him.

Angry Kokomo residents trailed Ryan toward Jacque Ridge south of Copper Mountain. Although they found a lighted cigar stump believed to be Ryan's, they couldn't catch up with him. He seemed to have vanished.

The aftermath of the shootings left the communities devastated. Two stalwart and respected men who had had families had been lost. Deputy Conrad was forty-two years old and left behind a wife and three little children. Sumner Whitney was taken by train to the Leadville hospital and didn't die of his wounds until almost a month later. He also left behind a wife and three children. But he was able to put his signature on a photograph of Pug Ryan, along with the inscription, "This is the man who did the shooting."

The wounded Manley lived long enough to confess in the Breckenridge jail. The information he gave led law enforcement authorities to begin a nationwide search. Bounty hunters heeded the call. The State of Colorado posted a two-hundred-fifty-dollar reward for Ryan's arrest and conviction. Summit County offered one hundred dollars, and El Paso County added five hundred dollars.

Even the city of Chicago had suffered from some terrible Pug Ryan deed and threw in one thousand dollars.

Regardless of all the publicity and attention given to finding Ryan, it would still be four years before he was successfully arrested and brought to trial. During that time he traveled to Seattle, Washington, and settled down. But he wasn't flourishing there, either. The Seattle police happened to pick him up along a local street one night in April 1902 as a vagrant. But once they saw the man's telltale tattoo, they realized they'd found the murderer Pug Ryan.

He was made ready for extradition back to Breckenridge, Colorado, with documents signed by Washington State Governor Henry McBride. Breckenridge Sheriff Detwiler and Deputy Lindsey traveled to Seattle to bring Ryan back to the scene of the crime and to trial.

Of course, all of the still-angry residents of Breckenridge and of nearby Kokomo were waiting for his return. It made news everywhere, including the *Denver Post*. A small jail like the one in Breckenridge was a sitting target for a lynch mob to break in and seize Ryan. So it was decided that the defendant would be sent to be incarcerated in Leadville.

Even Leadville's jail was not enough to hold Ryan securely—but it wasn't because anyone came to lynch him. Ryan's good behavior while in jail may have been what misled the Leadville sheriff, who decided to go fishing one afternoon. While he was gone, Pug and four other inmates sawed off the padlock on the sewer cover and fled through the underground waterway. All of them got away.

And once again, no one was able to find Ryan. It was his own misguided actions that brought about his recapture. Pug returned to his hometown of Cripple Creek and decided to consult with an attorney he had known there. Lawyer J. Maurice Finn was obligated by law to advise Ryan to turn himself in to the authorities.

But Ryan decided not to do that. Instead, he hung around Cripple Creek and was sitting on a bench late one evening on June 7, 1902, when a night marshal saw him and stopped to apprehend him. Once again, Pug tried to use another of his many aliases. This time he said he was Tom Davis, from Denver. But the marshal had recognized him as Pug Ryan, with his tattoo again foiling the murderer's attempts to lie about his identity.

Ryan's trial finally began on June 14, 1902, and the townsfolk of Breckenridge jammed the courtroom (which turned out to be the Grand Army of the Republic (GAR) Hall used primarily for social events). People were all dressed up, and even brought lunches so they didn't have to leave their seats. The trial was swift, and in his last remarks, the impassioned prosecutor reminded the jury about the loss of the two husbands and fathers, and ended by saying, "Oh, Pug Ryan, we got you! Four long years but at last. We cannot give you the gallows, but we will give you the nearest to it."

The jury went home for the night. The next morning, it took them only one hour to decide Ryan's fate: guilty of murder in the first degree. The law kept him from hanging, but not from prison.

The reminders of Ryan continued well beyond the discovery of the stolen treasures ten years after the crime. In 1975 the Pug Ryan Steakhouse and Brewery was opened in downtown Dillon, Colorado, in Summit County. As of 2015, the restaurant is still in business.

LOU BLONGER

Overlord of the Underworld

It was the year 1922 when Harry Tammen, called the "Little Dutchman," who copublished the *Denver Post,* said to one of his reporters: "You know, son, I'm sure sorry we had to print old Lou's name, but the story got so damn big we simply couldn't hold it out any longer."

Tammen was referring to one of the biggest stories in the news business and in Denver history. Lou Blonger had been arrested that day, and his crimes were finally exposed and out in the open. Up until then, Blonger had managed to befriend all the "right" people in Denver and had kept his name separate from his underworld activities. Apparently, even the *Denver Post* had not felt the need to make too much of Blonger's "business," because it seemed harmless enough—except to the victims. Blonger had spent years doing one thing very well, and that was to "catch a sucker." But on this day, his underworld and con game racket finally "caught" him.

Lou Blonger was short, rotund, and likable. His main physical characteristics were his large bulbous nose and protruding lower lip. At the theater and other public events, he enjoyed wearing full formal dress, which drew attention in a crowd.

His working life in Denver started in the saloon business in 1880. He was a French-Canadian who had previously operated a few illegal activities in New Orleans and Salt Lake City. He had also run a Denver dance hall.

Blonger branched out into the gambling business with the policy shop racket. "Policy" was considered the poor man's gambling game, because it made the poor even poorer. It was similar to the numbers racket, which paid off for picking the winning number. Like all numbers games, the odds were highly stacked against the bettor, but the reward for winning was very enticing. A "day number" paid five to one if any number up to seventy-eight was among the first fifteen numbers drawn. Or a bettor could win thirty-two to one if his two selected numbers, called a "saddle," appeared anywhere on the list. A "station number" paid sixty to one if the winning number was in a specific position on the list. Blonger soon became the kingpin of Denver's policy shop racket.

When Blonger arrived in Denver, Doc Baggs was already operating a con scheme that swindled men out of thousands of dollars at a time. Baggs donned a glossy stovepipe hat and carried a silk umbrella wherever he went. He could never understand why another Denver con game newcomer, Soapy Smith, settled for cheating a sucker out of five dollars when he could have conned him for so much more.

But Doc Baggs was growing old, and Soapy Smith had begun to dominate Denver's confidence racket, forcing Doc to join his gang. Soapy was interested in fast profits in mass volume. Lou Blonger would soon be forced to join with Soapy too, if he wanted to run his schemes in Denver.

Blonger would eventually take Doc's technique and develop it into a multimillion-dollar racket. Soapy later left Denver for Creede, Colorado, and when he returned a few years later, it would be Blonger who demanded and received a percentage of Soapy's profits. Blonger had become the leader of Denver's underworld by then, and every other con man had to report to him.

Blonger had learned a lot from Soapy in the early days. Just as Soapy had done, he and the members of his growing underworld group preyed only on visitors to Denver, not the local residents. Blonger also maintained protection from local law enforcement by contributing heavily to both parties during elections. His payroll included many highly ranked officials in the police department, the district attorney's office, and the local office of the US Department of Justice.

The summer tourist season was one of the best times for Blonger to operate his new scheme learned from Doc Baggs. One of Blonger's men, called a "steerer," would stand near the newsstands waiting for a prosperous-looking man to buy an out-of-town newspaper. He would then follow the man back to his hotel lobby and wait for an opportunity to sit next to him for a moment. Then the steerer would get up and walk away, leaving a wallet on his vacated seat.

The out-of-town stranger, seeing the wallet, would pick it up and look inside for information about the owner so the wallet could be returned. The stranger would find a ten-dollar bill, a newspaper clipping, and a document. The clipping told of a huge profit made in a stock market transaction by a man whose picture was shown. There was also a one-hundred-thousand-dollar bond, which guaranteed his ability to provide this service. The clipping and bond were both forgeries.

Usually the stranger would turn in the wallet at the hotel's front desk. The next day, the steerer would come to the hotel to claim the "lost" wallet. He would be accompanied by another man called the "spieler." The grateful owner of the wallet would ask the hotel clerk where he might find the person who had returned it. He and the spieler would then meet the out-of-town stranger to thank him. The stranger, now dubbed the "sucker" by the con men, would immediately recognize the owner of the wallet as the man whose picture was in the newspaper clipping.

The steerer would graciously thank the sucker and expound on the importance of the bond in his market transactions. He would then offer the sucker a
reward for finding the wallet and its contents. The spieler would then go into
action by interrupting this offer saying: "From his appearance, this gentleman
obviously is not the type who would accept a cash reward. Why don't you show
your appreciation by giving him a tip on the market? Give him a chance to make
some money."

The steerer would mildly object to this idea, saying he wasn't supposed
to give out tips, but, on the other hand, he was indebted to this man who had
returned his bond. The spieler would then take over by lauding the abilities of
the stock market operator. He would relate how he'd seen him make thousands
of dollars in the last thirty days. He would say that he had cleaned up on a couple
thousand as the result of a tip he'd been given by this talented man. The clincher
in the spiel was when he told the sucker that he was sending for more money
from his relatives back in his hometown, so that he could get into the next big
deal. It was expected to bring a huge return within the next few weeks. This suggestion was to encourage the sucker to think about what a "sure thing" this must
be if the man would do that.

The sucker usually showed interest since he had seen for himself the newspaper clipping and the one-hundred-thousand-dollar bond to back up the stock
operator's abilities. He would be offered an opportunity to go with the two men
the next day to visit the stock exchange. The sucker had nothing to lose by taking
a look, so he agreed to meet them. Little did the sucker know that the "stock
exchange" was a complete fake, created specifically to lure him in for the kill.

The stock exchange looked entirely real to the sucker, and he would overhear
the stock operator say that he had just made a profit that morning. He had earned
thousands of dollars when his stock had gone up two points. Then he predicted
that it was likely to double in a few weeks, so he decided to leave his cash in this
stock a while longer rather than cash out his profit.

The spieler, who also overheard this remark, would lean toward the sucker
and start talking to him in a low voice. He would say: "This is too good a chance
to lose. Let's go in together and make a killing."

The spieler would then buy a few thousand dollars of stock while the sucker
watched. No further pressure would be put on him, and they would all leave the
stock exchange, inviting the sucker to accompany them again the next day. The
next day their visit would be rewarded by more good news that the stock had
gone up again. With this good news as encouragement, the sucker would then
place a minimal buying order, putting up no cash. Each day they came back to
find the stock had continued to rise. When the stock appeared to have tripled,
the spieler would suggest they sell and take their winnings. The cashier would

actually place a huge stack of cash in the sucker's hands before realizing that the customer had not originally made a payment. The cash would be pulled back by the cashier, who would say: "Our customers must either establish a line of credit or put up the actual cash." He would add, "It's merely a formality, as soon as you produce the cash as evidence of good faith, we'll settle the account."

The sucker would have seen the money in his hands and believe he only needed to come up with the cash to be rewarded with triple that amount. The spieler, who had also supposedly bought a large amount of stock, would then suggest that the sucker go back home to get the needed cash. He would even be encouraged to mortgage his house if necessary to get the money. The sucker would go home to raise the cash and return to meet the spieler. Then they would go together to the stock exchange for the sucker to present the cash. The cashier would say that everything was now in order, and that they should return the next day to receive their winnings.

Unfortunately, they would be told the next day that the stock price had plummeted overnight and they had both lost all their money. The spieler would be outraged over this information and would start a fight with the cashier, even taking a swing at him with his fist. The brawl would be broken up, and the spieler and the sucker would leave empty-handed. The spieler would try to console the sucker, who would believe they both had been big losers.

Usually the sucker was never aware that he had been a victim of a confidence game. The spieler's final task was to get the sucker out of town. He was advised to go home and wait while the spieler promised he would try to get their money back somehow. Nothing would ever come of it, though, and the sucker would often be too ashamed to admit his loss. If he did suspect the scam, his pride usually prevented him from admitting he had been such a sucker. Either way, the con men were rarely reported.

If the ruse did happen to be reported by a victim, the police first tipped off Blonger, who would vacate the stock exchange location before the police arrived. The victim was then victimized once again by being made to look like a fool when he led the police to an empty office.

Blonger's gang is said to have swindled countless men out of a total of $645,720 in one season. Another account suggests the figure was as high as one million dollars. The typical victim was suckered for around five thousand dollars, but it could range as high as one hundred thousand dollars depending on his wealth. By 1920 only one gang member had ever been tried and convicted for this crime.

Blonger, in his early seventies, had enjoyed decades of success in maintaining a strong hold over his Denver operations. He was said to have had additional branches of his racket operating in Florida, California, and Havana.

He planned to continue to run his operation in Denver with the blessings of the corrupt officials. His mob did all the work, and he maintained the relationship with politicians by paying them off handsomely. A direct phone line was said to have been installed between Blonger and the chief of police.

What Blonger hadn't counted on was an honest district attorney. Philip S. Van Cise ran for the office in 1920. He had been a colonel in World War I, and he was a popular candidate among Denver citizens. Blonger tried his usual approach and offered Van Cise a twenty-five thousand dollar campaign donation. If elected, all Blonger wanted in return was for Van Cise to fix the bonds at one thousand dollars for any of his mob who might be arrested.

Not only did Van Cise turn down the offer, but he also won the election and immediately began to lay plans to bring down Blonger. It would take fifteen months of preparation while he used special investigators, hidden Dictaphones, and records gathered from victims of the gang from across the country. In one neatly planned operation, a surprise raid was about to end Lou Blonger's criminal career.

It began at dawn on August 14, 1922, when Van Cise gave the signal to begin the ambush of the entire Blonger gang, numbering sixty-three members. Deputies, special deputies, and members of the state ranger force went to work on their carefully designed actions.

One by one and in twos and threes, the gang members were quietly rounded up by the various deputies and rangers. Many were found at their homes, apartments, and other lodgings. Others were eating breakfast at local cafes, and some had just emerged onto the streets. They were not taken to the local city and county jails. If they had been, the whole operation would have been given away as soon as the first prisoner entered. Van Cise had thought of this in advance and obtained permission to use the Universalist Church as a temporary holding area. Blonger was among the first to be brought in, and all of the men were stripped and searched.

One startling side event almost undermined the whole scheme that Van Cise led that day. He had been painstakingly precise in every part of his strategy to get Blonger and his mob. However, he could not have accounted for an over-zealous *Denver Post* reporter who picked up a tip the night before the raid. The lucky part for Van Cise is that the reporter didn't know for whom the raid was intended. The reporter's information suggested it would take place at the statehouse, so he showed up at the capitol at daylight. He ran across various deputies who were leaving to get into their cars, but none of them would talk to him. He had overheard an earlier conversation by one of the officers that mentioned a church. He repeated this about a "church" to see if it got any attention. One of the officers heard him, feared that the reporter knew far more than he really did, and offered to take him there, hoping to detain him. At the Universalist Church the reporter still did not realize what was happening until he recognized Blonger being led into the building. Immediately he ran for a phone, but was blocked by a guard. Events were soon transpiring so quickly that the guard left the reporter unattended. He got away and was able to phone in the story to the *Post*.

Another lucky break for Van Cise came when the reporter returned and shamelessly announced he had called the *Post*. The district attorney had just enough time to phone the managing editor himself to convince him to sit on the story. The editor agreed to hold it rather than ruin the raid. Although the young reporter lost his big scoop, the story did run the next day. Blonger had always managed to keep his name out of the newspapers, but this time Harry Tammen felt they had to run it.

About thirty-four gang members were captured that day. Of those, twenty actually went to trial in Denver. A few were turned over to officials in other states. Six jumped their bond, and one was declared insane.

Lou Blonger and his chief assistant, Adolph W. Duff, alias "Kid Duffy," spent large parts of their fortunes to defend themselves. Legions of attorneys were hired to contend that the state could not prove its case against them. The two men were confident that they would be acquitted when the trial began in February of 1923.

Van Cise had done his homework, however, and the time spent on investigating Blonger, Duff, and the other con men paid off when all the evidence was presented to the jury. It took the jury four days to reach a guilty verdict. Blonger and Duff were sent to prison for seven years each. The other defendants received three years. Since Lou Blonger was already seventy-three years old, seven years turned out to be longer than he could survive. He died in prison, and so did an era of organized crime in Denver.

IDAHO OUTLAWS

THE EDDYS AND THE SPLAWNS

Counterfeiters

From a distance, Jim and Lewis Eddy looked alert and cheerful as they rode up the trail along Shingle Creek, past the small herd of cattle their families owned. The assorted Eddys and Splawns, members of the two families living creekside in this fold under the Seven Devils Mountains, peered out from the Eddy house into the brisk late fall day and figured that for a good sign. The meeting at Weiser with Emmett Taylor must have gone well. It meant the work they had been preparing for could begin.

Had anyone in Weiser taken note, the sight of the two backwoodsmen meeting with Taylor, a respected professional in town, must have seemed a little odd. But there's no record anyone noticed, and the Eddys casually rode off with the package from Chicago. They did not stop often on the road north, and only small communities lay between Weiser and their home anyway. Pollock was the closest, and it was ten or more miles away.

As they rode up to the house, checked the doors, and double-checked to make sure the family members on guard up and down the creek were in their places, they pulled out their supplies. Their supplies did not consist of food and sundries from town, but of manufacturing equipment. As everyone watched, they opened a box and pulled out the wooden mold pieces: one matching the shape of a five-dollar gold piece, another a ten-dollar gold piece, the third a twenty-dollar piece. And there were near-duplicate wooden pieces, also needed for the work ahead.

Over the next couple of days, they assembled their materials and were ready to produce US gold pieces—or at least reasonable facsimiles thereof. They decided to put in another order for more wooden molds immediately, as they would be needing them soon.

They carefully poured plaster into a set of molds. Most plaster took a long time to dry and cure; limestone plaster could take a month, which would have made it worthless. But this was a special mix developed through their research and it cured almost immediately. Once the pieces were set, they were taken to a kiln out back and fired there.

Now they were ready for metal application, which had three steps.

The plaster pieces were put inside another set of molds, which had small openings on the sides. The Eddys and Splawns melted down a batch of metals—

tin, copper, and lead—into an alloy, and then poured it thinly over the plaster. The layer was so thin that the coins' design remained sharp, but the alloy was strong enough to withstand wear, at least for a while.

The last step was the trickiest. The coins had to look as if they were made of solid gold, and the counterfeiters had prepared a liquid mix with a small amount of gold, together with other metals and chemicals, to create that impression. The surface had to be durable enough that the gold sheen wouldn't wear away too fast. This meant the backcountry families had to use a method that was high-tech for the 1880s. They acquired a large electric battery, able to supply a substantial current—this too had taken some research and effort. The coins were then placed in a tub with metal salts and other components, and a jolt of electric current from the battery was applied.

Not long after, the Splawns and Eddys were looking at their new pile of bright and shiny five-, ten-, and twenty-dollar gold pieces. They may have had plaster hearts, but on quick inspection they looked real, and they looked all the more real after the Splawns and Eddys jostled them around to test their wear and give them a well-used look.

The whole process took a few weeks, and a few months later the metallic odors and smoke in the little valley were long gone, cleared away by wind and rain. The stack of coins sitting in the Eddy house was their little secret.

Now all they had to do was spend them.

Where the Splawns and Eddys came from before Idaho isn't clear, and neither is whether they had a close relationship before their arrival in the Rapid River basin. They do seem to have had some earlier experience as cowboys or cattlemen.

They arrived quietly in 1886, and little notice was taken at first. Not many people lived in the Little Salmon River country; only a few in Pollock, south of the Rapid. There were a few people several miles to the north of Riggins, which had been first settled in 1863 by men who thought they had spotted some flecks of gold at the confluence of the Salmon and the Little Salmon. There was no gold rush in the area—though there had been to the northeast, in Florence—but every so often, someone came to the area hoping for a find. The Splawns and Eddys, to judge from their later history, may have been among them, looking for gold in the unpopulated creeks off the Rapid River. The Eddys settled on Shingle Creek, off the Rapid, and the Splawns a few miles north of them on Papoose Creek.

To the outside world, they appeared to be small-scale farmers and cattlemen. They didn't interact much with the few neighbors who did live in the area, and the cattle they had weren't purchased locally. They seem to have had generally self-sufficient lives in the backcountry for their first few years there.

They were tight families, as close as any. They lived together and worked together, did not fly off in different directions, and were intensely loyal. As many of them as there were, there was never a question of dividing them or turning one against the rest.

Then something gave them some ambition. We don't know what the precise motivation was, but it seems to have involved a combination of factors. The early 1890s were a time of excitement in the Seven Devils. Big finds of copper and smaller discoveries of precious metals were located, mining began on a large scale, and a good deal of ore money began to float around the area.

To the north beyond Riggins, White Bird, and Grangeville, the Nez Perce Indian Reservation was opened for settlement by non-tribal members. That meant the tribes were suddenly receiving money for land from the white settlers; conservative in finance, they preferred gold coins rather than paper money for their payments. In all directions money was changing hands on a regular basis.

Maybe, too, after most of a decade scratching by, the Eddys and Splawns were simply getting tired of the way things had been and were growing weary of livestock. The Eddys had a history as horsemen, as alongside the cattle they raised horses. They especially loved horse racing—an urban endeavor, engaged in informally in many places around Idaho but especially popular at Lewiston.

At first the families decided to counterfeit gold coins for use at the horse races in Lewiston and other tracks around the Northwest. The technical details eluded them at first, but during a visit to Weiser, members of the family met a well-educated local man named Emmett Taylor, who bought into the scheme and helped them devise their manufacturing operation.

The families began using the coins, and they were accepted routinely at the Lewiston track and other locations. For several years they traveled around the region and often exchanged the coins for paper cash. Money exchanged quickly and easily at the track, and once passed it was hard to track. They also exchanged money at county fairs—six of the group managed to work fairs around the region—and other big events, wherever they could easily blend into the crowd. Besides, the families must have figured, counterfeiting was usually assumed to be an urban crime, especially counterfeiting involving the minting of coins. Rapid River was not a suspect town for an illicit mint.

They also made sure never to spend any of their homemade money near Riggins or Grangeville. The spending and exchanging had to be farther afield. That way, they assumed, even if the coins were uncovered as fake, they'd never be caught.

Charley Reavis, a clerk in a Salt Lake City hardware store, was a young man with motivation. In the 1890s the profession of detective had just come into national prominence, and Reavis overflowed with ambition. Having just graduated from high school, he wanted to take a course in detection, if he could find one. But the opportunities in Salt Lake seemed slim. He had no immediate path to get himself from store clerk to polished detective, but one day the unlikely opportunity opened to him as he worked in the store.

A man who seemed to be unfamiliar with Salt Lake, and had a backcountry manner about him, had walked into the store looking for a box of nails, an item available for only a few cents. Reavis collected the box. The man apologized and said he had only a twenty-dollar gold piece to pay for it. Reavis opened the cash drawer and made change for the twenty, handing back nearly that much to the customer, along with the nails. The man thanked him and walked out.

Something about the exchange struck Reavis as peculiar—a backcountry man with only a large-denomination coin available to pay for an item costing a few cents? He strolled from behind the counter and over to the front window, and looked down the street. He saw the man casually walking along and then, a block or so away, he saw him toss the box of nails into an alley.

Reavis saw his opportunity and ran with it.

He took the coin to federal officials in Salt Lake, where they quickly determined it was a fake. Then they told Reavis something else: A big reward, a thousand dollars from the US Department of the Treasury, was waiting for anyone who could help federal authorities bring in the counterfeiters. Reavis was highly interested—he already knew what one of them looked like. He soon learned that the investigation was being run out of Lewiston, Idaho, where the largest number of bad coins had been found. Reavis made his way there.

The US marshal at Lewiston, Eben Mounce, had not been sitting quietly amid the counterfeiting. He knew the horse tracks, especially the Lewiston horse races, were the main distribution points for the bad coins. He and his men quietly interviewed people around the tracks, trying to get a sense of the money flow. Gradually the prime suspects began to emerge: the Eddy and Splawn families. One or another of the family members always seemed to be around when the bad gold coins appeared. And while people could recall them handing them out, no one could recall their taking one.

The research into the families continued, and what the law learned matched with the passage of bad money. The families traveled a lot, and they seemed to spend more than they ought to have been able to afford. But although they were good suspects, there was no proof. The hideaway off the Rapid River was well guarded, and any attempt to storm the place would fail before it began. No one knew when the gold pieces were made, or how, or where the incriminating evidence might be. There always seemed to be family members in the area to stop anyone who ventured near. Even getting through at all with anything short of a small army seemed to be unlikely.

Reavis knew another route needed to be taken. His route would begin at the horse track. Reavis searched around for the fastest horse he could find that hadn't already become visible on the track. He finally located a mare named Nancy Hanks, a little horse that was nonetheless very fast. He entered her in the Lewiston races, opposite a couple of Jim Eddy's horses. Nancy Hanks beat Eddy's horses.

Reavis made a point of introducing himself to Jim Eddy, and of making sure that what started as a competition developed into a friendship.

The amateur detective told parts of the truth. He had no good source of income, he said, and Nancy Hanks was his only big asset. As he met the Eddys and the Splawns a second time, and a third, he suggested that he was nearing destitution, looking for some kind of an opportunity.

They asked him whether he would be willing to part with Nancy Hanks. The answer was no, because she was his main opportunity. But he suggested maybe a half-interest, in return for some other enterprise that might also, on some level, be a moneymaker.

The Eddys and Splawns talked it over. The kid—still not much more than a teenager, certainly presented as no kind of law enforcement official—seemed to be on the level. They had never let an outsider into the family business before, but, well, this looked like an unusual case. Nancy Hanks was a special horse, and they wanted her. Their recent prosperity had eaten away at their long-running discipline and started to infect it with the idea that whatever they really wanted, they could have because they could afford it.

Jim Eddy sent a message north to Lewiston inviting Reavis down to the Rapid River. Reavis jumped at the opportunity. He took a stage south to Grangeville, met there with Mounce to tell him what he was up to, and then headed into the wilderness, up the Rapid River, and into the compound of two families having an unaccustomed internal battle.

Jim Eddy, the group's most fanatic horse watcher, had extended the invitation to Reavis without telling the others. The family had managed its operations successfully so far by letting no one else inside except for Emmett Taylor, and he had been a necessity. Domestically the Eddys and Splawns may not have taken kindly to this outside partner.

Once Reavis was there, however, they had a problem. He had told people where he was going, and if he simply disappeared, there might be trouble. And besides that, Jim Eddy was fiercely determined to have Nancy Hanks, which Reavis had left behind in Lewiston. The families finally concluded that he could stay, and they would observe him and make their decision when they felt comfortable with it. So for the next three months, Reavis spent his time at the Eddy and Splawn houses, helping with the chores. The families did not let him actually witness the counterfeiting. But he learned a good deal about it anyway, and he persuaded them over time that he might be able to pass some of the coins himself, over in Oregon, where he was unknown.

After three months the families' attitudes eased, and they decided Reavis could be trusted. They effectively let him into the family, explained the operation to him, and put the offer to him: half of Nancy Hanks for a slice of the counterfeiting revenues. Reavis eagerly accepted.

He helped the families where he could. He also learned where the supplies were kept, where the molds and dies were located—some of them buried in the yard—and where the coins were stashed before being taken into town.

Over time Reavis came and went between Rapid River and Lewiston. Watching his tracks closely, he stayed in touch with Mounce, and the two of them worked with the Idaho County sheriff, W. M. Williams. Eventually they hatched a plan to finally nail the counterfeiters.

It would go down during the sale of a nearby cattle ranch, owned by the Allison family. A story was concocted that cattle were missing, and Williams issued a warrant for the arrest of Jim Eddy, on a charge of cattle theft. When two members of the families showed up in Grangeville, they were arrested and jailed at the county courthouse at Mount Idaho.

Reavis made his way back down to Rapid River and told the tale: The charges were thin and could be beaten, but it would take a show of force to do it. Everyone the family could muster should show up in that courthouse at Jim Eddy's arraignment. Together, they could provide the evidence and the force to get this legal problem quashed. Otherwise, he warned, the prosecution likely would continue.

They accepted his advice, and one morning in 1896 the rest of the two families, except for Ike Splawn, who was at Lewiston, set off for Mount Idaho. When they arrived in the courtroom, the doors were shut behind them, and all were arrested. The charges: counterfeiting gold coins.

The Eddy women were soon freed, however, and they returned to Rapid River. Reavis showed up, and with his help they buried all the evidence—all the equipment, machinery, molds, and metals. They did not yet know Reavis was undercover, but they soon would.

At the trial in May of 1897 at the federal courthouse in Moscow, Reavis took the stand and told how he had infiltrated the clans and how the operation worked. The equipment and supplies for counterfeiting were all produced; Reavis had helped the federal agents who went searching and unearthed what the sisters had buried.

The trial lasted six days. The jury was sent out for supper, returned, and within a couple of hours had verdicts. They found Jim Eddy guilty on all eight counts, John Eddy guilty on all eight counts, Emmett Taylor guilty on six counts, Charles Scroggin guilty on four counts, Ike Splawn guilty on four counts, and

Stan Splawn and Newt Eddy guilty of conspiracy. Two minors were "recommended to the mercy of the court."

Jim and John Eddy and Emmett Taylor were sentenced to sixteen years of hard labor. The rest received lighter sentences.

The few Eddys who remained out of prison eventually sold off the property at Shingle Creek and were said to have left for Oregon.

The fake gold coins seem to have disappeared from sight. None of them appear to have surfaced in recent years.

Nancy Hanks, the horse whose speed was used to bring down the families, was poisoned at Meadows while Reavis was testifying in the case at Moscow.

And Reavis?

A few accounts float around as to the rest of life. According to one story, he was beaten to death near Culdesac; in another version he was fatally shot; and a third says he lived out his life near Enterprise, Oregon, where he ran a livery stable.

Just possibly, Reavis had had enough excitement for one lifetime.

DIAMONDFIELD JACK

Out on the south Cassia County hills, in the land claimed as grazing territory by the cattlemen, where the sheepmen grazed their flocks and visitors were few, the sight of a new face was welcome, even though some new faces meant trouble.

Not long past daybreak on the morning of February 4, 1896, two young Mormon sheep tenders, Daniel Cummings and John Wilson, saw a horseman riding their way. Although they were in the middle of fixing breakfast, they were glad to see him. He was Davis Hunter, another sheepman whose flock was also located in the no-man's-land a few miles to the west. He was pulling a two-wheeled cart, and unloaded for Cummings and Wilson a small stack of firewood he had chopped. He and the cart were headed to the small town of Oakley, about thirty miles away, to pick up supplies.

All seemed well at the camp. The sheep were nearby, under close observation, close enough that the two sheepdogs were still tied to a wheel of their wagon, not yet needed to rein in the stragglers. The camp was neatly kept, and supplies were adequate. Their wagon, a supply carrier that doubled as a makeshift bunkhouse under a canvas cover, was in good shape.

As he rode off, Hunter was pleased to see things going so well, especially in a time of tension and some risk from the cattlemen. For the sheepmen had all been warned: Work this territory at the risk of death. All of the sheepmen were armed for protection from predators, but now the wolves and coyotes were the least of their fears.

And no one had warned them more often than a talkative, tough man named "Diamondfield" Jack Davis, a gunman for the Sparks-Harrell ranch, which stretched from Cassia County, Idaho, deep into Nevada. Of all the cattlemen and all their hired guns, Davis was the man they feared the most. He had actually shot a man some months before, and word of his heinous reputation spread fast in Cassia County.

A couple of days after Davis Hunter's visit, two other men rode up to Cummings and Wilson's camp. One of them was Jim Bower, the general manager of the immense Sparks-Harrell cattle ranch. The other was a friend of his, Jeff Gray.

The encounter started tensely, with a series of warnings blasting back and forth. Bower warned the sheepmen to stay out of cattle territory; the sheepmen said they would graze where they liked. The cattlemen moved in closer. The two angry sides were only a couple of feet apart.

Exactly what caused Gray, who must have been a quick shot, to fire his weapon is unknown. But evidence does suggest that since he was closer to Wilson, Gray shot him first, a clean shot to the head, the bullet smashing through Wilson's chin into his brain. He crumpled to the ground. The shooter turned and fired at Cummings, hitting him in the stomach; he too fell in front of the wagon. Gray later said his shots were in self-defense; whether one of the sheepmen was brandishing a rifle, which was later found inside their wagon, remains a mystery.

Bower and Gray dragged the injured men inside the wagon, to keep them out of sight. They threw Wilson, who was barely alive but would not last long, onto the upper bed and dragged Cummings to the foot of the bunk. The sheepmen's rifle was there, along with supplies and a few bullets for ammunition; Bower and Gray took nothing. In the commotion and in his haste to leave the scene, Gray dropped his corncob pipe.

Wilson died, never regaining consciousness, within a couple of hours. Cummings's end was more protracted and painful—he died a slow, drawn-out death, taking several hours to leave this earth.

The sheepdogs, tied to the wagon wheel, were left alone. They had water but no food, and after a few days they began to starve.

About a week later another sheepherder named Edgar Severe was walking around the hills and saw scattered sheep to the southeast, in the direction of Cummings and Wilson's camp. He rounded some of them up and headed for the camp. When he discovered what had happened there, he released the nearly dead sheepdogs, returned to his camp, and sent for one of the other herders. He sent a fast horseman named Noel Carlson to race to Oakley. From there another rider and the sheriff were dispatched.

The investigation was haphazard. The scene was trampled not only by law enforcement but by curious sheepmen and cattlemen, and pieces of evidence such as bullets and clothing were passed around from person to person before the court got hold of them. The poor handling of the crime scene mattered little, because no one had any doubt that the killer was Diamondfield Jack.

Diamondfield's origins are unclear; he was sometimes said to have been born in Lynchburg, Virginia, around 1870, though a search for birth records there came up empty. Moving west, he started as a typical knockabout, moving from this job to that, distinguished mostly by a tendency to brag and exaggerate. He tried mining for a while in Nevada, and his claims of what he found there led to the dubious nickname "Diamondfield."

By the early 1890s much of the rangeland in the northern interior West had been staked out by cattlemen who had arrived early enough to stake claims. In the early 1890s overgrazing and fierce winters degraded the pastureland for cattle feeding purposes. Owners of large flocks of sheep, which needed to roam and could happily graze on poor rangeland, began to move in. The two industries had an uneasy coexistence, to say the least. They loosely agreed, in the Cassia County area, that the cattlemen would stay generally west of Oakley.

But irritating incidents kept happening. The cattlemen took the conflict to a higher level. They hired gunmen to ride the ranges, to chase the sheep operators off what they considered to be their land. Their intent was mostly to intimidate. They told the gunmen to try to avoid shooting, but if need be, shoot to wound. If it turned into a matter of shooting to kill, well, the cattlemen would stand behind their guns.

Despite a lack of practical experience, Diamondfield Jack talked himself into one of these jobs, hired by the enormous Sparks-Harrell ranch in Cassia County. The pay was good, but his employers demanded results: The sheepmen had to be genuinely held back. Jack's region-wide reputation as a braggart didn't help much at first.

For a while he simply talked big. He spread the word he was on "fighting wages." Encountering one pair of apparent sheepherders, he warned, "If the sheep come any farther, you'll be facing the muzzle of a Winchester."

The sheepmen were of split mind about Diamondfield. On one hand, he was a known braggart; on the other, some of his talk seemed so bloodthirsty that he might in fact be dangerous. One cold November day in 1895, a herder named Bill Tolman decided to call Jack's bluff. He found out where Jack was—at a shack on the Sparks-Harrell operation, in the Shoshone Valley—and rode up to it, his shotgun at the ready. A small crowd of sheepmen hung back, watching from a hill a quarter-mile away. He called out Jack, who emerged from the shed, his own gun at his side.

They talked and then argued for tense minutes and then an hour or more. Finally Jack Davis, either tiring of the debate or thinking that Tolman's patience was nearly ended, pulled his gun and fired, hitting Tolman in the shoulder. Tolman cried out in pain and dropped his own gun.

For all his rough talk, Jack Davis was no cold-blooded killer. A little startled by what he'd just done, he brought bandage material and water out of the shack to try to help Tolman. He called out to the sheepmen on the hill, telling them to collect their friend. None of them wanted to approach. So Davis, Tolman leaning on him, walked up to them and handed off the wounded man. Then he turned around and went back into the shack.

Once out of sight, Diamondfield Jack's bravado disappeared. He knew he was in trouble. For one thing, Tolman might die, and he might be arrested for murder. Even if Tolman recovered, the shooting might lead to trouble. A lot of law enforcement and a good portion of the politicians in southern Idaho sympathized more with the sheepmen than with the cattlemen, and the idea of taking out the most notorious cattle gunman of the day would be irresistible.

Jack Davis stopped in at Sparks-Harrell headquarters to collect his pay and to resign. He rode south to the nearest border, into Nevada. He spent several weeks at Wells, at the saloons and bordellos there. He ventured out a little further after the turn of the year, but he stayed mostly on the southern side of the Nevada-Idaho line, mainly hanging around the Middlestacks ranch, which was part of the Sparks-Harrell operation, carousing with the cowboys there.

One day in late January while he was staying there, Jack Davis rode off with another sometime gunman named Fred Gleason to look for two horses that had wandered off. The search took them into Idaho sheep country. That night, wandering around in the dark, they unexpectedly rode up to a sheep camp. Startled, Davis reached for his gun quickly, almost as a reflex, but his horse startled, too, and Davis's finger accidentally pulled the trigger and he shot into the ground. The sheepmen in the camp, alerted to the presence of two unexpected horsemen and probably quickly registering that Diamondfield Jack was one of them, grabbed their rifles and began to fire.

Maybe it was that no one was prepared and therefore shooting well, or maybe it was the darkness, but no people were hit by the dozen or so bullets that flew back and forth in the next few minutes. But Diamondfield Jack had added another shooting incident to his résumé.

The shooting of the Mormon sheepherders, Cummings and Wilson, occurred about a week later. Around that time Jack Davis was working around the Middlestacks, then said he was leaving there. He headed back south into Nevada, passed through Wells, then wound up in a string of ranches to its southwest, in the Lamoille Valley. There he regaled anyone who would listen with tales of his exploits, usually exaggerated—the sheepmen he had shot, the nighttime shooting at the sheep camp, and much more, real or imagined.

J. B. Green, who ran a general store in the valley, recalled later how a drunken Diamondfield Jack had wandered into his store, telling anyone who would listen about the sheepmen he had shot. That, as it turned out, was only shortly after news of the Cummings and Wilson murders had made its way there. People around northern Nevada and southern Idaho were beginning to put the pieces together.

Davis himself had not heard anything of the killings—yet.

He swung north, drifting through the Middlestacks area again, and finally chanced into the news about Wilson and Cummings, and the realization that he was the prime suspect. After a little discussion with some of the ranchers and hired hands seeking advice on how to leave the country, he then switched course and rode hard south, through Nevada and into Arizona. He appeared to be headed to Mexico. Davis covered the desert, and the large distance, quickly. He was within a couple hundred miles of Mexico and he might have made it, but for a dog.

In the middle of the street in downtown Congress, Arizona, a barking cattle dog alerted everyone to Jack's presence on the day in April 1896 when he rode into town. Barking and nipping at Davis's horse, it was sufficiently annoying that Davis shot it.

And with that, Diamondfield Jack's days at liberty ended for a long time.

A tearful boy, the dog's owner, quickly found a police officer, who was easily able to locate Jack Davis. Davis might have been able to escape that scrape with a fine and an apology, but he was spooked by the arrival of the officer. He pulled his gun on the officer and disarmed him, and did the same to a second officer who showed up. Plenty of other people were armed as well, however, and one public-spirited citizen pulled his weapon and shot Davis with a well-aimed bullet that didn't kill but did knock him down.

Mainly for his behavior toward the cops, Jack Davis—traveling under the name of Frank Woodson and held by officials who knew nothing of the murder case building to the north—was sentenced to a year in prison. He was manacled and shipped to Yuma to spend time at one of the most notoriously awful prisons in the old West, the Arizona Territorial.

Davis did not settle down there; he may have realized that law enforcement across the jurisdictional lines might soon figure out what had happened. He escaped on one occasion, briefly, but after three hours at large in Yuma, he was back in prison and in solitary confinement. Returned to the normal prison population, he was soon in a fight with another prisoner and was sent back to solitary. Davis was in confinement when Cassia County Sheriff Oliver Anderson, with two deputized sheepmen in tow, finally showed up. He and others in Idaho had just figured out where Davis was, around the time his original sentence was due to end in March 1897. Anderson was carrying a warrant for his extradition to Idaho on charges of the murders of Cummings and Wilson.

The case was listed as the state against Jack Davis, but it turned into something more expansive—two large teams arrayed against each other, even apart from the teams of lawyers. Davis discovered that the promise the cattlemen had made to their operatives—that they would stand behind them no matter what—was sound. John Sparks, who ran the Sparks-Harrell ranch, hired the attorney widely regarded as the best Idaho had seen since the territory was created: James Hawley, a Boisean who had handled hundreds of criminal cases—more than three hundred in his whole career, he once estimated. He was famed as one of the best attorneys anywhere in the West. And he wasn't alone. The cattlemen hired others to help him. One of them was Kirtland Perky, a former law associate of William Jennings Bryan and a future senator from Idaho. If they wanted to demonstrate to other gunmen that they would stand up for their own, they did it impressively.

The sheepmen were no less determined, and they had backing from large portions of the state's political establishment, along with—widespread word had it—leaders of the Church of Jesus Christ of Latter-Day Saints, of which the murdered sheepmen were members. They bought legal talent, too, even though the case was technically under the jurisdiction of the Cassia County prosecutor, John Rogers. The sheepmen wanted more insurance, so they made sure that first one special prosecutor from Utah was added to the case, and then another from Boise. The Boisean was a hot young attorney, fast rising in the law and in politics, named William Borah.

The case opened for trial in Albion before a jury of a dozen men, all farmers but for one miner. All of the jurors lived among the sheepmen and sympathized with them. They represented most of the people in Cassia County; Albion, the county seat, was a central town for the sheepmen.

The trial proceeded predictably, with evidence piling up about Jack Davis's conflicts with the sheepmen, many of whom were called to testify.

Hawley delivered a powerful rebuttal, which made a strong case that Davis was too far south from the murder site in early February of 1896 to have committed the crime. He developed several arguments for Davis's innocence. But the outcome may have been set from the beginning, even without the career-making case developed by the future senator Borah. After discussing the case for three hours, the jury returned to the court with a determination that Davis was guilty of murder.

Judge C. O. Stockslager sentenced Davis to be hanged, two months hence.

Hawley appealed to the Idaho Supreme Court. It upheld the sentence. Davis was rescheduled for the noose.

Only then did the cattlemen's real willingness to help Davis emerge. Ranch manager Bower went public, telling the story of how he and Jeff Gray had visited the sheep camp, and how Gray had shot the herders—in self-defense, he said.

Hawley took that confession to the pardons and parole board. The board reaffirmed that Davis had to hang.

That didn't stop the Cassia County prosecutors from trying Bower and Gray for the murders of Cummings and Wilson, or a jury from acquitting them on grounds of self-defense.

Hawley kept appealing for Davis, now in federal courts, where he finally began to win some rulings. He sought a new trial in Cassia County; it was denied. More appeals to the state parole board led to new dates for execution, until the board reversed itself and sentenced Davis to life imprisonment instead. Finally, in December of 1902, after reviewing the case over and over, the pardons and parole board formally pardoned Davis for the crime the State of Idaho still maintained he had committed.

When Diamondfield Jack Davis was released from the rock penitentiary building east of Boise, he hit the road. He walked about a mile toward town, stopping at the city's new natatorium, where he shared a few drinks with his attorney, Hawley, who was now Boise's mayor.

Then he made his way to the train station and took trains south to Tonopah, Nevada.

He never did find diamond fields. But, scouting the hills around Tonopah, he did find some precious metals and had the one big stroke of luck in his life. For a short time Jack Davis became a wealthy man, a prominent citizen in central Nevada, and he was even renowned for breaking up a lynch mob at one point.

But his wealth and his health soon dissipated, and Davis became, again, another Western wanderer. He died in 1949, after being hit by a taxicab in Las Vegas.

LYDA LEWIS

Serial Wife

When Lyda Lewis and Ed Meyer married in September 1920, the nuptials must have struck their neighbors as the cap of a happy story, a reversal of several bad episodes in their lives. And now here they were at the Twin Falls Hospital only a month later facing an emergency.

Meyer was the manager of the Blue Lakes Ranch, having worked many years for the patriarch of Twin Falls, Ira Perrine. But it had not been an easy time; the ranch life was wearying, and now he had the chance to settle down.

Lyda Lewis, after growing up in the shadow of the Perrine spread, had married at a young age, only to become a widow just three years later. And then a second marriage—widowed. And a third—widowed. And now her fourth husband was desperately ill. And she was only twenty-eight. But hardly anyone who saw her, hardly anyone male at least, thought about any of that when she came by. She was a striking beauty, her red hair, perfect figure, and pretty face bringing her instant attention wherever she went.

Ed Meyer could only groan in pain because his insides seemed to be on fire.

Doctors had not been able to reach a diagnosis. Ferocious strains of the flu were still sweeping around the country—the disease was said to have carried off one of Lyda's previous husbands—and this latest illness could be that. They asked what he had been eating. For a time they settled on inadvertent food poisoning, from the sardines and milk he'd been consuming.

They kept him at the hospital under observation, and the days dragged on. Grasping for anything that might work, the doctors tried a battery of tests. None of them seemed to do much good. For a time Meyer was only hanging on.

Then, after six days, Ed Meyer seemed to turn a corner. His fever went down, he breathed easier, and the pain faded. The doctors still weren't sure what was wrong with him, but his stay at the hospital seemed to be helping.

Lyda visited him regularly. The day after he seemed to be on the mend, she approached one of the nurses with a request. The two of them were still newlyweds, she said, and they'd had hardly any time together. She wasn't sure how much longer he'd be cooped up in this hospital and Lyda wanted some time alone with her husband. She'd brought a picnic basket with the fixings for lunch and was hoping for a little private time. The staff was sympathetic. There was not much bureaucracy; the hospital at Twin Falls had opened its doors only two years before. Things were still informal.

Lyda happily took her picnic basket into the room where her husband, still weak from fighting his way back to health, was waiting. They were in there for several hours. Nurses walking past heard their conversation into the mid-afternoon.

Then Lyda threw the door open, panic on her face once again. Something was wrong! Ed was sick again and doubled over with horrific pain, stumbling and falling.

The doctors went to work, trying rapid-speed some of their earlier treatments. Nothing worked.

Early that evening, he died.

They were stunned; puzzled. He had seemed to be doing so well.

They might have been less puzzled if, during the admissions process, Lyda had been required to make a full statement about the couple's insurance policies. They might have found useful a notation that, only a couple of weeks before, she had taken out an insurance policy on Meyer's life, which was now set to pay out to her in the amount of twelve thousand dollars.

If it is true that children learn about domestic life, and as adults fashion their own, after their childhood family experiences, you have to wonder what it was that Lyda Trueblood could have learned from her father. She might have learned from him the concept of the easy opportunity, and how quickly it can slip away. She might have learned how a lifetime of backbreaking work could only lead to a bare, drab, unsatisfying life.

Certainly she came away with a craving for the fast buck and a taste for the high life. But she failed her final exam. All her efforts, all her schemes, and all her killings yielded in the end a sad and dreary life shrouded in obscurity.

But once, she was an international femme fatale—and Idaho's most notorious serial killer.

Lyda was born in 1892 in Keytesville, Missouri, a farming community no bigger today than it was then, now a little more than an hour's drive from Kansas City but then out of reach for ordinary farmers. The 1890s were a desperate period for farmers nationally, a time of populist political unrest, and almost all badly wanted to improve their prospects.

William Trueblood was in that frame of mind when, on a visit to town, he spotted a poster advertising spectacular opportunities in Idaho. Federal water had just become available in the south-central part of the state, and the whole region was considered almost magical, even being called the Magic Valley.

In late 1906 the Truebloods—William, his wife, a son, and two daughters—packed up and headed west, across the empty deserts, over mountains and streams, much as the Oregon Trail pioneers had decades before. When they arrived, William Trueblood promptly bought a tract of land.

The big profits, made by people like irrigation planner Ira Perrine, were coming from the lands near the Snake River. Trueblood's land was well south of that, watered by the Salmon Falls Dam, but not watered well. As his daughter Lyda, now fourteen, watched him struggle to survive, doing no better in Idaho than he had in Missouri, she picked up on some life lessons.

Brightly red-haired and with a good figure, Lyda attracted plenty of male attention, and she quickly concluded it was the big advantage she had in escaping her father's life. She graduated from Twin Falls High School in 1910, and by then she had her pick of suitors.

Robert Dooley was a young man with family tendrils both in the Magic Valley and in Missouri, and by a few degrees more prosperous than the Truebloods. He had known Lyda back in Missouri, and now offered to take her there. She accepted. They were married in March 1912 in Twin Falls, and then drove back east to Keytesville, where Dooley took over part of the family property. Those two years were not as prosperous as they had hoped, so they returned to Twin Falls with Dooley's brother Ed and a daughter named Laura Marie in tow and bought a small farm.

The young family had just started to develop that farm when their neighbors were surprised to hear that Ed Dooley had died of ptomaine poisoning. They were even more surprised to hear a few months later, in late 1915, that Robert Dooley, too, had died, apparently of the typhoid epidemic that was sweeping the country.

The deaths were investigated, but only lightly. Accidental poisonings sometimes happened on farms, and epidemics were rampant. Only later, after extensive checks and research, would authorities learn that a life insurance policy had been taken out on Ed Dooley, with the payoff of twenty-five hundred dollars going to Robert and Lyda, and that another policy on Robert had been taken out too for five thousand dollars, with Lyda as the beneficiary. The insurance companies paid and did not think much of it.

Lyda spent some time on the small farm but more often was seen in town, at first the demure widow but soon catching appreciative attention again. Stopping at a cafe in Twin Falls, she fell into a conversation with its owner, Billy McHaffie, and then another, and before long he asked her to marry him. They were married in May 1917 and seemed to people in town to be a happy couple.

All seemed well for a year and more. McHaffie prospered with his cafe and other properties he owned outside of town. Then in the fall of 1918, as headlines around the country warned of a fast-spreading influenza epidemic, Billy McHaffie abruptly fell ill. The speed and the depth of his illness shocked his friends and customers; he had always been a robust, healthy man.

And then the daughter, Laura Marie, died too, evidently of the same disease. To the doctors, both deaths looked like cases of the feared influenza, and they certified them as such.

And then, days after McHaffie's funeral, Lyda Trueblood Dooley McHaffie sold all her property and vanished from Twin Falls.

Only one man knew where she went. Some weeks before Bill McHaffie's death, a farm machinery salesman named Harlan Lewis had come to their door, trying to make a sale. McHaffie noted that Lyda seemed struck by him, and neighbors reported that the couple started arguing a lot more from that point on. When McHaffie died, Lyda split from Twin Falls, apparently not with Lewis but with plans to meet him. They married in Denver in March 1919.

The happy couple drove north to Lewis's business headquarters at Billings, Montana. But the new marriage did not last long. In July, just three months after the wedding, Harlan Lewis was dead at Billings. Lyda Trueblood Dooley McHaffie Lewis stayed around long enough to collect on the ten-thousand-dollar life insurance policy—double most of the previous ones—she had just taken out on Lewis's life. As soon as she cashed out his estate, she vanished again.

So far she had managed to run under the radar of law enforcement, and had she moved on to a new community, she might have extended her streak much longer. But instead she returned to Twin Falls, early in 1920.

There she soon began to socialize with Ed Meyer, a large, powerfully built man who was manager of the Blue Lakes Ranch for businessman Ira Perrine, one of the founders and pillars of Twin Falls.

A few days after Ed Meyer died, Lyda tried to collect on the twelve-thousand-dollar life insurance policy. The company rejected the payout. For all her experience around insurance policies, Lyda had made a mistake with this one because an initial payment had been late. Furious but determined not to hang around, she disappeared again.

It was this second abrupt disappearance from Twin Falls that caught local attention. The Perrine family applied pressure to get to the bottom of this odd sequence of events. The sheriff needed no pressure to go after the case, since he was an old friend of Meyer's. He assigned Deputy Sheriff Virgil Ormsby to look into it and to find Lyda and clear up the nagging suspicion that something wasn't right.

Ormsby's investigation would take on almost epic dimensions.

Starting with the suspicion of murder, he thoroughly explored the old McHaffie house, now under new ownership. The new owners drew his attention to something unusual in the basement, which had been left over from the McHaffie tenancy: a huge stack of flypaper supplies. Ormsby put the pieces together: Lyda had boiled the flypaper, extracting the arsenic from it, and then poisoned the food of her husbands, and presumably her daughter as well. Arsenic poisoning could be hard to detect if law officials weren't looking for it.

Ormsby began to look for it. He started exhuming bodies and found trace amounts of arsenic in Meyers's and McHaffie's bodies. He developed a strong circumstantial case, with but one problem: Lyda Trueblood Dooley McHaffie Lewis Meyer was nowhere to be found.

She had wandered down to California, working jobs and conserving her money, and finally seizing on Vincent Paul Southard, then the chief petty officer on the USS *Monterey*. At this point Lyda described herself as a nurse, though she never tried to work as one. Southard fell hard, and within weeks the two were married in Los Angeles in November 1920. Southard was transferred to Pearl Harbor and Lyda followed him there.

Following one thin lead after another, Ormsby figured that Lyda had moved to the coast. With the help of California law enforcement, he tracked her from one city to another, at one point south of the border into Tijuana, and finally back to the Los Angeles area. There he discovered she had just left for Hawaii, where Chief Petty Officer Southard had been transferred.

Hoping to block another poisoning, Ormsby called law enforcement at Honolulu. They followed both of Ormsby's instructions: to arrest Lyda and to check around to see if any life insurance policy had been taken out on her new husband, with Lyda the beneficiary. One had been, and it consequently was canceled.

Brought back to Twin Falls to stand trial, Lyda Southard became an international celebrity, tracked by news photographers on her trip back to Idaho and during the trial. Her latest husband, Southard, accompanied her, not believing that his new bride could be a killer. Lyda generally seemed to enjoy the attention, and she gave interviews. But one profile of her in the *San Francisco Call and Post* seemed to shake her: "Her face is that of a weak woman capable of committing the crimes of which she is accused, yet unconscious of her guilt."

Lyda Trueblood Dooley McHaffie Lewis Meyer Southard was jailed and in September 1921 was tried in the same courthouse where she'd signed three marriage licenses. But despite the hoopla, her trial was a somber affair, detailed and protracted. Prosecutors pulled out bottles of liver and spleen—the exhibits were called "grisly." Lasting seven weeks, it was the longest criminal trial in Idaho up to then.

She was convicted of second-degree murder; speculation ran that jurors blanched at the idea of hanging a woman. But they had no doubt about her guilt, and after watching the trial neither did Paul Southard, who finally filed for divorce.

Prisoner 3052 was sentenced to life imprisonment. Walking around the old rock penitentiary, she developed a schedule of her own, ironically a more domestic one: Her hours were spent sewing, gardening, and listening to music on an old Victrola. She was a little shy of thirty years old.

As the years passed, the quiet and demure prisoner was gradually given more leeway at the prison. Rumors of relationships with staff at the prison were of questionable authenticity, but in 1931, as she approached a decade behind bars, she definitely established a romantic relationship with an inmate named David Minton.

In the middle of the night in May 1931, two weeks after Minton was released from prison, Lyda broke through the bars on her window and climbed down a hand-fashioned rope, and then down the trellises of the roses she had so carefully tended. Minton met her outside, and they drove off in his car.

A frantic search ensued for months, but it came up empty. Police finally caught Minton in Denver, but Lyda wasn't with him; he maintained that they'd split up weeks before and he didn't know where she was. For several weeks he stuck to that story. But after he was rearrested (for helping her escape) and returned to Idaho, he admitted he did have a clue.

Authorities were closing in on Lyda when she got married again in Denver to Harry Whitlock. Just before detectives arrived at their house, she split after getting some travel money from Whitlock. Calling herself Fern at this point, she had hooked up with him initially by doing housekeeping work. She had sug-gested a twenty-thousand-dollar life insurance policy on him, but it hadn't been purchased by the time she left.

Lyda was finally picked up in Kansas, and the Whitlock marriage was annulled. She was returned to Boise fifteen months after her escape.

Lyda stayed in prison most of the next decade, but then public attitudes toward longtime prisoners began to change. In October 1941 she was released to the home of her sister, Blanche Quigley, and Blanche's husband, John, at Nyssa, Oregon. She lived a quiet life there and was fully pardoned in October 1943. For a couple of years, she stayed there, but then wanderlust hit. She returned to the family farm at Twin Falls, but her relatives and other townspeople didn't welcome her presence.

After some months she moved on to Provo, Utah, where she wasn't known, and there scraped together enough money to buy a small secondhand shop. She met a man named Hal Shaw and married him. Then Shaw's children found out about Lyda's past, and one day Shaw vanished from Lyda's sight. She later moved to Salt Lake City and worked as a housekeeper and waitress. She died in February 1958, apparently of a heart attack.

She was buried in Utah, under the name of Lyda Shaw.

KANSAS OUTLAWS

KATE BENDER

Femme Fatale

An Independence, Kansas, man by the name of Wetzell suffered from excruciating neuralgia. Medical remedies being what they were in 1872, Wetzell had little choice but to live in pain. So when he read an advertisement for the supernatural healing powers of a German woman near Cherryvale, he readied his horse and carriage for the fourteen-mile journey across southeast Kansas.

The ad likely read something like this one, which began circulating in the summer of that year:

> *Prof. Miss KATIE BENDER*
> *Can heal all sorts of Diseases; can cure Blindness, Fits,*
> *Deafness and all such diseases, also Deaf and Dumbness.*
> *Residence, 14 miles East of Independence, on the road from*
> *Independence to Osage Mission one and one half miles South*
> *East of Norahead Station.*
> *Katie Bender*
> *June 18, 1872*

It was autumn when Wetzell made his way to see Kate Bender, with his friend Gordan riding along. As the leaves fell around them, Wetzell must have been full of hope—hope to be cured, to live a normal, pain-free existence. Perhaps he was skeptical of the woman's claims, or perhaps he had heard of her work as a medium in the area and was impressed. Either way, he had decided to pay her a visit.

Wetzell and Gordan entered a hollow of cottonwood and plum trees, cut by a shallow stream called Drum Creek. There they found the Bender residence and pulled up near dinnertime. It was a primitive, square structure on the much-traveled road from Fort Scott or Osage Mission to Independence. The place was just eighteen miles from the border of Indian Territory, now the state of Oklahoma. It was sparsely populated frontier, and the Bender family—four German immigrants—had set up an inn for feeding and boarding travelers just over a year prior.

Wetzell and Gordan entered the place to meet John Bender, perhaps sixty years of age, a thin man of average height and few English speaking skills; his wife, around the same age, with blue eyes and brown hair and only slightly better English; John Jr., a mustached young man with a thick accent; and finally Kate, the young daughter with auburn hair and a commanding presence. Kate, with her perfect English and outgoing persona, seemed to be the leader of the small pack.

The inn was a one-room house with a large canvas hung to separate two sections: the front, with shelves of basic groceries for sale and a table for serving meals, and the back, with beds for the family and guests and a trapdoor to a cellar. Behind the house were a garden, an orchard, and a few livestock in a barn.

Kate flashed her pretty dark eyes at the men and insisted that they have dinner before Wetzell's healing session could begin.

As they sat down to eat, the men found that their chairs had been situated snugly and awkwardly against the canvas partition. Then they noticed that the two Bender men, John Sr. and John Jr., were bustling behind the curtain. Something didn't feel right. Nervous, the men insisted on eating while standing up. They moved away from the table, and charming Kate transformed into an angry whirlwind, chastising them for their bad manners.

Wetzell and Gordan quickly left the uncomfortable situation, hopping into their carriage as the Benders stood outside staring and consorting. Two wagons happened by, and the men raced to join them on the road, looking back to see the odd family watching as they went. They didn't notify authorities and went back to Independence, Wetzell still ailing from neuralgia but happy to be out of the Benders' midst.

When the two men finally shared their story, they decided that they had overreacted. What had happened? A family of innkeepers tried to feed them dinner. Nothing more, right? Unbeknownst to them, others would have similar tales from the inn.

William Pickering, a wealthy man from back East, noticed disturbing stains on the canvas partition and hurried away. Father Paul Ponziglione, a middle-aged Catholic missionary who established several churches in the state, rushed out of the house for his horse when he saw John Sr. holding a hammer behind the canvas.

People from all walks of life reported that something wasn't quite right at the Bender Inn.

The Benders had arrived in Labette County in the fall of 1870, when they built their first shanty on the property of country grocer and fellow German immigrant Rudolph Brockmann. By the time they moved on to their modest inn near the Osage Mission Trail, the Benders were known to be a quiet, even strange lot. But Kate was a different story.

Vivacious and outgoing, Kate made appearances at country dances and briefly waited tables at a hotel in Cherryvale. She even went to church on Sunday, spreading the word there that she was deeply in touch with the spiritual world. In fact, she claimed, she was a medium. Kate claimed she could summon and commune with the spirits of dead loved ones—for a price. She began holding séances for locals and found such success that she took her act on the road. During the summer of 1872, Kate toured small Kansas towns such as Parsons, Labette, Oswego, and Chetopa, lecturing on spiritualism in theaters and halls. In those days it was rare to see a lone woman professing on stage, and her show was a hit. Kate herself was a hit too—for her sharp eyes and dark auburn hair.

By the fall of 1872, when Wetzell and his friend met Kate and her family, the clairvoyance road trip was over. Kate had more important business to tend to at the Bender Inn.

That fall, people started disappearing. Travelers making their way past Cherryvale would go missing, and by March 1873 perhaps a dozen individuals had traveled into the area and never come out. Locals wondered what sort of bad luck was in their midst. Little was done about the situation, though, until a prominent, wealthy doctor was among the missing.

Dr. William York was among the most esteemed citizens of Independence, not far from Cherryvale and the Bender Inn. He had the finest things—a well-bred horse, a quality saddle, luxurious clothes and boots, and an expensive gold watch. And he came from good stock. One of the good doctor's brothers was a state senator and among the most powerful men in the state. Another brother, Col. A. M. York at Fort Scott, was a man of great wealth.

William visited Colonel York in Fort Scott in March 1873, leaving on the ninth of the month to return to Independence. He stayed the night at Osage Mission and, upon leaving there on the tenth, told friends he planned to have lunch at the Bender Inn. He shared the same plans with another friend he met on the road just two miles from the Bender place. Then he disappeared.

Another story about Dr. York goes like this: He lent a horse and buggy to a man and his young daughter, who never returned. Dr. York went looking for them along the Osage Mission Trail and disappeared himself. The details of his trip might be disputed today, but it's certain that Dr. York was never seen again.

Days passed, then weeks. Colonel York made it his business to find his missing brother, hiring investigators and rounding up search teams. Sniffing around the area, Colonel York happened upon the man named Wetzell, who shared his story of his creepy encounter with the Bender family.

On April 3 a large group rode on horseback to the Bender Inn. The family said they knew nothing of Dr. York. Unconvinced, the colonel returned a few weeks later with a dozen armed locals. By then, though, the Bender family was gone.

The group found starving livestock in the barn and little remaining in the house but a sledgehammer and a knife. It was obvious that the Benders had no plans to return.

Searching the property, the group opened the trapdoor to the pitlike cellar beneath the house. They found the dark hole streaked and splattered with blood.

Fanning across the property, they would find ten bodies buried in the orchard behind the house, as well as another in Drum Creek. One of the victims was Dr. York. All the bodies had their skulls crushed and their throats slit—all except a small girl, who may have been buried alive. She was identified as the daughter of George Loncher, who was among the slit-throated bodies. The father and daughter had been en route to Iowa after Loncher's wife died.

Investigators surmised that the Benders had run their deadly inn with a consistent strategy. First the guest would be seated for a meal with his back to the canvas room divider. He would be seated so close to the canvas that his head could easily be detected from the other side. While Kate and her mother served the food, one of the Bender men would swing a hammer to crack the victim's skull. The victim's throat then would be slit before his body was robbed of any valuables and dumped through the trapdoor in the floor. Later the body would be buried in the orchard. Because they preyed on people far from home, they had been able to carry on this way for many months before arousing real suspicions.

Once the Benders' serial killing was revealed, posses of vigilantes were formed. Colonel York offered a reward for the capture of his brother's murderers, as did state and local officials. The governor's proclamation of the award, posted throughout the area, described the four Benders, including the "good looking, well formed, rather bold in appearance" Kate. The statement also suggested that John Jr. might actually be one John Gebardt, but the true nature of the four suspects' relationships would never be known.

Vigilantes got hold of Rudolph Brockmann, the German farmer who first met the Benders in Labette County and let them squat on his land. Rumors flew that he and Kate were lovers; surely he knew their whereabouts. The posse strung Brockmann up by a noose, demanding that he divulge any information he had. After several tries at strangling him into submission, the men finally let him go.

Meanwhile the Bender Inn had become a grisly tourist attraction. People came from great distances to see the place, be photographed there, and tear pieces from the structure for souvenirs. Before long the place had been destroyed, but its former occupants remained at large.

Stories about the Benders' escape, or possible demise, filled streets and newspapers across the country. Some reported that the four had split up at the train station to avoid identification as a group. Other reports had them escaping to Mexico. Or Canada. Or returning to Germany. Still others suggested that the Benders had run into other criminals and met their demise. Vigilantes had caught the Benders and hanged them, some said. No, they were shot. No, burned to death.

Three years later a Chicago man claimed to have gotten the real story when he met a Kansas man on a train to Washington Territory.

"During the conversation," the man wrote to the local paper, "knowing that he was from the vicinity of the Bender murders, I expressed my astonishment that these people, ignorant of and unfamiliar with the geography of this country as they must have been, had been so successful in making their escape from the officers of the law, especially as a large reward had been offered for their apprehension. In a half-confidential tone, and in a manner which lent credence to his statement and impressed me with a belief of his honesty, he said that so far as he was concerned there was no mystery about it." According to the report, the Kansas man went on to say that Colonel York's posse indeed had apprehended and killed the Benders.

This theory was thrown for a loop the next year, though, when a man and woman believed to be John Bender Sr. and his wife were arrested in Omaha. Their identity could not be confirmed, and they were released.

Then, in November 1889, two women were arrested in Oswego, Kansas, believed to be Kate and her mother. But their identities were confirmed to be otherwise, and the women finally were released in January 1890.

In 1901 four individuals were apprehended near Fort Collins, Colorado. Again, no dice. But in 1908 a new development revived the old theory that the Benders had themselves been killed. On his deathbed former Independence resident George Evans Downer said he had been among a five-man posse who chased the Benders over the prairie on a dark, cloudy night. The Benders fired from their wagon, killing one of the vigilantes, Downer said. The group finally caught up with the family, shooting all but Kate, who jumped from the wagon, cut one of the horses loose, and sped off. The posse shot her horse, which fell on Kate, killing her.

But wait! In 1910 a California woman announced that she had been a friend of Kate Bender, now known as Mrs. Peters, and that Kate had died recently of natural causes.

The case continued to fascinate for decades. The minutes from a 1938 Kansas State Historical Society report that the organization received a call asking whether Kate Bender had been captured or killed. And for some years the town of Cherryvale hosted an annual Bender Day celebration, complete with a nineteenth-century costume contest and a living descendant of a Bender victim.

The "bloody Benders" lived on in infamy, but it's still unknown whether they lived on in the flesh. A Kansas state historical marker outside Cherryvale reads, "The end of the Benders is not known. The earth seemed to swallow them, as it had their victims."

HENRY BROWN

Good Rifle, Bad Marshal

On the first day of 1883, the town of Caldwell presented its beloved new marshal with a fine gift—a customized rifle. It was a fitting gift for a man whose line of work called for top-notch weaponry. And it was a beauty. The Winchester featured inlays of precious metals—silver and gold—and a lovely silver plate engraved with a sincere tribute: "Presented to city marshal H. N. Brown for valuable services rendered in behalf of the citizens of Caldwell Kas." The inscription included the name of the town's approving mayor, A. N. Colson. Marshal Henry Brown was the toast of Caldwell.

Caldwell was a particularly raunchy cow town just north of Indian Territory. Reckless cowboys, six-shooters never far from their dirty hands, menaced morally upright citizens and had their run of the saloons. Then Henry Brown rode into town. He had served as deputy sheriff of Oldham County in Texas, and he had a cool, quiet, commanding presence. In June 1882 Caldwell hired Brown as assistant marshal. He quickly made a name for himself as a tough customer, a fast draw, and a reasonable official. Six months later he received his big promotion and his gorgeous rifle.

Brown brought Ben Wheeler—an impossibly tall stretch of a Texas man—to town to serve as his deputy, and together they tamed one of the wildest towns in the West. Gun ordinances were enforced. Unruly drunks were jailed. Violent offenders were arrested. Weary Caldwell residents saw true order and civility for the first time, and Brown's popularity only grew. When he killed two renegades in the line of duty, the town applauded. Just a year after his appointment as marshal, Brown married and bought a house, delighting the town with his obvious intentions to stay in Caldwell. After living in fear of bandits, drunks, and wayward cowboys, residents felt lucky to have a hero in their midst.

Had they only known.

Henry Brown might have cleaned up Caldwell, but his own past was very, very dirty.

Brown was born in 1857 in Cold Spring Township, Missouri, and was orphaned as a child. He stayed with his sister on their uncle's farm close to Rolla, Missouri, until he was seventeen, at which point Brown rode west to see where life might take him. It was 1875, and the frontier promised adventure.

Brown found work on a ranch in eastern Colorado and then hunted buffalo for some time. In 1876, though, he found himself in trouble in the Texas panhandle. He killed a man there and headed farther west to Lincoln County, New Mexico.

In New Mexico Brown got on with a rancher named L. G. Murphy. He worked for Murphy for a year and a half, during which time Murphy was embroiled in a bitter battle with competing ranchers John Chisum and John Tunstall and lawyer Alexander McSween. When Tunstall was murdered, a gang of his supporters formed—including a young fellow known as Billy the Kid. In early 1878 Brown, angry over a salary dispute, dumped Murphy and joined Billy's group, known as the Regulators. Violence over cattle ranges, known today as the Lincoln County War, then raged for weeks. Brown was indicted with two others for the murders of Sheriff William Brady and Deputy George Hindman. He managed to evade law officers, though, and hit the trail with Billy the Kid.

By the fall of that year, Brown had plenty of blood on his hands, and he fit right in with Billy the Kid and fellow gang members John Middleton, Tom O'Folliard, and Fred Wait. The Lincoln County War and the New Mexico law behind them, the group stole an entire herd of horses and made their way to the area of Tascosa, Texas. At this point Billy and O'Folliard daringly returned to New Mexico, Middleton to his home in Kansas, and Wait to his home in Oklahoma. The gang had dissolved; so too had Brown's patience for the outlaw life.

Staying on in Tascosa, Brown worked as a cowhand for George Littlefield before taking supremely ironic work tracking horse thieves. His next job, as deputy sheriff of Oldham County, was short-lived, and he drifted north to work for ranch foreman Barney O'Connor in Indian Territory. Finally, a bit farther north, he was in Caldwell, offering a very selective résumé to the townspeople and receiving the marshal's star-shaped badge.

Henry Brown seemed to be the answer to Caldwell's prayers. His square jaw and stern face belied his criminal past. It's been said that one resident, small business owner Charles Siringo, might have known Brown's true identity. Siringo had helped track Billy the Kid some years ago and might have crossed paths with Brown. If that's the case, he didn't share the information, perhaps fearing for his own life. Besides, it was information the town of Caldwell didn't want to hear. Brown was their knight in a shining badge. He had helped a federal deputy marshal capture a band of horse thieves in nearby Hunnewell. He had killed what the town thought to be a menacing Pawnee Indian brandishing a gun in the town grocery. He had used his rifle to shoot down a drunken Texas gambler making threats against the town. Yes, Brown was a good marshal.

So when Brown requested permission from the mayor to leave Caldwell and track down a wanted man in Indian Territory, the mayor agreed. He knew Brown had fallen into debt, and the twelve-hundred-dollar bounty on the man's head would come in handy. Could he take his deputy, Ben Wheeler? Sure. Wheeler's real name was William Robinson, and Brown had met him during his outlaw days in Texas. Again, Caldwell was none the wiser.

In late April 1884, Brown, Wheeler, and two mustached cowboys, William Smith and John Wesley, rode out of Caldwell with extra horses in tow; they were headed for Medicine Lodge, Kansas, seventy miles west of Caldwell.

As they neared the town, they entered the Gypsum Hills—slopes, small canyons, and buttes of red dirt just north of what is now Oklahoma. It was a curious landscape with sinkholes and natural bridges, and its many caves were ideal for waiting out the night with the snakes and prairie dogs. The men tied their extra horses in a shallow canyon and readied themselves for a big day.

In a torrential downpour on the morning of April 30, the men made a mental note of their hidden horses' location and rode toward Medicine Lodge. It was miserable weather, turning the earth into a red paste, but fine conditions for their plans that day—sheets of rain meant that the riders might go completely unnoticed about town.

Brown and his men hitched their horses behind a shed near Medicine Lodge Bank. Around 9:00 a.m. they burst into the bank with guns drawn—Brown's fine Winchester gleaming—and demanded money. Bank president E. W. Payne reached for his gun, but Brown shot first and killed him. Cashier George Geppert threw his hands up, but another member of the outlaw gang shot him anyway. Before he collapsed and died, Geppert lunged for the vault and locked it, ensuring that the robbers wouldn't get what they had come for. For Brown, that was money to pay off his debts.

Outside the bank, the thieves had more trouble awaiting them. Due to the rainstorm, a pack of cowboys was waiting out the bad weather in a livery stable across the road from the bank. They had meant to join a roundup at nearby Antelope Flat, but for now they sought refuge from the storm. Thus they heard the gunshots at the bank and saw Brown's group making off on their horses. Several of the cowboys mounted up and followed the outlaws at breakneck pace out of Medicine Lodge. The rain hadn't worked to Brown's advantage at all.

The pursuit lasted for two hours, pushing the men's horses to exhaustion. Brown and the three others made their way across the sometimes-confusing formations of red earth to the canyon where they had hidden fresh horses. Unbeknownst to them the landowner had moved a fence they had used to mark their horses' spot. They rode into the wrong box canyon, which was more than thirty feet deep. By the time they realized their mistake, they were trapped within the canyon's high walls, their horses growing anxious as water from the downpour collected at their hooves. A posse of nine men—led by Barney O'Connor, who had once hired Brown as a cowboy—had them cornered. As the canyon flooded, Brown and then Wheeler, Smith, and Wesley gave themselves up.

The posse and their captives returned to Medicine Lodge. When they arrived in town, it was still light outside, and the prisoners posed in their leg irons for a very glum photograph in which Brown still wears the handkerchief he had surely pulled over his face during the robbery. The crowd shouted for the men to be hanged, but the robbers were locked up in the Medicine Lodge jail.

Inside the log structure, the men had a much-needed meal and Brown wrote a letter to his new wife, Maude. "This is hard for me to write this letter but, it was all for you, my sweet wife, and for the love I have for you," he wrote. "If a mob does not kill us we will come out all right after while. Maude, I did not shoot any one, and did not want the others to kill any one but they did, and that is all there is about it." Brown went on to instruct her to sell his possessions to cover any existing debts. But not the Winchester rifle, he instructed. That item was too special to pawn.

Wheeler made attempts at a letter to his own wife, but he was a blubbering mess and couldn't write anything coherent. The tension he'd felt in the crowd of locals seemed to promise death. J. J. Burns, editor of the nearby *Belle Plaine News,* also sensed something foreboding when reporting the incident. "Citizens immediately organized and followed the outlaws," Burns wrote, "and before this they are probably hanging from a tree." Darkness fell on the town, and by 9:00 p.m. the prisoners' fears were realized. An angry mob of citizens was at the jail door, hungry for vigilante justice. Firing their weapons, they overpowered the guards and busted inside.

In the chaos Brown made a break for it, but a local farmer with a sawed-off double-barrel shotgun had other ideas. He pumped Brown full of bullets—the crooked marshal collapsed, dead at the age of twenty-six.

Wheeler took the chance to make his own escape, fleeing in the opposite direction, but a gun flash set his vest on fire and made a bright, obvious target against the night sky. He ended up with three bullets in his torso, a shattered right arm, and bloody stumps where two fingers once resided on his left hand.

Bleeding and in agony, Wheeler was dragged with Smith and Wesley to a tall elm tree. Long ropes were thrown over a sturdy branch. Wheeler begged for his life, promising to disclose information "that would interest the community at large" if he were spared. But the mob would have none of it. They strung him up with the other two. The three bodies were left hanging from the tree, a warning to any other would-be robbers.

Today the spot where Brown and his comrades found themselves trapped is known as Jackass Canyon. As for Brown's Winchester, his widow did get rid of it. The rifle made its way through several hands before ending up at the Kansas Museum of History in Topeka.

GEORGE "BITTER CREEK" NEWCOMB

Romantic Robber

"I'm a wild wolf from Bitter Creek, and it's my night to howl," the young cowboy sang. It was his favorite song, and he hummed it every day as he went about his work moving cattle, putting up fence, or tending horses. He sang it to whoever might be listening—cows, dogs, people, no one at all.

He wasn't from a place called Bitter Creek at all but rather Fort Scott, Kansas. Still, his affinity for the folk tune earned him the nickname "Bitter Creek."

His real name was George Newcomb, and he was born in 1866 in far eastern Kansas just after the Civil War came to a close. Though his uncle ran one of the largest grocery stores in the state, his own family was poor, and he left home early. In 1878, when a Texas rancher came through Fort Scott selling horses, twelve-year-old Newcomb followed the man back to his Long S Ranch on the Colorado River. His time there earned him another nickname, "Slaughter Kid," though that one didn't stick quite as well as "Bitter Creek."

Newcomb eventually drifted north into Indian Territory, where he gained a reputation as a hard worker for rancher Oscar Halsell. Newcomb had grown into a dark, handsome young man, and he loved women as much as he loved his free, cowboy existence. But when he met a man named Bill Doolin, his life changed forever.

Bill Doolin ran with the Dalton boys, a gang of robbers that had terrorized Kansas and surrounding states for the last two years. No train or bank was safe with them nearby.

Doolin recruited Newcomb into the fold, and in the summer of 1892, the young Kansan joined them for a little train-robbing fun.

One July night the outlaws rode their horses into Adair, a small train stop in Indian Territory, just before the 9:45 train. There they robbed the depot and seized the train. Newcomb kept the passengers at gunpoint to avoid a revolt while the others raided the express car for valuables. Shots flew between the robbers and guards, resulting in injuries for three of the officials but none of the thieves.

Newcomb reveled in his share of the booty. It was much easier money than working on the ranch, that was for sure. Emmett Dalton, one of the outlaw brothers, would later describe Newcomb as a perfect fit for the group—a solid shot with a rifle, good on a horse, and exceedingly reckless.

For the Dalton Gang, it was just another success story in a long list of crimes. Drunk on their seeming invincibility, the Daltons came up with a most ambitious scheme. The men would rob not one but *two* banks in one day—in broad daylight. Plus, their location of choice was Coffeyville, the Daltons' hometown. It was a wildly bold plan that would make history.

The Dalton Gang did make history when they knocked over two banks in Coffeyville on October 5, 1892, but for the wrong reasons. The robbery was a massive failure—four of the robbers ended up dead and another was captured. A sixth gunman was said to have escaped, and it's thought the man was Bill Doolin.

Luckily for Newcomb, he and fellow bandit Charlie Pierce had been left out of the Coffeyville raid and thus lived to see another robbery.

It didn't take long, either.

After the Coffeyville mess, Newcomb, Doolin, and Pierce wanted to make sure the town didn't breathe too large a sigh of relief at the death of their friends. They sent a letter to one of the townspeople who had helped gun down the bank robbers:

> *Dear Sir:*
> *I take the time to tell you and city of Coffeyville that all of the gang ain't dead yet by a hell of a sight and don't you forget it. I would have given all I ever made to have been there on the 5th. There are three of the gang left and we shall come to see you . . . we shall have revenge for your killing of Bob and Grat and the rest. . . . You people had no cause to take arms against the gang. The bankers will not help the widows of the men that got killed there and you thought you were playing hell fire when you killed three of us, but your time will soon come when you will go into the grave and pass in your checks. . . . So take warning.*
> *Yours truly, DALTON GANG.*

News of the ominous letter rattled the town, still reeling from the bloodshed of the failed robbery. The climate of fear reached fever pitch when the Coffeyville mayor received a message by wire from a detective hunting for the remaining outlaws. According to him, a massive group of forty desperados—led by Doolin, Newcomb, and Pierce—had just passed Wharton, Indian Territory, en route to Coffeyville. They intended to "wipe out" the entire town, according to the informant.

The town obtained weapons and reinforcements all the way from Kansas City and lit a bonfire in the town square to keep the streets well lit.

The band of outlaws never showed up.

Presumably deterred by Coffeyville's vigilance but still brimming with angry energy to conduct a crime, the surviving gang members instead donned masks at the Caney train station eighteen miles west of Coffeyville. When the train arrived on the Missouri Pacific Railroad tracks at 10:15 p.m., the men were waiting. They climbed onto the train, one of them pointing a gun in the engineer's face, and after a short distance ordered that the express car be quietly disconnected from the rest of the train. As ordered, the engineer moved the express car another half mile down the track. A shot was fired, signaling the others to empty valuables from another car. They sprang into action, forcing a railroad employee—bleeding from a shot in the arm—to unload the safe.

Although the robbers got away, they didn't have much to show for it—around fifteen hundred dollars at best. Most of the train's valuables had been transferred to another train at Conway Springs. Still, it was a victory for the rebel pack's morale—survivors of the Dalton Gang, they had pulled off their first robbery without a Dalton. The small gang, led by Bill Doolin, would be known as the Doolin Gang, or the Wild Bunch.

Coffeyville remained on alert, news of the nearby heist fueling fears that a murderous posse indeed would emerge. But the Wild Bunch had other matters to tend to.

First they recruited a new man, Oliver Yantis. A thick fellow with a dark face and a dark moustache, he had helped harbor the Dalton Gang after a horse theft several months prior. Hiding and feeding the bandits, Yantis's sister had fallen for the handsome Newcomb, and Yantis himself had fallen for the outlaw lifestyle. Now Yantis would fill in for Charlie Pierce on a trek to Garden City, a hundred miles away.

It was late October, and the air was crisp. They arrived in Garden City on the twenty-first, staying in the Ohio House while they scouted the area over the next week. They liked the looks of a little town called Spearville. Less than twenty miles east of Dodge City, the place was a stop on the Santa Fe Railroad and had just two hundred residents, hardly enough to mount a real fight against armed invaders. On the twenty-ninth the outlaws were spotted on an area ranch sporting copious numbers of weapons. Then, on November 1, it was time to get serious.

The weather had turned cold, and most of the people of Spearville were holed up indoors. Doolin, Newcomb, and Yantis rode right up to the Ford County Bank. Doolin and Newcomb left their thoroughbreds with Yantis and entered the bank. In a matter of minutes, Newcomb filled a bag with $1,697, while Doolin stuck his Winchester rifle in the face of physically handicapped cashier J. R. Baird. Newcomb and Doolin rejoined Yantis and their horses, fired a few victorious shots, and rode away. They encountered a small pack of locals who exchanged a few shots, none of which struck anything but air.

When County Sheriff Chalkey Beeson caught wind of the robbery, he led a posse southeast along the river.

The menacing trio was spotted a number of times traversing the country south of Dodge, and they ultimately split up to avoid detection. Doolin and Newcomb would follow different routes but meet up back at their Cimarron hideout, while Yantis would go to his sister's home in Orlando, Kansas.

Sheriff Beeson gave up the trail and sent postcards to nearby towns and train stations, offering a four-hundred-fifty-dollar reward for capture of the thieves and warning people to be on the lookout for crisp, new five-dollar bills that had made it into Newcomb's bag. Beeson described the three suspects, whose names he didn't yet know: The "small dark complexioned man 23 years old, small, very dark mustached and dark clothes" was Yantis; the "medium sized man, sandy complexioned, short beard, light hat and clothes" was Doolin; and the "dark man, 25 years old, medium size dark mustache" was Bitter Creek Newcomb.

A couple weeks later, the sheriff got a break. A Stillwater, Indian Territory, man believed he had seen the small, dark man in question. Sheriff Beeson sent a Garden City man who had seen the trio at the Ohio House during their scouting week. When the man found Yantis at a home near Stillwater, he recognized him but didn't let on. Still, Yantis sensed that something was amiss, shifting nervously and keeping his hand near his holster. In a week or so, Sheriff Beeson arrived with authority to make an arrest in Indian Territory, far outside his normal jurisdiction.

In the early morning fog, the lawman and his aides reached the homestead where Yantis was staying. When Yantis finally walked out of the house, Beeson yelled. Yantis grabbed his pistol and fired. His sister, Newcomb's old flame, ran out to try to stop the madness, but it was too late. The lawmen had gunned Yantis down, and the novice outlaw slowly bled to death. Bills from the Ford County Bank were found in his wallet, confirming his identity, and the sheriff collected a reward. Once again, though, Doolin, Newcomb, and Pierce remained at large.

Over the winter months, the Wild Bunch found a couple more able outlaws by the names of Tulsa Jack and Dynamite Dick. In June 1893 all five donned masks and hit a train just west of Cimarron. This train they mounted with particular flourish, swinging down from a bridge as the locomotive passed underneath.

The outlaws moved past the Kansas borders into Indian Territory, holding up trains and vulnerable travelers in Bartlesville, Ingalls, Sacred Heart, and Dover. They struck wherever and whomever they pleased. The Dalton Gang was dead, and thanks to the wiliness of Newcomb and Doolin, the Wild Bunch was the new gang to fear.

By 1895 Bitter Creek had a five-thousand-dollar prize on his head, though his true identity—George Newcomb—remained unknown. He'd spent the last few years successfully evading the law, amassing wealth by robbery, and killing men who got in the way. But he was still a young man with a soft spot for women.

Newcomb met a pretty teenage girl named Rosa Dunn at a country dance in Cimarron, and the two developed a romance. They made a good-looking pair; Rosa would become known as "the Rose of Cimarron." Newcomb and Pierce also made friends with Dunn's brothers. The Dunns provided a hideout, while the outlaws shared their considerable loot.

But on May 2, 1895, the Dunn ranch would go from a safe haven to a deadly trap. When Newcomb and Pierce arrived that day to see Rosa and collect a large sum of money owed by her brothers, the Dunn boys turned on them, unloading lead into the two outlaws and tossing their bodies into a wagon bound for Guthrie. When Newcomb somehow gasped another breath the next morning, he got another bullet for his trouble and was finally dead. The Dunns would have their reward, in the process putting it on the record that their lovely sister had known nothing of their plans.

Newcomb's body was identified a few days later, sending his hometown of Fort Scott into shock. A former resident told an area paper that the people of Fort Scott would "learn with horror that the little pale faced, well-mannered boy, George Newcomb, who played around the streets and about his uncle's store, was no other than the daring highwayman, Slaughter Kid. . . . It hardly seems credible that a boy surrounded as he was with influential friends, a kind, honorable and industrious father could go so astray."

MISSOURI OUTLAWS

THE SLICKER WAR

Vigilantes and Vendettas in the Early Ozarks

Screams cut through the night as the hickory switch slashed across the man's bare back. He was tied to a tree in front of his Ozark cabin, his crying wife and children held at bay by the barrel of a shotgun. A group of vigilantes stood around the tree where they had bound their victim, cheering and laughing as the strongest among them used all his muscle to whip the thin length of wood across bloody flesh. The man sagged against the tree, barely conscious as blood streamed down his legs and onto the ground.

"Get out of Benton County in ten days or we'll be back to finish the job!" one of his attackers warned.

Whooping with glee and firing their revolvers in the air, the group mounted up and rode off into the night, leaving the family to care for the battered victim as best they could.

They had just been visited by the Slickers.

It all started when the Turk family moved to Benton County in 1839 from Tennessee, settling on the Twenty-Five Mile Prairie just north of modern Quincy. At first the newcomers appeared to be prosperous, educated farmers, but what people didn't know was that Hiram and Martha Turk and their sons, James, Tom, Nathan, and Robert, had moved there to dodge thousands of dollars of debt and Hiram's charges of affray (brawling), trespassing, gambling, attempted murder, and murder. He'd managed to get free because of his connections with powerful people, but it had become distinctly uncomfortable for the Turk family in Tennessee.

The Turks dressed well, spoke well, and had money to spend, so they appeared to be an excellent addition to the community, but soon people learned otherwise. Hiram and his eldest boy, James, drank heavily, and as the whiskey flowed, their tempers turned foul. Tom, the middle boy, stood an intimidating six feet six inches. Most of his three hundred pounds was muscle, the rest anger and bad attitude. Nathan and Robert were still in their teens, but followed in the footsteps of their father and older brothers. Together they made a frightening group.

True to their nature, the first thing they did was open a tavern where the rougher element in the area lounged around, gambling and guzzling whiskey.

Within months the Turks got into trouble with their neighbor John Graham when he paid a twenty-dollar debt to Hiram with a counterfeit note. Twenty dollars was a lot of money at the time, so Hiram flew into a rage when he discovered the trick.

Later that day Hiram's son James was riding along and saw Graham riding toward him. James dismounted and approached, wielding a club. Graham warned him off, but James grabbed the bridle of Graham's horse and whipped out his Bowie knife.

Narrowly avoiding the sharp blade as it slashed by, Graham leapt off his horse and ran away, James hot on his heels, swearing he'd kill him. Suddenly Graham spun around and pointed a pistol at James, telling him that if he took another step, he'd be a dead man.

But James had his blood up and kept on coming. Graham pulled the trigger, but instead of a loud bang, he only heard an ineffective click as the gun misfired. James smacked him to the ground with his club and struck him on the head with his knife. Just then a neighbor intervened and held James back long enough for Graham to stagger to his horse and gallop away. He returned minutes later, having retrieved another gun, and it became James's turn to run.

The next day the justice of the peace showed up at the Turk home with a posse and took James into custody. For some unknown reason they didn't disarm him and let Tom and Hiram come along. When they arrived at the Graham home to hold a hearing, James refused to enter, and Graham refused to come out until they disarmed James. The officers moved to take James's gun, but Tom Turk pulled out a pistol and told them to stay back. The Turks went home, but their troubles were far from over.

The entire affair ended up in the courts. Hiram accused Graham of passing counterfeit currency, but the fake twenty-dollar bill had disappeared and the charges came to nothing. Somehow all the charges against the Turks got dropped as well.

Only two months later, Hiram Turk broke into the home of another of his neighbors, Archibald Cock, and threatened to kill him for reasons that have since been forgotten. The court dropped these charges too. It's not clear why the Turks seemed immune to prosecution, but the family apparently had friends as well as enemies, and the local law seemed reluctant to take sides.

Worse came that summer.

Just to the northeast of the Turk place flowed the Pomme de Terre River. Andrew Jones and his large clan had lived there in simple cabins since the earliest days of settlement. They were crude, illiterate folk, more interested in gambling and horse racing than education. Many locals said Andrew was a horse thief, but they said this only in whispers, because the Jones clan was related by marriage to many of the prominent families in the county.

Considering his character, it's not surprising Andrew liked to loaf around the Turk tavern. On Election Day of 1840, a large crowd gathered to vote, drink, and watch horse races. Andrew Jones and James Turk bet on a race, but fell into dispute about who won. In typical Turk family style, James struck Andrew with a rock. People jumped in on both sides, and soon the election party became a swirling mass of shouting men and flying fists.

Three of the Turk brothers were fined one hundred dollars each for rioting, but Hiram used his mysterious connections to get a remit from the governor. The courts also charged Hiram and James with rioting but put off the case until the following year.

Hiram had something else to celebrate as well. On Election Day he got elected justice of the peace. Now he and his sons could drink, gamble, and fight with little fear of the consequences.

James Turk hated one of their neighbors, a man named Abraham Nowell who had been a member of the jury that indicted his father and brother for helping him escape the posse, and now Nowell planned to be a witness at their trial for the tavern riot. James swore he would "take the damned old son of a bitch off his horse and whip him, so he can't go to court."

On the day of the trial, Nowell and some friends rode through the countryside toward the courthouse. As they stopped at a stream to drink, James rode past. He taunted Nowell, hinting he would settle on his land, and the conversation grew so heated, James drew out his revolver and advanced on Nowell, who grabbed a pistol and told him to stop. When James kept coming, Nowell killed him with a single shot.

Fearing the Turk clan more than the law, Nowell fled the county, only sneaking back in April 1842 to stand trial. The court ruled he had fired in self-defense.

The Turks wanted blood. It was all right for them to go free after committing crimes, but when someone raised a hand against their family, they had to pay. Unfortunately for the residents of Benton and Polk Counties, lots of people would pay.

Many of the Turks' neighbors had tired of the family's arrogance and violence, and since the law obviously wasn't going to help, they decided to take matters into their own hands. Archibald Cock organized a small group, including Andrew Jones, to oppose the Turk clan and their allies. They signed a solemn oath to kill Hiram.

On July 17, 1841, they got their chance.

Hiram and his followers were riding along a road through a brushy hollow one day when a shot rang out from the bushes. Hiram toppled off his horse, shouting, "I am a dead man!" The shooter disappeared into the thick brush before anyone could identify him. Hiram's friends carried him to a nearby cabin and summoned a doctor, and the spirited man lingered between life and death for three weeks before breathing his last.

Everyone suspected Andrew Jones. The courts indicted him for murder, and several of his friends for conspiracy to commit murder, but found them all innocent for lack of evidence. Jones celebrated his victory by stealing a neighbor's bull, cooking it, and inviting his friends to a big feast. Now the Jones clan, not the Turk family, got its way in Benton County.

This was too much for the surviving Turk brothers. Tom Turk organized a group of about thirty men who swore to uphold the law against horse thieves, counterfeiters, and murderers. While this sounds a bit hypocritical considering how the Turks treated their neighbors, on the rough frontier people had more loyalty to their families and friends than they did to any abstract concept of law and order.

One of the new recruits was Isom Hobbs, an old friend of the Turk family from their Tennessee days. Like Hiram, he had been accused of murder back home and decided to move to Missouri. Many in the group had similar characters, but others were respectable folk in Polk County. These men probably took the group's oath at face value, thinking they had joined a vigilante group, but it was really a vendetta of one band of outlaws against another, a turf war over who got to terrorize the region.

The Turk faction had deeper motives than revenge. Most of the men were relative newcomers interested in opening up the region to commerce. They generally voted Democratic, disliked paper currency (much of which was counterfeit and all of which had dubious value), and came from educated families. They opposed older settlers like the Jones clan, who led a simpler life of hunting and fishing and had little use for "development." Turk and his allies were mostly based around Warsaw, the Benton County seat, while the older settlers concentrated to the south around Bolivar, the seat of Polk County.

On January 28, 1842, the Turks' new group claimed their first victims. Two men complained that while they had been racing horses with Andrew Jones and his friend Thomas Meadows, some of their horses had been stolen. That's all the evidence Tom Turk and his crew needed. If the name Andrew Jones was in any way related to horse thievery, he must be guilty, him and his friend. Tom led his men on a fifteen-mile ride to Andrew's house, but only found his brother and another man. They threatened them with a whipping and ordered them to leave the county, and then proceeded to the home of Thomas Meadows. Tying Meadows to a tree, they stripped the bark off of some hickory switches and whipped him until his back was crisscrossed with bloody stripes. Witnesses claim that his blood created a gory stream that flowed a full six feet away.

Taking the bark off a switch was called "slicking" in local parlance, so Tom Turk's vigilantes became known as "Slickers" after their favorite method of punishment. That same day the Slickers went to the home of William Brookshire, a friend of Jones and Meadows, and gave him the same treatment.

As the hickory switches slashed into his back, Meadows admitted that Andrew Jones had stolen those horses. Brookshire named Jones and two other men as the murderers of Hiram Turk. Of course, being whipped is liable to make someone say anything he thinks his torturers want to hear, but these tales were proof enough for the Slickers.

Over the next few days, the vigilantes slicked three more friends of their enemies. In one case Robert, the youngest of the Turk brothers at only seventeen, gave the first few licks before letting a more experienced hand take over.

The Slickers didn't just whip people to punish them and to extract information; they also used the raids to scare families off their land so the Slickers could buy it. The terrorized families usually sold at any price so they could get out of the county as quickly as possible.

By this time the more law-abiding members of the community had had enough. On March 21 the militia set out to capture Andrew Jones, which they did after he tried to shoot one of the militiamen who also happened to be a Slicker. Jones's gun misfired, which was good for him because the court only charged him with attempted murder and let him out on bond. The sight of large numbers of armed, trained militiamen marching along the country roads helped calm the situation for a time.

Like before, when guns didn't work the two sides tried to get their revenge through the courts, filing countless charges and countercharges. The streets of Warsaw filled with large bands of armed Slickers and their enemies, while the militia cast a nervous eye on both. Several fights ensued, and in one incident a group of anti-Slickers threatened to storm a building where the Slickers had gathered, and the Slickers scared them off by sticking a stovepipe out the window and announcing they had a cannon.

As usual, people were either found not guilty or simply skipped town. Andrew Jones decided not to risk trial and fled. While this got rid of the Turk family's main rival, it couldn't have been very satisfactory to them.

On October 18 Abraham Nowell, an old rival of the Turk family from the very start of the troubles, walked out the front door of his cabin and bent over a barrel to get a bucket of water. Just then a shot rang out from the bushes. Nowell stood up in surprise, and another bullet tore through his chest. His wife rushed to his side, screaming for help. She saw two shadowy figures slip away through the brush but couldn't identify them.

The killers soon identified themselves. Within hours of the shooting, Isom Hobbs bragged that he'd "bagged a deer" and hinted that Tom Turk was a coward. Apparently Tom had taken the first shot, and Isom thought he'd missed on purpose to avoid responsibility for the murder.

Soon both sides took to erecting fake graves by the side of the road bearing the names of their enemies. A Baptist minister gave a sermon against the Slickers, and one loudmouthed Slicker swore all Baptists would be run out of the area. This united the more peaceful citizens against the Slickers.

One night three shots rang out near the cabin of William Metcalf, a neighbor of the Turks who had become one of their many enemies. One bullet cracked through the door and hit Jacob Dobkins, Abraham Nowell's son-in-law. Dobkins lingered between life and death for two days. A judge claimed he heard the young man say Hobbs and the Turks shot him, and so he called out the militia, led by Major Nathan Rains, to arrest every man in the Hobbs and Turk families. A bunch of anti-Slickers from Benton County, as well as a group of angry Baptists, came along too. They rounded up Nathan Turk and surrounded a cabin where Isom Hobbs and several other Slickers were hiding out. The militia told them they had the place surrounded and would set it on fire, and the Slickers soon surrendered.

Once again the wheels of frontier justice turned, and creaked to a stop. Prosecutors had no real evidence against the Slickers and eventually released them, but not before the Turks filed suit against Rains for false arrest. The Slickers turned out to have a better case than their enemies and got Rains court-martialed for misconduct of office.

Despite several brushes with the law, Isom Hobbs didn't keep his mouth shut. He kept bragging about killing someone and took to calling his rifle "Old Abram." He boasted it was accurate to ninety-six yards, the distance from which Abraham Nowell had been shot.

At harvest time in 1844, Isom Hobbs and Tom Turk were working in the same field. It must have been a tense situation, because Hobbs still felt Tom had been cowardly during the shooting of Nowell, and Tom would have heard of those accusations. Soon tempers flared. The two men faced off with scythes, but a deadly duel was averted when Tom fled the field.

Humiliated and afraid for his life, Tom announced he would leave the county. But it was not to be. On August 9, as Tom rode home from a blacksmith shop, Isom Hobbs hid in the brush, waiting for him. One shot from "Old Abram," and Tom pitched from the saddle. Neighbors carried his body to a nearby home, and Isom showed up to "pay his respects," rubbing the victim's head and saying, "You have been a brave fellow, Tom, but they got you at last."

"They" might have gotten Tom, but his younger brother Robert still lived. A few weeks later he hid beside a road outside Warsaw where he knew the Hobbs family would ride. Robert created a blind out of brush, like he was going to hunt deer, and set in for a long wait. When the Hobbs family came into view, he was frustrated to see Isom wasn't among them. Shrugging his shoulders, he aimed at Isom's brother Jeff and took him out with a single bullet. It wasn't the revenge he wanted, but it was a start.

A posse grabbed Robert a couple of days later, but once again the courts couldn't gather enough evidence to convict and he walked free. Authorities captured Isom Hobbs soon after, but he somehow managed to get the key to his cell. After he escaped, he hid the key in a tree stump and wrote a letter to the sheriff telling him where he could find it. He wouldn't enjoy his freedom long, however. After fleeing to Mississippi, he got into more trouble with the law, and a posse gunned him down.

Andrew Jones came to a bad end too. In 1844 he and some accomplices savagely murdered and robbed three Indians in Texas, one of them a young boy. Two Indians who escaped identified the killers, and Andrew Jones ended his long career in crime at the end of a rope. Nathan Turk died shortly thereafter in Shreveport, Louisiana, knifed during an argument over a card game. Robert, the last surviving Turk brother, took his mother, Martha, to Kentucky to start a new life.

It had been seven long, brutal years. Benton and Polk Counties were nearly bankrupted from the costs of conducting so many trials, but the troubles finally subsided. Most criminals had been killed or run out of the area, and those who remained feared another cycle of vendettas and kept quiet. Peace had finally returned to the rugged Ozarks.

FRANK AND JESSE JAMES

Legendary Bandits

It had been a good day at the Kansas City Exposition. As night fell, a huge crowd headed for the gates after enjoying a day listening to brass bands, watching trick riders, trying to guess what bushel of corn or fat hog would win the farming contests, and stuffing themselves at the concession stands. It was September 26, 1872, and Missouri was at peace. The economy was improving after the long years of the Civil War, and everyone just wanted to have a good time. Well-fed and content, the crowds headed toward home.

But three riders rode through the throng in the other direction. Murmurs and a few laughs scattered through the crowd when people noticed the men wore checkered bandannas over their faces. Were they entertainers, or local kids up to some prank?

One man dismounted in front of the ticket booth, and to everyone's amazement the other two pulled out pistols and aimed them at the hundreds if not thousands of people around them. Anyone who had been laughing stopped immediately.

The man strode over to the ticket booth, reached his arm through the window, and grabbed the cash box. The ticket seller shouted a protest and ran out of the booth to grapple with the robber. One of the riders fired a shot, but the ticket seller ducked and the bullet hit the leg of a young girl standing nearby. The robber leapt into the saddle and the three rode off, the crowd parting before them in panic.

Kansas City had just been visited by the James gang.

Frank and Jesse James were born to Robert and Zerelda James on a farm near Kearney, Clay County. Robert was a highly educated Baptist minister and one of the founders of William Jewell College in Liberty. In 1850 he left his young family and set out for the gold fields of California, where he soon died. Zerelda kept the farm going and eventually married Dr. Reuben Samuel.

Despite having lost their father, the James boys seem to have had a happy childhood. They loved their new stepfather and lived on a prosperous farm tended by slaves, but they must have been aware of the growing tensions in the region. Pro- and antislavery factions fought it out along the border with Kansas to determine whether the territory would become a slave or free state. Abolitionist

Jayhawkers often raided border counties in Missouri, and the James brothers probably knew some of their victims.

This fierce border war, known as "Bleeding Kansas," was the prequel to the Civil War, which started in 1861. By then Frank was eighteen and Jesse just fourteen. Frank promptly enlisted in the pro-Southern Missouri State Guard and fought in the early Confederate victories at Wilson's Creek and Lexington. While things seemed to be going well for Missouri secessionists in 1861, they would be kicked out of the state the following year after a series of bloody engagements that gave the Union control of Missouri. While the Confederates launched several large raids, they never seriously threatened to take Missouri again.

But the fight was far from over. Frank had contracted measles and been left behind during the Confederate retreat from Lexington. Union troops captured and paroled him, making him take an oath not to fight the Union before allowing him to go home. He lived there peacefully until 1863, when the Missouri government required all able-bodied men to enroll in a Union militia. This was too much for Frank. While he would take an oath not to fight, he would never fight for the North. Local authorities arrested him for failing to join up, but he managed to escape from the Liberty jailhouse and ended up joining the guerrilla band of William Clarke Quantrill. He would spend the rest of the war roving the countryside, making hit-and-run raids on federal outposts and destroying train tracks and telegraph wires. Quantrill's wasn't the only guerrilla band operating in Missouri, and these innumerable groups of bushwhackers would be the main rebel resistance in the state for the rest of the war. While the Union had taken Missouri, they had a great deal of trouble holding it.

Unfortunately for the James family, everyone knew Frank had broken his oath and was fighting for the South once again. They might have also suspected that Zerelda and Jesse paid close attention to federal troop movements and ran messages for the bushwhackers.

One day in May 1863, the Union militia showed up at the James farm. This was the same outfit that Frank would have joined if he could have stomached fighting for the North. The militia questioned Dr. Samuel about Frank's whereabouts, and when he said he knew nothing, they put a noose around his neck, threw the rope over a branch of one of the trees in his yard, and strung him up. Jesse tried to intervene, but they whipped him until he lay limp and bleeding on the ground. The militiamen, laughing and teasing Jesse's stepfather, let him drop and then hauled him up again. The tortured man finally admitted that Frank and his friends were camped nearby, so the militia left on a fruitless chase after them. The frustrated soldiers soon returned to drag Dr. Samuel off to jail and force Zerelda to take a loyalty oath in court.

After this treatment the young Jesse asked to join Quantrill's guerrillas too, but they rejected him as too young. They also weren't impressed when he shot off the tip of his finger while cleaning a pistol, screaming "Dingus!" As a good Baptist boy, he wouldn't swear even when losing a finger. For the rest of the war, "Dingus" would be his nickname among the bushwhackers.

Jesse finally got a chance to join his big brother in the spring of 1864. By that time Frank rode with "Bloody Bill" Anderson, leader of a faction that had split away from Quantrill's outfit.

Jesse didn't get to stay with his brother long. That summer he snuck into the yard of a Unionist farmer to steal a saddle and the man shot him. The bullet pierced Jesse's chest and passed right through his body. This laid Jesse up for two months, but as soon as he could get back on his horse, he rode off to rejoin his brother, just in time for Bloody Bill's greatest killing spree. The band carved a crimson path through the state in support of General Sterling Price's raid in the autumn of 1864. Both brothers nearly got killed in a failed attack on a federal blockhouse in Fayette and went on to Centralia, where Anderson's band slaughtered twenty-two unarmed Union soldiers on furlough.

There is debate about whether Frank and Jesse were present for the Centralia Massacre, because much of the group stayed in camp that morning, but they were definitely present that afternoon when the bushwhackers wiped out a federal pursuit force. The gleeful guerrillas scalped and mutilated some of the dead, but there are no reports that the James brothers participated in this. Anderson got killed by a Union militia the next month, and Frank went to rejoin Quantrill.

After successive defeats on the field, the Southern cause seemed doomed, and Quantrill, one of the most wanted men west of the Mississippi, led his men east to Kentucky. It would not save him, however, and the Federals tracked him down and killed him. Frank went with him on that excursion, but managed to survive. Meanwhile Jesse raided around Missouri with another guerrilla group under the command of one of Anderson's former lieutenants.

As the war ended, the authorities in Missouri offered amnesty to bushwhackers who would surrender and take an oath of loyalty. Jesse spoke against surrender, but the other members of the band outvoted him. Deciding all was lost, he too rode toward Lexington to turn himself in, but before they made it to town, they got ambushed by federal troops. It's unclear why this happened; perhaps the troops thought they were one of the many bushwhacker groups who weren't surrendering, or perhaps they simply wanted revenge for all the suffering the guerrillas had caused. Missouri was chaotic at the time, and no one could tell friend from foe. In any case, Jesse had his horse shot from under him and took a bullet in his lung. Lying half dead in the Virginia Hotel in Lexington, he managed to raise his right hand and take the oath of loyalty on May 21, 1865. This action made him a rehabilitated rebel in the eyes of the federal government. Over in Kentucky on July 26, Frank took the oath as well.

Jesse took a long time to recover from the bullet that hit his lung and had to be nursed back to health by his cousin, who like his mother was named Zerelda. Jesse called her "Zee." As the former guerrilla lay recovering, the two fell in love and got engaged, although the wedding wouldn't happen for another nine years.

Frank, on the other hand, had more serious business to attend to. Apparently he couldn't adjust to peacetime life and on February 13, 1866, rode into Liberty with about a dozen men. They wore Union-style blue army overcoats, and some wore wigs and false beards and mustaches. Two of them walked into the Clay County Savings Association Bank, asking the cashier for change for a ten-dollar bill. When the man turned to address them, he found himself staring at the business end of a pistol. They pushed the cashier and clerk into the vault and cleaned out the money before closing the vault door on them.

The robbers hadn't actually locked the door, however, and the cashier ran to a window to call for help as the bandits mounted up. Just then a student at William Jewell College, which Frank's father had helped found, passed by. He took up the call and one of the robbers shot him dead. They galloped out of town as the citizens of Liberty gathered a posse.

It was too late: The robbers were well ahead, and a snowstorm soon blew in and obscured their tracks. The gang got away with more than fifty-seven thousand dollars in cash, gold, and government bonds.

The choice of the bank hadn't been random. Frank knew the area well, and the bank's president had been a Union informant during the Civil War, causing trouble for Dr. Samuel and friends of the James family. Liberty had another bank, but Frank had a score to settle with this one.

While Jesse has been said to have joined in the robbery, he was still recovering from his gunshot wound and unlikely to have been up for the job. He seems to have lived a quiet life at the time, joining the local Baptist church. Frank may or may not have engaged in other robberies in the state, but generally seems to have kept a low profile except for the occasional bender in town.

On a rather ominous note, in September 1869 Jesse made a formal request to be taken off the rolls at his Baptist church, saying he was unworthy.

In December of that year, Frank and Jesse committed what may have been their first robbery together. They and possibly one other man rode into Gallatin, hitched their horses in an alley near the Daviess County Savings Association, and walked inside. They shot cashier John Sheets before running to their horses. One of the men, probably Jesse, had trouble mounting up and got his foot caught in the stirrup. The horse dragged him down the street before he could break free. Battered and covered in dust, the robber staggered to his feet.

"Let's get him!" someone shouted, and an angry crowd closed in on him. He pulled out a pistol and the townspeople fled in all directions. The bandit vaulted onto the back of a companion's horse and they rode away.

Outside of town they came upon an unsuspecting traveler and relieved him of his horse, then kidnapped a traveling preacher to guide them for part of the way. The robbers boasted to him that they had killed Major Samuel Cox, who had led the militia that killed Bloody Bill Anderson near the end of the Civil War. The raid on Gallatin may have only been for revenge because, contrary to the first newspaper reports, apparently no money was taken.

Actually they had killed Sheets, thinking he was Cox, but their desire to kill Cox implicated the James brothers in the robbery. Both had ridden with Anderson. The third robber may have been Jim Anderson, another former bushwhacker and Bloody Bill's brother. The authorities traced the horse that one of the robbers left behind to Jesse James. Furthermore, a posse that went after them lost the trail but noted they were headed in the direction of Clay County, home of the James/Samuel family.

Four men showed up at the James farm to capture them, but just as they arrived a young boy ran to the stable, opened the door, and Frank and Jesse galloped out, guns blazing. One of the posse's horses was killed and they lost the chase.

The James brothers laid low for a while, with Jesse writing to the newspapers protesting his innocence and saying he had fled because he didn't want to get lynched. The horse found at Gallatin, he claimed, had been sold to a "man from Kansas." Otherwise, they seem to have drifted from state to state. The law accused them of other robberies, but it is hard to separate fact from fiction. By this time the brothers had become famous, and any major heist usually got laid at their door. Furthermore, other bandits would claim to be them, either to enhance their reputations or direct suspicion away from themselves. So many stagecoach, train, and bank robberies happened at this time that they couldn't have all been done by the Jameses, but a few probably were, including the Bank of Columbia in Kentucky and the infamous heist at the Kansas City Exposition.

That last robbery, certainly their most daring, guaranteed their national fame. The editor of the *Kansas City Times,* an alcoholic ex-Confederate soldier named John Newman Edwards, turned the thieves into noble Robin Hoods out of some epic ballad, effusing, "These men are bad citizens but they are bad because they live out of their time. The nineteenth century with its Sybaric civilization is not the social soil for men who might have sat with Arthur at the Round Table, ridden at tourney with Sir Launcelot or won the colors of Guinevere. . . . What they did we condemn. But the way they did it we can't help admiring."

Edwards would continue in this vein throughout the James brothers' careers, and his paper often received letters from the bandits themselves. Sometimes they would sign their own names, claiming their innocence. At other times they signed themselves "Dick Turpin, Jack Shepherd, and Claude Duval," famous English highwaymen from the previous century. They even offered to pay the medical expenses of the girl they accidentally shot at the Kansas City Exposition. It's not recorded if her family ever took the robbers up on their offer.

In 1874 the gang resurfaced in Arkansas, robbing a stagecoach at Malvern before heading north to hold up a train at Gads Hill, Missouri, pulling off the state's first peacetime train robbery. This last crime got the Pinkerton detective agency on their trail. The Pinkertons had gained a reputation for success in tracking down outlaws, and the railroad hired them to get the James brothers in case they decided to repeat their trick on another train.

While the Pinkertons claimed to be crack detectives, they didn't go about collaring Frank and Jesse James in a very intelligent manner. At first only a single agent, Joseph Whicher, went off to the James farm, posing as a farmhand looking for work. He must not have been very convincing, because his body turned up in another county. Next they sent two more agents, along with a local deputy sheriff, but the Younger brothers, former bushwhackers and accomplices of Frank and Jesse, got to them first and killed the deputy and one of the agents.

All this bloodshed didn't seem to affect Frank's and Jesse's personal lives much. On April 24, 1874, Jesse finally married his beloved Zee, and Frank married Annie Ralston sometime later that summer. The two couples enjoyed a fine honeymoon in Texas with their stolen money.

But things started heating up for the brothers. Their daring robberies had become a political issue, with the Republicans demanding they be brought to justice, while the Democrats, mostly made up of former Confederates, pointed out that corrupt Republican politicians and railway tycoons stole far more than the James brothers could ever dream of. Reward money, offered by the railroads, various banks, and eventually the state, began to pile up.

Unlike the politicians, the Pinkertons didn't just talk. They had lost two agents and wanted revenge. On the night of January 25, 1875, a group of Pinkerton detectives snuck up to the James farm, thinking the bandits were inside. Actually, only their stepfather, Dr. Samuel, their mother, Zerelda, and their thirteen-year-old half-brother, Archie, were at home. The lawmen broke open a window and tossed in an incendiary device. It rolled into the fireplace and exploded, killing Archie and mutilating Zerelda's hand so badly that it had to be amputated.

The Pinkertons claimed they were "only" trying to burn the house down, but the senseless killing of a young boy and the maiming of an aging woman enraged the population. The Pinkertons worked for the railroads, the corrupt companies that overcharged farmers for freight and had put dozens of counties deep into debt. Edwards and other newspapermen wrote scathing editorials denouncing the Pinkertons as child killers. Sympathy for the James brothers rose to an all-time high. One of their neighbors, who apparently helped out in the raid, turned up dead.

While Frank and Jesse had become legends in their own time, law-abiding citizens began to stock up on guns and get ready in case the outlaws visited their town next. The brothers would find their heists becoming increasingly dangerous. When Frank James, Cole Younger, Tom Webb, and Tom McDaniel hit a bank in Huntington, West Virginia, netting more than ten thousand dollars in cash, a posse got on their trail right after they left town. The robbers fled into Kentucky, where a second posse chased them halfway across the state while the telegraph wires hummed across the countryside, warning citizens to be on the lookout. They fought at least three gun battles, and McDaniel got killed before the rest made good their escape.

Worse was to come in 1876 when the James brothers once again teamed up with the Younger brothers to raid a bank in Northfield, Minnesota. Northfield citizens greeted them with a hail of gunfire, and Frank and Jesse barely got away with their lives. The Youngers got the worst of it.

The Northfield affair badly shook the brothers and their new wives. They decided to take on aliases and settle as farmers in Tennessee. Mr. and Mrs. Woodson (Frank and Annie) and Mr. and Mrs. Howard (Jesse and Zee) did well for a time, racing horses and tending crops, but they acted too differently from their run-of-the-mill neighbors to escape notice for long. People began remarking that the men seemed a bit jumpy and that the women had a lot more jewelry than people of their station would be expected to have. In one episode Jesse James/John Howard attended a county fair and watched a contest where men tried to blow out a candle by shooting at it with pistols. As contestant after contestant missed the mark, Jesse could stand it no longer and went up, drew his revolver, and shot out the candle on the first try. Jesse, always more showy than his quiet and reserved brother, was beginning to make people talk. This, combined with various lawsuits from creditors, made him pick up stakes and move in with Frank.

But settled life didn't sit well with Jesse, and soon he headed down to New Mexico Territory to assemble another gang. He briefly tried to get Billy the Kid to join, but Billy preferred cattle rustling to bank robbery and turned him down. Jesse did manage to collect a group of outlaws, but of inferior quality to the old crew. They included Bill Ryan, who had no previous criminal record and spent much of his time drunk; Dick Liddil, a horse thief; Tucker Bassham, a slow-witted farmer; Ed Miller, brother of Clell Miller, who had died at Northfield; and Jesse's cousin Wood Hite. Another cousin, Clarence Hite, would join later. Their first holdup was of a train at the Glendale station, just south of Independence, where the express mail netted about six thousand dollars. This heist led the United States Express Company to offer a twenty-five-thousand-dollar reward, and the Chicago and Alton Railroad offered another fifteen thousand dollars. With all the rewards that had accumulated on Jesse's head, anyone who nabbed him would be a rich man.

Things began to turn ugly for the new gang. Bassham got captured and sentenced to ten years for the Glendale robbery. Ed Miller died under mysterious circumstances, and everyone believed Jesse killed him so he wouldn't talk. The gang continued to rob stagecoaches, trains, and payroll shipments, but often got away with very low stakes. Soon Ryan also found himself behind bars, after foolishly shooting off his mouth while on a bender. Jesse's earlier successes were due in no small part to the fact that he allied himself with former bushwhackers such as the Younger brothers whose skill and daring helped them get out of almost any scrape. Now Jesse kept company with lowlifes and amateurs. It would cost him.

Meanwhile, political pressure had been growing to do something about the new James gang. Missouri Governor Thomas Crittenden got the railroads to offer another fifty-thousand-dollar reward. State law prohibited Crittenden from offering a large reward himself, but he'd be a key player in stopping the gang's crime spree.

But by this time there wasn't much of a gang left to chase. Liddil got into an argument with Jesse's cousin Wood Hite and gunned him down for allegedly taking more than his share in a robbery. Two new gang members, Bob and Charlie Ford, were there too. Bob got into the gunplay and his bullet might have actually killed Jesse's cousin. The three men dreaded what Jesse might do if he found out.

The Fords decided to stay close and watch Jesse's every move. Hiding out first in St. Joseph and then at the James farm near Kearney, the bandit leader planned more robberies, but Bob Ford had secretly met with Governor Crittenden, who promised him a rich reward for Jesse's capture. Bob claimed it was to bring in the bandit "dead or alive," something the governor would vigorously deny.

Soon Dick Liddil surrendered to police, and this made Jesse nervous. While he was still ignorant of Liddil's part in his cousin's murder, he didn't trust him and worried he might talk. Jesse discussed killing Liddil and acted more and more suspicious of those around him. Bob and Charlie Ford realized they needed to get him soon.

They got their chance on April 3, 1882, as the Fords and Jesse sat in the living room in Jesse's home in St. Joseph. Jesse complained about the heat and took off his coat and threw open the windows. Worried someone outside might see his gun belt, he took that off too. Then he stepped onto a chair to dust a picture on the wall. Bob gave Charlie a wink and they both drew their pistols. Jesse heard them cock their revolvers and began to turn just as a single shot from Bob's gun took Jesse in the back of the head. He fell to the floor, dead in an instant. Zee raced into the room, and Charlie claimed that a pistol had accidentally gone off.

"Yes," she snapped, "I guess it went off on purpose."

The Fords beat a hasty retreat and turned themselves in to the law. Within hours of the news being made public, a stream of visitors came to the James farm to view the body of America's most famous outlaw. The Fords were initially charged with murder but gained a pardon from Governor Crittenden.

The press, of course, took sides. The Democratic papers, led by John Newman Edwards, railed against Crittenden, calling him an assassin. The Republican press was just as eager with their praises for the termination of the state's worst outlaw.

Frank, meanwhile, was still living the quiet life in Virginia. He hadn't participated in a robbery in several years and hoped this clean living would help him get pardoned. He sent out feelers to Governor Crittenden via Edwards, and the newspaperman reassured him that if he gave up, he would be given a fair trial and not be extradited to other states to face charges there.

Frank decided to take a chance and turned himself in to the governor, handing over his pistols and telling him he would fight no more. People thronged to see the famous outlaw, and when he went to trial, he was found innocent of all charges. His case was helped by the fact that so many fellow gang members, the only ones who could truly say what he had done and when, were dead or on the run. The cases may have also been helped along by the governor himself, who felt convinced that Frank had turned over a new leaf and simply wanted the whole affair to be over. Frank walked out of jail a free man.

While the legend of Frank and Jesse James had been made in their lifetime, with cheap novels about their exploits being published while they were still out robbing banks, it would continue to grow to the present day, helped in no small part by those involved. Frank eventually joined Cole Younger in a Wild West show, and Jesse's son, Jesse James Jr., would make a silent Western movie in which he played his father. This would be followed by dozens of others, few having anything to do with the real story. Charlie and Bob Ford even toured with a theater troupe, playing themselves in a production called *The Killing of Jesse James*. In one performance they were booed offstage to the shouts of "Murderers!" and "Robbers!"

Frank and Jesse's mother, still living on the James farm, buried Jesse in the yard and erected a fine monument over his grave. She sold tickets to tour the farm, regaling visitors with tales of Jesse and Frank's nobility and the evils of the Pinkertons. One stop on the tour was Jesse's grave, where she offered pebbles from the grave at a quarter apiece. When the supply got low, she'd go to a nearby creek and gather more.

A distinctly American bandit has been remembered in a distinctly American fashion, through tourism, mass media, and show business.

THE PENDERGASTS

Running a City Ran in Their Family

It was Election Day in Kansas City in the year 1900. A new century had dawned. For more than a hundred years, America's great experiment in democracy had flourished, and now voters once again prepared to freely and fairly elect someone who would honestly reflect the will of the people.

Long lines snaked toward the polling stations, proof of the thriving democratic spirit of the century's first election. But a shrewd observer, or even one not so shrewd, would notice that the lines moved awfully slowly, and that men carried chairs up and down the line, asking people what candidates they intended to vote for. If the answer was acceptable, they got a chair to relax in while they waited. Voters who answered incorrectly had to stand and often ended up leaving in disgust.

And then there were the homeless people, crowded around polling stations in the worst neighborhoods. They seemed content, as if they had just eaten their first big meal in a long time, and they proudly went up to vote for the same slate of candidates the men with chairs supported. When they were done voting, they returned to the back of the line to vote again.

All across the working-class neighborhood of the West Bottoms, drunken mobs poured out of saloons and stumbled to polling stations, convinced by several rounds of free drinks that the saloon owner's candidates were the best men for the job. Not surprisingly, these were the same candidates the homeless people voted for, and the same ones the men with chairs supported. Now if only the drunks could remember the candidates' names . . .

No fear on that score: The saloon owner had men working the polling stations to remind them.

And who was this man? He started life as a nobody, just another working-class Irish American coming to the big city in the hopes of becoming rich and famous. He became both, but not in the usual manner. Like the heroes of other American success stories, he was a shrewd, hardworking businessman who built up a network of important connections, but he was more than that. He was a huckster who rigged elections and virtually ran the Kansas City Democratic Party for decades.

His name was James Pendergast, and he built one of the most successful political machines this country has ever known.

James Pendergast was born in 1856 and grew up in a working-class neighborhood of St. Joseph. Many of his neighbors were Irish Americans like him, but there were also Germans, English, and some African Americans. This eclectic upbringing made him comfortable with a wide variety of people, a skill that would help him in his political career.

In 1876 James, who usually went by "Jim," headed to Kansas City to seek his fortune. Kansas City was a boomtown, acting as the industrial center of the West, and had huge milling and meatpacking operations. The railroad had arrived less than a decade before, and steamboats still chugged down the Missouri River, bringing the city's products to the rest of the world. Pendergast rented a room in a boardinghouse in the crowded West Bottoms, on the Missouri side of the state line. In this raucous neighborhood, working-class families of all ethnicities labored, played, and drank together in crowded but exciting streets lined with saloons and illegal gambling houses. People called the area "the Bottoms" because it sat below a tall bluff called Quality Hill, where the rich lived in giant mansions and frequented the grandiose opera house, the singers doing their best to drown out the sound of the carousing drinkers and churning factories in the Bottoms below.

Pendergast was a muscular, stocky man weighing two hundred pounds, and he had no problem finding a job. At first he worked as a meatpacker in one of the many plants that processed the huge herds that came from as far away as Texas. Then he got a better-paying position as a smelter in an iron foundry before being promoted to the position of puddler, the highly skilled task of pouring molten metal into molds. He made good money, but not enough to satisfy his burning ambition. People didn't come to Kansas City to do well; they came to get rich, and the fine houses on Quality Hill showed him what he could have if he could just figure out how.

Local legend says that he got his first break through sheer luck. Jim had always been a gambling man, and he put a stake down on a long-shot horse named Climax who pulled ahead and won him a pile of money. With it he bought the American House saloon in 1881, in the West Bottoms near the old location for Union Station. A more prosaic theory is that he hoarded his money, working long hours until he could earn enough to make a down payment. Whatever the truth, he had made an excellent choice of businesses. Even though Kansas City had no shortage of saloons, the people never seemed to get enough of them.

The American House also had a boardinghouse and hotel in the same building, which added to his income. The location was good too, right in the center of the red-light "tenderloin" district where men flocked to gamble and meet prostitutes. Jim opened a gaming room in the back of the American House and rented rooms by the hour for any "couples" who didn't need to stay the whole night. He soon had enough money to expand into the building next door. He also set up a banking service to give loans to workers and cash checks. Since many working-class people, especially immigrants, didn't have bank accounts, this earned him a lot of gratitude. Of course he took a small percentage, but that was only to be expected, and his winning personality made people think of him as a friend, not a business owner. Soon everyone knew him as "Big Jim."

Jim now looked set to become one of Kansas City's leading men, but he had other ideas. The snobbish circle of aristocrats and nouveau riche held no interest for him. He stayed in the West Bottoms, where people knew and liked him. He decided a big house on Quality Hill wasn't what he was after. What he really wanted was power.

As an Irish American, the obvious choice was to join the Democratic Party. In 1884 he attended the Democratic City Convention and became one of eleven delegates to represent the Sixth Ward of the West Bottoms.

A bit of political power earned him even more customers, as everyone wanted to get on his good side. Soon his saloon gobbled up more buildings on the 1300 block of St. Louis Avenue, and he brought in many of his younger brothers and sisters to work for him. His brother Tom started coming up from St. Joseph in 1881 when he was only seventeen. Tom liked the excitement and easy money of the big city, and when he was twenty-two he moved there permanently. Tom was much like his brother, a burly man who would be friendly until crossed, and then snapped into a dangerous rage. He worked for Jim as a bartender and was the man to come to if you couldn't see Jim.

Around 1890 Jim bought another saloon, a high-class place right downtown at 520 Main Street. As always, his businesses weren't just for making money but for gaining influence. The new saloon happened to be right near the city hall and the courts, so when influential lawyers or politicians came in to get a drink or engage in a little backroom card playing, Jim would be there with a ready smile and an attentive ear. The savvy lawmakers were probably not fooled by this, but they recognized political talent and ambition when they saw it and made sure to be friendly to him.

From 1887 to 1892 Jim served as a First Ward Democratic committeeman. The First Ward included most of the West Bottoms and pulled a lot of political weight because of all the businesses there. He became well known within the party (and soon across the entire city) for how he handled elections. At this time primaries were done informally by getting people together and having a voice vote. Jim would tell only his friends the time and place for the vote, usually by throwing a free party at his saloon and then getting the drunken crowd to show up at the polling place and scream at the top of their lungs for the candidate of his choice. Whoever got elected knew to whom he owed his office. When more modern techniques were introduced, with supposedly secret ballots, he found that the drunks could be relied upon to do the right thing, and he always had a few other tricks to make sure his candidates won.

Pulling the strings behind his favorite politicians whetted Jim's appetite for more direct power, and he got his large personal following to elect him alderman for the First Ward. Nobody dared oppose him in the primary, and he soundly defeated his Republican opponent in the general election.

Once in office, Jim ran the First Ward much as he ran his saloon—anyone friendly to him and his goals would be treated like gold, and everyone else had better leave. He would get drunks out of jail quickly so they wouldn't lose their jobs, helped policemen who were in trouble with their superiors, gave coal and turkeys to the poor, and basically lent a hand to anyone so that on Election Day he could call in those favors.

High finance in Kansas City at the time was dominated by the small group of white, Anglo-Saxon Protestant businessmen who ran the Commercial Club. This club had no interest in having some grubby Irish saloon owner as one of its members, so Jim merely sidestepped its influence and built a power base of his own. He noticed the club never did any charity work, so he made a name for himself, and made lots of friends, by giving assistance to those in need. Someone who needed a job or some food for their family could always turn to Big Jim.

He became known as "King of the First" and easily won reelection. He kept his Republican rivals from clamping down on gambling, which was his political cashbox and the main source of income for many of his friends. Although gambling was actually illegal, Jim's friends in the police department gave him protection. They also ran rival operations out of town, making it appear to the public that they were doing something about illegal gambling.

An important aspect of Jim's political job was patronage. Since he got to appoint some posts, and had influence over other politicians who did the same, he could put his own men in the jobs or give contracts to businesses he had invested in. The beneficiaries, of course, would know to whom they owed their allegiance. Patronage was, and still is, one of the ways politicians create a power base.

His little brother Tom worked out well as a bouncer and barkeep, so in 1894 Jim got him a job as a deputy constable in a First Ward city court. Two years later he became deputy marshal in county court. This job paid one hundred dollars a month, a lot in those days, but still left Tom with plenty of time to be on committees where he could assert his big brother's interests. Soon Tom became precinct captain, helping Jim cheat on Election Day.

Jim also had another brother, Mike, who helped rig elections but was a bit crazy. He once entered an opposition saloon, bought everyone beer, then threw his own drink in their faces. His political rivals piled onto him, and although he got pummeled in the fight, he enjoyed himself thoroughly.

Jim wasn't the only political boss in town, or even in the local Democratic Party. Joseph Shannon moved to Kansas City and had crawled up the ladder of power in a similar fashion to Pendergast. An Irish-American Democrat like Big Jim, he had his base of support in the Ninth Ward, southeast of downtown.

Pendergast and Shannon started running opposing candidates, and sometimes even allied themselves with the Republicans to beat each other. The origin of their rivalry is unclear; perhaps it was as simple as each not wanting to share the lucrative patronage that came with the jobs.

In the 1900 elections, their greed got the best of them and they spent so much energy fighting each other that the Republicans won several important offices. After this they made a truce such that they fought in the primaries but cooperated in general elections. Their "fifty-fifty" agreement dictated that whoever won, patronage would be split between both factions equally, but of course both sides cheated any chance they could.

One of Jim's best political investments was James A. Reed, a lawyer he and Tom chose to be county counselor, equivalent to the county prosecutor of the modern era. In 1898, backed by Jim's gambling money, Reed won the race for prosecuting attorney in Jackson County. He became mayor in 1900, got reelected 1902, and went on to become senator in 1910.

With such a powerful politician in their pocket, the Pendergasts reaped huge rewards. Reed made Tom Pendergast superintendent of streets, an important job earning two thousand dollars a year and coming with 250 jobs to hand out as patronage. Jim got to fill 123 police jobs, which made his gambling ring safe from any pesky raids by do-good policemen who actually wanted to enforce the law.

Tom worked out well as superintendent, greatly improving the city streets and gaining public support in the process. He had learned from his big brother that the best way to keep power was to give people what they wanted. He listened to complaints about potholes and litter and treated black neighborhoods and workers the same as white ones, something blacks in Kansas City, or anywhere else in the country for that matter, weren't accustomed to enjoying. In 1902 Tom became county marshal, earning twice his previous salary.

With money rolling in from big government contracts and a wide range of businesses, Jim worked on several charitable projects to improve the quality of life in Kansas City. He organized the building of parks and pedestrian boulevards, assisted by William Rockhill Nelson, a powerful real estate magnate and owner of the *Kansas City Star*. Nelson's paper usually railed against the corruption of the Pendergast family, but Nelson realized that property values would go up with the addition of parks and sidewalks. His paper managed to look the other way while Jim's companies and followers gobbled up the lion's share of building contracts. Apparently Nelson learned something from the Pendergasts about doing well while doing good.

While most of Jim Pendergast's "charitable" projects had ulterior motives, he did seem to have a genuine concern for the people of Kansas City. When the Missouri River overflowed its banks in 1903, displacing hundreds of citizens, Jim provided food and shelter. The good press this generated surely helped him, but in this case at least, he probably spent far more than he earned. He also supported the relocation of Union Station away from the West Bottoms. While this would hurt his saloon business, he saw the new location as more central to the expanded city and in the best interest of the city as a whole.

By the first decade of the twentieth century, Jim's power was at an all-time high, but his health had begun to fail. His beloved wife, Mary, died in 1905, and Jim lost much of his spirit after that. He left his city council seat in 1910, a position he had held for eighteen years, and gave it to Tom, who easily won the "election." Jim died the next year.

In the years to follow, Tom Pendergast built up the political machine his brother had founded until he practically ruled Kansas City. He could make or break politicians, and even helped get an aspiring politician named Harry Truman elected Eastern District judge of the county court, the first step in a political career that would lead to the White House. While Truman tried to distance himself from the Kansas City political machine, in his private papers he referred to Tom Pendergast as "the Boss." When Truman got elected to the Senate, many referred to him as "the senator from Pendergast." Not even someone as ambitious as Jim Pendergast could have dreamed that the machine he built would one day reach so high.

But it all came crashing down in 1939 because Tom got too blatant with his election rigging. Times had changed, and the federal government was clamping down on political machines all over the country. Many members of the Missouri Democratic Party saw the Pendergast machine as an embarrassment, opening up the party to accusations of corruption. While nobody could pin any specific corruption on Tom Pendergast, the Treasury Department discovered he had cheated on his taxes and sent him to prison. He only stayed behind bars for fifteen months, but that was long enough for the political machine his brother had built to disintegrate.

In a fitting epitaph, the *Kansas City Times* published an interview with Jim Pendergast on November 11, 1911. Big Jim, in his last months of life, confided, "I've been called a boss. All there is to it is having friends, doing things for people, and later on they'll do things for you. . . . You can't coerce people into doing things for you—you can't make them vote for you. Wherever you see a man bulldozing anybody he don't last long."

While his claim that you can't make people vote a certain way isn't exactly borne out by the facts of his career, Jim Pendergast was right about one thing: One of the only ways to live a life of crime and die a free man is to make more friends than enemies.

MONTANA OUTLAWS

CON MURPHY

The *Helena Daily Herald,* the newspaper of the Montana Territory's capital, proclaimed Con Murphy "one of the worst desperados that ever infested the [Rocky] Mountains, the 'Jesse James' of Montana." He bore another dubious honor: In 1885 Murphy became Helena's last outlaw to be hanged by a mob.

By that date, the vigilantes of Montana's Virginia City–Bannack area had executed twenty-two thieves and murderers, and Helena's hangmen had added thirteen more. Before Murphy the last two, George Wilson and Arthur Compton, were hanged for the brutal beating and robbery of George Lenharth, an elderly prospector and rancher on the Missouri River. A crowd of more than three thousand people witnessed the April 30, 1870, execution at the old Hangman's Pine tree in Dry Gulch. Six years later, the tree was cut down by a Methodist minister named Shippen. The lack of a hanging tree didn't prevent a large number of men from hanging the twenty-eight-year-old Murphy—"a famous horse thief and badman," according to a local newspaper—from a railroad trestle across a small coulee between Helena and East Helena.

Versions vary somewhat, but what follows is the story of the relatively short and turbulent career of Con Murphy.

Known to his friends as "Red" or "Jack," Con Murphy was described as a slender but wiry and well-muscled man of about 150 pounds with an innocent-looking round face. His hair was a light reddish brown, and he had a matching mustache and closely clipped beard. The outlaw's complexion was described as both sallow and freckled, and his blue eyes (with red-hooded eyelids) were said to have produced a glossy stare. Murphy was supposedly good-natured and was not noted for either gunplay or killing, although he had briefly been associated with the vicious George "Big Nose" Parrott gang.

He said he took the name "Con" in Montana "because I fancied it." Murphy's real name was either Henry or John Redmond, and he reportedly came from a well-to-do family that lived between Hannibal and Palmyra, Missouri. He was said to have come west to live in southern Idaho at some time in his youth, possibly with relatives. In 1876 he became a teamster-packer with Gen. Alfred Terry's Montana military command, campaigning against the Sioux (Lakota) Indians in the Yellowstone River country during the Great Sioux War of 1876–77. He barely escaped being dispatched with Lt. Col. George Armstrong Custer and his Seventh Cavalry on their fateful ride from Fort Abraham Lincoln into the Little Bighorn River valley.

Murphy decided to abandon the military life while stationed at Terry's supply camp on the Yellowstone River; he first began his outlaw career as a horse thief and later as a stagecoach robber. He also worked at legitimate jobs out of Miles City, Montana, such as driving a freight wagon, and apparently he owned some property there at one time.

As an outlaw, Murphy began operating in the Gallatin, Jefferson, and Madison River valleys of Montana, then went west to the Malad River and Big Camas areas of eastern Idaho. One writer, Andrew Garcia, said that Murphy knew every trail, hole, and corner of the freight-stage road between Corinne, Utah, and Virginia City, Montana, and that his earlier attempts at robbing heavily guarded stagecoaches had ended in failure.

Reportedly, he also drove and sold horses to the Mounted Police of the Dominion of Canada's North West Territories. Murphy obtained some horses "legally" by trading with a few Indians and Métis (French-Indian) peoples for rotgut whiskey. He eventually drifted into the Helena Valley area, which proved to be a fatal mistake.

After three years on the outlaw trail, Murphy was captured in 1878, and in 1879 he was sentenced to the Montana Territorial Prison at Deer Lodge. He escaped—something at which he became an expert—after serving only seven months. He was recaptured about a year later by Lewis and Clark County Sheriff C. M. Jeffries in the Dearborn River country northwest of Helena. Murphy completed his sentence in 1882 and spent several months working as a cowboy in the Snake River country of Idaho and at other occupations at various mining camps before returning to the Helena area in 1884.

Upon his return he teamed up with the Edmondson brothers and a Texan named George Munn. The Edmondsons operated a ferry on the Missouri River near Spokane Creek. With Munn, Murphy robbed the Helena–Fort Benton stage on May 27, 1884. The holdup occurred at Mitchell's stage station, about thirty miles north of Helena in Prickly Pear Canyon on the Helena–Fort Benton stage line and the Mullan Road.

The bandits intercepted the coach about six hundred yards beyond the stage station, just after the Helena-bound coach passed by. The holdup went smoothly, with no opposition. The booty consisted of registered letters containing money, plus watches, revolvers, and two hundred dollars taken from the three passengers.

Perhaps Murphy believed he had found an easier, more lucrative way of life, but stage line superintendent Jacob Powers was determined to bring Murphy's new career to an abrupt halt. John Mead, the stage and ranch manager, gave

Powers and two deputy sheriffs a detailed description of the two men and their horses and saddles. Mead said the bandits had arrived early in the morning on the previous day and had left about noon. Mead's suspicion was aroused in part because the thieves' horses were muddy, showing they had crossed the creek instead of using the road. In addition, he had observed that one suspect had a rip in one of his boot's insteps, and that it had been repaired.

The deputies stayed at the scene overnight, but Powers immediately began his pursuit. Two men had been seen riding in an easterly direction from the general area of the relay station after the robbery. Powers believed the pair might cross the Missouri River at the town of Canyon Ferry, and he set out for the Judith Basin country to the northeast.

The superintendent arrived at the ferry landing early the next morning, but no one had crossed recently. After resting briefly, he turned south and followed Spokane Creek, which paralleled the Missouri, to the old Helena-Bozeman stage station. The station was run as a traveler's halfway house by Bruce Toole, who told Powers that Murphy often stayed with the John O'Neil family a mile and a half northeast of Toole's place.

Powers had ridden more than one hundred miles in twenty-four hours with no sleep; he had talked with several ranchers in his line of travel, and he had located Murphy's and Munn's hideout. And what of the two deputies at Mitchell's? They leisurely returned to Helena, after spending the night in comfort and filling their stomachs. Powers also returned to Helena with the information he had rounded up and reported to the sheriff's office. He then traveled back to Toole's place with the two deputies to watch the O'Neil homestead.

Before arriving, the lawmen learned that two men matching Murphy's and Munn's descriptions had stolen two gray horses from the Clancy area south of Helena in Jefferson County. It was mistakenly believed they were returning to the O'Neil ranch.

Powers talked to O'Neil while the deputies stood by in the general area. After a lengthy, confidential discussion, O'Neil admitted that Murphy had stayed there and that the Edmondson brothers had collected all their stolen horses and had left for an unidentified park near the Snake River in the mountains of northern Idaho. Murphy and Munn were to follow, he said, planning to add to the stolen horse herd on their way south. He told Powers that he doubted if the gang could be taken alive.

This ended Powers's participation in the search for Con Murphy, because the action shifted about one hundred miles southward to Madison County, Montana. In spite of the fact that the outlaws were handicapped with both a large herd of horses and a covered wagon driven by John Edmondson, along with his wife and two children, the Edmondson-Murphy bunch was not detected until it neared Idaho.

Once they had located the outlaw bunch, the two Lewis and Clark County deputies took the train to Dillon, Montana, to cut them off, but they were too far to the west to make contact. A contingent of Jefferson and Madison County deputies finally caught up with them at Wall Creek in the Madison River valley and attempted capture on June 5, 1884. Many shots were fired (several hundred, some claimed), but no one was injured save a posseman who had his mustache singed by a stray bullet. Although the outlaws lost some of the stolen horses in the fracas, the outgunned posse couldn't dislodge them from their hiding place in a narrow canyon. After expending all their ammunition, the deputies retreated. The two-hundred-dollar reward was hardly enough incentive to get shot.

The outlaw band continued twenty miles south, crossing the Continental Divide and going over Raynolds Pass into Idaho. They stopped at a naturally secluded park on Henrys Lake as originally planned.

The outlaws apparently thought the chase was over. But as they rested, a new eleven-man posse was forming at the Madison County seat at Ennis, and was soon close behind them. The outlaws were spotted at their place of rest by local residents, the Switzer brothers, who passed the information on to the posse.

On July 9, John Edmondson's slow, lumbering wagon was at last overtaken a mile from Camas Station. It contained the camping outfit, rifles, and ammunition, and three stolen horses were tied on behind. The other outlaws had gone into town with just their handguns. They were captured the following day during a carefully staged ambush when they stopped for breakfast at the home of Latter-day Saints Bishop Brigham Ricks in Ricksville (now Rexburg).

Murphy's partner Munn died in the exchange of gunfire and was buried in Idaho. His gear and personal effects were confiscated by Mormon authorities to defray the costs of an inquest and burial. Murphy (using the first name of Neal), Albert Edmondson, and John Edmondson were returned to Helena and incarcerated in the Lewis and Clark County Jail on July 19. Two nights later, Murphy cut his way to freedom through the jail roof. He wasn't missed until morning.

The old wooden jail was described by a Helena newspaper as a "poor insecure building, no stronger than a pigeon box." It was learned that the night guard had left for a period of time to watch a boxing match. The US marshal's office had recommended that Murphy be kept in irons because of his frequent escapes, but this advice was ignored, and he was allowed to roam freely among the other prisoners and talk to outsiders as well. This must have allowed him to either plan a break with a confederate or hire someone. The roof hole measured fourteen by sixteen inches, and a rope was dangling from the roof into his cell. The opening had been worked on from both sides.

A Helena paper called Murphy "the most hated villain in the county." The night of his escape, he reportedly rode thirty miles in the first two hours on his stolen horse, swam the Missouri River, and reached the Big Belt Mountains by daylight. On the third day he arrived at Big Timber, Montana, having survived on berries and handouts from various farms. In Big Timber, he sold the horse and bridle for seventy-five dollars to an Englishman and entered the Bliss Saloon to drink and gamble.

Murphy did more of the former, so it was no problem for the sheriff's department to arrest him after local citizens telegraphed Helena. There was little worry of him leaving—they had tied him down.

Murphy stayed in the Silver Bow County Jail at Butte until new steel-clad cells arrived in Helena from St. Louis and were installed. While being transported back to Helena, Murphy almost escaped from the undersheriff by jumping, fully cuffed and shackled, out the window of the train's water closet.

After he was incarcerated again in Helena, his jailers relaxed: Murphy was in an escape-proof lockup—or so they thought. They should have been more cognizant of his determination to remain free. Three months later, when law officers entered his cell to take him before a US grand jury, he had vanished. One report read that Murphy had skipped out the previous week; another said that he had secreted himself in the boxed compartment under the sink and escaped only after the cell was opened and they thought he had already disappeared. Apparently none of Murphy's jail mates had been invited along.

The reward for Murphy's capture was now boosted from two hundred dollars to one thousand dollars.

Something else happened as a result of the jailbreak. Several arson fires occurred in Helena about the time of Murphy's escape, and a number of men—probably members of the fading vigilante movement—decided the outlaw must have set them. These men also surmised that the fires were a way to divert attention from a planned escape by the Edmondson brothers before they could be transferred to the state prison at Deer Lodge.

To further stir things up, Murphy's younger brother, whose name might really have been Con, appeared on the scene, trying to locate his brother. He had journeyed from Deer Lodge, and he told various Helena residents that their mother was very ill. She wanted her older son to return home to Missouri and mend his ways before she died.

Meanwhile, the Helena fires continued, and a witness claimed he saw Murphy at the scene of one. Hence the law and a resurrected vigilante "people's committee" made Murphy's capture (at the height of winter) a high priority.

Just before Murphy's second escape, the Jefferson and Boulder stagecoach had been held up by five or six masked men. The stage contained fifteen passengers, nine on the inside and six on top. Two more wagonloads of passengers followed, along with two county sheriffs in a buggy. The group of prominent lawyers, judges, politicians, lawmen, and others were on their way to Boulder for the trial of the Edmondson brothers. This Helena group had transferred to the stage from a Northern Pacific train at Jefferson City.

The bandits were not after their money or valuables. They thought that John and Henry Edmondson and Con Murphy were aboard, and they had brought extra horses to rescue them. Warren Toole acted as spokesman for the passengers, asking the outlaws to be careful with their guns and not shoot anyone by accident. Toole told them that the prisoners they wanted were still in jail at Helena and warned them that more in their party were in wagons just behind the coach. The holdup men cut off their conversation with Toole and were about to beat a hasty retreat when lawmen arrived and opened fire.

One of the masked men, identified as Charley Warfield, was killed. Warfield had been one of the defense witnesses for the Edmondson brothers, and another Edmondson was thought to have been among the masked group, as was "Sleepy" Johnny Rothwell. The Edmondson trial was moved to Helena because of prisoner security problems and threats by the brothers' father and friends against the judge, sheriff, and jury. But the trial proceeded, and the boys received prison terms of fourteen and twelve years.

In the interim, jail escapee Con Murphy had been having a rough time surviving in the snow-covered and frigid Rocky Mountains. In January 1885 he stopped for two days at Paul's Saloon in Pipestone, a small community in Jefferson County near Whitehall. Murphy traded horses there and obtained a rifle and revolver. It wasn't until later that the saloon owner realized that Murphy had combined rewards of seventeen hundred dollars on his head.

Finally, the cold and lack of food drove Murphy to return to the John O'Neil ranch on the Bozeman Road. There, somehow, his brother found him and convinced him to go back home. He bought railroad tickets to St. Louis for them, and they planned to depart from Missoula, where the outlaw Murphy was unknown.

O'Neil made contact with the Helena authorities, perhaps while buying supplies, and agreed to help in Murphy's capture if he would see the reward money. Murphy's would-be captors were not Lewis and Clark County officers, however, but special officers George Bashaw, a city policeman, and J. H. McFarland, a liveryman. They were after Murphy for setting the Helena fires, not for the federal or state charges.

There had been about five arson fires in the vicinity of the county jail, and "people were in a state of alarm," according to a Helena paper. Henry Edmondson had escaped during the confusion generated by one of the fires, but he was quickly recaptured. The fourth brother, Jeff Edmondson, considered the leader, was captured a year later on a ranch near the Green River in Wyoming by Uinta County Sheriff Ward. Edmondson was brought back to Helena for trial on cattle-stealing charges in Meagher County by Montana Stock Inspector Jeff Conley, and shortly he joined his brothers in the state prison.

The three-man party of O'Neil, Bashaw, and McFarland set out in a sleigh for the fourteen-mile journey south, arriving at the O'Neil place early the next morning. The two officers waited in a nearby coulee while O'Neil entered the cabin and found the Murphy brothers still in bed. O'Neil asked the younger Murphy brother to feed the horses, and he was captured outside the cabin. Con Murphy was taken while still in bed. After leaving the O'Neil place in the sleigh during a blinding snowstorm, the party was forced to lay over at Toole's halfway house, only a mile and a half down the road. The two officers stayed awake all night with their prisoners.

The following morning after breakfast, Murphy had one of his handcuffs removed so that he could put on his coat. When Bashaw glanced out the window to see if the sled was ready, he allowed Murphy enough time to draw a secreted revolver from either a shoulder holster or boot. Murphy shot Bashaw in the wrist.

With his captor temporarily disabled, Murphy ran up the stairs and hid in a closet. After several shots were fired up through the floorboards and walls, Murphy was told to surrender or the cabin would be torched. The outlaw said he would agree if promised safe passage to Helena and the return of his gun in the event a mob should attempt to seize him. Supposedly Murphy received such assurances, and he gave himself up.

Soon afterward, however, other law officers arrived from Helena and took custody of the Murphy brothers. The Helena newspaper's headline read "Con Murphy Will Be in the City This Evening, Dead or Alive." The twelve lawmen and their prisoners began the journey back to Helena on January 27, 1885, only to be intercepted four miles south of the capital city by a "people's posse" of about 150 men. The mob took the prisoners despite the helpless peace officers' protests. Murphy's revolver was not returned, preventing him from going out in a blaze of glory.

A short trial of sorts was held. Murphy was questioned about the fires; he said he had no knowledge of them, and did not admit to having confidantes who did. The mob leaders told Murphy that his career had ended and said if he had anything to say he should "make it damn quick." Murphy asked them to spare his younger brother because he was innocent of any crimes. He also asked for a fair trial, but the mob had already decided to hang him.

The crowd took Con Murphy to a nearby telegraph pole. A rope was thrown over the crossbars, and fifty men pulled him skyward. But the crossbar broke, and the half-strangled prisoner tumbled to the ground. After a short conference, the mob threw him back into the sleigh with the rope still around his neck and took a ten-minute ride to a nearby railroad trestle.

Before his second hanging, Murphy and his brother exchanged embraces and a few last words. Afterward, his swollen and purple-faced body was cut down from the fifteen-foot-high makeshift gallows and removed to Helena to be put on exhibition, with the noose intact, at the old firehouse in Courthouse Square.

Con's brother, who had not been harmed by the mob, was arraigned before County Judge Davis the following day for harboring and protecting a known criminal. The twenty-three-year-old Murphy explained (in a different version of the earlier story) that he had come from Morris, Illinois, at his coal miner father's request after receiving a letter from Con, who had been gone for ten years. He said he had arranged a meeting near the railroad tracks twenty miles northeast of Helena, and that neither he nor his family knew anything of Con's outlaw career. Before he was scheduled to appear before a grand jury, Murphy was released by Judge Davis, escorted under heavy guard to the station, and given a ticket to St. Paul, Minnesota.

Apparently, his family never claimed the body, and Con Murphy was said to have been buried in the pauper's section of Helena's Benton Avenue cemetery. In October 1894, old letters addressed to J. T. Murphy were found at the local post office; who had sent them was not revealed.

Whether Con Murphy would have gone straight if he had returned to his home in Missouri (or Illinois) can only be speculated upon. We do know, though, that the outlaw once remarked to a fellow cellmate that he could have died an honorable death at the Battle of the Little Bighorn with Custer and saved the people of Montana much grief and expense. In the end, it was Murphy and his family who suffered the grief. His mother supposedly died soon after from a broken heart.

Special officers Bashaw and McFarland, who had risked their lives to capture Murphy, weren't happy either; they were denied the reward money, which was to be given for a live capture only.

And lastly, the real culprits in the Helena fires were finally discovered. After the rest of the Edmondsons were banished from Montana by secret order of the Citizens Committee, the fires ceased. The mystery of who helped Murphy escape from the Helena jail, however, was never solved.

Although fate had dealt Murphy a dishonorable death, he gained a place in history as the last victim of the local vigilantes' rope—ironically, for crimes he didn't commit. After his death, it seemed the vigilante movement, which had begun in 1863, had run its course. Popular opinion weighed against it, and a strong court system replaced it.

GEORGE "BIG NOSE" PARROTT

On a hot, dusty day in the summer of 1879, the US Army paymaster's wagon proceeded slowly northeast on the rough, spine-jarring (Fisk) Montana-Minnesota wagon road. The journey had begun at Camp Ruger, located at the Coal Banks–Missouri River steamboat landing near present-day Virgelle, and would conclude at Fort Assinniboine, about forty miles distant. The wagon, carrying the soldiers' first payroll, was escorted by a detail of Second Cavalry soldiers.

The construction of the new ten-company military post on Beaver Creek, a tributary of the Milk River, had commenced recently on land formerly used legally as a camping and hunting site by the Blackfoot Confederacy (made up of Blackfoot, Blood, and Piegan tribes) and by Gros Ventre and River Crow (Absaroke), and not so legally by the Assiniboine (Nakoda), Plains Cree (Kinnis-to-no), and Sioux (Lakota) Nations. The mostly brick fort would eventually have more than one hundred buildings surrounding its rectangular half-mile-long by one-fifth-mile-wide parade grounds.

Waiting for the wagon in a coulee off Beaver Creek was a party of gunmen led by George "Big Nose" Parrott. They had been led to believe that the payroll would be easy pickings, with only a handful of guards. But the cloud of dust they saw coming from the south was too big for just a wagon and a few horses; in fact, there were some thirty bluecoats guarding the payroll. Swearing profusely at their bad luck, the men spurred their horses and headed southwest, back toward the community of Sun River.

Meanwhile, the military party reached the fort site and reported seeing the men to their commander, Col. Thomas Ruger. US Deputy Marshal John X. Beidler of Helena was at the post on business concerning horse theft, robbery, and murder; Ruger told him to go and investigate.

The short but stocky ex-vigilante was a brave man with a reputation for toughness, but he wasn't foolhardy. When he asked for an escort, Ruger refused; the commander said the men were needed at the military post because there were so many hostile Indians in the area. Beidler ended the conversation by telling Ruger that he wasn't yet prepared to meet his maker, and the gang was allowed to go on its way.

This was not Parrott's and his men's usual stomping ground. Parrott had been making his home at Miles City, Montana, since he was wanted for murder in Wyoming. The outlaw was about 5 feet 10 inches tall and weighed 160 pounds. He was in his mid-thirties and had a large mustache, dark curly hair, heavy eyelids, and a large potato nose. He was a little on the homely side.

Little is known of the early life of the man who also called himself George Reynolds in Montana, George Francis Warden in Wyoming, and George Manuse at other times. One historian states that Parrott was born in Indiana and reared in Iowa. Other reports had him living at St. George, Utah, once he came west. His earliest and perhaps only legitimate job would have been in 1876, as a bull team freight-wagon driver, or bullwhacker, carrying supplies to the gold-rush town and gulch of Deadwood, Dakota Territory, in the Black Hills mining district. Parrott probably hauled gold ore shipments south to the Union Pacific Railroad depots at Sidney, Nebraska, and Cheyenne, Wyoming, also going eastward to a Northern Pacific Railroad depot at Bismarck, North Dakota, and the steamboat landing at Fort Pierre, South Dakota, on the Missouri River. Parrott quit this work after learning all the routes so he could easily ambush the gold-laden stagecoaches and freighters or travelers he came upon. Ambushes were easy to execute from the trails through the dark and narrow gulches. The gold shipments were not easy to take, however, because the gold came in two-hundred-pound bricks; mine payrolls were easier marks.

Parrott's gang members at the time were believed to have been Jack Campbell, "Dutch" Charlie Burris (or Bates), Frank Towle (or Toule), and a man named McKinney. The gang reportedly had a robbers' roost near Cheyenne, Wyoming, close to the Black Hills stage route. They also had access to the old Oregon Trail along the North Platte and Sweetwater Rivers, the north-south Black Hills–Cheyenne route, and the Bozeman and Bridger Roads that broke off into Montana. They were said to have had another hideout in the Sheridan Valley on Goose Creek where the Bozeman Road skirted the Big Horn Mountains, and a third hideout shared with other outlaws in the lush mountain setting of Jackson Hole in the Grand Tetons of western Wyoming.

Parrott and his gang were well known in the lower Yellowstone River valley once Milestown (later renamed Miles City) was established near Fort Keogh at the confluence of the Yellowstone and Tongue Rivers. The same was true farther west at Bozeman, a farming community in the Gallatin River valley. Parrott and his band sold stolen horses from Wyoming in Montana and north to Canada, and they brought stolen animals back with them. In the winter months, they stayed at one of their hideouts, playing cards, drinking whiskey, racing horses, and fattening up horses to be sold in the spring.

Their exploits were recorded in the memoirs of Andrew Garcia in July 1878. Garcia had decided to leave the employ of the army as a wrangler-packer at Fort Ellis near Bozeman, and had set out with a partner to hunt and trap in the Musselshell River country to the northwest. They fell in with five men who used them and their pack outfit as a cover while they peddled whiskey to certain Indian and Métis people, who in turn stole horses from the tribes for them. One of the peddlers was Parrott; another was Con Murphy, soon to be known as a notorious Montana outlaw. Yet another was Al Shinnick; he is believed to have had a brother, John, who had a saloon-brothel in Miles City. Parrott stayed there when in town. A man called Brock Adams, perhaps from Utah, was also traveling with them, as well as a Métis (French-Indian) called Hypolite La Brie, a most unstable and dangerous man.

These men kept Garcia's partner drunk during their journey—a feat that took little effort—and spoke freely to Garcia of their activities, perhaps trying to recruit him. They told him that they sold the ill-gotten horses to the Mounted Police in the North West Territories for about a hundred dollars each through a contact of La Brie's. In addition, Garcia learned that Parrott and Shinnick had attempted several holdups of stagecoaches in Utah and Montana, but had failed at all of them. The gang claimed to be headquartered at Green River, Wyoming, near the Utah border.

Garcia and his partner were allowed to leave the outlaws after journeying south from Otter Creek to near Sweet Grass Creek, near the future town of Big Timber. La Brie wanted to kill the two men, but Adams wouldn't allow it. Reportedly, La Brie and Adams finally shot it out when they reached Canada, killing each other in the exchange.

The following month, Parrott returned to Wyoming and rejoined the old gang. After buying supplies at Medicine River, the group settled in a hideout in the thickly wooded Rattlesnake Creek canyon near the community of Elk Mountain in the Medicine Bow Range of the Rocky Mountains. It was believed that Parrott had previously been in the northern part of the Carbon County country, robbing stagecoaches, after he left the St. George, Utah, area.

In the group besides Parrott were regulars Dutch Charlie, Frank Towle, a "Mack" (possibly McKinney), Jack Campbell, and two men identified as Thomas Reed and Sim Wan. Reed was supposedly a Younger brothers gang member, and Wan was said to be an alias used by Frank James, the outlaw brother of Jesse James.

This bunch formulated plans to rob a special Union Pacific Railroad train carrying the railroad workers' payroll along a stretch of track west of the town of Carbon. Then a major coal-mining town, Carbon was six miles west of Hanna, where the rail section crew was headquartered, and about forty miles west of Rawlins, the seat of Carbon County. The gang put its plan into action on August 19, 1878.

Using a James brothers technique, they pulled the rail spikes on a downhill curve and tried pulling the rails off, but their crowbars were not long enough to get sufficient leverage, so they planned to build an obstruction of ties on the track to derail the train. But a section crew showed up before they could accomplish the work, and the outlaws had to lay low in a gully all day waiting for them to leave. The maintenance crew did not discover the loosened rails until they were ready to quit for the day. They hurriedly packed up and headed back to report their discovery. Meanwhile, the gang went back to work on the rails and once again had their plan thwarted when a passenger train came by and drove them into hiding a second time. When the special didn't show up, and since the section crew had found the sabotaged track, they decided to head back to their hideout. What they didn't know was that the section foreman had flagged down the special and warned the crew of the danger ahead.

With the train stopped and the gang in retreat, the Carbon County sheriff instructed deputy sheriffs Tip Vincent of Rawlins and Ed Widowfield of Carbon, along with six special deputies, to proceed to the aborted robbery scene. The lawmen were fairly sure of their quarry because the Parrott gang had been seen earlier in the week at Laramie, about eighty miles to the southeast, and had left in a westerly direction.

Vincent and Widowfield became separated from the posse when they struck the outlaws' trail, and they followed it to the gang's camp. Seeing no one, they advanced into the campsite and examined the ground, including the recently extinguished fire. In the ashes the lawmen found the remains of the railroad spikes the gang had cut off.

That was enough for gang member Frank Towle, who shouted, "Let's fire!" Both deputies were killed as the outlaws, who had been hiding nearby, emptied their guns into them. One officer was killed immediately, but the other made it about fifty yards on horseback before he fell to the ground, mortally wounded. The bodies were thrown into the thick brush and lightly covered, after being stripped of their valuables, weapons, boots, and so on. The men hurriedly broke camp, took the extra horses, and started north, crossing the railroad tracks at Carbon and later fording the North Platte River above Muddy Creek.

By this time, the other posse members had returned to town, thinking Vincent and Widowfield had done the same. Search parties were sent out to find the two deputies after three days, but their bodies weren't discovered for ten days. Although the dim trail of four of the outlaws was picked up, it was soon lost. A reward of two thousand dollars was offered for Parrott, and one thousand dollars was offered for each gang member, dead or alive.

Dutch Charlie was supposedly arrested soon after at Green River, Wyoming, and transported across the state to the county jail at Laramie. But another report is more likely: that he was arrested in Laramie after hiding out for several months on Rock Creek. Carbon County Sheriff Rankin was in the process of bringing the outlaw back to Rawlins for trial when the train stopped at Carbon for fuel at 9:25 p.m., and a party of masked men broke into the baggage car. It would have been useless for the sheriff to resist the mob; besides townspeople, there were several hundred miners to contend with. They took Dutch Charlie to the nearest telegraph pole and hung him high. He reportedly confessed his guilt before the execution, but would not identify the others. His body was cut down the next day and thrown into a Rawlins-bound coal car, the rope still around his neck.

The remaining gang members were credited by some authorities with robbing a stagecoach at Canyon Springs on the Deadwood-Cheyenne route near present-day Four Corners, Wyoming. Perhaps twenty-seven thousand to forty thousand dollars was taken in the holdup. One outlaw died of the wounds he received. Frank Towle died near the Black Hills when the gang tried to rob a stagecoach bound for the Hat Creek sheep station in country south of Canyon Springs. The mysterious Mack died of fever in the Yellowstone country of Montana, according to Parrott.

The equally mysterious Reed and Wan apparently disappeared, but they were hardly Younger or James brothers gang members. The Youngers were in prison at the time after committing the Northfield, Minnesota, bank robbery; the Jameses were in hiding in Mexico until the summer of 1879, when they returned to their Nashville, Tennessee, homes, where their families were in hiding. From there they began a crime spree throughout the South before returning to Missouri, where Jesse James was killed. A Thomas Reid (or Reed) from Arkansas pops up in the Dutch Henry Ieuch gang at Culbertson, but whether there was any connection with the Thomas Reed involved with Parrott is unknown.

In the fall of 1878, Parrott and some gang members returned to the Miles City, Montana, area. When in town, Parrott frequented John Shinnick's saloon on North Fifth Street. John and Nell Shinnick's saloon and home ranch were widely known as desperado hangouts. Parrott stayed at Shinnick's cabin on the edge of town. The other gang members apparently had a hideout at Buffalo Rapids on the Yellowstone River.

Miles City, the seat of Custer County, was at the time a wild and rough young cowboy town near the end of Texas cattle trails. A combination of buffalo hunters, soldiers, and cowboys made it a lively place. Main Street had a solid block of saloons, brothels, and gambling dens. Its location at the mouth of the Tongue River made it an excellent fording place and steamboat landing on the Yellowstone River. Several large cattle companies established ranches near there because of the good grass and water. But at the time of Parrott's residence, it was still "a long way from nowhere," according to locals.

If Parrott and his gang had indeed robbed the stagecoach at Canyon Springs, they were broke by the following winter. Perhaps their attempted robbery and a successful stage robbery by another gang became confused, because a bandit died in each.

Parrott probably believed his luck was changing when Morris Cahn, former Fort Keogh military post trader and then prosperous town merchant, decided to take a trip back East. Cahn, who wasn't well liked and didn't have an honest reputation, planned to buy merchandise on the trip. He feared carrying a large amount of cash on the first leg of the journey from Miles City, before he boarded a Northern Pacific train at Bismarck, North Dakota. His worries were legitimate because the local people resented their money leaving town.

Cahn was able to hitch a ride with a military ambulance and an escort of fifteen soldiers going that way to pick up the fort's payroll. Some claim that Parrott saw to it that each soldier was furnished with alcohol, but that cannot be substantiated. The party consisted of the lead scout, Sergeant Green, the ambulance carrying the officers, and Cahn, followed by the soldiers in the escort wagon.

About ten miles beyond the Powder River crossing, near present-day Terry, they came off a five-mile plateau into a steep-walled valley. Sergeant Green and the ambulance were stopped at the bottom at a sharp, dark corner by three men with rifles. When the soldiers in the escort wagon appeared, they also were captured. All the men were robbed, and Cahn was relieved of his thirty-two hundred dollars and some peach brandy. Adding insult to injury, the robbers took the sergeant's horse—but they gave the wagon driver a cigar.

Even though Parrott had the brim of his hat pulled down and stood in shadow, his big nose was still visible to the victims. The gang crossed the Yellowstone River and doubled back north, eventually reaching a ranch near present-day Kinsey, halfway between Terry and Miles City. The next day they reappeared in Miles City, spending freely.

For several years afterward, when folks in Miles City wanted to treat a friend to a drink, they would say, "Come up, old boy, and have something on me, for I still have one of old Cahn's dollars left." Although Cahn lost his bankroll, he did have some solace: The coulee where he was robbed was later named in his honor. Apparently Parrott was arrested and tried for the robbery (at least in a preliminary hearing), but he was acquitted because of sworn testimony that he was at the Buffalo Springs camp at the time of the robbery. Cahn feared for his well-being after the trial, but to his relief, Parrott decided to move on four days later, broke once again.

Parrott's gang had good reason to move on. The army swore vengeance on the men; plus, with wanted posters still up in Wyoming, the Cahn robbery gave them unwelcome attention. And perhaps one or two gang members had bragged of their Wyoming killings one time too many.

The gang moved to an even more isolated area some three hundred miles to the northwest. The community of Sun River was at the main crossing on the Mullan Road, which started at Fort Benton and ended at Fort Walla Walla in Washington Territory. More locally, it was the route of the Helena stage from Fort Benton to Sun River and south to the Helena-area goldfields. About five miles to the west of the Sun River crossing was another military post, Fort Shaw. The adobe post had been built in 1867 to oversee the Blackfoot Confederacy and protect the north-south trail.

The new Montana Central Railroad tracks were just being laid from Helena to Great Falls, Fort Assinniboine, and Pacific Junction, where it joined the main east-west line. The tracks would bypass the old crossing; this was the gang's last chance at any treasure-laden coaches.

The Parrott gang established headquarters at the Hardy place, in the nearby hills at Rocky Gap. The gang members, except for Parrott, took jobs at different ranches to allay any suspicion about their activities. They spent their free time at Johnny Divine's, the local saloon-hotel, planning to rob the army payroll from the paymaster's wagon bringing the money from Helena. The plan was to lie in wait in Prickly Pear Creek canyon north of Helena.

(Their old comrade Con Murphy would rob a stagecoach in the same vicinity a few years later. Murphy's booty was sparse, and it was the beginning of the end of his outlaw career—and his life.)

The story goes that Divine overheard Campbell telling of their plan, and being a former soldier, he hurried to Helena to warn the military authorities. Riding through the canyon, he was stopped by the gang, but he bribed his way through with whiskey and cigars. He arrived in Helena and warned the military of the outlaws' plan. A changed trip date and a more formidable escort prevented any robbery.

This story raises questions, however. Why would Johnny Divine journey the ninety-some miles to Helena when all he had to do was report to Fort Shaw only a few miles away? Fort Shaw personnel could have telegraphed to Helena to stop the shipment, and could have sent out their own column to capture the outlaws. And was it typical for a horseman to carry whiskey and cigars? It would appear the storytellers embellished a bit.

The boys tried one more army payroll robbery in the isolated stretch between Fort Benton and Fort Assinniboine, but again the party had a large escort. The soldiers were lucky not to run into any of the hostile Plains Cree who were opposing the military move into north-central Montana. Crime definitely wasn't paying well in northern Montana, so the Parrott gang returned to Wyoming, despite the price on their heads.

At this point, the waters muddy considerably, because the lives of George "Flatnose" Currie and George "Big Nose" Parrott merge at times. Currie was part of the Wild Bunch, along with Kid Curry, Butch Cassidy, and the Sundance Kid. He had first operated out of the Hole-in-the-Wall valley in Wyoming's Powder River country. But the Wild Bunch's notoriety came after all the Parrott gang members were resting eternally in Boot Hill.

The Parrott gang went back to horse stealing, but incidents of hot pursuit and shootings by ranchers and lawmen were making horse theft tougher. It is believed the stubborn outlaws planned yet another army payroll robbery not far from the site of the Union Pacific Railroad robbery attempt and subsequent murders.

The payroll for Fort Fetterman, at the junction of the Bozeman and Oregon Trails, came in by train at Medicine Bow and was taken from there to the fort. Because of the high number of robberies, the payroll was supposedly secreted on a freighter wagon, and the gang didn't find it in the teamster's grocery shipment.

The year 1880 continued to bring the Parrott gang misfortune. In a saloon in South Pass City, Wyoming, northwest of Rawlins on the Continental Divide at the Wind River Range, Parrott and some new associates were fleecing a cowboy during a poker game. The cowboy, Tom Albro, accused gang member Tom Rutledge of dealing from the bottom of the deck. Rutledge went for his gun. Albro shot him, but Parrott then killed Albro and rode away in the dark before Albro's friends could find their target.

The following month, Parrott and a sidekick named Bill Carey (perhaps he was actually old gang member Jack Campbell) were in the vicinity of Fort McKinney and the town of Buffalo. Here they reportedly stole a large amount of supplies from an old man camped near Deep Creek. With their new cache and a string of stolen horses, they headed north and dropped some of the animals off with a "squaw man friend" before following the Tongue River back into Montana.

However, the welcome mat was no longer out at Miles City. Reward posters for the Wyoming train holdup had reached Custer County Sheriff Tom Irvine at last. No one would tolerate the harboring of Parrott this time around.

Parrott arrived in town and stayed at the Shinnicks' cabin as usual. The stolen horses were housed in the adjacent stable, while Carey stationed himself at Shinnick's saloon-brothel. The law officers made a deal with a prostitute known as "Beavertooth," who was on calling terms with Shinnick's wife. The saloon woman was to frequent the cabin, report back on Parrott's movements, and keep Carey happy at the downtown saloon. Shinnick's cooperation probably wasn't hard to obtain; Parrott was sharing the cabin with Shinnick's wife.

Next, the sheriff hired two special deputies, Lem Wilson and Fred Schmalsle, both former Fort Keogh packers unknown to Parrott. The first trip to the cabin and grounds consisted of crossing the pasture to look at the horses. Parrott came out of the cabin with rifle in hand, but he believed them when they said they were prospective buyers. They had a friendly discussion. Wilson and Schmalsle returned the next day. This time Parrott came out unarmed, and the two arrested him either as they sat on the front porch or while talking horseflesh in the stable. The sheriff and his deputy came out of their hiding place in the nearby brush and handcuffed the outlaw. Carey was arrested at the saloon. As he lifted his drink, a revolver was stuck under his chin.

Carbon County officials arrived to extradite Parrott after a local blacksmith riveted irons on his hands and feet. Because there was still a significant outlaw element in the town, a large posse escorted Parrott to the steamboat landing. He was taken up the Yellowstone River to the Missouri, and down that river through the Dakota Territory to Omaha, Nebraska. What happened to Carey isn't clear. In one story, he escaped or was released; in another he was sent to prison for horse theft and later was transferred to the state mental hospital, from which he subsequently escaped. Whatever his fate, his part in the tale ended. Two other supposed gang members were arrested, one in Ogden, Utah, and one in Deadwood, Dakota Territory, but neither was convicted of involvement in the Wyoming murder and train robbery attempt.

At Omaha, Parrott was taken to the Union Pacific Railroad headquarters, where his only known photograph was taken. The authorities tried unsuccessfully to link him to other train robberies, but he wouldn't even admit to the robbery in Carbon County or to the murders. Departing Omaha, Parrott and his captors went by train to Cheyenne, Wyoming, where the lawmen tried to link Parrott with unsolved state robberies. Once again they were unsuccessful.

The party left for Rawlins the next day, August 14, 1880, on the same fateful railroad journey that Dutch Charlie had taken and that ended in his death by hanging at Carbon. As the train pulled into Carbon for fuel and water, the passengers saw that the stores were lit up and a street dance was in progress. It is said the lawmen graphically recounted to Parrott how Dutch Charlie had been dragged off the train and lynched. As if on cue, a dozen armed and masked men entered the car. Another group had already neutralized the crew and conductor. It looked as if Parrott's fate would be sealed in Carbon too.

But Sheriff Jim Rankin chose not to cooperate. He drew his revolver and called upon the compartment's passengers to help him resist the taking of Parrott. This proved fruitless, however, and his weapon was confiscated. Unable to find handcuff keys on the sheriff (another officer had them), the intruders broke Parrott's manacles with an ax, destroying his seat in the process. Parrott was marched out with a rope already around his neck.

Apparently, Parrott grabbed a revolver from one of his captors for a few seconds, in spite of overwhelming odds and being bound. Once outside, though, his toughness faded. He denied any involvement in the attempted train robbery or killings and asked to be shot rather than hanged. He was taken to a corral and a rope was thrown over a beam. At that Parrott changed his mind, telling the mob he was badly scared and wanted a few minutes to compose himself before confessing. The mob leaders told Parrott he could have all the time he wanted, within reason.

Parrott confessed to having been one of the party who had attempted the train robbery near Elk Mountain and killed the two law officers. He named the gang members, said that they had separated that fall, and claimed that most of them were dead. When asked why they had killed the lawmen, he replied, "On the principle that dead men tell no tales."

To Parrott's surprise, the group's leader ordered the outlaw returned to the sheriff's custody and sent on his way to Rawlins for a legal hanging. Back on board the train, Parrott slid down between the seats and burst into a hysterical fit of weeping.

A short intermission was called at the Carbon dance. The people expressed their satisfaction at how well the abduction had been executed and their relief that Dutch Charlie had actually participated in the murders. This was the first hard information that anyone had as to the gang's makeup.

One could speculate as to whether the Carbon County sheriff collaborated in obtaining Parrott's confession. The editor of the *Carbon County Journal* remarked that "the only wonder is that Big Nose George did not climb the golden stairs via that route."

Although the town of Carbon outlasted Parrott, it began a gradual decline in 1902 when the coal mines closed. Soon the town and railroad siding were bypassed by the new Union Pacific main line.

Perhaps it was a small consolation to Parrott that no mob waited at the Rawlins railroad station when the train pulled in. The outlaw was hustled off to the county jail. He pled guilty at his preliminary hearing in September 1880, fearing a lynch mob if he pled otherwise. Upon legal advice he then recanted his confession and requested a trial. Judge William Peck stopped the trial to say it was useless to go on; he was satisfied with Parrott's guilt. The outlaw broke down again when he received his death sentence and had to be physically supported by two bailiffs.

For a short time Parrott tried a hunger strike, but he gave up when it became obvious it wouldn't help his cause. Next he supposedly converted to Christianity. Perhaps because of this "conversion," his jailers relaxed and, as the months rolled by, even allowed him to roam the cell-block corridor.

Somehow, between September and March, Parrott obtained a small case knife with one blade and a piece of sandstone with which to sharpen it. He used the knife to file the rivets on his leg shackles. The night of Parrott's escape attempt,

Sheriff Jim Rankin was out of town. The sheriff's brother, Robert Rankin, was the jailer on duty. When he entered the cell-block corridor to lock the prisoners in their cells for the night, Parrott came from the water closet compartment and struck Rankin three times on the head with the seven- to eight-pound shackles. But Rankin turned, struck Parrott with his fist, and slammed him against the wall. Rankin's wife, Rose, heard the commotion and locked the outer corridor door to prevent an escape, then ran to grab her husband's revolvers. She covered Big Nose George while her bloodied husband exited the cell. Meanwhile, Rose's sister ran for help.

Parrott returned to his hiding place in the water closet, but when another prisoner was called out of his cell to light a corridor lamp, Parrott was found and ordered back to his cell.

Reinforcements arrived presently, and new rivets were fashioned for Parrott's leg irons. He was returned to his cell for the night, and as an extra precaution, another guard was added.

Parrott expressed remorse for attacking Rankin, although no one believed him. In fact, the townspeople were already on the streets in small groups discussing Parrott's irritating behavior—and how to end it.

Around 10:00 p.m., these smaller parties merged into a large assembly in front of the jail. About an hour later, there was a rap on the jail door, and several voices demanded entrance. A guard inquired who was there. The answer was, "Friends." The guard said it was too late to admit anyone. "The door was immediately burst open," the *Rawlins Daily Tribune* reported. The well-armed visitors covered the jail personnel and removed Rankin's keys from his room. They used an ax to enter Parrott's cell because they couldn't make the key work. The group—said to have been some of Cheyenne's best citizens—marched Parrott to a place near the railroad station where more than one hundred people awaited him. A half-inch rope had been hung from a telegraph pole, with an empty kerosene barrel as a platform for Parrott to climb. According to local folklore, Elizabeth Widowfield, sister-in-law of one of the murdered deputies, kicked the barrel out from under Parrott, saying, "This will teach you to murder my brother-in-law!"

On this first try, the rope broke and Parrott went sprawling to the ground. Undaunted, the group obtained a twelve-foot ladder and made Parrott climb it, with two men "assisting." The ladder was pulled away when the doomed outlaw was at the eight-foot level. In desperation, Parrott was able to untie his hands and cling to the telegraph pole, pleading to be shot. Finally, he lost his grip and agonizingly strangled to death.

The assembly dispersed, Parrott was cut down by the coroner, and his body was removed from the scene. Several other outlaws were said to have left the city in a hurry after word of the hanging spread.

Rose Rankin, wife of the jailer and sister-in-law of the county sheriff, received a gold watch and key in a velvet-lined box for preventing Parrott's escape.

Ordinarily, this would have marked the end of Parrott's story, but there is a bizarre epilogue involving Dr. John Osborne, a recent arrival from Vermont. Osborne had witnessed the lynching, and he and his partner desired the outlaw's corpse for "anatomical study and dissection." When no kin claimed the body, Osborne took it and preserved it with a strong saline solution in a whiskey barrel. He made a plaster cast of Parrott's head and neck and then sawed off the top of Parrott's skull, supposedly so he could examine Big Nose George's brain to find out why he had such a mean disposition. He noted that Parrott didn't look very intelligent—but how many dead people do? He gave the skullcap to his young assistant, Lillian Heath, who used it at times for a doorstop or a container for rock specimens. (Heath later went on to become a doctor herself, specializing in obstetrics.) Finally, the physician removed skin from the dead man's thighs and chest and had it tanned for use in a pair of two-toned shoes and a medicine bag. Reportedly, he wanted to keep the nipples on the shoe skin, but the shoemaker ignored his bizarre instructions.

His body of no further use to the physician, George Parrott was buried, using the barrel as a casket, in a secret location. His remains had finally come to rest—at least until May 1950. That month workers from the Metcalf Construction Company were digging a foundation for the stone Hested store on West Cedar Street in Cheyenne when they found the whiskey barrel with Parrott's corpse (minus the top of his head) and items of clothing and shoes. Dr. Heath's memento was taken to the scene; it matched perfectly. Parrott's bones were offered to the Carbon County Museum, which declined, and Parrott was reinterred in a more suitable but still undisclosed location. Like folks said, "Big Nose George Parrott sure has got around!"

And parts of him still are around: A piece of his tanned skin, his skullcap, and his leg irons remain on display at the Union Pacific Railroad Company museum at Omaha, Nebraska. The bottom part of his skull and the shoes he was wearing when he met his death are in the Carbon County Museum. And lastly, his death mask and the doctor's shoes made from his flesh are on display at the Rawlins National Bank.

But what of Dr. Osborne? Did he go to Hollywood and produce horror movies? Or start a wax museum? No, he became the governor of Wyoming and later assistant secretary of state under President Woodrow Wilson. He died in Rawlins in 1943 at the age of eighty-nine. And yes, he received a conventional burial.

If the local citizens thought the end of the Parrott gang spelled the end of outlawry in the area, they were sadly mistaken. Soon Butch Cassidy and associates were on the scene, rivaling the exploits of the James and Younger brothers.

The latter gangs frequented the same country and became quite successful at robbing Union Pacific trains, in contrast to the Parrott gang's failures.

Nonetheless, Parrott's notoriety in Western outlaw lore was secure, not only because of his scattered remains, but also because of his frequent confusion with George "Flatnose" Currie of the more famous Cassidy Wild Bunch.

NEBRASKA OUTLAWS

BLACKBIRD

An Omaha Chief's Gruesome Game

As leader of one of North America's most powerful tribes in the late eighteenth century, Omaha Chief Blackbird encountered many challengers. Like a bull elk in autumn, Blackbird locked antlers with innumerable foes who sought his power and his prestige. But, unlike those who sought to command his people, the most dominant tribe on the Great Plains, the wily chieftain pulled no punches; instead, he employed poison to defeat his rivals. He performed dastardly acts that would create a legend and Nebraska's first outlaw.

As he was known to his people, Wazhinga-sah-ba was fearsome, brave in battle, and possessed strong "medicine" that allowed him to foil his foes. Blackbird was, however, not without his faults. When a favored wife embarrassed him in front of his tribe, he hastily threw a knife at her, killing her where she stood. As chief in a lawless land not yet settled by whites, his only punishment came not from the courts, but from his own lingering conscience.

Assuming control over the Omaha tribe in the late 1770s, Blackbird was among the first Native American leaders to establish trade agreements with the Spanish and French fur traders who roamed what was then the Western frontier, now the state of Nebraska. Under Blackbird's leadership, the Omaha also became the first tribal warriors on the Great Plains to master the fine art of equestrianism, which, for a brief period, allowed his people dominance over the Lakota Sioux and other major Plains Indian tribes.

Although his tribe was not as large as other clans in the region, Chief Blackbird's skill in establishing favorable relations with white traders and explorers further helped the Omaha fend off other warring tribes for the more than three decades that he remained in power.

In 1600, more than 170 years before Blackbird rose to chief, evidence indicates the Omaha had begun as a much larger woodland tribe comprised of both Quapaw and Omaha bands, inhabiting a vast tract between the Ohio and Wabash Rivers. The bands eventually migrated westward, and the Omaha split from the Quapaw. When French cartographer Guillaume Delisle stumbled on the "wandering nation" of "the Maha" in 1718, he found them along the northern stretch of the Missouri River. Two decades later, French fur traders located the tribe on the west banks of the river, near present-day Cedar County, Nebraska.

Sometime around 1755, the tribe established the new village of Ton won tonga (translated as "Big Village") near the Missouri River in extreme northeastern Nebraska, north of the present-day Omaha Indian Reservation. This would be the home of Chief Blackbird and as many as 4,000 members of his tribe. And, a century later, the largest city in Nebraska would be named Omaha, for the powerful tribe that never was known to take up arms against the United States.

As a young brave, Blackbird reportedly proved his worth in a number of skirmishes against competing tribes. Captured by the Sioux as a boy, he escaped and later fought them and other tribes until all inhabitants of the region feared his name and his reputation. He purportedly took scalps from the Otoe and Kansas tribes, burned a Pawnee village to the ground, and employed strange medicine that allowed him to overcome the enemies of the Omaha.

According to the late Nebraska historian Addison Erwin Sheldon, Blackbird was once in pursuit of a hostile war party when he fired his rifle into the hoofprints of their horses, telling his band the unusual action would cripple their horses and allow them to be overtaken. When Blackbird and his warriors did indeed overtake their enemies and slay them all, the Omaha were convinced of the strength of Blackbird's medicine.

Further enhancing Blackbird's reputation as a fierce rival was an incident involving the Ponca Indians, who lived as neighbors of the Omaha near the mouth of the Niobrara River. Although the two tribes were related and spoke similar languages, conflicts occasionally occurred that needed to be addressed. When a band of young Ponca men raided the Omaha encampment, stealing horses and kidnapping a few Omaha women, Blackbird's response was swift and decisive.

Gathering all the fighting men of the Omaha, Blackbird led them against the raiders and quickly began "to eat up the Poncas," according to Sheldon. When the vastly outnumbered Poncas were eventually cornered in a crude fort, a furious Blackbird and his warriors were ready to kill them all.

"The Poncas sent a herald carrying a peace pipe," Sheldon wrote before his death in 1943. "Blackbird shot him down. Another herald was treated in the same way. Then the head chief of the Poncas sent his daughter, a young girl, in her finest Indian suit of white buckskin, with the peace pipe. Blackbird relented, took the pipe from the girl's hand, smoked it and there was peace between the tribes."

The beautiful Ponca maiden eventually would become the favored wife of the Omaha's fiercest fighter and legendary leader, wielding great influence in Blackbird's lodge and in his dealings with fellow tribesmen. But it would be short-lived. When his Ponca wife angered Blackbird over some minor transgression, the chief flew into a fit of rage and hastily drew his knife from its scabbard and plunged it into the handsome maiden, instantly killing her. As his anger turned to grief over what he had done, Blackbird buried his head in a buffalo robe, slumped down near his wife's body, and refused to sleep or eat for days. Entreaties from his tribesmen were met with silence, and all around him feared they were witnessing the last days of their leader.

In a final act of desperation, another tribal head carried a small child to Blackbird and laid it on the ground before him, placing the chief's foot upon the child's neck. The tender gesture apparently touched Blackbird's heart, for he threw off the buffalo robe, shed his sorrow, and resumed his duties as chief of the Omaha Nation.

As French and Spanish explorers and fur traders tracked across their territories on the Great Plains of North America in ever-increasing numbers in the late 1700s, the free-roaming herds of buffalo began to dwindle. Blackbird was prescient enough to know that the white man's culture was wending its way across the prairie like a gathering storm. Reluctant to migrate further west as many of his brethren had done, Blackbird instead made a conscious effort to create a trading relationship with the newcomers. In this he was not beneficent, only insightful.

Living on the banks of the Mighty Missouri and in the deep, surrounding coulees that afforded protection, the Omaha had developed a sophisticated society based on the inseparable union between the earth and the sky. Divided into two moieties, or kinship groups, Sky people attended to the tribe's spiritual needs, while the Earth people focused on the physical welfare of the tribe by hunting, fishing, and fighting off other bands.

In winter Omaha tribesmen lived in villages consisting of timber-framed lodges covered with thick soil. Some lodges measured 60 feet in diameter and were capable of accommodating several families and a few treasured ponies. In summer the Omaha often adopted the ways of the Sioux, hunting migrating herds of buffalo by day and sleeping in tepees at night.

It was into this well-established society in the latter years of the eighteenth century that French fur traders and Spanish explorers first strode, rode, and steamed with a collection of Western paraphernalia that dazzled the native inhabitants. No Omaha was more astonished by the variety of material goods and wonderful elixirs than was Chief Blackbird.

Shrewd, clever, and never shy about taking advantage of his position, Blackbird customarily greeted traders personally and then invited them to his lodge. Traders were directed to assemble all their goods and spread them out in the spacious lodge of the chief. According to historian Sheldon, Blackbird would then select the very best items for himself—warm blankets, colorful beads, and fine tobacco, as well as whiskey, powder, and bullets—and place them to the side, with no expectation of compensating the trader.

Summoning an underling, the chief would order him to climb atop the lodge and tell the entire tribe to collect their furs and come trade with the friendly white man. Shortly, the lodge would be crowded with anxious Indians bearing piles of buffalo robes, beaver pelts, and otter skins.

"No one was allowed to dispute the prices fixed by the white trader, who was careful to put them high enough to pay five times over for all the goods taken by the chief," Sheldon wrote. "Thus Blackbird and the traders grew rich together, but his people grew poor and began to complain."

Faced with increasing dissent created by his own greed after three decades of dictatorial leadership, Blackbird feared for his exalted position at the top of the tribe. Obviously aging and no longer the fine physical specimen he'd been in his youth, he was likely viewed with suspicion by his people for his close relationship with white settlers. Nonetheless, Blackbird had grown accustomed to the perks of being at the peak of his power, and he had no desire to change the status quo.

Consequently, when a friendly trader suggested a magical solution to get rid of those who would oppose his power or question his directives, Blackbird immediately grasped his proposition and reveled in the conspiracy. In his ongoing quest to maintain power, the chief accepted a large amount of arsenic from the trader, who provided helpful suggestions for how it might best be used. Thus began the legendary Omaha chief's deadly plan to thwart any and all rivals.

About the same time, one of five European expeditions to explore the Upper Missouri River, prior to Lewis and Clark's fabled Corps of Discovery, stumbled on the Omaha tribe in present-day Nebraska. The Spanish expedition's leader, Jean Baptiste Truteau, operating under the charter of the Company of Discoverers and Explorers of the Missouri, commonly known as the Missouri Company, sought to reach the Mandan villages of present-day North Dakota and establish a trading post.

Although Truteau failed to reach the Mandan, only traveling as far as present-day South Dakota, he did return from the Western frontier with journals that would later aid Lewis and Clark in planning their journey to the Pacific, as well as a candid assessment of the notorious Omaha chieftain known as Wazhinga-sah-ba. After meeting Blackbird on December 18, 1794, Truteau wrote:

> *This great chief of the Omahas was the most shrewd, the most deceitful and the greatest rascal of all the nations who inhabit the Missouri. He is feared and respected and is in great renown among all strange nations, none of whom dare to contradict him openly or to move against his wishes. . . . [H]e is a man who by his wit and cunning has raised himself to the highest place of authority in his nation and who has no parallel among all the savage nations of this continent. He is able to or cause to be done good or evil as it pleases him. It is not his war-like actions that have brought him so much power, for he has been*

*inclined towards peace, but because of the fear that his men and
his neighbors have of certain poisons which he uses, they say to
kill off those who displease him.*

As his reputation expanded beyond his own people and neighboring tribes
to include white settlers stretching their tentacles across the land, Blackbird
grew more emboldened and decidedly more deadly. Armed with a mysterious
power and an innate desire to maintain control over his tribe, Blackbird became
a prophet as well as a chief.

When younger, stronger, wiser, or nobler contenders for the position of
chief arose, Blackbird would simply counter their logical succession by foretell-
ing of the rival's death within a specified time. Indeed, when the challenger would
inexplicably suffer a sudden and agonizing death, tribal members were astounded
by Blackbird's abilities to see the future and safeguard the well-being of the tribe.
Not surprisingly, in short order, all of Blackbird's rivals disappeared and his people, undoubtedly fearing his deadly gaze, acquiesced to the chief's every whim
and desire. There were no critics to be found.

Secure in his leadership and surrounded by loyal tribal members, Blackbird
would live a few more years in absolute power atop the most dominant tribe on
the Plains. But, in the earliest years of the nineteenth century, an enemy arrived
among the Omaha that was destined to decimate the tribe, divert history, and
deal Blackbird a challenge from which Nebraska's first outlaw would never
recover. And, in a strange twist of fate, it was delivered by the same white man
that Blackbird had befriended.

Smallpox, the scourge of the Native peoples who populated the Americas,
first arrived in the New World with Europeans and Africans in the sixteenth
century. The first major outbreak occurred between 1616 and 1619 on the
northeastern Atlantic coast, when smallpox reduced the Algonquin tribes from
an estimated 30,000 members to 300.

As the newcomers to America headed west over the ensuing centuries, so too
did the spread of the infectious disease. Without any prior exposure or resistance
to smallpox, Plains Indian tribes such as the Omaha were faced with an invisible
enemy that even Blackbird's strange and powerful medicine couldn't counter.
The effect would be devastating.

Although Natives would also suffer from other deadly diseases that included
cholera, bubonic plague, influenza, measles, typhus, and yellow fever, those
diseases combined didn't kill as many American Indians as did the smallpox
epidemic. According to widely accepted estimates, the epidemic killed more
than a third of the Aztecs; half of the Cherokee, Huron, Catawba, Piegan, and
Iroquois; two-thirds of the Blackfeet and Omaha; nine out of ten Mandan; and
all of the Taino.

Baffled by a faceless enemy that could mysteriously travel from lodge to lodge and village to village, the unwelcome visitor finally arrived at Chief Blackbird's well-established town of Ton won tonga in 1800. Before it departed smallpox would take the lives of more than 400 of the defenseless Omaha. According to historian Sheldon, in a matter of months, smallpox had decimated the entire tribe:

> *This was smallpox, the white man's disease which the Indians had never known. It came among them like a curse. . . . The fever and the fearful blotches drove them wild. Some of them left their villages and rushed out on the prairies to die alone. Others set fire to their houses and killed their wives and children. Two-thirds of the Omaha tribe perished and it never after recovered its old strength and power.*

Eventually, even the old warhorse was stricken. As friends and eager successors gathered around his deathbed, Chief Blackbird delivered his final command: a desire to be buried seated on his favorite steed at the summit of a hill overlooking the Missouri River.

When he had taken his last breath, the Omaha obeyed their chief's dying order, placed his corpse on the back of his horse, led it up the hill, then buried both under a great mound of earth and rocks. A pole bearing the scalps Blackbird had taken in battle was placed at the top of the mound. Four years later, when Lewis and Clark passed through the Omaha village on their epic journey to the Pacific, the explorers climbed what forever after has been known as Blackbird Hill—a lingering reminder of Nebraska's first and, perhaps, deadliest outlaw.

FLATNOSE CURRIE AND THE WILD BUNCH

The career of crime attributed to George Sutherland "Flatnose" Currie began and ended in Nebraska. Between those bookends in the Cornhusker State, Flatnose Currie was involved in innumerable horse thefts, cattle rustling, bank heists, train robberies, and the murders of several lawmen charged with bringing him and his associates to justice.

As a member of the notorious Wild Bunch, whose members also included Butch Cassidy, the Sundance Kid, and a quick-tempered killer known as Kid Curry, Flatnose Currie led a life on the lam, hiding out in places that ranged from Nebraska's Sandhills and Wyoming's Hole in the Wall to Utah's Robbers Roost, Montana's Hi-Line, and, by some accounts, as far south as Bolivia.

Born on Canada's Prince Edward Island around 1864, accounts of Flatnose Currie's early life are relatively unknown. At some point in his youth, he moved with his family to the vast expanses of Nebraska Territory, where his parents settled near the small ranching community of Chadron. Nearing manhood, Currie allegedly found the work of rustling cattle and horses from neighbor's ranches far preferable to the backbreaking labor it took to establish a homestead and "prove up" the land, as so many settlers were then doing.

Sometime during his colorful career, which entailed the repetitive theft of horses not under his ownership, one of the equines apparently kicked George in the face, producing his signature feature. At various times, he was known as "Big Nose" and "Flatnose" Currie, a sobriquet that would catch on with the legions of lawmen who sought to apprehend him over the ensuing years, making the bandit readily identifiable.

The misdeeds attributed to Flatnose Currie have long been mixed in history with those actually performed by a mean and menacing man named Harvey Logan, who may have been Flatnose's nephew. Shortly after forming the Wild Bunch and in testament to his admiration for Flatnose Currie, Logan would adopt his name and become known as Kid Curry.

To further the confusion, Kid Curry's brothers—Lonny and Johnny Logan—also adopted Curry as a surname and ran rampant with the Wild Bunch. After Kid Curry's quick and remorseless gunplay left at least two lawmen dead, he would be widely regarded by authorities as one of the most dangerous and unpredictable men to ever roam the Wild West.

Flatnose Currie, however, started his career of crime on a softer note. He began his illustrious march into the annals of Nebraska outlaw lore by rustling cows and stealing horses from ranches, reservations, and even the US government, which maintained herds of ponies at numerous forts throughout the West. Among them was Fort Robinson, some 30 miles southwest of his childhood home in Chadron. The Pine Ridge Indian Reservation and its large herds of stock were found to the northeast, just over the border in Dakota Territory. Following in the footsteps of other thieves who had practiced the same vocation for two decades before Flatnose arrived on the scene, he and his associates would hide out in the rolling hills, canyons, and forests of the Sandhills.

However, by the late 1880s and early '90s, lawmen were becoming as familiar with the Sandhills as the outlaws. Consequently, when the law came too close once too often, Flatnose and his band headed west into the lonesome country of eastern Wyoming. They settled at a then-little-known sanctuary known as the Hole in the Wall near present-day Sundance, in extreme northeastern Wyoming. Over the next several years, the bandits made frequent forays into the Dakotas, Montana, Utah, and Colorado to rob trains, banks, stages, and the occasional unlucky rancher. Then, they would take their loot and hightail it to the hinterlands of eastern Wyoming, still among the least populated places in the US.

It was during one of Flatnose Currie's extended stays at the Hole in the Wall that he met and befriended Harvey, Lonny, and Johnny Logan. As a measure of respect for their uncle, each of the Logans adopted Flatnose's last name, although historians have traditionally spelled them with slight variations. Nonetheless, by many accounts, Flatnose was a man who commanded respect.

One longtime friend of Flatnose Currie, who some knew as Geo Carver, would later remark that most of his close friends and associates in crime called Flatnose "Colonel, because he was such a large, well-proportioned man, with a military appearance, straight as an arrow and strong as a horse."

The sheer, crimson canyon wall featured a "hole" or gash through which rustlers could herd their stolen cattle and horses away from the prying eyes of the law. Sentries stationed on top of the sandstone outcroppings could see posses or other riders approaching from miles away, allowing ample time to send warning to those outlaws who were hiding in ramshackle cabins scattered near the Hole in the Wall.

In her well-researched biography of the Sundance Kid, author and historian Donna B. Ernst retraces the Outlaw Trail, which was comprised of a series of hideouts and safe houses throughout the Old West. The Wild Bunch, as the gang was known, would become one of the best-known groups of bandits to ever roam the West, earning the moniker by shooting up saloons and main streets as easily as they raided trains and banks.

According to Ernst, the Wild Bunch had "a loose membership of about twenty-five men, but any given robbery seldom involved more than two or three of the same men from any previous or future holdup." The core group consisted of five men: the leader, Robert LeRoy Parker, alias Butch Cassidy; Harvey Alexander Logan, alias Kid Curry (who would murder nine men); Benjamin Arnold Kilpatrick, known as the Tall Texan; William Richard Carver, alias Will Causey; and Harry Alonzo Longabaugh, known forever after as the Sundance Kid.

When Kid Curry arrived at the outlaw outpost in the 1890s, Flatnose had been content with spending his days stealing cows and horses—easy pickings in the Old West. But the Kid's influence, coupled with that of newcomers Butch Cassidy and the Sundance Kid, soon had Flatnose eyeing the cash stashed in the vaults of the region's banks.

As Currie and his gang advanced from rustling to robbing, all conducted with a distinctive flair that included the liberal use of firearms and dynamite, they became the Wild Bunch. Following lucrative raids and robberies, and during the winter months, the bandits hid out in the Hole in the Wall until law enforcement officers raided it in 1897. In the off-season, the outlaws frequently took legitimate work at area ranches, where local residents were keenly aware of their nefarious activities but tolerated the Wild Bunch, as long as they didn't foul their own nest. Other hideouts used by the gang included Robbers Roost in the high desert canyons of Utah; Powder Springs, in extreme southwestern Wyoming; and the Hi-Line of Montana, near the present-day towns of Malta and Culbertson, just south of the Canadian border.

By 1897 the Wild Bunch was experienced enough to take their game to a whole new level. Flatnose Currie and the Wild Bunch set their sights on the big bank in Belle Fourche, a sheep, cattle, and commerce hub on the northern fringe of South Dakota's Black Hills. The town had been destroyed by a major conflagration in late September 1895, but just two summers later, the bustling community had been rebuilt and was ready to roll out the red carpet for a reunion of Civil War soldiers. The affair promised to be one of the major celebrations of the year.

Flatnose Currie and his gang had learned of the impending festivities and had decided it would provide an opportune time to relieve the Butte County Bank of its excess currency. Located in the town center, where the Civil War reunion was taking place, Flatnose surmised that all the bank deposits would swell the bank's coffers, while the strange faces in town would provide the ideal cover for their illicit activities. They headed toward Belle Fourche, today located just a few miles from the geographic center of the US.

Accompanied by brothers Harvey and Lonny Logan, Tom O'Day, and Walt Punteney, Flatnose camped just outside of Belle Fourche during the weekend celebration. On Monday morning, June 28, 1897, Flatnose sent O'Day into town to reconnoiter. But O'Day promptly forgot his assignment, stopped at a downtown saloon, and got liquored up with a bunch of newfound friends. When he didn't return, Flatnose elected to proceed with the planned robbery anyway.

As the town clock struck 10:00 a.m., the remaining four outlaws hitched up their horses near the bank and walked in the front door. Flatnose and company ordered the two bank employees and five customers in the lobby to reach for the sky. As they did, a hardware store owner across the street happened to notice their actions and slowly walked onto the boardwalk for a closer look. Just then O'Day, who had by then remembered his assignment, came sauntering up Sixth Street, noticed the merchant eyeing the bank, pulled his six-gun, and fired several rounds at the fleeing busybody.

Alerted to the robbery by the gunfire, the townspeople took up arms. The hostages in the bank took advantage of their startled captors and fled outside. Head cashier Arthur Marble scooped up a revolver from behind the counter and fired a couple rounds at the now-fleeing bank robbers. When O'Day's horse, spooked by the gunshots, ran away, the still-tipsy outlaw hopped on a mule that elected not to work that day. Frantically hustling to an outhouse located between Sebastian's Saloon and the *Times* printing office, O'Day sought to discard his weapon. But an alert butcher named Rusaw Bowman watched O'Day enter the outhouse and took him into custody at gunpoint when he left the latrine. The suspect's handgun was retrieved with a rake, and bullets were discovered on his person, along with nearly four hundred dollars in cash and a pint of whiskey.

Unfortunately, another drunk had burned down the town's jail at the onset of the Civil War festivities two days earlier, so the marshal simply locked O'Day in the same bank vault his friends had attempted to rob earlier that day. The suspect was transferred to Deadwood the next day, where he was held in the Lawrence County Jail pending trial.

Meanwhile, Flatnose Currie and his three compatriots headed southwest into the familiar territory of Wyoming. Once they had crossed the state line, Flatnose and Lonny Logan headed for their refuge at the Hole in the Wall, while Harvey Logan and Punteney rode for Powder Springs, a hideout on the border with Utah. Since the bandits were successful in their escape, the holdup at the Belle Fourche bank would become larger than life. In fact, the outlaws probably garnered only ninety-seven dollars grabbed from a bank customer's hand as they were heading out the door.

Nonetheless, Pinkertons and law officers traced Flatnose Currie, Butch Cassidy, and the Sundance Kid, as well as several of their known associates, for the next several years. Innumerable train robberies, bank holdups, and the like were attributed to the Wild Bunch, although it is doubtful even these prolific criminals could have staged so many crimes.

In the early morning hours of July 14, 1898, a Southern Pacific passenger train was leaving Humboldt, Nevada, when two outlaws jumped on board the tender car and pulled six-shooters on the train's engineer and fireman, ordering them to stop the train. Met by a third outlaw in waiting, the three desperados ordered the trainmen to open the express car door. When the express messenger refused, the outlaws struck a match and lit a stick of dynamite, which exploded at the rear door to the express car. Warned that the next blast would kill him and destroy the train car, the express messenger slowly opened the door to the waiting outlaws, who stormed inside. A second dynamite blast opened the safe, blew the roof off the express car, and devastated its interior.

In addition to a few pieces of jewelry, the bandits carted off twenty-six thousand dollars in currency and coin. For this and other alleged robberies, Flatnose Currie and his friends soon had a one-thousand-dollar price on their heads. When a small saloon in Elko, Nevada, was robbed about a year later, the deed was attributed to Flatnose, Sundance, and Kid Curry. And when three men held up the bank in Winnemucca, Nevada, eighteen months later, the same trio was named as suspects.

Although not the first time, the use of dynamite in the commission of the train heist attracted national attention and put the outlaws' names before a public eager to know everything that happened on the Western frontier. When the Wild Bunch struck the Union Pacific's Overland Flyer at Wilcox, Wyoming, less than a year after the Southern Pacific train robbery, their fame was assured.

This latest exploit began shortly after 2:00 a.m. June 2, 1899, as the Union Pacific's Overland Flyer was chugging down the tracks near Rock Creek, Wyoming, a tiny railroad town servicing the needs of area ranchers as well as the federal government at nearby Fort Fetterman. When two men were seen standing in a driving rain, waving a lantern along the side of the tracks, the train's engineer feared an approaching bridge may have washed out, and he hit the skids. When the train finally halted, two masked men forced their way on board at gunpoint and ordered the engineer to proceed with all haste past the bridge up ahead.

When the engineer hesitated, one of the crooks pistol-whipped him with his Colt revolver. What the engineer could not have known was that the outlaws had already set and lit dynamite charges on the trestle to prevent any posses from pursuing them via a similar mode of transport. Just as the train cleared the trestle and stopped, an explosion rocked the locomotive. After disconnecting the passenger cars from the steam engine and express, baggage, and mail cars, the train proceeded up the tracks for a couple of miles, where four more bandits were waiting.

With practiced patience, the robbers used the next two hours and a healthy supply of dynamite to blow the doors off the express and mail cars before blasting open the safe. However, unschooled in the appropriate use of dynamite, the outlaws set a heavy charge on the substantial vault, which succeeded in getting it open but, as an unintended consequence, also blew the roof off the train car and obliterated its sides.

Bolstered by their haul of fifty thousand dollars in cash, gold coins, unsigned bank notes, and jewelry that included four exceptional Elgin watches, the outlaws scattered for the hinterlands.

The Union Pacific immediately offered a reward of one thousand dollars each for their capture, dead or alive, and the federal government and the Pacific Express Company, which owned the safe, matched the reward. Posses formed, boarded specially outfitted train cars capable of accommodating them and their mounts, and arrived at the scene of the crime seven hours after it had occurred. Wyoming Governor DeForest Richards called out the state militia, and by the time the Pinkerton Detective Agency and the Burlington Railroad added their agents, more than a hundred gun-toting, reward-hungry men were pursuing the culprits.

The Wild Bunch was immediately suspected of staging the holdup, and when several of the train's crewmen described one of the bandits as five-foot-nine, 185 pounds, with blue eyes and "a peculiar nose, flattened at the bridge," authorities matched that with the likeness of George Sutherland "Flatnose" Currie.

The outlaws had planned in advance for their getaway, posting fresh mounts along their escape route to allow them to stay ahead of the posse. But a rancher near Horse Ranch, Wyoming, saw the thieves and reported the sighting to authorities in Casper. Sheriff Josiah Hazen and his posse caught up to the crooks and a brief gunfight ensued, wounding only a few ponies, before the outlaws fled further north.

Hiding beneath a rock ledge on Teapot Creek three days after the train robbery, and believing they had evaded the posse, Flatnose, Kid Curry, and the Sundance Kid were catching some rest when the posse stumbled onto their hideaway. In the hail of gunfire that soon erupted, Sheriff Hazen was hit by a shot fired by Kid Curry, a wound from which he would soon die. Taking advantage of the posse leader's mortal wound and heavy rains that began to fall, the outlaws escaped up the creek on foot, losing a portion of their loot in the swollen stream. The only thing the posse captured was a few of the outlaws' horses, left tethered in a nearby canyon.

Meanwhile, Flatnose, Curry, and Sundance "borrowed" a few horses from a nearby ranch and headed for their Hole in the Wall hideout. Encountering a lone deputy sheriff, William Dean, near the north fork of the Powder River, Kid Curry dispatched him with a gunshot just as he had Sheriff Hazen.

Eight months later, Lonny Logan (Curry) was shot and killed by Pinkerton agents as he attempted to flee his aunt's home in Kansas. In August 1900, the Wild Bunch, sans Flatnose Currie, struck the Union Pacific train near Tipton, Wyoming, using dynamite to blow the safe and riding away with fifty-five thousand dollars in cash and jewelry. Two weeks later, members of the same gang, led by Butch Cassidy and the Sundance Kid, robbed the bank in Winnemucca, Nevada, nabbing more than thirty-two thousand dollars, including thirty-one thousand dollars in gold coins. When one of the bank bags containing the loot broke open during the escape, the thieves scooped up what they could, but purportedly left six to seven thousand dollars in twenty-dollar gold pieces scattered in the street.

With an ample stake, Butch Cassidy and the Sundance Kid fled the West, stopping over in Fort Worth and New York City before boarding a steamer headed for Buenos Aires, Argentina, and their South American adventure. Some say other members of the Wild Bunch, including Flatnose Currie, accompanied the Western legends. However, a photo of the Hole in the Wall Gang taken in November 1900 in Fort Worth, Texas, doesn't include Flatnose. In fact, Butch Cassidy and the Sundance Kid would settle for a time and attempt ranching in Argentina. But their past eventually caught up with them, and wrongly accused of robbing a bank, they in turn did stage a series of robberies. In 1906 they were working as payroll guards for the Concordia Mines near La Paz, Bolivia.

But the legitimate work wouldn't last. On November 4, 1908, Butch and Sundance robbed two payroll guards of 80,000 pesos, roughly one hundred thousand dollars today. Two days later they were cornered by militia in a San Vicente, Bolivia, home, and it was here that their days as the most-revered Western outlaws would end. After exchanging gunfire with the troops, the nighttime scene grew silent. The next morning, an officer entered the house to find both men dead. An inquest in the ensuing days would find that, with no escape, Butch had apparently shot Sundance, and then turned the gun on himself. The duo's exploits would be immortalized nearly six decades later in the classic Western film *Butch Cassidy and the Sundance Kid,* starring Robert Redford and Paul Newman.

Meanwhile, the sands of time covered the outlaw trail of George Flatnose Currie. Some reports had him shot by lawman Jessie M. Tyler in April 1900, as the outlaw was rustling cattle in Grand County, Utah. Kid Curry allegedly avenged his uncle's death and that of his brother, Lonny, by riding to Utah and gunning down Sheriff Tyler and his deputy, Sam Jenkins. Kid Curry was imprisoned in the early 1900s, escaped from jail in June 1903, and then maintained tradition by robbing a train in Parachute, Colorado, a few weeks later. When a pursuing posse wounded the desperado, he elected not to return to jail and took the easy way out, putting a bullet in his own head.

But Flatnose Currie, who had begun his career of crime on the Nebraska Panhandle, purportedly returned to his home range and lived out his life with his daughter.

ANNIE COOK

Evil Incarnate

Steeped in the Prohibition years of the 1920s, the story of Annie Cook is one of a venomous Nebraska outlaw who never had enough, and didn't hesitate to cajole, belittle, bribe, beat, or exterminate anyone who stood in her way. Indeed, slender little Annie Cook's true story is more terrifying than the legends and lore of any of the Cornhusker State's many cattle rustlers, bank bandits, train robbers, and gunmen.

Annie Cook was born on July 15, 1873, in Denver, Colorado, the daughter of moderately wealthy Jewish parents who had emigrated from Russia and opened a thriving livery stable in the fledgling community. Every member of the large family worked hard to get ahead, even Annie and her sister, Lizzie. Annie didn't mind the day-to-day drudgery of life on the Western frontier, but as a young woman, she did experience a growing resentment over the fact that she didn't get paid for her honest labor, while the men in the family, including her brothers, did.

When a tall, handsome young farmer from Nebraska, Frank Cook, stopped at the livery stable for supplies one day in 1893, nineteen-year-old Annie saw an opportunity that could help define her future, while removing her from the unappreciated labors of her family's business. She befriended the likable man, who owned a farmstead near Hershey, Nebraska.

By all accounts, Frank was an earnest, well-liked young farmer content to work his small 80-acre spread and enjoy his neighbors. He didn't necessarily want to own the largest farm in Lincoln County; Frank just wanted to live a life free of major stress and worry. When he took Annie as his wife, the odds of that tranquil existence actually coming to pass vanished like topsoil in a tornado.

You see, Annie wanted it all—money, land, and power. And for the next few decades, she would expend all of her nastiness to pursue her own dreams, even if they were contrary to her husband's. Once she arrived on his diminutive farm outside Hershey in the winter of 1893, Annie assessed her husband's operation and found it wanting in virtually every respect. The house was too small, there was an insufficient amount of tillable land, and, without acquiring additional property, there would be no prospect of living the kind of life she had planned for herself.

In this regard, Annie wasn't alone. In the last part of the nineteenth century, many Americans were transfixed by the possibility of creating something from nothing, of living a life of luxury in which their well-considered schemes and lucrative deals could replace the hard work and endless toil on which the nation had been built. From Wall Street to Main Street, promoters and confidence men were striking it rich by wheeling and dealing their way to wealth.

The same year Annie was born in Denver, Mark Twain and Charles Dudley Warner penned *The Gilded Age,* presenting a satirical account of political corruption and financial greed in post–Civil War America. The book's central character, Colonel Beriah Sellers, was a honey-tongued promoter whose eloquence served as "a magician's wand that turned dried apples into figs and water into wine as easily as it could turn a hovel into a palace and present poverty into future riches."

Armed with the notion that she, too, could create something from the nothing that was her husband's farm, Annie set about exploiting everyone around her. Frank was constantly belittled, and when a daughter, Clara, was born three years after they wed, she was engaged in involuntary servitude essentially from the time she could walk.

When things became too bleak on the isolated farm in 1905, Annie boarded a train to travel east to Nebraska's largest town of Omaha, ostensibly to see a doctor for a recurring bladder infection. The doctor quickly diagnosed the problem, prescribed medication, and told her to return to see him in a week. While in the waiting room, Annie met the madam of a local "sporting house," who would spend the next week moving Annie from a low-end hotel to her own establishment, buying her fashionable clothes, educating Annie on the application of rouge, eye shadow, mascara, and lipstick and the proper etiquette of entertaining moneyed men.

As her one-week stay stretched into a month, Annie found herself with a suitcase of stylish clothes she could never wear in Hershey and more money than she had ever had in her life. She reluctantly returned to the drab surroundings of the farm with a renewed purpose, and the realization that she now had the means to execute her plan. She told Frank that the doctor had diagnosed a chronic condition that would require her periodic return to Omaha, and thus the stage was set for the thirty-one-year-old farm wife. For the next two decades, Annie's occasional work as a prostitute would provide the continuing income with which to fund her fondest desires.

Neglecting her young daughter, Annie set about improving the farm, and nearly drove her husband to exhaustion in the process. They raised poultry, sold eggs and holiday turkeys, planted corn and potato crops, tended apple and cherry trees, milked cows and churned butter. Following the harvest of 1898, with the help of Annie's supplemental income, the couple paid off the mortgage and Annie set her sights on buying the neighboring farm.

That same fall, Annie's parents came to visit from Denver with her sister, Lizzie. By the time their parents departed, Annie had agreed to let Lizzie stay on the farm. The arrangement was enticing to Annie because, first, her sister could be another free hand for the farm and, second, their parents planned to leave their large Denver home and a portion of their estate to Lizzie. Annie had little doubt that Lizzie's inheritance would one day be her very own.

Before their parents' train had even left the station, Annie was barking orders to her shy sister, telling her that she must pay her way by milking the cows, churning the butter, collecting eggs, planting and harvesting, and dressing poultry. In addition, Lizzie must make little four-year-old Clara into a productive member of the family. Intimidated by her older sister, Lizzie quickly agreed.

Unknown to Annie, Lizzie had developed a relationship with a rancher named Joe Knox from the Nebraska Sandhills. The two kept up a clandestine relationship through the mail. One day, when Frank, Annie, and Clara were in town delivering cream, butter, and eggs, Knox came to call on Liz. When he presented her with a Christmas present, Lizzie broke down and wept, confessing that she had never worked so hard in her life, providing details of her domineering sister. Knox promised to return in the spring to marry her and take her back to the Sandhills, where she would never have to work that hard again.

When Knox wrote to Lizzie again in the spring, he said he would be in North Platte on the night of May 28, 1901, and that she should meet him at the courthouse the next morning for their marriage ceremony. And that's exactly what Lizzie did. While Annie was busy in the farmhouse kitchen, Lizzie stole away down the country lane toward town, eventually catching a ride to the courthouse with a soft-hearted farmer headed in the same direction. Finding Knox waiting in front of the courthouse, the two quickly bought their license to wed, walked down the hall to the office of the justice of the peace, and were married. The couple then climbed into Knox's wagon and traveled two days to the Sandhills and their new home together.

Meanwhile, Annie was despondent over Lizzie's defection. She had lost a valuable farm worker and was likely to lose Lizzie's inheritance as well. When Annie learned where Lizzie had gone, she traveled to the Sandhills, but couldn't convince her sister to return to the farm. She also journeyed to Denver, lied to her parents about her sister's absence, and found out everything she could about Joe Knox. Later that year, when their mother died, Annie returned to Denver for the funeral, making excuses for Lizzie's absence. When their father decided to move in with one of his sons, Annie quickly put the big house, bequeathed to her sister, up for sale and returned to Hershey.

Angered that she now had to tend to the farm chores previously performed by Lizzie, Annie worked hard on the farm and plotted her revenge. In July 1902, Lizzie gave birth to a daughter, and she and Joe Knox named her Mary. As the months turned into years, Annie bided her time and schemed to get her sister back into her fold. In the spring of 1905, Annie wrote Lizzie a well-crafted letter, inviting her and her daughter to come back to Hershey for a visit, promising that she wouldn't have to work, and that Annie would buy her beloved little sister some new clothes. Unfortunately, Lizzie took the bait.

When she arrived in Hershey that spring with her daughter in tow, Lizzie quickly realized that nothing had changed with Annie. Her gruff sister ordered her to milk the cows that very night, and the next day Lizzie was forced to clean the chicken coops and the cow barns and care for the poultry. Secretly, because Annie wouldn't even let her go near the mailbox, Lizzie sent her husband a card that implored him, "Don't write, just come."

In a matter of days, Joe Knox showed up at the Cook farm and demanded that his family be allowed to leave with him. Annie's answer was decidedly succinct: She grabbed her shotgun, pointed it at Joe's chest, and demanded that he get off her property. Unarmed, Knox relented, promising his wife that he would return. A few days later, over Lizzie's objections, Annie sent little Mary off to live with their brother in Colorado. Joe did return several times and was run off at gunpoint. When he came with a lawyer, Annie only laughed and pointed her shotgun at the pair. Joe Knox would never return.

Bolstered by her sinister success, Annie put Frank, Lizzie, and Clara to work every morning at 4:00 a.m. When Lizzie's daughter, Mary, turned five, Annie traveled to her brother's residence in Denver, told them that Lizzie was very sick, and that she needed to take Mary back to Hershey to be with her mother. When they returned to the farm a few days later, Annie immediately put the five-year-old to work collecting eggs. Mary was punished for every one she broke. And one night, when an innocent little mole on Mary's right cheek caught Annie's attention, the villain put a poker in the stove, heated it to red hot, and then burned it off her niece's face.

As Prohibition came to the land in the 1920s, North Platte—just 15 miles from Hershey—became known as "Little Chicago." City officials turned a blind eye to the gambling, illegal alcohol, prostitution, and extortion in their town in exchange for copious quantities of hush money. Annie Cook wasn't above paying bribes to any of them.

When her daughter, Clara, reached the eighth grade, Annie wondered how she might best be put to use in her grand plan. Annie decided to enroll her in the high school in North Platte and purchased a home where she and Clara could live while they were in town. It all looked innocent enough, until Annie took on a "boarder"—an attractive young woman who would live at the house and watch Clara when Annie had to be out at the farm. In fact, Annie had hired the woman away from the best bordello in town. By the end of the school year, Annie had four "boarders" living at the house, and she was able to purchase a beautiful new two-seater carriage with a fringed canopy top.

Back at the farm, Annie remained a wicked taskmaster, barking orders and beating little Mary with a buggy whip until her legs bled.

When Clara turned thirteen, her mother decided it was time for a coming out, although it didn't involve a party. Annie and Clara boarded a train for Omaha, where Annie's old friend, the sporting-house madam, introduced the teenager to the rewards of prostitution. Two years later, when Clara turned fifteen, Annie entered into negotiations with an older North Platte businessman of Japanese descent who was infatuated with Clara. At the conclusion of the talks, Annie had agreed to sell her daughter to the man for the princely sum of five hundred dollars. There were conditions: The gentleman was not to visit Clara more than three times a week, and she would have to finish high school.

The next year, when a Union Pacific railroad crew set up camp near the Cook farm, Annie met with the supervisor and made an arrangement. For several weeks, she and her sixteen-year-old daughter serviced the crews, enriching their bank account by several hundred dollars. A year later, Annie established her second "house" in North Platte and hired an experienced madam to run it. By now she was well on her way to wealth and creating the life she had always dreamed of for herself.

In her definitive biography of Annie Cook, titled *Evil Obsession,* author Nellie Snyder Yost tells of the dirt-poor itinerant farm workers hired by Annie to work their sugar beet fields in the summer of 1915. With a thunderstorm fast approaching, Annie was worried that the work wouldn't get done and that the rain would delay a return to the fields for several days. As she approached a pregnant Hispanic woman whose family had been hired to work the fields, cracking her whip and yelling at everyone to work faster, the pregnant woman stood up and gripped her sides.

"'Missus,' the woman gasped, her face twisting in pain as she tried to tell Annie, with her few English words, that she needed to go back to the shack, her baby was coming.

"'No,' Annie shouted. 'You're not stopping work. You lazy bitches sluff [sic] off on the job every chance you get, but you damn well won't get away with it in my fields. Get to choppin', damn you,' and she swung the whip at the woman. With a look of despair, she bent to her task again."

Half an hour later, the Mexican woman simply fell to the ground and, in a matter of minutes, gave birth to twin sons right there in the furrows of the sugar beet field. Ordering young Mary to cart the newborns to the itinerant family's shack, Annie then berated and whipped the woman who had just delivered the babies until, reluctantly, she bent down and continued her field work.

With her mounting wealth, Annie continued implementing her grand plan in incremental steps. By 1923 she had greased enough palms of city and county officials—and threatened others with exposure for their sexual proclivities—to gain the contract for the Lincoln County Poor Farm, which forever after was known as Cook Poor Farm. While the patients had previously been treated with dignity and respect, Annie treated them with contempt and made them work on the farm as slave labor. Some ran away. Others who too strenuously objected to Annie's treatment mysteriously disappeared or were found floating facedown in the farm's irrigation ditches.

Meanwhile, Frank was despondent over the way Annie treated her sister, Lizzie, and young Mary. But, in a contest of wills, he was powerless to fight Annie. Finally, when Annie accused her husband of sexually assaulting Clara, whom he loved, Frank moved his quarters into the barn, where he would stay until he died in 1936.

Bolstered by her success, Annie began dabbling in bootleg whiskey and buying tax-delinquent properties, bribing the local sheriff to evict the unfortunate tenants, then reselling them at a handsome profit. She built a gleaming new white farmhouse to replace the old one, which was now being used to house the indigents of Lincoln County. By 1920 she was driving around town in a sparkling new Ford touring car and hoarding all her cash at home.

For a dozen more years, Annie's life went on this way: badgering and bullying her family and the Poor Farm workers, and bribing city and county officials to look the other way over conditions at the Poor Farm, her houses of prostitution, her bootlegging, and her other nefarious activities. With regularity she also argued with her daughter, Clara, who had gradually tired of her mother's meanness. They screamed and swore a blue streak and didn't care who knew it.

On May 29, 1934, the constant bickering and battles came to a head. Clara screamed at her mother for the last time, then exited the house and stormed into the yard. Enraged, Annie followed her out the door with a heavy lid-lifter from the stove in her hand; without thought she threw it at her retreating daughter. The lid-lifter struck Clara on the back of her head. Dazed by the blow, Clara ran around a tree in the yard two or three times, "like a chicken with its head cut off, and then just fell down dead."

The next day, the *Daily Bulletin* erroneously reported in a front-page headline, CLARA COOK DEAD, VICTIM OF POISON. The newspaper claimed in its story that the thirty-eight-year-old operator of the county Poor Farm died after an inmate of the home allegedly prepared a dose of disinfectant for her, believing it was the medicine she had requested. Further, the county attorney, clerk, and commissioner had investigated the incident and did not believe an inquest was warranted, the *Daily Bulletin* reported.

Annie showed up at her daughter's funeral and grieved in a manner appropriate to the occasion. She soon lost the contract to maintain the county Poor Farm, which she and Clara had held for the previous twelve years. But her daughter's untimely death was not without its rewards. Shortly after the funeral, she met with insurance investigators and demanded that they pay double indemnity on the ten-thousand-dollar insurance policy Annie had taken out on Clara, because she had died in an accidental manner. With the ill-gotten gains, Annie was able to purchase the 80 acres of farmland that she had coveted for nearly forty years and buy a new car, which coincidentally she had denied her daughter when she was alive.

Annie Cook would live for another eighteen years after murdering her daughter in a fit of rage. Those who knew her say she didn't get any nicer, didn't play any fairer, and didn't really give a second thought to the manner in which she had lived her life. Only when Annie died on May 27, 1952, did her sister, Lizzie, escape from the clutches of the woman who was, perhaps, Nebraska's meanest and most feared outlaw.

NEVADA OUTLAWS

ANDREW JACKSON "BIG JACK" DAVIS

Master Stage Robber

Andrew Jackson "Big Jack" Davis started out as an honest miner in the California Sierras. The intelligent, well-educated, fine-looking man, tall and strong, earned an excellent reputation that extended from the Tuolumne diggings as far north as Nevada and Sierra Counties. But he didn't find much gold, so he came to the Comstock Lode of Nevada Territory in late 1859, shortly after the discovery of silver there.

Perhaps Jack had grown tired of digging ore out of the ground in California. Blister-raising, knuckle-busting toil under the glaring sun of summer, followed by vainly seeking warmth in the thin tents pitched against the freezing winds of winter, made many give up and return to eastern homes. They had seen the elephant and would let others seek riches in a forbidding land. Jack was willing to keep trying, but he had figured out that very few of those who made money in a mining camp were the ones who mined the ore. He wondered if he should try something different. When he reached Nevada, he built the first stable in Gold Hill.

Boarding horses for other people and renting out his own was easier than mining, but Jack soon tired of that, too—he tired of hunting for hay and grain, shoveling manure, repairing damaged buggies and wagons, and worrying about abuse to his own and leased horses. He moved over to Six Mile Canyon, a few miles east of Virginia City, leased a quartz mill, and built a cabin nearby.

Now he would grind the ore that others brought in, mix the pulverized product with mercury to extract the silver, and refine that amalgam into silver bullion. The work was still hard, but most of it could be done with heavy machinery operated by employees.

It appeared to outsiders that Jack prospered. He worked hard in his mill during the day, played poker in the evening, and became noted for his generous nature. Wanderers and wayfarers found his cabin door always open and his larder well stocked. He was even elected recorder of claims for the Flowery Mining District. He might have been mistaken for a scholarly professor or a wealthy merchant. Judges, lawyers, and bankers welcomed him to their high-stakes poker games.

"That big fella sure looks out fer a man down on his luck," one hard-luck prospector would say.

"And he hobnobs with all them high muck-a-mucks, too. Jist like he was one of 'em."

But gradually close observers of Davis's mill began wondering if he was shipping more bullion than could be reasonably extracted from the ore he seemed to be buying. He appeared to be a prosperous mill operator, but no one knew where he got his paying rock. He kept turning out a steady stream of bullion, and rumors even cropped up that the purpose of the mill was re-melting and marketing bullion that had been obtained in robberies.

At that time western mining communities disliked Wells Fargo for fares that seemed extortions to the people. They laughed at stage robberies, considering them a wrangle among thieves over spoils extracted from the common worker. When stages began hauling bullion out of the growing mining camps and returning currency to the mine owners and to the merchants so they could cash checks, the robberies increased. With stages coming into Virginia City from six or seven different directions, news of a robbery could be expected almost every day.

When a few people began wondering about Jack's source of prosperity, most just winked and nodded and said nothing that might reach the authorities. The Robin Hood possibility that their generous friend was taking advantage of the rich stage company was even more enjoyable when the masked robbers recruited by Jack added flair to their robberies.

On October 30, 1866, two stages traveling together moved out of Reno toward Virginia City. It was close to midnight, and the Sierra Range in the west was bathed in moonlight. The stages, each carrying seven passengers, rumbled past Steamboat Springs and out onto the Washoe Plain.

The lead coach, driven by John Burnett, carried a large express chest made of boilerplate bolted securely to the frame of the coach. Its six horses labored up the winding Geiger Grade, with the other coach close behind. They topped the grade at a slow walk three miles north of Virginia City. Before the horses could catch their breath and trot on into town, five masked men stepped forward out of the rocks and sagebrush.

"Hold up!" one shouted, waving his shotgun. Some carried Henry rifles.

Burnett's foot hit the brake, and the relieved horses stopped and breathed deeply, their ribs heaving as they sucked in the cool mountain air.

"Better point that gun the other way, young feller," Burnett said. "It might go off, you know."

"Well, we don't want to shoot you but will if you don't follow orders."

"Your passengers, too," another said, nodding his head.

The leader stepped up and spoke in a gruff voice, obviously trying to disguise it. "You will all step down, as we have some business to transact with Wells Fargo. You drivers unhitch and move your horses a ways up the canyon. This will take us some time and some blasting powder."

The fourteen passengers filed down from the coaches. Only one was armed, and he tried to keep his revolver hidden. Another tossed his wallet and its four hundred dollars to the roof of his coach. No one noticed. But the robbers got the sixty dollars from his pocket and another sixty dollars from Judge Baldwin. They made similar extractions from the other passengers, but not from either driver or from the only woman passenger, "You fellows work hard for your pay," the leader said to the drivers, "and don't get much anyhow. And this young lady here"—he bowed deeply—"is also excused from the evening's business. The rest of you just stand aside and don't get in our way."

The woman, a Miss Crowell, was returning from a shopping trip to San Francisco, and she clutched her hoop skirt carefully as she tried to find a level place to stand. The leader of the robbers gently took her elbow and led her to a rock while another robber brought a cushion out from the coach.

"Now, you just sit here, young lady," the leader said. "We won't bother you at all." He looked at one of his men. "Bring out a lap robe for the lady. The air is cool and we have work to do." He bowed and made sure she was comfortable while two men climbed into the forward coach with hammers and cold chisels.

Two of the masked robbers chiseled the hasp off the iron express box. While they worked, others brought out overcoats and more robes. Then someone found a small cargo of champagne in a rear boot.

The leader looked at his watch. "Now, would you look at that—just what we need. It's Halloween, exactly two years to the day since President Lincoln signed Nevada into the good old U. S. of A. This calls for libations while we work, and let's pour some for the little lady, too. We'll start with a toast to Miss Crowell."

As the two men continued working on the hasp and another kept the drivers and passengers under close watch, the leader and another man handed out champagne. They drank toasts to Miss Crowell, to President Lincoln, to Wells Fargo, to the Comstock Lode, and to the new state of Nevada. Then two cans of blasting powder were packed around the express box's lock and a long fuse installed and ignited. Miss Crowell covered her ears and grimaced until the loud blast shook the air. The coach trembled as though held by a large giant. The blast blew out the end of the box and ignited the inside of the coach, but the robbers threw dirt in until the fire went out. Then they scooped out five thousand dollars from the box and added it to the coin and watches they already had.

"You'll have to finish the party without the pleasure of our company," the leader said as they ran to where their horses were securely tied.

The passengers all got back into the undamaged coach. The lead coach wobbled like a drunk out too late at night as the coaches and passengers moved on to Virginia City. They arrived about 3:00 a.m. with another tale of Nevada stage robbing.

But some passengers had heard enough of Big Jack Davis's talk, even though he tried to disguise his voice, that they reported their impressions to the police. No one listened more sympathetically to the stories about the holdup next day than Big Jack. Finally he was arrested, but the jury refused to convict.

But Wells Fargo began putting shotgun-carrying messengers on their stages, and the bandits had more to think about than one busy driver with four or six horses under his control. After they began adding an occasional second messenger, Big Jack started looking for a supplementary source of income. Robbing stages had become a hazardous occupation!

He studied the operations of trains coming east out of Oakland through Reno to carry silver and gold to eastern destinations. He gathered seven confederates, and he planned and carried out the West's first train robbery. Although the overall planning and the coordination between confederates were superb, a curious woman innkeeper and a skilled lawman combined to put the entire gang in custody in less than four days after the 1870 robbery. Davis confessed and showed the officers where he had hidden almost twenty thousand dollars in a culvert, a short distance from the robbery site.

Officers on the Comstock had suspected that Big Jack and John Squires, one of the train robbers, had been involved in many holdups of Wells Fargo stages in the area for years. But every time their work was sufficient to bring the robbers before a jury, the jury would be convinced that a reasonable doubt existed and would acquit. The railroad robbery turned out differently. Two men were released after they testified against the others. Squiers got the longest sentence, twenty-three years. Four others got sentences of twenty-two, twenty, eighteen, and five years. Big Jack Davis, the leader, got ten, entering the prison on Christmas Day.

Davis claimed with righteous indignation that Wells Fargo had forced him into train robbery when it put so many shotgun messengers as guards on its stages.

Davis was pardoned early. In 1871, less than nine months after his sentence began, twenty-nine inmates of the Nevada State Prison broke out in the largest prison escape in the West. They included four of Davis's train-robbing accomplices, but not Davis or the man who got the five-year sentence.

Davis could have gone out of the prison, but he refused. He cooperated with prison officials and was pardoned on February 16, 1875, after P. C. Hyman, the prison warden, wrote to the board of pardons and explained Davis's help in investigating the escape. His letter said that Davis's conduct had been exemplary and it ended: "If good conduct is to be taken into consideration, in my judgment he deserves the leniency of the board." One week later, Davis was released.

But Big Jack Davis hadn't forgotten his difficulty in earning an honest living. He returned to stage robbery, again determined to use his fine mind in outwitting Wells Fargo. He had never worried about the stage driver, whose first concern was controlling his horses. He worried about the messengers, whose only concern was fighting off robbers, and he particularly wanted to know whether the stage carried one or two messengers. One messenger usually rode on the seat behind the driver, and a second messenger would ride inside the coach. So, if Big Jack knew that the stage had one messenger and the driver was alone on the seat, or that it had two messengers, he would look out for the armed man or men inside the coach.

Big Jack decided that a signaling system would enable a confederate, seeing the stage leave a station, to signal how many messengers were aboard to the robbers who lay in wait on the stage road. And he realized that such a system would work better in the sparsely settled country of eastern Nevada. There the confederate, after a stage left at night, could hurry to a nearby mountain and signal with small fires about the number of messengers. One fire meant one messenger aboard, and two meant a pair.

Big Jack's well-organized plan worked fine until September 3, 1877. On that day Jack's signaler, Tom Lauria, watched the stage leave Eureka in the evening dusk, southbound for Tybo. Lauria saw two messengers get aboard, and he hurried to his horse and galloped away toward Pancake Mountain.

Big Jack with two brothers named Hamilton rode up to the Willows Station, forty miles south of Eureka. This first station on the road to the Tybo mines was usually tended by William Hood, a horse wrangler and blacksmith. The three masked bandits crept up on Hood and a surprised visiting rancher, Josh Tingley, who had stopped at the station to visit. Jack and the Hamilton brothers bound and gagged their two prisoners and tied them to a center post in the barn. Then they waited, watching for the signal that Tom Lauria would light on Pancake Peak, ten miles away.

Well after dusk had turned to darkness, Eugene Blair, riding as messenger behind the driver on the stage to Tybo, looked up and spoke.

"Jack, you see that star low in the sky over there?" He pointed. "I never did see one right there before."

Driver Jack Perry looked and responded, "Probably a hunter out late on Pancake Peak. Got him a fire to keep warm."

"Maybe so."

"It'll be a cool one tonight." Perry shivered.

At about nine o'clock the stage approached Willows Station and Big Jack recognized Blair, riding as messenger behind the driver. Big Jack stepped out of the darkness at the barn and shouted, "Blair! Throw up your hands."

Eugene Blair was a good man and a determined one. Seven months before, while working on the Hamilton-to-Ward stage run about forty miles east of his present route, his stage had been held up by two men as it approached the Ward station. He wounded one robber, but the other fled. He carried the wounded man into Ward, where he died. Then Blair returned to the holdup site to follow the tracks of the other bandit. Ten days later, lighter in weight, his skin darkened by the winter sun and his chapped lips grimly set, he returned to Ward Station, his prisoner in tow.

This time, as Blair's stage approached the Willows Station, he was on his usual alert. When he heard the surrender demand, he jumped down, shifted his shotgun to his right hand, and crouched instinctively. The blast from Davis's two shotgun barrels seemed to slam into Blair's body, but the lead sailed overhead. Then he felt Davis's shotgun muzzle push against his chest.

Eugene Blair had never lost a fight and didn't intend to lose this one. He knew he was fighting Big Jack Davis, the brainiest bandit in Nevada. Blair grabbed the gun barrels and swung Davis around. He grappled with Davis, looking for an opening. He could see another man dancing about in the darkness, trying for a clear shot at him. Then he spun Davis squarely into the light from the stage's lamps, jumped away, and shouted, "Get him, Jimmy!"

Jimmy Brown, the second and unexpected messenger, shot from inside the stage, and Big Jack Davis fell in the dust and darkness. As Brown put his foot on a wheel to jump down, one of the Hamiltons shot him in the leg. The other Hamilton never appeared. Presumably he held the bandits' horses.

Tom Lauria's two fires were either too close together or at the wrong angle for viewing from Willows Station. They had appeared as one fire from ten miles away.

Blair and the stage driver released the wrangler and his visitor, tied up in the barn. Then they carried Davis and Brown into the station cabin.

"We got to be going on," the driver said to Blair. "Will yuh have to stay here with Jimmy and the prisoner? Yuh know what we got in the cargo."

"You don't seem to be hurt bad, Jimmy," Blair said, turning to Brown. "Reckon you can keep an eye on Big Jack until the morning stage gets in from Tybo? You could haul him back to Eureka on it."

"I'll be fine," Brown said. "I been hurt worse in the mines. I'll see he gets back to the sheriff in Eureka."

"You take care now, Jimmy," Blair called out as he climbed back on the stage. He spoke to the driver as he pulled up his collar against the evening chill. "Don't look like Big Jack's gonna rob any more stages for a while."

"He didn't rob this'n, thanks to you and Jimmy." The driver slapped the reins down on the horses' rumps, and the stage moved away.

Davis had nine buckshot in his back, and he begged, in his intense agony, to be mercifully killed. Brown's wound was painful but not dangerous. The northbound stage had one passenger when it made its brief stop the next forenoon. He helped load the two wounded men in for the trip back to Eureka.

As the stage lumbered along, crossing the high, rocky, sagebrush-covered land, the September sun glistened from distant hills. Andrew Jackson Davis wondered how he could have misread the signal. Tom Lauria was a good man. He must have seen the two messengers on the stage.

Davis thought the air should warm as the sun rose in the sky, but he shivered as he shifted his weight to get comfortable. A back full of buckshot did pain a man. The wounded messenger would get well, but what about him? He had never been hurt so bad.

Brown looked out the window, ignoring his enemy, but the stage's lone paying passenger stared at Big Jack with contempt.

"To hell with him and the rest of the world," Big Jack might have thought. "I tried to be better than the rest, but sometimes they just had better luck. That Eugene Blair was some kind of a man in a fight."

When the stage reached Page's ranch early in the afternoon, it turned into a hearse. Big Jack Davis, the smartest stage robber in Nevada, had reached the end of his career.

NICANOR RODRIGUES

The Spanish King

Nicanor Rodrigues was born into the hidalgo class in the mountains of Spain about 1840. He inherited from his father, an important member of the aristocracy, the class's noble disdain for labor or business. After living for a time in both Paris and Rome, he told his father that he wanted to follow the examples of ancestors who had spread Spanish influence to the New World. His father gave the boy, barely a teenager, a few hundred pesos and wished him well in Mexico City.

But Nicanor found life dull in the capital of New Spain, and he followed the gold rush north to California. Seeking excitement without the drudgery of manual labor or the boredom of business, he joined a band of robbers operating in the northern mines. The leader of the band had been as unusual in his choice of a second profession as his newest neophyte—age fifteen—was in the choice of his first.

Dr. Thomas J. Hodges had just graduated from medical school in Tennessee when he joined the army to serve in the war against Mexico. But instead of going home after the war to start a medical practice, he followed the gold rush to California, changed his name to Tom Bell, and recruited a band of robbers. The well-educated southerner may have felt a bond with the highborn Spanish youth. We don't know how long Nicanor was in Bell's band, but it was long enough for one robbery and a shootout.

On March 12, 1856, five of Bell's men, including Nicanor, robbed four travelers in the Trinity Alps of northwestern California. Exactly a month later a different band of Bell's robbers, not including Nicanor, held up a stage near Marysville, California. In the investigation that followed, robber William Carter was found with a watch that had been taken in the earlier robbery. This led to a shootout when police barged into a tent-cabin near Folsom on April 24. The police fired twenty-five shots, killing one robber and wounding Nicanor twice. A third robber escaped.

Nicanor fired two shots before he fell with bullets in his arm and his leg. The police found four pistols, a double-barreled shotgun, and a large bowie knife in the tent-cabin.

Sentenced to the California State Prison for ten years, Nicanor was moved to Angel Island in San Francisco Bay, then the location of the prison. When the authorities learned that he was barely sixteen, they notified the governor and he granted the boy a pardon. Young in years but old in ambition and determination, Nicanor went immediately to the Comstock in Nevada.

The bright young man thought that wealth should be collected at its source and had no interest in robbing individuals of small amounts. So he turned his attention to the quartz mills that refined gold and silver bullion from the ore that hard-working peons dug from the ground. One of his earliest adventures in Nevada was the theft of precious amalgam from the retorts of the Imperial Mill at Gold Hill. Later he removed an entire wheelbarrow load of amalgam from the Pacific Mill. He buried it in the Silver City cemetery until the uproar about the brazen theft died down.

Nicanor's most daring robbery occurred when he saw three bricks of silver bullion being loaded into the front boot on the Virginia City to Reno stage. He ran into the stage office, bought passage on the stage, and asked the driver, Baldy Green, if he could ride on the box with him. Baldy's stage had been robbed so often that miners had made up a ballad about "Baldy, Hand Down the Express Box," but this time no one would stop the stage and make such a demand. Of course, Baldy let him ride on the box. He had heard about the linguistic skills of the young Spaniard, and he looked forward to some highfalutin conversation.

The spur-of-the-moment robbery demonstrated the skill of a dashing young man who saw in other people's carelessness opportunities for sudden wealth that others missed. Taking advantage of those opportunities with courage and skill was, to Nicanor, his right. He felt more entitled to the world's wealth than the unimaginative people who produced it.

When the stage left the long Geiger Grade and turned north on the flat meadows of Steamboat Springs, Nicanor diverted Baldy's attention by asking him if he could see an eagle flying in the distance or something on the mountains to the west. Then he quickly and silently extracted a brick from the boot and dropped it over the side into the roadside dust. He seared into his memory the appearance of the roadside willows and sagebrush that marked the location.

The audacious bandit repeated his actions twice more, each time after diverting Baldy's attention by some innocuous question. When the stage reached Reno, Nicanor hurried to the nearest stable and rented a team and buggy. He drove back up the stage road and made the three stops necessary to recover his treasure before Baldy knew it was gone or anyone else had seen the bricks lying along the road.

This time, however, suspicion implicated Baldy's passenger. When Nicanor left the bricks at an assay office in Gold Hill to be melted into smaller ingots, the assayer told him to come back in a few days. Nicanor, immediately suspicious that something was amiss, forgot about the bricks and quickly moved his operations out of town.

Nicanor did not know that the Washoe County sheriff had found his fresh buggy tracks and followed them the next morning to the assay office. There the officers learned that an unidentified man had left the bricks and was told to return. They posted a guard, but, of course, their suspect never showed up.

Although Nicanor never considered Mexicans socially equal to hidalgos like him with pure Spanish blood, Nevada's Mexicans treated him as a folk hero. He became a legendary Robin Hood who robbed the rich and gave to the poor. This adulation from Mexican workers seems strange. By the time the debonair young man left Virginia City, he was noted for hosting elaborate dinners, where he displayed the most impeccable taste in the town's best restaurants. He often asked them to serve wild game accompanied by the best European wine. A handsome man, Nicanor invited the area's loveliest ladies and its most esteemed young gentlemen to his soirees, entertaining them with his quick wit and worldly conversation. Suave and cultured, he captivated his guests with stories of European and other capitals. But he did not have the reputation of opening his door to down-on-their-luck miners that Andrew Jackson "Big Jack" Davis enjoyed. Contemporaries on the Comstock, both Nicanor—by now called the Spanish King—and Big Jack led double lives. Each hobnobbed with law-abiding judges, bankers, and public officials until suspicion of criminal activities became too strong and forced them into the open. While Big Jack patronized the wealthy and powerful, he kept his door open to the poor, something the Spanish King did not do. So it is surprising that the Mexican workingmen thought of him as a Robin Hood.

The two men differed in another respect. Davis was finally sent to prison. Nicanor, while arrested many times, was never convicted.

Nicanor was known for his immaculate dress and his Old World manners. The budding young socialite women, in the beginning, had individual dreams of conquering the cultured young Spaniard. And he soon added to his laurels the beauty of his chosen mistress. We don't know her name, but she worshiped her dashing young lover. This, too, has a strange element. She was a Mormon woman and brought up in the strict moral demands of that faith.

Nicanor's prejudice against operating a business apparently abated after he discovered some of the handicaps of a criminal career. After leaving Virginia City in 1867, he stopped in Austin and set up a saloon in partnership with Jack Harris, another robber of Wells Fargo stages and an all-around bandit on the Comstock. In fact, it was Harris's cabin to which Billy Mayfield moved Henry Plummer, the California fugitive, to hide him from Marshal John Blackburn. Eventually, Plummer, a notorious Montana sheriff, was hanged by vigilantes on his own gallows.

But the Austin mining camp fell on hard times, and several rich strikes had just been made at Hamilton and Treasure Hill, farther east. The partners closed their saloon, and the Spanish King moved on with his mistress to White Pine County. In a few years Harris, too, would be hanged by vigilantes.

Shortly after Nicanor arrived in White Pine County, he robbed the Shermantown Mill of a sack of amalgam. A posse of 250 men scoured White Pine County for the robber and found Nicanor. But he hired his close friend and former fellow socialite back in Virginia City, Judge Jesse Pitzer, to come and defend him. The evidence seemed clear to the police, but Pitzer argued to the jury that a man of Nicanor's stature would never run around with hoodlums. The jury agreed and acquitted—one of a long line of acquittals that the Spanish King would eventually receive.

Nicanor returned to stage robbing. He concentrated on the Gilmer and Saulsbury stage line. Agents for Wells Fargo, this line covered eastern Nevada from Pioche all the way north to Battle Mountain. Two or three holdups a week were soon reported, not all, of course, by one band of robbers.

But more and more the drivers mentioned a handsome young man leading the robbers. By this time Wells Drury, ace reporter for the *Territorial Enterprise,* considered Nicanor the king of Nevada stage robbers. But with pressure increasing from more frequent arrests, in 1872 Nicanor moved his operations again, this time to Pioche, the busiest mining camp in Nevada. There two of the half-dozen or so inmates from the 1871 prison escape appeared to have joined his gang. We don't know who they were, but none of the men who escaped and remained uncaptured had Mexican names.

Booming Pioche had doubled its population in four months. Prices soared as beef became scarce. At first Nicanor's men rustled steers in Utah, drove them over the state line, and sold them to butchers in Pioche. But he soon returned to stage robbery.

Nicanor and his men stopped a stage two miles from Pioche one night and found the express box nearly empty. After robbing all the passengers, they took the mail sacks and got two thousand dollars that was being mailed to Nevada State Bank. This time Nicanor was arrested and charged.

But the jury acquitted him after a dozen of his friends supported his claim of an alibi. However, the same stage was robbed a week later, and this time Nicanor fled to the mountains. Officers and posses tracked him through the mountains for several weeks and were about to give up when Nicanor sent word to Gilmer and Saulsbury that he was tired of being hunted and would like to negotiate an agreement with them.

By this time Gilmer and Saulsbury had been reduced to the brink of bankruptcy. They were willing to do most anything to stop the robberies. They sent word to Nicanor that they were ready to deal. Nicanor sent a Mexican guide to bring their representative to him.

The stage company sent its lawyer, Colonel W. W. Bishop, to meet the Mexican. Bishop described the meeting:

> *A young Mexican acted as my guide. We left Pioche on burros at midnight and went over Spring Mountain. Taking a long sweep to the right we soon struck a rugged ravine and started up it. I could see armed Mexicans behind every clump of sagebrush. We passed safely through the defile until we reached a grove of stunted pines. These, we found, hid the entrance to a natural cave or tunnel, which ran into the side of the mountain.*
>
> *Our burros were tied behind the trees, and torches were furnished to us by an old woman who emerged from the darkness of the cavern. After going about seventy-five yards into the tunnel my guide whistled, and seven or eight big fellows came cautiously out from behind the rocks and advanced to meet us. Without a word they seized a large flat stone, which looked like a part of the floor of the tunnel and, moving it aside, disclosed a lower chamber, oval in shape and about the size of an ordinary church.*
>
> *A ladder was thrust up, and following my guide downward I found myself in the presence of Nicanor and some dozen or so of his most trusted friends, several women being of the number.*
>
> *Nick was very brief. He said all he wanted was to be left alone. If the stage line and the express company would let up on him and not prosecute him, he would protect their property until one side or the other should see fit to terminate the contract, in which case fair notice should be given. I was authorized to act, and at once agreed to his terms.*

It was rumored that the stage company had agreed to pay Nicanor two thousand dollars a month besides, but they never admitted that. A few days later, Nicanor appeared in Pioche and told Colonel B. F. Sides, the stage agent, "If I can prevent it, your stages will never be stopped as long as you're the agent here."

Nicanor kept his word, and the stage line's holdups decreased. But when the company sent a new agent to Pioche, Nicanor terminated the agreement, giving the company fair notice of his decision. He called on the new agent, one Seibert.

"I am very regretful, Señor, but I am no longer able to take care of your treasure boxes. You must protect your own property."

Then the robberies resumed.

But Nicanor was finally arrested, and bail was set so high he could not post it. Feeling that conviction and imprisonment was near, he escaped with the help of two other prisoners. They knocked the jailer down as he made his nightly round of inspections. The jailer fired his pistol, and they knocked him unconscious. They stole some horses in Spring Valley, and rode to the Utah ranch of Mormon James Maxwell on the headwaters of the Sevier River.

After a period of rest, and perhaps to return for his mistress, Nicanor and one of his co-escapers, Eugene Billieu, a Frenchman, returned to within a dozen miles of Pioche, robbed a stage, stole more horses from the C. H. Light ranch, and quietly returned to Utah. There they picked up the other escaper, a horse thief named Yank, and headed for Mexico.

Like all of us, Nicanor learned to compromise as he grew older. He gave up his ideal of stealing wealth only from its source. First, he shifted away from the quartz mills, which he thought exploited their workers, and began robbing the express boxes on the stagecoaches. From this to robbing the passengers may have seemed to him a small step at the time.

But the compromise he made as he fled to Mexico was unusual indeed. All Nicanor's followers thought their leader, with his charmed life, could be trusted for his loyalty. Billieu, who only robbed with Nicanor once, and Yank, merely a horse thief, were fleeing from the law together, and they reasonably expected loyalty from their co-escaper. When Nicanor's last pursuers from Nevada got fifty miles south of Maxwell's ranch, they found Billieu and Yank dead. They had been shot in the back by the man they trusted, obviously to make it harder for lawmen to follow.

A miner who had once worked in Pioche returned from Sinaloa in 1888 and reported that a man he thought was Nicanor had a huge ranch in the mountains near Mazatlán. He had a large band of horses and called himself Don Felipe Castro Estrada. But the miner wasn't sure, and he said nothing about the man having a mistress.

If the man was Nicanor Rodrigues, his years of robbing mills, stages, and people in Nevada probably contributed to a small fortune that the once proud hidalgo, who turned into a back-stabbing killer, was finally able to invest in Mexico upon his retirement.

WILLIAM THORINGTON

The Hanging of Lucky Bill

William "Lucky Bill" Thorington came to Nevada's Carson Valley in 1853 and established a farm near present-day Gardnerville. He enjoyed gambling, and he never seemed to lose.

Rollin Daggett, a San Francisco newsman later elected to Congress from Nevada, described Thorington's advertisement of his shell game: "Here gentlemen is a nice, quiet little game conducted on the square, and especially recommended by the clergy for its honesty and wholesome moral tendencies. I win only from blind men; all that have two good eyes can win a fortune. You see, gentlemen, here are three little wooden cups, and here is a little ball which, for the sake of starting the game, I shall place under this one, as you can plainly see—thus and thus—and thus: and now I will bet two, four, or six ounces that no gentlemen can, the first time trying, raise the cup that the ball is under; if he can, he can win all the money that Bill, by patient toil and industry, has scraped together."

Thorington soon opened a toll road west through the mountains to California. The road ran through a difficult canyon filled with huge boulders and a fast-running river. Now called Woodfords Canyon, the road through it became the final link in the emigrant trail from Salt Lake City to Placerville.

In 1854 Thorington's wife, Maria, and their twelve-year-old son, William Jerome, joined him. Forty-five years old and over six feet tall, with powerful shoulders and mirthful gray eyes, Thorington was a handsome man. Maria, with her coal-black hair and huge brown eyes, was described as "strikingly beautiful."

In the words of Myron Angel, editor of Thompson & West's *History of Nevada,* Thorington was "generous and brave, and his sympathies were readily aroused in favor of the unfortunate. The county had no merrier citizen in it than Lucky Bill."

Within a few years Thorington's neighbors considered him quite wealthy. Many people talked about him. In addition to his impressive appearance, his deep baritone voice made his barroom stories sound like biblical parables. But early historian Asa Fairfield pointed out that Thorington's "associations in life, however, had been with individuals that had led him to look upon murder or theft as a smaller crime than would be the betrayal of a person who claimed his protection . . . and this characteristic proved his ruin."

Thorington's suave urbanity, described by the locals as "nobility," was his greatest asset. Henry Van Sickle, a quiet, patient man who would hunt down and shoot Nevada's most savage killer, described Thorington as "a man having many good qualities, a good worker at anything to be undertook; a better neighbor never lived near any man, nor a better friend to the weary traveler."

As Lucky Bill's prospects continued to improve, he added a mill and a trading post, built a house in Mormon Station (present Genoa), brought the first fruit trees to the valley, and dug its first irrigation ditches. When Kit Carson and his crew of sheepherders drove five thousand sheep from New Mexico to California in 1853, Thorington allowed them to pass over his toll bridge free of charge to hungry California prospectors.

In 1857, when the Mormons—the majority of Nevada's settlers—were called back to Utah Territory to defend their church against the approaching United States Army, the Gentiles who remained sought to stamp out all reminders of the hated polygamy that had been practiced in their community. By this time Maria and William Jerome were living in their town house in Mormon Station, and a Martha Lamb lived with Lucky Bill on the farm.

The 1853 move to the Carson Valley was not Lucky Bill's first trip west. Three years earlier he left Maria and eight-year-old William Jerome behind in Michigan and moved to California. He then returned in 1852 and persuaded three young girls to move to California with him. Parents and friends of the girls overtook him in Peoria, Illinois, and two of the girls went back to their homes; the third, Martha Lamb, continued on west with Lucky Bill. Martha would bear his son, named William R., in 1858. By this time Lucky Bill's popularity was declining as his herds and flocks seemed to grow faster than one would expect from natural increase, and he never bought any livestock. The loose living arrangement with Martha also fueled rumors that perhaps Lucky Bill wasn't the paragon that his Nevada neighbors thought at first.

In December 1857 William Edwards introduced himself to Thorington and told him that he had killed a man in self-defense in Merced County, California, and needed help to avoid vigilantes who were after him.

"What can I do? asked Thorington.

"I got friends in Honey Lake Valley, but I need to hide some money that I got in a sack before I go up there," Edwards replied.

"I can take care of that."

Honey Lake Valley was a long two-day ride to the north from Carson Valley. Thorington buried the sack, containing about a thousand dollars, under a tree on his ranch.

Also in 1857 Mormons in Honey Lake Valley, before moving back to Utah Territory to defend their church, sold a fine herd of almost one hundred head of Durham cattle to Henri Gordier, a French settler in that valley. A few months after Edwards left for Honey Lake Valley, he wrote to Thorington, asking him to dig up his buried money and add enough to it to buy the herd together, as Gordier wanted to leave the valley. Thorington replied that he was not interested in buying the cattle. By this time Edwards was living with John Mullen and Mullen's hired man, Asa Snow, in Honey Lake Valley.

In late March or early April 1858, Edwards and Mullen told Gordier that he had a sick cow and offered to take him to it. Neither Mullen nor Gordier was ever seen again. Soon Asa Snow moved into Gordier's cabin. He and Edwards told neighbors that the Frenchman had sold out and returned to France. By this time some of Gordier's cattle were reportedly seen in Lucky Bill's herd.

Gordier's body was recovered from a deep hole in the Susan River in May 1858. Soon after, Edwards showed up at Thorington's farm in Carson Valley, swore to Thorington that he had nothing to do with the murder of Gordier, and asked for help to avoid arrest.

The next day Lucky Bill sent his son Jerome to Merced to collect a debt owed to Edwards. Jerome returned with three hundred and fifty dollars and a mare in partial payment of the debt. By this time Edwards was hiding out in the mountains on the west side of Carson Valley. He came down to replenish his food supply once in a while, and to get the money Jerome had brought back from Merced.

On June 10, 1858, the San Francisco *Daily Alta* reported that the *Marysville News* had carried the following note: "We are indebted to Mr. Whiting, of Whiting's Express, for the information that a man named Snow was hung in Honey Lake Valley Monday last, by the citizens. He confessed having been accessory to the murder of the Frenchman, some weeks since, in the valley. He implicates two other men, now supposed to be in the lower country."

In fact, Snow did not confess to anything. It was an unusual hanging, though, and that is probably why Snow never confessed.

A defiant Snow denied knowing anything about Gordier's murder. He insisted that he was innocent and dared the Honey Lake vigilantes to hang him. They decided that a little hanging might refresh his memory, so they strung him up on a pine tree for a while and then lowered him for more questions.

Still Snow insisted that that he knew nothing, and he continued to defy and curse the vigilantes.

A second hanging produced the same result. But when the vigilantes pulled Snow up the third time, they let him hang too long. He was beyond answering questions when they lowered him to the ground.

On Monday, June 14, the Honey Lake vigilantes rode into Carson Valley just before daylight. The San Francisco *Daily Alta* reported: "On Monday morning last before daylight a body of armed horsemen, numbering about 100 men, charged into Carson Valley and took possession of all the roads and trails leading from the valley into the mountains. All egress was cut off from the valley by a strong armed guard, and those wishing to pass out of or into the valley are furnished with passports."

After securing the roads, the armed riders rode on to Lucky Bill's house as the sun came up. They first brought out Lucky Bill, then Jerome. Maria followed, pleading for their son. By early afternoon the vigilantes had arrested five more men and had moved their prisoners to the Richard Sides ranch on Clear Creek near present Carson City.

Carson Valley had its own vigilantes, formed by Richard Sides and Major William Ormsby. Organized before the Honey Lake vigilantes, the Carson Valley group cooperated with the later group. Shortly after the Carson Valley vigilantes had been organized, Lucky Bill Thorington helped form the anti-vigilantes to oppose the Sides-Ormsby group.

Sides's Clear Creek ranch in the north part of Carson Valley would serve as temporary headquarters for the Carson Valley and Honey Lake vigilante groups for the next few days. It included a large barn where the vigilantes would keep their horses, hold their prisoners, and conduct a "trial." The ranch, located on flat land with few trees on it, was not considered vulnerable to a sneak attack by the anti-vigilantes.

The Honey Lake vigilantes made their plans to capture William Edwards, whom they correctly believed was hiding out in the mountains west of Carson Valley. They used sixteen-year-old Jerome Thorington for help, and the promise they made and broke is probably the ugliest part of this weird story.

The vigilantes told Jerome that if he would bring Edwards to a remote cabin that Lucky Bill used, they would release his father and let him go free. Otherwise, his father would hang. Jerome knew that it would be perilous to go to Edwards, a powerful, well-armed, dangerous man.

"Can I just show you where his hideout is?" asked the desperate boy.

The vigilantes, afraid to attack Edwards in his hideout, replied, "No. You either bring him to your father's cabin, where we can talk to him, or your father will hang. We mean business, Jerome."

Willing to do almost anything to save his father, whom the boy knew was innocent of any involvement in the murder of Gordier, Jerome set out for a secluded canyon in the mountains southwest of Lucky Bill's Mormon Station home. He found Edwards, who did not know that Lucky Bill had been captured. Jerome told him that his father wanted Edwards to come to the cabin so they could make plans together to avoid arrest. Edwards, suspicious, refused at first.

"We can stay hid out better if we keep apart," Edwards insisted.

But with the burden of his father's life on him, the boy continued to plead, assuring Edwards that no harm would come to him. Finally Edwards agreed.

"But if this is a trick," he warned the boy, "you're as good as dead, you know."

Edwards followed the boy through the woods and down the mountain. They reached the cabin long after midnight. Edwards had no reason to suspect the cabin's darkness; obviously Lucky Bill, trying to avoid arrest, wouldn't have a light in the window.

When Jerome reached the door, Edwards grabbed his shoulder and pulled him back. He listened for a long time, his ear pressed against the door. Then he put his revolver in the front of his shirt where it would be handy, cocked both triggers of his shotgun, and carried it in front, ready for immediate use. Finally he opened the door and stepped inside.

Two men, Rough Elliott of the Carson Valley vigilantes and John Gilpin of the Honey Lake vigilantes, clubbed Edwards down. Their first blow hit his shotgun, breaking both barrels away from the stock. The second landed on his head. Edwards regained consciousness in the vigilantes' barn and found that he had been bound securely with a rope.

While his assailants were still counting the money they had taken from him, Edwards managed to untie the rope and run out of the barn. Vigilantes hiding outside fired at him but missed. Rough Elliott, a "good foot-racer," caught up with Edwards as he jumped into a slough. After they pulled Edwards out, the vigilantes took him to blacksmith G. W. Hepperly, who riveted irons to his legs with a chain attached. They then took him back to the barn for trial.

The Honey Lake vigilantes set up a trial with three judges and an eighteen-man "jury." John Neale, one of the Honey Lake vigilantes who had ridden with the others into Carson Valley on June 14, served as one judge. A verdict would be reached if any twelve of the jury agreed.

Chauncey Noteware served as reporter to take down the testimony. Years later he would serve as secretary of state for Nevada. Noteware recorded the testimony, but no copy has ever been found. He did say that Edwards was "convicted on his own confession." The judges, jurors, and spectators were all armed as they sat in the courtroom and the trial proceeded. The anti-vigilantes stayed in hiding, afraid that what happened to Thorington might also happen to them. Only persons approved by the vigilantes were allowed inside the barn.

After reading Noteware's entire transcript of testimony some years afterward, before the document was lost to history, Myron Angel, editor of Thompson & West's *History of Nevada,* reported, "Not a thing appears there implicating Lucky Bill in anything except the attempt to secure the murderer's escape. Edwards swore positively that he had assured Lucky Bill that he was innocent, and no one else testified to the contrary."

Although Edwards had been captured, the vigilante "court" did not try him. They used his testimony in the trial against Lucky Bill.

Thorington's trial started on Thursday, June 17. The sounds of the gallows being built could be heard the day before. On Saturday morning, June 19, the vigilantes found Thorington guilty. He was sentenced to be hanged that afternoon.

The vigilantes shackled Thorington and hauled him to the gallows in a wagon. After positioning the wagon under the gallows, two vigilantes placed the hangman's noose around Thorington's neck and then jumped out of the wagon.

Staring defiantly at the assembled crowd, Lucky Bill shouted, "I ain't never lived like a hog and I ain't gonna die like one screamin' about bein' butchered." With that he threw his head back and burst into his favorite song, "The Last Rose of Summer."

Lawrence Frey, the teenaged son of one of the "jurors," had been tricked into driving the team that pulled the wagon to the gallows. A few vigilantes drew straws to determine the driver of the wagon, and they secretly marked the straws so the Frey youth had no choice but to take the short one. He was bothered for the rest of his life by what he had done.

After the noose was dropped around Lucky Bill's neck, the plan was to drive the wagon forward, leaving the prisoner hanging from the improvised gallows. As Thorington neared the end of his song, the wagon still hadn't moved. Some vigilantes shouted at the Frey boy to go ahead and start the team, but he was crying and shaking his head. Thorington stopped his song and said, "Don't worry, boy. I'll take care of it." With that he jumped out of the wagon to a painful death by strangulation.

Friends of Lucky Bill obtained his body and buried it in a secret place. In July 1941 the grave was discovered in the mountains near Woodfords, California, about twenty-five miles from Carson City.

The morning after the hanging, the Honey Lake vigilantes rode away with Edwards in their custody. They refused to let any Carson Valley vigilantes ride with them. Conflicting reports followed about whether Edwards had been hanged, turned loose, or escaped. No one knows; he was never heard from again.

Within a few years, Jerome Thorington died a drunkard's death. His mother's mind failed, and she died in the Stockton, California, insane asylum around 1900.

Martha Lamb stayed in the Carson Valley a few more years. After a friend of Lucky Bill's was divorced by his wife on grounds of his adultery with Martha, the friend married Martha. The couple moved to Bishop, California, and raised several children. Martha's first son, William R. Thorington, became the father of Cecil Thorington, who was elected sheriff of Mono County, California, in 1938. A popular sheriff, this grandson of Lucky Bill served for twenty-eight years.

This is not the typical story of an outlaw opposing lawful authority. Here a friend of the outlaw who was himself innocent of murder was murdered by a law-defying mob of citizens. No reliable evidence exists that Lucky Bill knew of Edwards's involvement in the murder of Gordier. Thorington made it clear that he welcomed a trial before a legal tribunal. The vigilante actions of citizens of both Honey Lake Valley and Carson Valley resulted in the execution of a man who only offered friendship to the scoundrel who, if he did not murder Gordier as he did the man in Merced County, California, certainly was implicated in the crime. Furthermore, if Edwards did "escape" from the Honey Lake vigilantes, either through their assistance or from their negligence, we have the result that vigilante action both killed an innocent man and allowed a guilty one to go free. It would not be the only instance of such a tragedy, which always undermines the concept of law on which any civilization is necessarily based.

NEW MEXICO OUTLAWS

VINCENT SILVA

The Man Who Fooled a Town

On October 23, 1892, the residents of Las Vegas, New Mexico, woke up to a picture-perfect winter scene. The previous night's storm had covered the streets and walkways in brilliant white. Shop fronts gleamed with a just-scrubbed look from the night's fierce wind. Windowsills laden with snow glittered and gleamed.

The brilliant sun, reflecting off the icy streets, caused early risers to view the main street with squinted eyes. Then eyes fell on the town bridge. There, gently swaying back and forth in the slight breeze, was Patricio Maes, hanging from the metal girder on the bridge. His clothes, stiff from cold and ice, fit him like boards; his cocked head faced heavenward, as if he were viewing the sky; his sightless eyes saw nothing.

The night before, a bitter wind had swept along the streets of Las Vegas, bringing with it a cold that settled into the marrow of a man's bones. This weather had driven an unusually large crowd to seek comfort in Silva's Imperial Saloon. The conversations thundered off the walls. Red-bearded Vincent Silva, looking dapper and handsome as usual, oiled his way around his customers, stopping here and there to have a quiet word with someone.

Meanwhile, the wind quieted and snow began falling. The white flakes piled up quickly and covered the dusty roads of Las Vegas. As midnight approached, Valdez, the bartender, shouted out that he was feeling sick and was closing the bar. Complaints and surprised looks were exchanged among the men. Silva's never closed; it was a twenty-four-hour-a-day operation. Reluctantly, the men left the saloon, faced with the choice of going home or freezing outside in the cold.

When the bar emptied, Silva locked the door and started for home. However, a short time later, shadowy figures began making their way through the snow to the saloon's side door. Vincent Silva had called an emergency meeting of his secret outlaw band, the White Caps. Silva, a respected and wealthy citizen of Las Vegas, was not all he appeared to be.

Silva's handsome looks, powerful bearing, and red hair made him a charismatic man. Most of the townspeople held him in high regard as a successful businessman and the owner of the Imperial Saloon, a large affair with a bar, billiards, and a dance hall.

Silva came to Las Vegas with his wife, Telesfora, in 1875 and started his business. Four years later the Atchison, Topeka, and Santa Fe Railway arrived, making his saloon even more successful.

Wealth and success were new to Silva. He was born to poor parents in the countryside of Bernalillo County, New Mexico. He married Telesfora Sandoval, a plain-looking village girl who presented a remarkable contrast to his handsome looks.

Before moving to Las Vegas, Silva and Telesfora lived in the mining town of San Pedro. Silva operated a grocery store, and his wife took care of the candy counter. An avid hunter, Silva spent his weekends looking for game. His familiarity with the countryside served him well in later years.

In Las Vegas people admired Silva as a family man. He was the doting father of an adopted daughter. Eight years earlier someone had abandoned the newborn Emma in a Las Vegas stable. Unable to bear children, Telesfora begged her husband to adopt the baby. It was not long before both parents were completely enamored with the child. As further evidence of his family responsibilities, Silva had welcomed Telesfora's younger brother, Gabriel, into his household and employed him as a bartender in his saloon.

Silva was more than a family man, however. He had another side—a dark, evil side that only his outlaw band knew. His greed had slowly turned a simple man into a crime lord. While he smiled and sympathized with the citizens of Las Vegas, his men were rustling cattle, robbing, and murdering innocent people.

Vincent had built an organization with some of the cruelest, most immoral men in the West; men with no conscience and no compassion. Some of his gang members bore very descriptive names. They called Martin Gonzoles y Blea "the Moor" because of his dark complexion; Manuel Gonzales y Baca, "Toothless"; Antonio José Valdez, "the Ape"; and Ricardo Romero, "Pugnose." Antonio José Valdez earned the name "Pussyfoot" for the way he walked.

Not all of the outlaws were tagged by their physical appearance. Guadalupe Caballero, "the Owl," was Silva's spy and personal aide. Five feet tall and weighing about one hundred and ten pounds with crossed eyes, the Owl had the appearance of a helpless and harmless man.

The Owl looked so inconsequential that people often ignored him. He would sit on his haunches on the side of the street or by a storefront and appear to be slumbering. However, he was wide awake; he would listen, take everything in, and then report his findings to Silva.

Also in the gang were three men of extreme importance to Vincent: Julian Trujillo, José Chavez y Chavez, and Eugenio Alarid. These three were members of the Las Vegas police force. They had worked over the years to see to it that Vincent Silva was not accused or even suspected of crimes.

Vincent Silva was an uneducated man; he could barely read and write, but his cunning, ambition, and ruthless manner made him the leader of this group. His men followed him without question.

To keep his façade of respectability in the community, Vincent had to keep his unlawful acts away from public scrutiny. He bought a ranch, Monte Largo, in an inaccessible section of the San Pedro mining district. Monte Largo was a place of deep gorges and scissor peaks, an ideal hiding place for his rustled cattle and horses.

It was to Monte Largo that Refugio Esquivel, a local rancher, traced his stolen horses. There he found his brand altered into Silva's brand. After rescuing his stock, Refugio stormed into Silva's saloon and accused him of cattle rustling.

Silva feigned innocence. There was no proof, so who would believe Refugio? However, the humiliation of a public accusation in his own saloon shook Silva's confidence. For years missing cattle and unsolved murders had plagued Las Vegas, but no one had ever suspected the respectable Vincent Silva. Someone must have talked. Silva believed that there was an informer in the White Caps, and he thought he knew who it was.

Silva acted the part of a fair man, and the fair thing to do was to have the alleged traitor put on trial and judged by his peers. And so it was on that snowy night in October that the band of thieves gathered on the second floor of the Imperial Saloon for a clandestine meeting.

Just days before, Patricio Maes, a Silva gang member, had placed a notice announcing his resignation from the Partido del Pueblo Unido political party. He stated he was now a member of the Republican Party.

The Herrera brothers, who wanted a party that represented the people, originally started the Partido del Pueblo Unido. These men rode around the countryside punishing those they believed had stolen or illegally obtained land from the poorer peasants. While they threatened people and destroyed barns and crops, they never physically attacked anyone. The party was nicknamed the White Caps after the headgear they wore on raids. When Pablo Herrera was murdered, the party was leaderless and disbanded. Vincent Silva secretly reformed the party into a gang of thieves, murderers, and cattle rustlers. He took on the name the White Caps for his gang. They were also called the Forty Thieves, a name that accurately described the membership.

Silva took the published announcement of Maes's resignation personally. To him it was not a resignation from a political party, but a display of disloyalty and untrustworthiness. He also believed that Maes was the leak.

Silva set up court to try Maes on the charge of being a White Cap traitor. He appointed himself attorney general and fellow outlaw Polanco the defending lawyer. Toothless, also called the Dull One, was the judge.

Both sides presented their arguments. The gang members voted on a verdict, but "Judge" Toothless felt the verdict was unfair and refused to announce it. Manuel Gonzalez y Baca hurled insults at the men, reminding them of the importance of capital punishment. The discussion heated up as men chose sides and began to make their points physically. It was apparent to Silva that each member of his band had his own opinion about the accused and was not willing to listen to other arguments, or to blindly follow Silva on this matter.

Silva stopped the trial, ordered three gallons of whiskey, and after the refreshing break called for another vote. The vote was unanimous—death to the traitor. Patricio Maes fell to his knees pleading for mercy, proclaiming his innocence, and begging for forgiveness for any transgressions. But the liquor had done its job, and the gang members were now in agreement with Silva and unmoved by Maes's pleading.

A noose dropped over Maes's head, and the gang led their victim through the deserted, stormy streets to the iron bridge spanning the Gallinas River. When they reached the bridge, the assassins allowed Maes to say his prayers. When he finished, one end of the rope was tied to a girder. Then Silva and a gang member picked up Maes and threw him over the bridge. Unfortunately, the rope knot was not tight, and it slipped, causing Maes to fall, smashing against the ice of the frozen river.

Two men climbed down to the ice, threw the loose end up, and the men on the bridge hauled Maes's body up. They tightly secured the rope end to the metal bridge girder and let him hang. Then, in ones and twos, the gang members drifted off, leaving Maes to his death dance in the howling wind. The next morning a large crowd gathered around the bridge to view the swinging corpse of Patricio Maes.

The *Las Vegas Optic* reported the hanging with a small notice: "Patricio Maes was taken by a mob early Saturday morning and hanged from the Gallinas River bridge at Las Vegas." That seemed to be the end of the matter.

Meanwhile, Captain Esquivel, the father of Refugio, was quietly investigating the rustling of his family's horses. Captain Esquivel had enough evidence to prove the illegal activities of the White Caps. Unfortunately, it was all circumstantial. Even so, he was able to get a grand jury indictment against Silva. On November 7, 1892, Vincent Silva's trial began. At the trial Silva's alibi could not be broken. The charges were dropped, and Silva was freed.

After that Silva became a very cautious man. He did not fear the local police, but the Sociedad de Muta Protection, a vigilante group. Taking several gang members with him, Silva went into hiding in a cave near the village of Coyote (now called Rainsville). From this hideout, a mere twelve miles from Las Vegas, Silva and his band continued their criminal activities.

A deserted Telesfora was forced to find a way to support herself and Emma, by now a student at the Las Vegas Academy. She opened a lunch counter in town and then, fearing for the safety of her brother, Gabriel, insisted that he give up his work at the saloon, which continued operating under the management of a gang member. Although he was no longer managing the saloon, Silva did not stay completely away from the town. He made clandestine night forays into West Las Vegas to visit his mistress, Flor de la Peña.

Silva knew his safety depended on stealth and secrecy, and he worried about the two people closest to him. His young brother-in-law, Gabriel Sandoval, knew too much about Silva's illegal activities. His other worry was for the safety of Telesfora and his child.

Telesfora was the opposite of Silva in many ways. Her short, dark, and fat appearance made a sharp contrast to his large frame and redheaded good looks. Despite her unattractiveness she was well respected in the community and known as a kind and compassionate woman. Her demeanor was quiet; Silva's was one of boldness and bravado. She was blindly dedicated to Silva and very much in love with him; he openly kept a mistress. What the two had in common was their love for their daughter, Emma. Now Silva was to use that love to protect himself.

On January 23 Guadalupe Caballero pulled up to the Las Vegas Academy in a horse-drawn carriage. He told Emma he was taking her home for lunch. Instead, he drove her to Silva, who took her to Taos and enrolled her in a local school.

When Telesfora found her daughter missing, she was frantic, consumed with worry and fear for her beloved child. By kidnapping Emma, Silva hoped to silence both his brother-in-law and his wife. He planned on using Telesfora and her brother's love for Emma and their fear for her well-being to force them into cooperating with him. But Silva soon worried that even this measure was not enough. Enlisting the help of his three police officers, José Chavez y Chavez, Julian Trujillo, and Eugenio Alarid, he planned a murder.

The three policemen met with Gabriel Sandoval. Convincing him that he was aiding in the rescue of Emma, they led him to an abandoned mill in West Las Vegas. There Silva jumped out of the darkness and stabbed Sandoval, his own brother-in-law, to death, while the three police officers held his arms. The policemen, with the help of the Owl, carried the body to the back of Silva's saloon, where they stripped it and threw it in the privy pit.

Silva had plans to leave for Mexico with his mistress, but he needed more money. Silva and five of his gang members broke into the William Frank mercantile store in Las Vegas and helped themselves. They also stole the safe. The *Las Vegas Optic* described it as "the most audacious act in many years."

The thieves dumped the broken safe by the road about a mile from the store, setting fire to the accounts, books, and papers. They took the cash, amounting to twenty-five dollars. The merchandise, which was worth more than five hundred dollars, was never recovered.

On May 19, 1893, a notice of a reward for the capture of the outlaws appeared in the *Las Vegas Optic*. On the list was Vincent Silva, wanted for two indictments for stealing. Also on the list were rewards for the capture of the robbers of the William Frank Store and the murderers of Jacob Stutzman and Abran Abulafie, all by persons unknown. What the authorities did not know at the time was that all of these crimes were perpetrated by Silva and his band of forty thieves.

On the day this notice appeared, events took a horrific turn in Vincent Silva's life. Needing more money for his flight with his mistress, Silva sent his wife a message. The message told Telesfora that he, her brother, and Emma were all well and that she was to pack her things and join them.

That evening Silva's man Genovevo Avila picked Telesfora up and headed toward Silva's ranch. Along the way Vincent joined them. When they reached the ranch, Silva dragged his wife into the small house and demanded money. She handed him all she had—two hundred dollars. Not satisfied, Silva demanded her jewelry. When she protested, he pulled out his knife and killed her. He dragged her body to a deep arroyo at the southern end of the village and flung her to the bottom.

Furious, Silva jumped on the bank until it collapsed and covered her body. After he'd killed his wife, his mood drastically changed. Pleased with himself, he opened up his stuffed money belt and gave each of his five gang members ten dollars.

The men were in a state of shock over the killing of Telesfora. But shock turned to anger when Silva handed out the meager sum of ten dollars each from his bulging money belt.

As the men headed for the village, Antonio José Valdez walked up to Silva, put a .45 to his head, and shot him. They dragged his body back to the bank of the arroyo, tossed it over, kicked sand down to cover it, and went their separate ways after dividing up the money and jewels.

The fact that Vincent Silva, Telesfora Silva, and Gabriel Sandoval were all now dead did not slow down the activities of the White Caps. Over the next few years, innocent men were murdered, and cattle continued to disappear. Finally, William T. Thornton, the governor of New Mexico, offered pardons to anyone who came forward with information on the crimes.

It was not until April 10, 1894, that Manuel Gonzales y Baca told the district attorney about the crimes of Vincent Silva and the White Caps. Among the many crimes he reported was the hanging of Patricio Maes and the murder of Gabriel Sandoval. He said nothing of the murder of Telesfora and Vincent Silva.

When the news of Vincent's heinous crimes became public, the townsfolk were appalled. A man they had respected, trusted, and admired had betrayed them. An intense hunt for Silva turned up nothing. Vincent Silva and his wife seemed to have disappeared without a trace.

Vincent's mistress, Flor de la Peña, took Emma into her home and raised her along with her son, Hilario, who may have been Silva's child.

Eventually, the Silva gang began to fall apart. Several gang members had been captured and hanged. Dishonest policemen Julian Trujillo and Eugenio Alarid had earned life sentences in prison. José Chavez y Chavez escaped and went into hiding. And Vincent Silva was still "missing."

A year later Guadalupe Caballero, the Owl, solved the mystery of Vincent and Telesfora Silva's whereabouts and explained to the authorities how they had been killed. On March 17, 1895, Antonio José Valdez led the officials to their graves in the arroyo. The March 18 edition of the *Las Vegas Optic* reported the events:

> *Some excitement was caused here yesterday by the bringing in of the bodies of Vincent Silva and his wife. Silva was the leader of the gang of cut throats who made so much trouble in this county two years ago. He has been badly wanted by the officers since the gang was broken up, and there were rumors that he had been killed and also that he was in Arizona or Colorado. Yesterday Hon. Manuel Baca and a party went out about twelve miles north of here on information obtained from some of the former gang, and found the bodies of both Silva and wife buried near each other. It is understood that Silva was murdered to obtain money supposed to be in his possession and his wife was killed to keep her from informing on the murderers.*

Finally, after two years of searching, the authorities found Vincent Silva, a man who led two lives. It was a shock to the town to discover that the man they respected as a successful businessman, loving husband, and devoted father was a killer, thief, adulterer, and kidnapper. With his cleverness and wit, Silva had managed to fool a town for more than twenty years.

PANCHO VILLA

The Raid on Columbus, March 9, 1916

The men moved noiselessly, surefooted on the desert sand they had called home for generations. There were no shadows in the moonless night. They were men with little education, all with a hunger for a better life. Pancho Villa had gathered these men and boys from small, poor villages, promising them work, money, a white woman for each man, and schooling for the boys. It was dreams of wealth the men followed, not thoughts of power. In the middle of the night, the men made their way in small groups to a point about three miles west of the border gate.

While most held a military rank, they were not a legitimate army. One in twenty was a general, and there were many colonels. Villa handed out ranks as favors, not as positions earned. He believed titles gave an air of legitimacy to his ragtag army of banditos called "Villistas."

Villa himself had humble beginnings. He was born Doroteo Arango Arámbula in Durango, Mexico. An uneducated man, son of a peasant, he killed his first man at sixteen when he discovered the son of an hacienda owner had seduced his sister and then abandoned her. After the killing he stole a horse, headed for the mountains, and began his outlaw life.

During his lifetime he was on both sides of the law. An outlaw, he robbed banks, trains, and stores and committed forgery and murder. He was a revolutionary leader, and at one time held the office of governor of Chihuahua and printed his own money.

However, when he mounted the attack on Columbus, he had lost his legitimacy and political status and was nothing more than an outlaw in charge of a band of thieves.

Pancho Villa placed Colonel Cardenas in charge of this attack. Villa opted to stay back in the mountains and await the news. As the banditos approached Columbus, New Mexico, Cardenas divided his men into two groups. Half stayed with him and were equipped with an 8-mm light machine gun, which he set up on a low hill facing the town. The rest went with Colonel Cervantes to attack the town from its east end. Then the men hunkered down and waited.

Pancho Villa had conceived a brazen plan—a raid on Columbus, New Mexico. This plan was his chance for glory and power. Spies had informed him that a safe stuffed with money was located in Sam Ravel's general store. Pancho had some unfinished business with Ravel. He had placed an order with Ravel and paid him for guns and ammunition. However, Ravel never delivered the merchandise, nor did he give back the money. Pancho was going to take care of that matter. With this raid he would get his money and the supplies he desperately needed. His orders to his men were simple. Surprise the gringos and loot all buildings.

Columbus was a small, dusty town of about five hundred people located just over the Mexican border. It had a thriving business district that included two hotels, a newspaper, a bank, and a post office. It also had Camp Furlough.

The US military set up small army outposts along the border in an attempt to stop the increasing incursion of Mexican bandits and rustlers. Camp Furlough was one of these outposts. It normally had about five hundred men and twenty-one officers, but on this day had fewer. Many of the officers were out of town, including the commanding officer, Colonel Herbert Slocum, who, with his wife, was visiting Deming.

The army camp at Columbus made the plan for a raid even more audacious and appealing to Pancho. However, Villa never counted on the heavy losses he would sustain. Four hundred Villistas started their trek toward Columbus. More than a hundred would never make it home.

Dawn was still hiding behind the mountains when Sergeant Ellery Waters finished checking his five posts and picket lines. That's when the guard, Private Fred Griffin, noticed movement in the darkness. He called for the password, and when silence greeted him, he started shooting.

The early morning peace erupted in gunfire. Then there were shouts of "viva Mexico," "viva Villa," "death to the gringos." The bandits overran Griffin, killing him. The charging Villistas shot indiscriminately. A wayward bullet hit the railroad clock, stopping it at 4:30 a.m.

When Sergeant Waters heard the shots, he took off for the orderly room, unlocking it as the Mexican raiders filled the streets. He stood by the door, guarding the rifles within and triggering off twenty-one rounds from his service pistol to keep the bandits at bay.

Sergeant Burns unlocked the rifle case as troopers came running in to grab weapons. The ammunition, however, was in the locked supply room, and no one could find the sergeant who held the key. Turns out he was hiding under the water tank. Burns and Waters broke down the door and rapidly handed out bandoleers of .30-06 cartridges to the scrambling troopers.

Two soldiers were early casualties when bullets pierced their wooden barracks walls, killing them. Corporal Harry Wiswell died near the border gate, and Private Jessie Taylor died from his wounds the next day at the Fort Bliss hospital.

Two of the Villistas had orders to go to Sam Ravel's home and capture Sam and his two brothers. They were to take them to the store, force Sam to open the safe, and then shoot him. But when Ortiz and Vargas arrived at the Ravel house, they found only the youngest brother, Arthur, a boy of fifteen. Louis was hiding under a pile of hides. The men dragged Arthur to the store and ordered him to open the safe. When it became apparent that the younger Ravel did not have the combination, the Mexicans attempted to get into the safe by shooting at the knob. The gunfire caused the gasoline drums in front of an adjacent store to explode, and both stores caught fire.

Meanwhile, Lieutenants John Lucas and J. P. Castleman went for the army's machine guns. They were able to answer the bandits' shots with a steady flow of bullets, and slowly the army's greater firepower began to take its toll on the raiders. Sergeant Harry Dobbs held the line for Lieutenant Castleman and the troopers as they prepared their defense line in front of the Hoover Hotel. Fatally wounded, Sergeant Dobbs stayed in position firing until he died from loss of blood. Sergeant Dobbs was recommended for a Medal of Honor; unfortunately, it was never approved.

A group of Villa's men headed for the hotel to sack the rooms. Here they met Uncle Stephan Birchfield. Awakened from his sleep, an irritated Uncle Stephan told the looters to stop making so much noise. They had him in their gun sights when he presented them with a proposition. If they let him go, he would write checks made out to cash for them. One man in the group had had dealings with Uncle Stephan and knew him to be good for his word. While machine guns and rifles were blazing around him, Uncle Stephan wrote checks and lived.

Mexicans set fire to the wooden-frame Columbus Hotel, but not before they captured the proprietor, William Ritchie. His daughter begged the raiders not to kill her father. Her pleas went unheeded, however. They shot him and burned his body along with the hotel. Juan Favela was able to rescue the rest of the Ritchies. Most of the Columbus Hotel guests fled the fire by running out the back door and through the backyard. John Walker and Dr. H. M. Hart died when they tried to escape out the front door.

When the shooting started, Charles Miller left his hotel room to get rifles from his drugstore. He made it as far as the hotel door. Milton James and his pregnant wife, Bessie, made a run for the Hoover Hotel and its protecting thick adobe walls. They were shot as they reached the door. Will Hoover pulled Bessie into the hotel. Her last words were, "Thank God we are safe."

Alice Bains, a sister of Bessie James, found the hotel office filled with Mexicans. In fear she ran between the buildings and out into the bush and hid until daylight, when she saw the Villistas retreating.

Later, Mrs. Sara Hoover wrote her brother about the shocking events:

> *Our soldiers and our citizens never dreamed that Villa would*
> *cross the border to murder innocent women and children.*
> *They did think he might cross to steal horses and cattle, and*

*our soldiers were scattered along the border. Our people think
Villa has had spies here who have kept him informed of the
troops along the border, and he could safely cross the line and
murder a lot of American citizens, which would bring on war
and unite the Mexicans. He must have known that in the end
the Mexicans would be defeated, yet he would hold a high place
in Mexican affairs . . . there will be no war and Villa will be
hunted down as a bandit and murderer and will lose his life.*

Young Arthur Ravel saved the life of Sara Hoover's son Will when he convinced the bandits that Will was out of town. Will Hoover was the owner of the
Hoover Hotel, the town banker, and its mayor.

As the Villistas headed for the bank, soldiers opened fire. One bandito lay
dead in front of the hotel, six others lined the street, and bandito bodies were
scattered over the other main streets of Columbus.

As dawn broke over the smoking, devastated town, a broken and beaten
bandito band regrouped and retreated. Except for the devastation, they had
accomplished none of their objectives. They left about one hundred of their comrades dead and seven as wounded prisoners. Ten American officers and soldiers
lost their lives, as did eight civilians. Two officers, five soldiers, and two civilians
suffered wounds.

One of the wounded bandits was a young boy of twelve. He pleaded for his
life, saying he was told the gringos would kill him if he were captured. Jesus came
from a poor village. His job with the banditos was to clean and care for their
horses. He told his captors that once, due to exhaustion on a long trail ride, he fell
out of his saddle, and the officers beat him and told him to keep going.

The *Deming Headlight* reported the boy's story on March 17, 1916. He told
the interrogators that he was the boy who held Pablo Lope's horse. Pablo was
Villa's second in command. The paper reported the interrogation:

*Twice as he talked he asked for a book that he always keeps with
him and reads whenever he can. It is a story of India and is
called A Fallen Idol. As the shadows lengthened the little bandit
spoke only in soft short sentences, the morphine was doing its
work, he was almost asleep, but he roused himself and said, "Me
bueno muchacho" (I am a good boy). He was asleep. Pancho
Villa has very, very much to answer for to his God.*

As the Villistas retreated, Major Frank Tompkins mounted up two troops
of cavalry and chased after them. He kept up a running fight, crossing the border
and venturing fifteen miles into Mexican land. Major Tompkins's troops did

severe damage to the Villistas. Seventy-five bandits were reported killed, and more wounded. The major's troops suffered no losses. Pancho Villa's bandits were badly beaten, scattered, and on the run. Unfortunately, the cavalry had to return to New Mexico Territory when they ran out of ammunition. Nevertheless, it was an exhausted and triumphant troop that rode into Columbus.

The United States would not let Villa's bandito raid go unpunished. Five days after the attack, General "Black Jack" Pershing organized a punitive expedition using the 7th, 10th, and 13th Cavalry Regiments. Also under his command was the aviation section of the Signal Corps. The squadron had eight outdated airplanes that were underpowered and weighted down with armor plate. Only three were armed. Their commander was Captain Benjamin, who had learned his craft from Orville Wright. Also assigned to Pershing were several motorized vehicles, including some that were the forerunner of the modern tank.

Mule trains carried fuel for the motorized vehicles. Motor vehicles were so new to the army that there were no experienced drivers. Accustomed to urging on their mounts and pack animals, the inexperienced drivers cried to their vehicles with yells of "whoa" and "giddyup." The "flying machines" and motorized vehicles proved to have many problems and were not effective in the desert.

Pershing's troops eventually traveled 1,400 miles into Mexican territory. They were engaged in several skirmishes, but never found Villa. After eleven months the punitive action was called off.

But Villa's bandit gang had been destroyed, and he was never again a major threat. The failed Columbus raid was his last chance for glory. In 1923 Pancho Villa was assassinated in Parral, Mexico, and his body was beheaded.

Ironically, the punitive expedition that the raid prompted was the last hurrah for the mounted cavalry, their last chance for glory. Lessons learned with the motorized vehicles and flying machines led to their successful use in World War I, when the roar of engines replaced the sound of hoofbeats forever.

The true motivation for Villa's attack has never been determined. Certainly Villa wanted to gain the attention and respect of his people at a time when his country was in turmoil and its leadership undetermined. Glory was another possible goal. In addition, if Villa had been cheated of the arms he purchased from Sam Ravel, revenge could have been another reason for the attack. But there is no proof he actually purchased merchandise from Ravel; it is more likely he was hoping to secure more arms and money by robbing the store. Although he had many men, some with military rank, his group lacked the discipline, the leadership, the recognition, and the formal structure of an army. They were a large number of bandits brought together with promises of riches and dreams and personal gain. Their attack on a small town was unprovoked, not driven by international politics, and amounted to nothing more than a large outlaw raid. Villa is still considered the Mexican outlaw who raided a town.

HOODOO BROWN AND THE DODGE CITY GANG

Black Magic and the Reign of Dirty Justice

In 1879 the railroad arrived in Las Vegas, New Mexico. So did Hyman G. Neill. Crowds watched the train pull into town on its first run. No one saw Neill arrive. One minute he wasn't there, and the next he was. Many said it was magic. If it was, it turned out to be black magic, for the kind of magic Neill performed captured Las Vegas in a net of evil, crime, outlaws, and terror. Because of that, Hyman G. Neill would be known from that time on as Hoodoo Brown.

There was nothing really distinguishing about Neill, nothing that stood out from the many men who ventured west. He was described by one newspaper as a tall, thin man with light brown hair and a mustache. The newspaper went on to note that he had a rakish look about him. The look was deceiving. He was anything but a charming rascal. He was a dangerous man.

Serious trouble started for Las Vegas in 1879. For the perpetrator of Las Vegas's trouble, Hyman G. Neill, it started after the Civil War in the small southern town of Johannesburg, Missouri. That's when Neill realized that he did not like hard work. He also did not like taking orders. Right then he had a belly full of both, and he made a decision. It was in the late 1860s, and he was working as a printer's devil, a job he detested almost as much as he disliked his boss. The teenager was sick and tired of the printer and his demands. When the printer ordered him to get clean rags for the printing, it was the last straw for the young man. He was not about to spend his life obeying someone else's orders and setting up presses. He was not interested in a life of hard, honest labor.

At the printer's latest demand, Neill headed out the back door, telling him he was going to "get your darn rags," and with those words Neill kept right on going. He left not only the printer, but also Johannesburg, Missouri, and never looked back. He hopped a freight train and followed the railroad out west.

Neill's father originally brought his family to Johannesburg, Missouri, from the southern town of Lexington. He was an ardent southerner and wanted to join the Confederacy, but as a lawyer felt he could not turn his back on his oath to support the Constitution. Therefore, he pledged to the Union. Torn between his love of the South and his loyalty to his profession, he felt it necessary to move to another location. The recent death of his wife further cemented his decision.

After Neill left his printing job, he spent the following years doing what he felt like doing—or what he had to do to keep alive. Around 1872 he did some buffalo hunting and hauled lumber. Much more to his liking, he became a gambler, confidence man, and trickster, what some called a conjure man. Neill worked the silver mines in Colorado, but it was hard work, not at all what he had in mind when he left Missouri. His wanderings took him down to Mexico, where he ran a successful opera house for a time. But even that was not enough to satisfy the ambitious Neill.

Neill was a man ideally suited by temperament and talent for the lawless West. When he arrived in Las Vegas, he found the perfect setting to practice his preferred way of life. It was a match made in hell for the town. In the late 1800s Las Vegas was a mere spot on the road, a stepsister to the bigger towns surrounding it. Located in the middle of nowhere, this sleepy town was 68 miles east of Santa Fe. Taos was 78 miles north, the big city of Albuquerque was 123 miles away, and the sinful city of Denver was just over 300 miles distant. Las Vegas was far enough away from the eyes of legitimate lawmen in the more populated towns and just big enough for Hoodoo to control.

When Neill arrived in Las Vegas, he found saloons and gambling halls, a few hotels, and several merchants supplying the needs of the five thousand townspeople and those who lived in the countryside. However, with the arrival of the railroad, Las Vegas would not remain a small village for long. Neill knew it would grow with settlers looking for a new start in the West, but he planned to have control by the time that happened.

Neill was not the only one to arrive with the railroad. The minions that would enable him to keep the town in his clutches came pouring into the village. Kicked out of the Kansas town from which they took their name by a vigilante group that had enough, these men became collectively known as the Dodge City Gang. One by one they joined up with Neill, who was now known as Hoodoo.

By the time these lawless men got to Las Vegas, Hoodoo was the elected justice of the peace, as well as the acting coroner. Must be black magic, the town grumbled, for no one remembered an election. No one remembered voting Hoodoo in. With the power now invested in him, he began appointing the kind of men he wanted to serve in the running of the town. That's when the quiet village of Las Vegas began changing.

The town soon discovered that the tough new faces in town were not just passing through; they were staying because Hoodoo gave them a reason to call Las Vegas home. He appointed them to law enforcement and judicial positions. Las Vegas law and order was now controlled by the lawless.

Hoodoo established a police force made up mostly of the Kansas gunfighters. He paid for his exclusive police force by collecting money from the town's merchants, who paid premiums for "protection." Well-known names served at various times on Hoodoo's police force. They included Joe Carson, Mysterious Dave Mather, Dirty Dave Rudabaugh, John Joshua Webb, Jack Lyons, Dan Miller, Charles Jones, Tom Pickett, and Tetchy Thunderbolt.

Hoodoo's law enforcers were not the only notorious men in town. Passing through, or settling for a brief time, were Doc Holliday and his companion Big-Nose Kate, Rattlesnake Sam, Cock-Eyed Frank, Web-fingered Billy, Hook Nose Jim, and Stuttering Tom. The Durango Kid and Handsome Harry the Dancehall Rustler called Las Vegas home at one time or another. Their names were more than colorful sobriques—they described personalities. Hoodoo's judicial policies made Las Vegas a safe haven for all sorts of questionable characters.

Among the numerous outlaws who were appointed by Hoodoo to public law enforcement positions were Carson, who was made the city marshal; Mather, who served as deputy US marshal; and Webb, who was hired as a policeman. Many of Hoodoo's law enforcers walked both sides of the line. The Dodge City Gang members committed acts of crime, and it was the job of Hoodoo, Mather, Webb and the others to cover their tracks and see to it that they were never accused. Hoodoo's aide-de-camp was John Dutchy Schunderberger, a big man with talented fists. He was the man you wanted with you if trouble started. The *Las Vegas Optic* considered it an obligation to report on Hoodoo and his law enforcement officers. Schunderberger was one of their favorite newspaper topics.

In a January 10, 1880, article, the *Las Vegas Optic* wrote of Dutchy's rescue of two of Hoodoo's policemen.

> *Last night Jack Lyons made an arrest of one of Montezuma's frail daughters, and two Mexicans came to her rescue and [she] was about to get away with Jack. He whistled for Joe Carson to put in an appearance, but the Mexicans were about to prove too much for both of them, when Dutchy suddenly turned up and dispensed a little Dutch justice by striking out from the shoulder and letting one of the Ms. have it under the butt of the ear. Joe thinks the fellow is turning somersaults yet. The daughter languished in the cooler last night.*

The men who served Hoodoo left a colorful outlaw history in their wake. They associated with the most feared men in the West and committed acts of violence and crime. Among those whose names are forever emblazed in the criminal annals of the West are Joshua (J. J.) Webb, who owned a saloon with Doc Holliday and rode with Bat Masterson during Bat's lawless days; Rudabaugh, who was a saddle mate and fellow gang member of Billy the Kid; and Mather, who cut a swath through the West with his robberies and murders. They all either met the hangman's noose, were gunned down, or disappeared from jail, never to be heard from again.

Hoodoo ran his town with a heavy hand. He opened court sessions by seating himself, then saying, "Myself and partner will now open court." At that he would point to his partner, a large, double-barreled Winchester resting against the side of his desk, well within view of the court attendees. His legal judgments were at times very unorthodox and certainly not based on any of this land's known law. The *Las Vegas Gazette* reported on this interesting case in their November 1, 1879, issue.

> *Thursday evening a young man named Marshall when settling his bill at the Parker house had a dispute with K.P. Brown and invited him outdoors. On getting out, Marshall drew a pistol and stuck it in Brown's face. Brown returned to the office but could not get a pistol. Later in the evening someone had Marshall arrested and taken before Justice Neill in the new town, who after hearing evidence complimented both parties on their good looks and genteel appearance and advised them to divide the cost, which done, the case was dismissed.*

As justice of the peace, one of Hoodoo's responsibilities was joining couples in legal matrimony. Since he was new on the job, he decided to practice before his first official ceremony. The rehearsal was recorded in the *Las Vegas Optic* on December 26, 1879.

> *Squire Neill spliced his first couple Christmas Eve. He stood Joe Carson and Dutchy up on the floor and practiced on them before starting for the house where the bride and groom awaited him. Passers-by thought he was reading the riot act to Joe and Dutchy. He has hoo-dooed them for life, though.*

Within one year of Hoodoo and his appointees becoming the law, there was an increase of killings in the Las Vegas area. The victims were either murdered, shot in what was determined to be self-defense, or, in a few cases, hanged by the vigilance committee—a "committee" closely controlled and regulated by Hoodoo.

On August 18, 1879, a Barlow and Sanderson stagecoach was robbed near the village of Tecoliote, New Mexico. Three men were arrested but never convicted. On August 30 the same stage line was again robbed by men with ties to Hoodoo's Dodge City Gang. They were arrested and charged but again not convicted, and they soon went free. Several years later Rudabaugh and Carson confessed to the robberies.

That same year, on October 14, a train was robbed on the outskirts of Las Vegas. The masked men got away with more than two thousand dollars, three pistols, and the train lanterns. In later years Rudabaugh confessed to his part in that robbery, but it was in order to avoid prosecution for a more serious crime. Charlie Bassett, Chalk Beeson, and Harry E. Gyden, all formerly of Dodge City, along with Webb, were hired by the Adams Express Company to investigate the robbery, even though Webb was one of the a suspects.

Hoodoo appointed some of his men to coroner's juries. It was their responsibility to determine if the victim committed suicide, was murdered, or killed in self-defense. Often Hoodoo's jurors were passing judgment on victims they had helped bring to their present state of death. Invariably in these cases, they determined the cause of the victims' deaths to be self-defense.

It didn't take long for the citizens of Las Vegas to realize that Hoodoo was not a man to defy. They believed that he would always get his own way either through his corrupt legal practices or with the arts of black magic.

The rest of the country took note of the happenings in Las Vegas. The town was getting a reputation as one of the most lawless and dangerous places in the West. The *Dodge City Times* reported that violence and thievery prevailed, and that "shooting scrapes are of frequent occurrence in that remote region." When twenty-nine men were killed in the Las Vegas area in one month, the future governor of New Mexico, Miguel Otero, wrote that Las Vegas had become the home to all the lowlifes from Kansas, Texas, and Colorado. It offered a safe haven to every outlaw that rode in the West. Even Billy the Kid and Jesse James passed through town. But neither joined the gang or stayed long enough to become part of Hoodoo's law enforcement.

By the beginning of 1880, the citizens of Las Vegas had had enough, and things started falling apart for Hoodoo and his justice system. The honest residents of the town gathered their courage and took matters into their own hands. It started when Webb was arrested for a shooting he insisted was self-defense, but because he was a member of the Dodge City Gang and was suspected of several robberies, he was sent to jail. Rudabaugh's outlaw ways caught up with him, and he too was sent to jail. Unfortunately, both Webb and Rudabaugh escaped and never served their sentences. The prisoners chipped a stone out of their cell wall in the old town jail, creating a seventeen-by-nineteen-inch hole that was big enough to set them free.

Over the next few months, gang members, seeing their power and protection eroding, left town. Their decision to depart was helped along by this notice posted in the *Las Vegas Optic* on April 8, 1880:

To Murderers, Confidence Men, Thieves;

*The citizens of Las Vegas have tired of robbery, murder,
and other crimes that have made this town a byword in every
civilized community. They have resolved to put a stop to crime,
if in attaining that end they have to forget the law and resort
to a speedier justice than it will afford. All such characters are
therefore, hereby notified, that they must either leave this town
or conform themselves to the requirement of law, or they will be
summarily dealt with.*

*The flow of blood must and shall be stopped in this
community, and the good citizens of both the old and new
towns have determined to stop it if they have to HANG by the
strong arm of FORCE every violator of the law in this country.*

—Vigilantes

In 1880 an important citizen known only as Kelliher was killed. The outraged citizens put up a seven-thousand-dollar reward for the killer. Hoodoo, who was still the law in East Las Vegas, formed a posse to capture the killer and, of course, the reward. Hoodoo's actions infuriated the citizens, who believed that Hoodoo had played a part in the murder and had also stolen money from the dead man.

A newly formed vigilante group got rid of the mayor and then went after Hoodoo, forcing him out of town and out of the state. Running for his life and realizing that a posse was now after him, Hoodoo hightailed it to Houston, Texas, where he was arrested and charged with murder and robbery.

Two months earlier one of Hoodoo's deputies had been shot and killed. The widow had the body exhumed and, traveling with her dead husband, also headed for Houston. She visited Hoodoo in jail, where they had a rather touching reunion. The reunion was reported by the *Parsons Sun* newspaper: "The meeting of the pair is said to have been affecting in the extreme, and rather more affectionate than would be expected under the circumstances."

The Parsons Eclipse wrote:

> *The offense committed at Las Vegas, as near as we can gather
> the facts relating to it, was murder and robbery, and the
> circumstances connected with the arrest here would indicate that
> the lesser crime of seduction and adultery was connected with it.*

Hoodoo wasn't about to languish in jail while his true love was so near. He hired a couple of local lawyers who proved that the police had no authority to hold him. Hoodoo was set free and being a wise man immediately left town.

Even the *Chicago Times* got in on this bizarre affair. In typical big city style, they reported that Hoodoo and the widow, accompanied by her dead husband and his coffin, "have been skylarking through some of the interior towns of Kansas ever since."

And, with that, Hyman G. Neill, aka Hoodoo Brown, dropped out of the public eye—but not, it seems, out of his family. Years later a descendant of Hoodoo reported that his famous relative had died in Coattail, or, as some reported, Torreson, Mexico. Two of his brothers went to Mexico and retrieved his remains. They brought his body back to Lexington, Missouri, along with a son born to Hoodoo and his common-law wife. Nothing is mentioned about the wife accompanying her son or what happened to her. Hoodoo was laid to rest in the family plot under a headstone engraved HYMAN G. NEILL.

Years later a woman in Leadbelly, Colorado, insisted she was Elizabeth Brown, the widow of Hoodoo Brown. She said he had died in a gambling argument in Mexico. Mrs. Brown was known to be a heavy drinker, so her report was viewed with some skepticism.

What happened to the most corrupt town in the West after Hoodoo's law and all the outlaws, thieves, and murderers were run out of town? Well, the *Las Vegas Optic* summed it up.

> *Not so many killings to chronicle this week. Indeed, Las Vegas is a civil, law abiding but lively place. Life and limb are as safe here as anywhere on the globe; however, if you want a shooting match, just for the fun of the thing, you needn't leave town for the purpose of hunting a cowboy. You can be accommodated here.*

OKLAHOMA OUTLAWS

NED CHRISTIE

A Man with Two Faces

Deputy US Marshal Dan Maples, a well-respected lawman, was in Indian Territory searching for outlaws. He and his small posse—which included his young son Sam—camped close to the Big Spring, a plentiful source of water. Maples and a posse man went into town for supplies and, on the way back, walked into an ambush. It happened as they were crossing Spring Branch Creek, using a log that served as a bridge.

Posse man Jefferson, in the lead, saw somebody's shiny revolver in a thicket ahead. The holder of the revolver fired twice, and Maples went down. He managed to pull his revolver and fire four times into the thicket, but the attacker vanished. Officers investigating the murder scene soon found a black coat with a bullet hole in it, what was left of a whiskey bottle in the pocket.

Maples died the next day, and at least one local citizen's life would never be the same. Ned Christie's existence in Oklahoma was about to become news.

Over the years a great deal of chatter has abounded over Ned Christie as a career outlaw, and most tales paint him as a wanton killer. Consider this passage from the WPA *Writers' Project* back in 1938.

> *Eleven murders were credited to Christie. Among his victims were two officers, an Indian woman and a half-breed boy. He was born a killer, cold blooded, ruthless; no one knew when or where he would strike next. . . .*
>
> *[A]long the isolated paths to the lonely cabins of settlers he stalked relentless in his maniacal hatred.*

Christie was a Cherokee, described as a tall, lean, good-looking man who wore his hair long in the old tribal fashion. He came from a well-known, respected family; he was one of the sons of Watt Christie, an expert blacksmith who came west sometime in the 1830s to settle in the Goingsnake District of the Cherokee Nation.

Watt was an active, successful farmer who also carried on the smithing trade. He had several wives, a common and legal practice. Watt's extended family eventually produced eleven children, seven boys and four girls . . . or maybe it was twenty-one, depending on what account you read.

Ned was deeply bitter over the encroachment of white immigrants into the Cherokee Nation, the advance of the railroads, the planned allotment of parcels of land to individual Cherokees, and increasing agitation for statehood for the entire territory. He certainly opposed all of these things as a violation of Cherokee sovereignty, and he did not mince words about his position.

Thus far he had been a peaceful man, save for a charge of killing a young Cherokee, of which he was acquitted. But because of the events on the dark night near Big Spring, now he was suspected of the murder of Deputy US Marshal Maples, a well-known veteran federal officer.

Maples and a small posse were camped close to Tahlequah, the Cherokee capital. Whatever Maples's mission, it appeared to be fairly routine, at least as routine as any job the marshals had to do. The territory was dangerous country, where any lawman was at risk. In the end more than sixty deputy marshals would die in the line of duty in this wild area, described by a newspaper of the time as the "rendezvous of the vile and wicked from everywhere."

At the time of the murder, Christie was in Tahlequah. As a tribal legislator, he had come to attend a special meeting of the Cherokee Council. The Cherokee National Female Seminary had burned down, and that tragedy had deprived the Nation of both a handsome building and the venue for the free education of young Cherokee women. The council met in emergency session to decide what action to take to replace their school.

The marshals arrested one John Parris, who lived in a disreputable part of Tahlequah called Dog Town and had spent some time on the wrong side of the law. Parris is variously described as a drinking companion or an accomplice of Christie in the Maples murder. After his arrest the hunt for Ned Christie began.

Christie and Parris were probably together on the evening of the shooting and ended up in Dog Town. That evening, according to one account, Parris and Christie left a friend's house very drunk. That was not long before Marshal Maples was murdered nearby.

In the most reliable version of what happened that night, Parris and Christie met three other Indian men. One of the three was the egregiously bad Bub Trainor, and one of the others had seen the inside of a federal prison at least twice.

A story later surfaced that another man had watched in the darkness as Bub Trainor had stolen Christie's coat as he had slept, then worn it to cut down the marshal. That same tale asserts that the dying Maples's return fire tore through Christie's coat and knocked the neck from a whiskey bottle in the pocket. Christie had bought a bottle of moonshine from Nancy Shell, who ran a Tahlequah bootleg joint, and the bottle in his coat was still plugged with a piece of Nancy's apron, torn off as a makeshift stopper. That bit of glass and strip of apron were damning evidence against Christie.

Christie woke the next day to find himself one of the suspects in the killing of Maples. Also on the short list of murderers were Parris, Parris's brother, and two other Cherokee men. All of them had been spotted near the creek at about the time of the murder. Nancy Shell identified the scrap of cloth that plugged the broken bottle's neck. She also admitted that she had sold the bottle to Christie and Parris.

Christie might have come in and surrendered to stand trial in Fort Smith, but he chose to stay away from the town. According to one tale, he wanted to turn himself in, but others convinced him that he should run. In another story Christie sent a messenger to Fort Smith, asking district judge Isaac Parker to set bail, something Parker could hardly do for a man accused of the ambush murder of a federal officer.

In September 1889 veteran Deputy Marshal Heck Thomas led a serious attempt to arrest Christie. He took a posse of four men, including Deputy Marshal L. P. Isbel out of Vinita. The lawmen managed to avoid Christie's watchers, moving in slowly at night, until Christie's house was surrounded. Then Christie's dogs started barking, and the fight was on.

Christie fired from a loft window while his wife and son reloaded his rifle and pistols and handed them up to him. In an effort to break the stalemate, the posse set fire to Christie's gun shop near the house. But as Isbel leaned out from behind a tree, Christie drilled him through the right shoulder. The marshal went down, badly hurt, and Thomas hurried to help Isbel, fixing a temporary dressing around the wound.

As the flames from Christie's shop spread through the brush around the house, Christie's wife ran from the house, followed by his son, then Christie himself. Thomas fired on the fleeing figures through the smoke, putting a bullet through the younger Christie's lung. Christie himself took a round from Thomas's rifle. It smashed into his temple, tore out his right eye, and ripped loose much of the structure of the nasal bones. Christie kept going, however, and vanished into the woods. Thomas and two of his posse men briefly looked for their quarry, but Isbel was badly wounded, and Thomas's most pressing task was getting him back to medical help at Fort Smith.

Christie, Christie's son, and Isbel would all recover from their wounds. Isbel's arm was paralyzed, however, and he bid good-bye to the marshal service. Christie was terribly disfigured, no longer the handsome man he had been. From that day forward, deeply bitter, he spoke no word of English but conversed entirely in Cherokee.

Christie's kin and his friends improved his fortifications while he recovered from his terrible wound. The new lair was not far from his old home but this time was built within a rock formation on a hill that afforded good views in every direction. The rock formed a thick wall that no bullet could possible pierce.

Christie was undisturbed for a while, because it was obvious that only a very strong posse had any chance to root him out. Some people thought it would take US troops. And in the interim Christie rebuilt his home on a new site, strategically close to a spring. The new place would be called Ned's Fort. The walls were two parallel lines of logs, the space between the logs filled with sand. The walls inside were lined with oak, giving even more protection against rifle bullets. Upstairs there were no windows, only firing ports for defense.

Christie finished his new place in 1891, and a little while later the law tried again. This time the leader was an experienced deputy marshal named Dave Rusk. Rusk was a one-time Confederate officer and a crack shot. He had been a lawman for more than fifteen years when he set off to besiege Christie.

He chose a posse composed mostly of Cherokees who were not well disposed toward Christie, but his first try at Ned's Fort ended in fiasco with four of his Indian posse men wounded. For the moment he retired, but Rusk was tough and persistent. He would come again.

Rusk was back on the hunt in October of 1892. This time he led five other deputy marshals, but again the mission ended in failure. Rusk called to Christie to give up, which may have been a mistake. For Christie answered the challenge to surrender with a gobbling sound one writer called the "Cherokee death cry" and gunfire, and two deputy marshals went down, badly wounded.

Now several women and children ran out of Ned's Fort, and they told the lawmen that not only was Christie inside the fortress, but also three other Cherokee men. Rusk looked about for a better solution than going head-on against this bulletproof house. He found his answer in a rickety wagon, which the lawmen soon filled with brush and logwood. They set fire to it and then rolled it flaming into the side of the fort, hoping to burn Christie out. Trouble was, the battered wagon disintegrated on contact with the log wall, and the fire went out before it could do major damage.

Their next weapon was several sticks of dynamite lashed together. The fuse was lit and one of the posse threw the package against the side of Christie's lair. As the dynamite struck the wall, however, the fuse fell loose, and so that attempt fizzled out. Now the deputies sent a messenger into Tahlequah with instructions to wire headquarters at Fort Smith for more help. The rest of the lawmen returned to their futile siege of the log building. In the end they ran out of ammunition and had to retreat.

Another expedition against Ned's Fort was led by Paden Tolbert, a tough, experienced deputy marshal. Tolbert talked the matter over with US Marshal Jacob Yoes and Judge Parker and quietly recruited four more men, plus a fifth man to cook for the posse. Even their initial meeting was held in the dead of night. Nobody was going to take a chance that some early warning might reach Christie.

The next day the group took the train to Fort Smith, where they met John Tolbert, Paden's brother, and five more men. The group then met up with three more posse members, including Sam Maples, young son of the dead deputy marshal. One version of the fight that followed has Christie besieged by no fewer than twenty-seven posse men.

And the posse acquired an unusual piece of crime-fighting equipment. It was a small cannon, about four feet long, with forty rounds to go with it.

Other lawmen joined the posse before it moved west across the Arkansas, including Heck Bruner, one of the best of the deputy marshals, and the experienced Will Smith, who was part Cherokee. The posse now numbered about twenty-five men, and Cherokee Sheriff Ben Knight—no partisan of Christie—agreed to guide them into the heart of Christie's lair.

Logically, Christie should have known this small army was coming. The lawmen could not move rapidly, and there could be no hiding so many armed men and a mule-drawn wagon loaded with a cannon and heaps of supplies from the vigilant eyes in Christie country.

The trip in was uneventful, however, and shortly after nightfall the party reached a spot behind a ridge not far from their target. Dinner was tinned sardines and crackers, for the lawmen did not build a fire. In spite of the size of their force, they still had some hope that their approach had gone undetected.

About four o'clock the next morning, the lawmen moved to their positions. Tolbert, Rusk, and two others moved the wagon to the point they had selected to get the cannon into position. With the little gun ready to fire across a creek in front of Ned's Fort, the law was ready.

About daybreak a man carrying a water bucket emerged from the cabin and headed toward the spring. Tolbert shouted to the figure to surrender, but the man dropped the bucket and dove back inside the house.

Tolbert shouted again. He is said to have told Christie they were prepared to stay this time until Christie was taken, and that he had no means of escape. Nothing happened. Then Tolbert shouted to Christie to send out any women and children who were inside the cabin. In response three Cherokee women and a child emerged from the cabin door. Cherokee lawman Knight asked one of them who was inside helping Christie, but the women would not speak.

Now Tolbert tried again, yelling to the cabin that the posse would not leave until Christie was captured or dead. The answer was gunfire. The battle continued as the morning wore away, and gradually a group of onlookers began to form. Among them was Christie's father, Watt. Ben Knight went to Watt and asked him to help persuade his son to surrender. The father refused.

The lawmen turned to the little cannon, loaded it with black powder and something called a "bullet-wedge" projectile, and opened fire. But the heavy log walls held up through thirty-seven rounds, dented and splintered but still intact.

With only three rounds left, Tolbert tried doubling the powder charge, but all that accomplished was splitting the barrel of the cannon. Night was falling by now, and Tolbert began to send his men back to camp in pairs for something to eat.

He began to explore other ways to get into the fort. His eyes lit on the rear axle of the wagon that had disintegrated during the earlier siege. It was still intact. He sent men to Christie's own sawmill then, and they brought back heavy boards and used them to build a rolling barricade atop the axle, a sort of mobile shield to cover an approach to Christie's fort. The thing would be guided by the tongue of the destroyed wagon, used as a sort of lever to push the structure near the building.

The plan was for Charlie Copeland, an officer, to carry an explosive charge, six sticks of dynamite, advancing behind the shield as three more officers pushed it toward the cabin with the remaining officers providing covering fire. When they got near enough, Copeland would dash to the cabin wall and place his charge of dynamite against it.

And so, about midnight, four officers rolled the oak shield close to the logs of the cabin wall. As planned, Copeland placed the dynamite, lit the fuse, and sprinted back to the protection of the shield. They pulled the shield back a safe distance as the fuse smoked and sputtered.

A colossal blast caved in the wall of the fort and knocked over a stove inside. Now fire followed the explosion, and by dawn great gouts of flame were shooting up from the structure, garish against the coming light. Gunfire from the fort had died away. All the posse had to do was simply wait.

With one side of his fortress blown out and flames enveloping the cabin, Christie had no options left. Out of the fire and smoke, he ran suddenly, a pistol in each hand, gobbling his war cry and firing on the marshals hidden behind trees and logs and rocks. He must have known he was running to his death, charging straight ahead into those flaming rifles. And, in fact, he overran lawman Wess Bowman, who was lying on the ground. Bowman simply rolled over and shot Christie in the back of the head as he ran by.

The rest of the posse closed in then, holding their fire, but young Sam Maples ran up to empty two revolvers into what remained of Christie. The marshal's son had waited a long time to avenge his father.

An enterprising photographer emerged from the crowd of spectators and took everybody's picture. The lawmen hauled Christie's body into town and thence to Fayetteville, where everybody, the living and the dead, was loaded on the Fort Smith train. At various points Christie was propped up to take the usual photographs. In one of them somebody laid a Winchester across his folded arms. The posse also had their pictures taken again, and there was general rejoicing at the fall of a man most white people thought was Lucifer incarnate.

Not so among the Cherokee Nation. Many people, especially fellow Kee-toowahs, saw the fallen man as a hero who had resisted the encroachment of the white man's law. He was admired for his courage as well. Watt Christie claimed his son's body and returned it to a family burying ground near Rabbit Trap.

So passed Ned Christie, both vilified and canonized by reams of prose of greater or lesser accuracy. His story was powerful fodder for any number of writers, some of whom were not above making up a "fact" or two to beautify their tale. Other more reliable authors simply uncritically accepted the original story that Christie cold-bloodedly shot down Marshal Maples from ambush.

The notion that Christie had murdered Maples was badly shaken when, in 1922, an elderly blacksmith came forward to insist that Christie was innocent. He had seen Christie lying on the ground drunk, he said, and watched Bub Trainor pull Christie's coat from him. The blacksmith, Dick Humphrey, somehow suspected dirty work and hid to watch what happened next. And he saw Trainor talk to Parris, then check his own revolvers, and head toward the log bridge across the little creek.

Why didn't Humphrey come forward? Because Trainor had a great many friends among the outlaw fraternity, he said, and even after Trainor was shot down a few years later, Humphrey was still afraid to speak. Only as an old man did he decide to tell his tale to a newspaper in Tulsa. Christie was, probably, innocent and became a hunted man only because of the lies Parris told the lawmen to save his own skin, plus the damning evidence of the coat with its hole and whiskey bottle's neck.

And so ended the saga of Ned Christie, hero or villain, wrongfully accused victim or callous murderer. Leaving aside the myths and legends, one thing is certain: Christie was a very tough cookie indeed, an exceptionally brave fighting man, a dead shot, and a man of conviction.

HENRY STARR

More Banks than Any Other Man in America

Ex-marshal Floyd Wilson was riding with a fellow detective, hot on the trail of a budding outlaw known as Henry Starr. Unfortunately, the second detective had fallen some distance behind Wilson when the lawman rode up on his quarry. Alone and unsure just how dangerous this new outlaw might be, the lawman pulled his Winchester out of the saddle scabbard and shouted to Starr, "Hold up. I have a warrant for you."

Starr dismounted and drew his own rifle, yelling to Wilson he should be the one to hold up, and both men opened fire at a range of only about thirty yards. Wilson probably fired first, although that shot may have been simply a warning. In his usual whiny manner, Starr later asserted that he had "pleaded with him not to make me kill him, but he opened fire, the first ball breaking my saddle and two others passing close by."

In fact, the officer's rifle jammed after that single round, and Starr shot him down. Wilson pulled his pistol as he lay on the ground, but Starr shot him again, and then once more, and finally drove a third round point-blank into Wilson's chest. The last round pierced Wilson's heart. Starr turned away from the fallen officer, whose clothing still smoldered from the muzzle blast of Starr's rifle, swung up on Wilson's horse, and rode away. Starr's outlaw career was off with a bang.

Starr was related by marriage to Belle Starr, the Bandit Queen, much celebrated in print and celluloid. Though Belle was one of the West's most enduring legends, she was no queen, and she was also one of history's all-time overrated criminals. But Henry himself was the real thing, all wool and a yard wide; the papers called him the "Bearcat," but his real name truly was Henry Starr.

Through the years Starr gained a reputation as the country's greatest bank robber. When he started taking other people's money, the outlaw's favorite means of escape was the horse; by the time he finished his crooked career, he and the rest of America's robbers were carrying off their loot in automobiles.

Henry Starr was part Cherokee, born in Fort Gibson, Indian Territory, in December 1873. His father was George Starr, called "Hop," son of notorious old Tom Starr and brother to Sam Starr, the husband of the celebrated Belle. His mother, Mary Scott, was a much-respected lady. Starr got what he described as a sixth-grade education, and then entered the hard adult world of work and choices.

Henry Starr did some plowing and cow punching for a while, then graduated to stealing horses. He apparently considered himself something of a free spirit, born of the Cherokee lands, not a man ever to be constrained by mere laws. As he himself told a Kansas newspaper:

> *It was God overhead and nothing around. The world, our*
> *world, was ours and none to dispute. . . . We had been taught*
> *that it was ours, to have and to hold so long as grass grew*
> *and water ran, ours to hunt on, ours in which to follow in the*
> *footsteps of our fathers, to do with as we wished.*

Although he fancied himself an unfettered soul, or maybe because he did, Starr was given to blaming other people for his own shortcomings. And he blamed quite a lot of them: his stepfather, his boss, a lying witness, peace officers he said were venal and crooked, even what he called the bloody and corrupt federal court at Fort Smith.

He said, for example, that as a youngster, on his way to the site appointed for tribal payments, somebody he didn't know asked him to carry a valise to the place. Later, again according to him, deputy US marshals stopped him and found whiskey in the bag. He was, he said, badly mistreated by the lawmen, feeling the "murder-breeding leg-irons and chains." "Let any young man of ambition," he declaimed, "be shackled to a worthless perjurer and be carried 200 miles away from home, all the time being pointed out as a horse thief, to face a charge for which there is no iota of evidence . . . and what respect would he have for a law with such representatives?"

All of these people and entities, as Starr believed, drove him to a life of crime. Starr's whiny self-justification predictably excused his passage down the paths of unrighteousness, straight to a long career stealing other people's money, beginning in the summer of 1892 when he started out robbing a country store with a couple of second-rate hoodlums for backup.

He also stuck up the railway station at little Nowata, in company with career thugs Ed Newcomb and Jesse Jackson. As so often happened with Starr's confederates, however, the law quickly caught up with his cohorts: Newcomb served a long prison sentence, and Jackson killed himself in jail. Starr got away.

With practice Starr got pretty good at larceny, and he raised his sights. In December of that year, he visited Coffeyville, Kansas, where he bought wire cutters and gun holsters, in preparation for greater things. Starr apparently saw nothing wrong in jumping bail after one of his early crimes, leaving people who believed in him holding the bag, nor did his conscience seem to bother him when he hid out at the home of a friend and then stole the friend's money, about three hundred dollars, a substantial nest egg.

Floyd Wilson was probably the only man Starr ever killed, but that was hardly due to Starr's peaceable nature. The outlaw surely did a lot of pistol waving in his robbing days, and a good deal of indiscriminate shooting as well. Fortunately for the general public, he never hit anybody else, unless he did some quiet murdering that is not recorded.

Despite the outright murder of Wilson, Starr the outlaw started slow. Much of his early robbing was bush league, holdups of country stores, stealing from store tills and individual citizens indiscriminately. For instance, he and one Milo Creekmore stuck up a little country store in Lenapah, looking for a stockman's seven hundred dollars that was supposed to be held there. They followed that with another store robbery, in which they robbed the clerk of some five hundred dollars, magnanimously giving back to the fellow ten of the five hundred dollars so that he might have something with which to do business.

Starr and his growing gang certainly were not getting rich. They were, however, beginning to create a reputation. Late in March of 1893, Starr and outlaw Frank Cheney struck the Caney Valley National Bank in Caney, Kansas, riding off with about two thousand dollars. According to Starr, he and Cheney had already "sacked the town of Choteau, just to keep in form, without any trouble at all." And then, on May 2, Starr and his embryo gang—six men in addition to Starr—stuck up a Katy train at Pryor Creek in Indian Territory, making off with some five thousand dollars in jewelry and money.

The gang members seem to have considered themselves professional criminals rather than warriors for the working day and lived high on the hog. They expended at least one hundred rounds of ammunition per day in practice, Starr boasted, and ate "every delicacy to be obtained."

In June of 1893 Starr followed up his success on the Katy with an ambitious attempt to rob a bank in Bentonville, Arkansas, but Starr was cautious at the start of this one as he had the gang's rifles brought into town in a hired buggy to escape attention. But once the robbery began, the citizenry of Bentonville quickly learned that their bank was being robbed. These stout people reached for their weapons, and Starr ran for his life amidst a torrent of gunfire. One of his men, Link Cumplin, was badly shot up, although he managed to stay on his horse and clear the town. Like other Starr accomplices, Cumplin would finish the year dead from his wounds. One townsman took a round in the groin and another was wounded in the chin, but the gang was in full retreat, with a posse hot on their heels.

The gang would never ride together again. One, a morose man inevitably called "Happy Jack," was shot down two months later; a second was killed by lawmen in 1895. And Cheney had eaten his last meal, which was an officer's bullet to the head, in 1894.

As for Starr, he evaded the posse but was arrested not long afterward in Colorado Springs. After an ill-conceived jailbreak attempt, he faced a multitude of charges at Fort Smith. He was convicted of several robberies, and to add insult to injury, the People's Bank of Bentonville sued Starr for eleven thousand dollars looted from the bank. Starr denied the claim, even though he was carrying much of the money when he was arrested.

But the big charge, the deadly one, was the murder of Wilson. That trial, too, ended in conviction, and Starr faced Judge Isaac Parker for sentencing. Judge Parker was famous for his stern lectures to condemned criminals, hanging sentences, and dwelling at length not only on the vileness of their earthly crimes but also on the imminent and daily danger posed to their immortal souls. The judge gave Starr a twenty-minute speech on morality and salvation and sentenced him to die.

That should have been the end of Henry Starr, but it wasn't. The US Supreme Court reversed the conviction, and the matter was remanded and set for a second trial. Meanwhile, Starr remained in the Fort Smith jail with as choice a collection of murderers and other worthless scum as any lockup has ever held.

Crawford Goldsby, the bloody-handed felon better known as "Cherokee Bill," smuggled in a pistol. Nobody could get at Cherokee Bill, however, and he seemed to have plenty of ammunition. The standoff might have continued indefinitely, except for Henry Starr. Starr boldly walked into the cell where Cherokee Bill had taken refuge and talked him out of his weapon.

On retrial Starr was again convicted of the Wilson murder and again sentenced to death. And again the Supreme Court reversed. Judge Parker left the bench not long afterward and was replaced by Judge John Rogers. Judge Rogers entertained a plea of manslaughter, and Starr went off for a stiff prison term of thirteen years and eight months. Starr could behave well when he wanted to, and after his mother appeared before the Cherokee Council, that body appealed for clemency to President Theodore Roosevelt. In 1901, impressed with the story of Starr's cool intervention with Cherokee Bill, the president telegraphed Starr: "[W]ill you be good if I set you free?" Starr said he would, and so, by the beginning of 1903, Henry Starr was a free man.

Starr settled in Tulsa and married a schoolteacher, Miss Ollie Griffin. Starr was not without worries, however, for the Arkansas authorities had still not forgotten Bentonville; Starr was safe, however, for Oklahoma authorities refused to extradite him, relying on an attorney general's opinion that that action was unlawful as it affected a member of the Civilized Tribes. So Starr remained free and, for a time, apparently stayed away from the outlaw trail.

Eventually, the lure of the bank heist and easy money were too much for Starr. With Kid Wilson, an old criminal associate now on parole from New York, he struck a country bank in Tyro, Kansas. Things got so hot as a result that Starr and Wilson fled all the way to Colorado, where they robbed a tiny bank in Amity. Moving on to Arizona, Starr settled there under an alias. Traced by a letter he sent to Oklahoma, he was arrested in Arizona and returned to Colorado, where an unsympathetic court gave him seven to twenty-five years in the Cañon City penitentiary. In the fall of 1913, after his usual good behavior, Starr was paroled, on the one condition being that he not leave the state of Colorado.

And for a while he didn't. He opened a small restaurant, but that venture did not prosper, and in due course Starr abandoned the eatery and left Colorado, taking with him the comely wife of a local merchant. There followed a long string of robberies in Oklahoma, none of them big paydays. Rewards were posted—"dead or alive" this time—but Starr was hard to find, even though he was living in Tulsa. He even had the audacity to write the governor of Oklahoma, denying he had anything to do with any robberies, a profoundly unconvincing tactic reminiscent of Jesse James.

But Starr's luck was about to run out. In March of 1915 he decided to replenish his funds by raiding the bank in Stroud, a prosperous town about dead center in Oklahoma. He rode into town on horseback with six hoodlums to help him, a force that should have sufficed to cow the citizens of peaceful Stroud. And this gang should have been enough to accomplish the bank robber's ideal, the dream for which the Dalton Gang had gotten itself destroyed in Coffeyville twenty-three years before. They were going to rob two banks at once.

On March 27, 1915, at about 9:00 a.m., Starr and his crew rode into Stroud and set to work. At first the robbery went according to plan. Starr divided his force into two parties of three men, and they entered simultaneously the First National and the Stroud State Bank. Starr led the column that would raid the State Bank, brandishing a short rifle he had carried stuffed down his pants leg. As his partners covered two bankmen and a customer with pistols, Starr got sixteen hundred dollars in loose cash, and then he demanded that bookkeeper J. B. Charles open the safe, or Starr would kill him.

"You'll have to kill me, then," said Charles coolly, "because I don't know the combination." Starr then threatened bank vice president Sam Patrick, who just as coolly told the outlaw leader that the safe had already been opened for the day's operating cash but was then reclosed and its time lock reset for the next day. Frustrated, Starr snatched Patrick's diamond stickpin and herded him, Charles, and a customer out into the street.

Over in the First National, Starr's companions found the safe open and swept up more than four thousand dollars. When Starr joined them, they collected four bank employees and five customers to use as human shields. Herding these nine men in front of them, along with the hostages from the State Bank, the whole bandit gang walked deliberately toward their horses. But word of the holdup had spread through the town, and armed citizens were beginning to collect.

Their first shots were ineffective, and Starr's gang blazed away up and down the street to keep the townsmen at bay. Starr, hiding behind bankman Patrick, snapped a shot at Charley Guild, a shot that drove the shotgun-toting horse buyer quickly to cover behind a building.

More of Stroud's angry citizens were opening up on the outlaws. One in particular proved to be an especially deadly marksman. Seventeen-year-old Paul Curry had seen the robbery unfold from the yard of his parents' home nearby. Curry now ran into a butcher shop and came out with a sawed-off Winchester rifle. Taking cover behind some barrels in front of his father's grocery store, young Curry smashed Starr's leg with a round that tore into the outlaw's left thigh. When the bandit raised his weapon to return the fire, Curry yelled, "Throw away that gun or I'll kill you!" Convinced that this cool, tough youngster meant what he said, Starr dropped his weapon and fell back on the ground.

By this time the rest of the gang, abandoning their leader, had run to the stockyards, where they had tethered their all-important horses. They mounted up in haste and began to ride hard for safety, but bandit Lewis Estes was having trouble controlling his horse. Young Curry fired once more, and the bullet smashed into Estes's shoulder, breaking it and tearing into a lung. Waving a pistol, the outlaw forced two of the hostages to help him climb into the saddle, and all five bandits rode clear of the town.

Estes managed to stay on his horse for about a mile and half until he fainted from loss of blood and was pitched out of the saddle. His companions, as compassionate for him as they had been for Starr, took his horse and left him on the ground. Recovered by a posse, he was returned to town and taken to the office of Dr. John Evans, where Starr already lay. The bandit leader readily admitted to his identity and encouraged the close-mouthed Estes to do the same.

As the doctor dug the rifle bullet out of Starr's leg, Starr asked, "What did the kid shoot me with?" A hog rifle, somebody said, and Starr reacted with embarrassment. "I'll be damned. I don't mind getting shot, knew it had to happen sooner or later. But a kid with a hog gun—that hurts my pride."

Starr did have the good grace to congratulate Curry on his courageous stand. The young man told Starr he would use the reward money, one thousand dollars, to get an education, and Starr is reported to have said, "You're all right, boy."

Meanwhile, a posse pursued the fleeing bandits, and the telephone—that new and handy crime-fighting tool—sent lawmen, volunteers, and even state militia chasing after the remains of the gang from all directions. Much of the pursuit was by automobile, and the pursuers came very close. But in the end they were foiled by the cross-country mobility of the mounted bandits and their own inability to quickly hire or borrow horses for the pursuit.

At the trial Starr entered a plea of guilty, to everybody's surprise, and then went off to prison in McAlester with a twenty-five-year sentence. Estes got five years. While in prison Starr went into his good behavior mode, and he was back on the street again in less than four years. His chief aide and support in this quick return to liberty was Kate Barnard, who was Oklahoma's first commissioner of "Charities and Corrections."

To her credit Kate was a holy terror to slothful or uncaring officials and did much good in improving conditions in state hospitals. She also cordially detested the penal system, which she considered medieval, and thought herself a perceptive judge of the character of those confined there. "I have studied men," she said, "until I know from the shape of their hands and head, the gait of their walk, and the contour of their faces, much of their mode of life and the character of their thoughts."

She was convinced that Starr would now walk the paths of virtue and thought he had made "one of the sincerest efforts at reformation of all the 20,000 convicts I have known." Maybe this redoubtable lady did have some powerful insight into the souls of felons, but in Starr's case she—and others, including the prison chaplain—had been thoroughly bamboozled.

Starr now settled in Tulsa and became involved in the burgeoning film industry. He bought an interest in a firm called the Pan-American Motion Picture Company, and with it produced a silent movie, *Debtor to the Law*. This film, an account of the Stroud debacle, used many of that town's citizens as actors, including young Curry, playing himself. *Debtor to the Law* was very successful, and a series of other films followed.

At that point in his life, after serving prison sentences in Colorado and Oklahoma, Starr had every chance to change his outlaw lifestyle. And for a while it seemed that he would do so. However, not even the bonds of matrimony—he was married twice—could wean Starr away from the excitement of being a professional criminal.

In spite of the fact that he had not had much luck robbing banks in Arkansas, Starr decided to hit yet another Arkansas town. This time he tried the People's National Bank in the little town of Harrison, not far from Bentonville.

On February 18, 1921, Starr and three other men drove into Harrison in a Nash automobile and entered the bank. None of them wore a mask, although Starr seems to have worn a pair of cheap glasses, perhaps as a rudimentary disguise. The outlaws had every expectation of a successful haul, for there was some thirty thousand dollars in the bank.

At first the holdup went just as planned. The robbers pushed up to the cashier's windows and covered bank president Marvin Wagley and cashier Cleve Coffman, pushing out of the way Ruth Wilson, a bookkeeper for a grocery firm who was in the midst of making a deposit for her boss.

"Hands up!" yelled the bandits. Then repeatedly warned Coffman to "keep quiet; don't move." One of them then went inside the working area of the bank while a second man began to herd everybody else toward the vault. Starr had thoughtfully brought along a pillow case, which he now opened. At gunpoint he told Coffman to do what he was told. "You work with me and I'll work with you." By now the robbers had to watch not only Coffman, Wagley, and Ruth Wilson, but two other female employees and three more customers. Starr and his men also leveled their weapons at sixty-eight-year-old William J. Myers, who was a director and onetime president of the bank.

Myers had just entered his office at the rear of the bank, walking right into the middle of the robbery in progress. Having no other option, he dutifully raised his hands and followed one of the robber's orders by walking into the bank vault. But Myers apparently believed in prior planning, because he had long since arranged for a back door to the vault—what he called his "bandit trap"—specifically for just such an occasion. He had also secreted a loaded 1873 Winchester at the rear of the vault.

Starr finished sweeping the depositors' money into a sack, and he now ordered Coffman to open the safe. Coffman began to turn the dial, with the outlaw leader looking over his shoulder. When the door swung open, Starr started to reach inside. At that moment Myers opened fire from inside the vault and Starr went down. "Don't shoot!" he is supposed to have yelled. "Don't shoot, don't shoot anybody. I am the one that is shot; don't shoot a man who is down."

Myers advanced out of the vault, his weapon trained on Starr. Oddly enough, the outlaw asked Myers to remove the cheap glasses he was wearing. Myers did so, and then pressed on after Starr's companions, who had not stayed to fight or save their leader. They ran for it, in fact, tearing out of town in their automobile and leaving their boss behind. Myers ran outside and blazed away at the Nash as it raced off down the street, hitting one tire and blowing out the windshield.

Hastily organized citizens' posses pursued, but all they found was the Nash, abandoned and set on fire. In the days to come, authorities would arrest three other men for complicity in the crime, but for now all eyes were on the desperately wounded Henry Starr. At first Starr would not reveal who his cohorts were and simply asked to see George Crump, once a US marshal. Crump was not in town, but his son was, and the younger man positively identified Starr.

So once again the celebrated king of the bank robbers was down and hurt and back in the hands of the law. Once more he had been shot down by an ordinary citizen who objected to Starr's larcenous ways, and this time the hurt would be permanent.

As he lay on a cot in a jail cell, Starr was visited by Coffman, the bank cashier, and on another occasion by an official of a bank in Seligman, Missouri, who identified Starr as one of the men who had robbed his bank the previous year, just before Christmas. Lawmen spent some time with him too, and at last Starr began to give them some information. He also told one physician, Dr. T. P. Fowler, that "I was in debt $20,000 and had to have money, so I turned bank robber again. I am sorry, but the deed is done."

Myers's bullet had lodged in the outlaw's spine, from which it was carefully removed by Dr. J. J. Johnson. The outlaw survived the operation, but the doctor opined that Starr's life was now chiefly in danger from blood poisoning. He also ran the risk of fatal uremic poisoning, the doctor said, because the slug had torn through one kidney on its way to the backbone.

The doctors did all they could for Henry Starr, but it soon became obvious to them, and to Starr, that he was finished. His present and ex-wife were both contacted, along with his mother and his son. Staring death in the face, Starr now began to lose some of his outlaw cockiness. "I am going to die," he said, "and I am anxious to make my peace with God." He also said he would give some useful information to the sheriff, which he did.

This time there would be no encore for the Bearcat. He lasted four days, slipped into a coma, and died.

A great many honest depositors and bank employees did not shed a single tear. They would not miss in the slightest a boastful professional criminal who lived off the sweat of other people. No amount of weeping and learned lamentation about society's evils would change the fact that Henry Starr was a career thug, a thug by choice, a thug who found it easier to steal what other people earned than work for himself.

Henry Starr was blessed by nature with considerable intelligence and an iron constitution, both of which assets he chose to squander in robbing other people, running from the law, and wasting his years sitting in prison. Boastful and arrogant, it is the real measure of the man that on the day before his death, sliding toward oblivion, he still bragged to his doctors that he had "robbed more banks than any man in America."

Where he was going, that dubious record would do him precious little good.

GEORGE BIRDWELL

He Robbed the Wrong Bank

The gang drove into Boley and turned up Main Street, and Pete Glass stopped the Buick, pointing north, just south of the bank. Glass waited in the car while George Birdwell and Champ Patterson got out, Birdwell carrying a 1911 Colt .45 semiautomatic pistol, Patterson with a sawed-off shotgun beneath his overcoat. As they entered the bank, treasurer Wesley Riley looked up from his conversation with Horace Aldridge, suspecting nothing. D. J. Turner, the president, got up from his desk and moved up behind the bars on the teller's window to serve Birdwell. He found himself looking into the bad end of the Colt pistol.

"We're robbing this bank," Birdwell said. "Hand over the dough! Don't pull no alarm!"

Turner said nothing but began to pull bills out of the cash drawer, sliding them under the bars to the bandit. Meanwhile, bookkeeper Herb McCormick saw what was going on, slid softly to the floor, and crawled back toward the vault, hoping to get to the rifle he kept there. And then, as Turner pulled out the last bills in the drawer, the alarm fired with a deafening din, both inside the bank and outside, and in the four other stores wired into the system. "You pulled that alarm," yelled Birdwell. "I'll kill you for that!"

And the doughty Turner looked the bandit right in the eye: "You bet I pulled it!"

Riley, standing helplessly in front of Patterson's shotgun, saw what was coming. "Don't hurt nobody, please!" he pleaded, but his only answer was obscenities. Infuriated by Turner's defiance, Birdwell's mercurial temper exploded, and he drove four .45 slugs into Turner at point-blank range. Turner staggered back and went down, clutching at the desk for support as he fell.

McCormick reached the vault and his rifle, and as the bank president fell, the bookkeeper put a bullet into Birdwell's neck. Blood spurting from the wound, the outlaw dropped his pistol and the sack full of about seven hundred dollars in loot. "I'm shot," he cried, no longer bold and arrogant. "Hold me! I'm . . . " And down he went.

Patterson ordered Riley and customer Aldridge to pull what was left of Birdwell to the bank door and get him outside. Under the malignant stare of the shotgun, they did. Glass, hearing the firing, now came running into the bank, pistol in hand. He fired random shots toward the back of the bank as he and Patterson fell back toward the door, still trying to scoop up bills scattered across the counter and floor and stuff them into their pockets.

Outside, the outlaws saw citizens headed their way, running toward the bank, carrying rifles and shotguns. The hostages took advantage of the confusion of their captors to drop what was left of Birdwell on the sidewalk and run for it, disappearing down a side street. Riley's coat was ripped by a bullet or buckshot aimed at Patterson, but both he and Aldridge escaped without being hurt.

His forced labor and human shields suddenly gone, Patterson bent over to pick up Birdwell. Hazel, who owned the town's big department store, had told the sheriff he and his shotgun were ready for a bank robbery, that he might "git me a pretty boy for breakfast." Now he took a shot at Patterson.

Glass crawled toward Birdwell, as Patterson saw shopkeeper Hazel on his store's veranda and fired at him. Glass realized that Birdwell was quite dead and saw the giant form of Sheriff McCormick heading for him, followed by more citizens who had armed themselves at the Masonic Temple. Glass, seeing that the fat was in the fire, abandoned Birdwell's corpse and ran to the Buick. Patterson, stubborn or stupid, or both, was still tugging at Birdwell's corpse when a citizen named Zeigler shot him again.

Miraculously untouched by the hailstorm of lead, Glass slammed the Buick into reverse and began to turn around and make tracks for the highway. At this point, enter retired sheriff John Owens. Kneeling in the center of Main Street some fifty yards from the Buick, Owens coolly put a bullet into Glass. Roaring backward, the car crashed into a parking lot wall and stopped. Everybody within range poured bullets into it until the car was junk and Glass was a corpse. Birdwell and his boys had taken on the wrong town.

In 1932 Boley's five-block Main Street boasted forty stores, including Hazel's two-story department store and the Farmers' and Merchants' Bank. Boley was a successful all-black community, one of about two dozen such towns in Oklahoma in those days. Across the street from the bank stood the Masonic Temple, an impressive three-story structure. The bank, whose president, Turner, had also served as mayor for ten years, was the town's centerpiece. He had been worried about bank robbery, with good reason.

In the first three months of 1932, bandits stuck up Oklahoma banks for some sixty-two thousand dollars, a lot of money to small depositors. In Boley a hoodlum named Charles Arthur Floyd began to create a reputation for himself. He was called "Choc" by his friends, but the rest of the reading public called him "Pretty Boy."

Then and later people who should have known better called Floyd a latter-day Robin Hood. They gave no thought to the little people whose savings were wiped out by his raids. There was no friendly FDIC to protect depositors if a bank was driven to bankruptcy by robbers, because unless the bank had insurance, the depositors were out of luck.

Floyd and his gang had already struck the banks at Paden and Prague, not far away from Boley, and they robbed both in the same day. And just the last January, a gang had robbed the bank in the little town of Castle, just six miles down the road from Boley.

Turner said flatly that he would defend the town's savings at all costs. When Turner said something, he meant it. His bank had installed a brand-new electric alarm system. It triggered automatically when the last bills were removed from a teller's drawer, whether the bills were snatched by a robber or removed under duress by a bank employee.

The alarm made a noise like the last trumpet and was tied into four businesses in downtown Boley: Hazel's department store, Shorty Bragg's barbershop, Aldridge's pool hall, and John Owens's meat market.

Butcher John Owens was a formidable man indeed, a retired peace officer who always wore a black Stetson with a bullet hole in the crown, a memento of a gunfight. He and other citizens of Boley kept their shotguns and rifles close at hand, and more weapons were stashed in the Masonic Temple.

Anybody who tried to hold up the bank would also have to come through Sheriff Lankston McCormick, all six foot seven of him, very tough and very capable. Anyone who wanted the hard-earned money of Boley's people would have to buck most of the rest of Boley's determined citizenry as well. But George Birdwell didn't have the sense to stay away.

Companion and sometime accomplice to Pretty Boy Floyd, Birdwell was later described by a lawman as "the man who planned these activities and handled the machine gun in their raids." Birdwell had been a cowboy and an oil field roustabout. At least one story relates that at one time he was even a church deacon. Whatever Birdwell's history, he had turned robber, presumably because there was more money in the larceny business. Birdwell was a veteran criminal and well known for his volatile temper. He nevertheless had the reputation of being a devoted father, who not only took care of his wife and his own four children but also looked after his two nephews.

Nobody knows for sure how many banks Birdwell and Pretty Boy Floyd stuck up together. They robbed the bank of little Morris a couple of times, and banks in Shamrock, Konawa, Maud, Earlsboro, and Tahlequah, in addition to the banks in Paden and Castle. They held up the American State Bank in Henryetta, Oklahoma, early in November 1932 and got more than eleven thousand dollars, a notable haul for those impoverished days.

Of Birdwell's helpers at Boley, Champ Patterson was an experienced outlaw, and Birdwell's brand-new bank robber was a black gambler from Boley called Pete Glass. It may have been Glass who suggested the Boley raid to Birdwell, for the cocky Glass boasted that he was going to "show the gang how to rob a colored bank."

Pretty Boy Floyd refused to join in the Boley venture. This disappointed Birdwell, but it certainly didn't stop him. He decided to take on the Farmers' and Merchants' Bank by himself, with only the two men he had.

Two days before Thanksgiving, Birdwell and his cohorts drove their big black Buick down to Boley to reconnoiter the town and its bank. They hung out at Horace Aldridge's pool hall, shooting a few games and watching the bank across the street. Neither Birdwell nor the rest of the bandits aroused suspicion until they left town. They made the mistake of saying something ungentlemanly to Bennie Dolphin, a pretty secretary who worked for Dr. W. A. Paxton, whose office was across the street from the bank.

After breakfast the next day, allowing time for the Boley bank to open, the three climbed in their Buick. Patterson, who usually drove the getaway car, took the wheel, but somewhere near Boley, he moved over so that Glass could drive. The outlaws' plan—insofar as they had any plan at all—was to drive up Main Street and stop just short of the bank. They would park on the wrong side of the street, pointed north, the direction away from the highway.

Once Patterson and Birdwell had the cash and returned to the Buick, Glass was to back up a short distance, making a U-turn as he did so, and then drive hard to the south, to the highway and safety. It would have made more sense to park facing south to begin with and save a few precious seconds when they ran. The right side of the car would face the bank, giving the men two doors to jump into instead of just one.

It was the day before Thanksgiving, and many farmers were in town to buy supplies. Some bought shotgun ammunition because quail season opened the following day. Also in the bank was Herb McCormick, the bookkeeper and brother of Sheriff Lank McCormick, and the bank's treasurer, Wesley W. Riley, who was talking to Horace Aldridge, a customer. Out on the street, Sheriff McCormick was making his rounds, dressed in high boots with his trousers stuffed into them, a plaid shirt under a sheepskin coat, and a cowboy hat on top.

Now the robbery had been defeated in blood, and the sheriff shouted for a cease-fire. Dr. Paxton ran across Main Street toward the bank, his shotgun in one hand and his medical bag in the other. Turner was semiconscious on the floor, soaked in blood. Herb McCormick knelt beside him, unable to help.

Turner, still clinging to life, was loaded into Dr. Paxton's car for the trip to the hospital at Okemah. Turner's wife drove up and jumped into Paxton's vehicle, but neither her love nor the doctor's ministrations could save the gallant bank president. He died on the road.

Patterson survived his multiple wounds to reach Okemah.

The next day, according to the *Daily Oklahoman*, Champ Patterson, unable to talk because of his neck wound, confirmed by nodding his head that the dead bandit was the infamous George Birdwell.

A crowd of over five thousand people turned out for Turner's funeral on November 28. Boley was jammed with mourners, only about a quarter of whom could crowd inside the church for the funeral services. Among those offering eulogies was a man representing the Oklahoma Bankers Association. Scattered through the crowd were more than fifty peace officers in plain clothes, alert to the possibility that Floyd might "come to claim revenge," as one paper put it.

Pretty Boy Floyd didn't show up. He left the state before the year was out, never to return except to get himself buried at the biggest funeral ever seen in Oklahoma. Within two years he would be cut down by lawmen in the dirt of an Ohio cornfield.

In addition to laudatory letters, Herb McCormick also received a five-hundred-dollar reward from the Oklahoma Bankers Association for killing Birdwell, and Boley's "vigilance committee" got another five hundred dollars for exterminating Glass. Governor "Alfalfa Bill" Murray invited Herb McCormick to Oklahoma City, where the governor conferred on him the honorary title of "Major."

So he was known for the rest of his life.

OREGON OUTLAWS

THE DEAUTREMONT BROTHERS

Oregon's Last Train Robbery

When Southern Pacific Railroad Train Number 13 came to a slow stop a little before 1:00 p.m. on October 11, 1923, in Tunnel 13 on the summit of Siskiyou Pass in southern Oregon, the eighty-plus passengers aboard must have thought it odd. They only had a few minutes to sit in the darkness and wonder what was going on before a huge explosion rocked the front of the train, breaking out windows on the passenger cars and sending a bright flash of light and billowing, thick smoke through the tunnel.

Conductor J. O. Marrett, assuming a boiler explosion, tried to calm and comfort the panicked passengers as best he could, then stepped out of the car into the black, smoky darkness of the tunnel and carefully began to make his way to the front of the train. It would be some minutes before he realized what the forward crew members already knew—that a brutal and vicious robbery was in progress.

Chugging south to San Francisco, California, Train Number 13 had originated out of Portland, Oregon, and was carrying, in addition to paying passengers, twenty deadheading railroad employees and was pulling four baggage cars.

Tunnel 13 is located just south of Ashland in the Siskiyou Mountains, a remote and wild place in those days. The steep, winding grade through the mountains to the tunnel required additional "helper" engines to get trains to the summit. Just before reaching the tunnel, the trains stopped at Siskiyou Station where the helper engines were unhooked. Then, because the ride down the other side of Siskiyou Pass was also steep and a train could gain four or five miles per hour extra speed before reaching the tunnel, company policy required its engineers to conduct a brake test, slowing down the train before reaching the east end of Tunnel 13 on its way down the mountain. It was all a routine, except for today.

On this day three brothers—nineteen-year-old Hugh DeAutremont and the twenty-three-year-old twins Roy and Ray DeAutremont—were waiting for the train to reach the tunnel. They were out to make a big, one-time heist that would set them up for a life of leisure, forever free from financial worries. Rumor had it that Train Number 13, called the Gold Special because in past years it transported gold between Portland and San Francisco, was carrying forty thousand dollars in cash on this run.

Now, hidden in the brush along the tracks, Hugh and Roy, armed with Colt .45 automatic pistols, waited at the east end of the tunnel where the train would enter, while Ray, clutching a 12-gauge automatic shotgun, positioned himself at the west entrance.

Their plan was simple. The train, having conducted its brake test before entering the 3,100-foot-long tunnel, would be traveling slowly enough for Hugh and Roy to hop aboard. They would then make their way to the engine car cab and order the engineer to stop the train with the engine outside the exit end of the tunnel and the rest of the train inside. Ray, waiting with his shotgun at the tunnel exit, added extra firepower if needed. They would then blow open the mail car door with dynamite, uncouple the rest of the train, and order the engineer to pull the mail car out of the tunnel, where they would take its valuable cargo, and then disappear into the rugged mountains as rich men.

An hour earlier they had run wires from a detonator hidden in the woods to the tracks and stashed a suitcase filled with dynamite in the bushes so that everything would be ready to go. The brothers had stolen the explosives and accessories, ironically, from a Southern Pacific Railroad Company work site. Everything was in place, and now all they needed to do was wait for the train to arrive. They had planned it out so well that nothing could possibly go wrong.

The DeAutremonts were not an atypical family for that time period in American history. Ray and Roy were born on March 31, 1900, in Iowa, and Hugh in Arkansas in 1904. They were the middle children in a family of five brothers. Their father, Paul, was of French extraction and their mother, Belle, German. They were Catholics and regular churchgoers.

A barber by trade, the father also tried his hand at farming and ranching and owned a general store for a while. In addition to Arkansas and Iowa, the family also lived for a time in Colorado and New Mexico. Eventually Paul and Belle divorced, and he moved to Eugene, Oregon, to work as a barber.

Following in their father's footsteps, Roy and Ray moved to Oklahoma to attend barber school, but Ray did not care for the profession and jumped a train one day and rode the rails to Portland, Oregon, arriving in 1918.

While Roy remained in Oklahoma and opened his own barbershop, Ray became involved in the labor movement, specifically with the Industrial Workers of the World party. In November 1919 he was arrested, which was not an uncommon practice for harassing labor activists, and sentenced to one year in a Washington State reformatory on charges of "criminal syndicalism."

Roy came to Oregon when he heard about his brother's arrest, and upon Ray's release, the two lived together in a Salem apartment, scraping by on what work they could find. Some scholars of the DeAutremont case believe that this was a radicalizing period for the two brothers, with Ray's anger and bitterness over his arrest eventually affecting Roy as well.

Ray took off for Spokane, Washington, in 1921 to find work and then went to Chicago where he hoped to join up with "gangsters." Failing to make a connection, he returned to Oregon by the end of the year and hooked up once again with Roy.

The twins, who were always close, began talking about pulling off some major heist that would permanently solve all their financial problems—an idea that first occurred to Ray when he was serving his reformatory sentence from 1919 to 1920. In 1922 the two even went so far as to plan several bank and general store robberies in Oregon and Washington, casing the locations but backing out at the last minute.

Over the next year the brothers spent time with family in Oregon, attended church, and worked at a number of jobs. Then Ray hopped a train during the winter of 1922–1923 and went to visit his younger brother Hugh, who was attending high school in New Mexico, where his mother, Belle, remained after her divorce. It was here that he pitched to Hugh the idea of helping him and Roy with a holdup, suggesting that the younger brother come up to Oregon after he graduated.

When Hugh graduated in June 1923, he headed up to Oregon to join Ray and Roy, and they began discussing a plan to rob a Southern Pacific Railroad mail car. Their date with destiny was drawing closer.

The brothers began exploring the Southern Pacific Railroad's route from Portland to northern California, looking for a promising ambush location. But the three just weren't finding a place they liked until Ray remembered Tunnel 13 and the Siskiyou Summit, over which he had traveled on his way to visit Hugh in New Mexico. Their spot was chosen, and they began to plan the details for a late October robbery of the Gold Special.

They went to Portland in early September 1923 and bought a used Nash car, which they drove to Eugene, where their father lived, taking the opportunity while passing through Oregon City to steal the explosives, detonator, and wire they would use in the robbery.

They visited with their father for a few days, then loaded the Nash with camping gear and other provisions and departed on September 18, telling him they were going hunting in Washington's Puget Sound area. Then they turned south, down the Pacific Highway to the Siskiyou Mountains.

Just a little below the summit of Siskiyou Pass, they pulled off the road and concealed the car. Here they camped for about a week, and then moved to another site not far away to spend a few days practicing setting up the explosives and getting familiar with handling their weapons. They did a good deal of target shooting. They also burned their tent and other belongings that might be used to identify them if discovered by the authorities before relocating to a small cabin they found on nearby Mount Crest.

They stayed here for the better part of a week, making their preparations for the robbery, for which they had set a date of October 11.

Next, they sent Hugh to get the car with orders to drive it back to their father's house in Eugene, store it there, and then hop a train for a lift back to the Siskiyou Summit. Because of the very limited road system in the area, attempting a getaway by car would almost certainly result in capture by the authorities. The plan, instead, was for Roy and Hugh to hide in the mountains once the robbery was successfully completed. Ray would make his way back to Eugene, pick up the car, then come and retrieve his brothers and the loot. At that point they would be free to make their escape.

But things went wrong. On the way down the mountain on September 26, Hugh crashed the Nash into a cow that was loitering in the road, crunching in the touring car's front end. He made it into Ashland, where he got it repaired, but had to spend a couple of days in town while the work was being done. He finally pulled into Eugene on September 29, leaving the car at his father's house and hopping a train to Ashland. While hanging around the Southern Pacific Railroad yard waiting for a train to come by so he could hitch a ride to the Siskiyou Summit, Hugh was questioned by suspicious security guards. Although they let him go, the episode unnerved him. Instead of waiting for a train and risking getting caught, he hiked up to the Mount Crest cabin from Ashland, reuniting with Ray and Roy on October 9.

The appointed day finally arrived. At noon the brothers set out from the cabin on foot for Tunnel 13. In addition to their weapons, they carried with them the detonating machine wrapped in a pair of blue overalls, three backpacks to carry away the loot, three pads that had been soaked with creosote that they would strap to their feet to confuse bloodhounds, a one-pound can of pepper for the same purpose, flashlights, and a suitcase containing sticks of dynamite.

Upon reaching the tunnel, they attached the wires from the detonator and hid the suitcase by the tracks. Hugh and Roy made their way to the east tunnel entrance. Ray hefted his shotgun, sat down at the west entrance, lit a cigarette, and waited.

But now the waiting was over. The brothers could hear the train approach, slowing down enough during its brake test to allow a person to leap aboard as it passed by. Just before the train entered the tunnel, Hugh and Roy emerged from the brush and swung themselves onto the engine car.

Hugh stole up on engineer Sidney L. Bates and fireman Marvin L. Seng. With pistol drawn Hugh ordered that the train be stopped with the engine outside the west end of the tunnel and the remaining cars inside. Roy watched from the back of the engine car by the oil tank.

As the engine emerged from the tunnel and the train came to a halt, Ray suddenly appeared, brandishing his shotgun. Mail clerk Elvyn E. Dougherty opened the door of the mail car to see what was going on. When he poked his head out, Ray fired his shotgun, but missed. Dougherty quickly slid the car door shut and locked it. Hugh Haffney, in the baggage car, was also peering out his car door. Seeing what was transpiring, he, too, slid his car door closed and locked it.

Now the DeAutremont brothers had everything under control and everyone where they wanted them. All that was needed now was to blow the door off the mail car, grab the forty thousand dollars, and make clean their escape. The high life was in their grasp.

Ray and Roy went up to the engine cab where Hugh was covering the engineer and fireman. They ordered both trainmen to get down off the cab and marched them out the tunnel to the front of the train where they would be protected from any debris thrown by the explosion they were about to set off.

They placed the suitcase of dynamite by the mail car door, attached the wires, and ran for cover as Roy rammed down the detonator plunger.

But the robbers had no experience using explosives and used far more dynamite than the job required. Instead of just blowing off the door, the explosion tore apart poor US Postal Service mail clerk Elvyn E. Dougherty and virtually demolished the mail car. Baggage man Haffney, in the next car over, was knocked unconscious by the blast.

Immediately after the explosion, while conductor Marrett was still attending to the passengers, brakeman Charles Orin "Coyle" Johnson jumped from one of the rear cars onto the tracks and made his way through the dark smoky tunnel to see what had happened, holding a red lantern to light his way. Rail accidents including derailings and boiler explosions were not unheard of—between 1890 and 1905 there were as many as seven thousand such incidents in the United States. That is probably what Johnson was expecting to find. Instead, he ran into Roy DeAutremont.

The brothers now had a dilemma on their hands. The plan called for uncoupling the mail car from the rest of the train so the engine could pull it out into daylight. At that point the trio could search it until they found the forty thousand dollars they sought. But the explosion filled the tunnel with smoke and flames, making it difficult to see and breathe. They brought fireman Seng back to uncouple the car, but he was overcome by the fumes and had to retreat. Now there was a problem. Then the brakeman blundered into Roy's clutches.

Roy told him that that it was a robbery and demanded that Johnson help uncouple the mail car. The brakeman explained that once the uncoupling lever was raised, the engine had to be moved forward to separate the cars. So Roy sent Johnson forward to tell engineer Bates, who was being covered by Hugh and Ray, to pull the engine and mail car out of the tunnel. But when the brakeman suddenly appeared out of the smoky tunnel, red light in hand, Ray and Hugh panicked and opened up on him with both pistol and shotgun. Johnson fell to the ground, dying. One of the two DeAutremonts, it's not known who, shot Johnson one more time to finish him off.

Now Hugh brought engineer Bates back into his cab and ordered him to pull forward. Unfortunately for the brothers, the mail car had been so badly damaged by the explosion that, even after several tries, it wouldn't budge.

Stunned at how badly things were going, the brothers examined the smoldering carcass of the mail car, strewn with the body parts of the mail clerk, and considered their options. The mail car was so hot and smoky that, in their estimation, by the time it was safe to go inside to loot, the law would probably have arrived on the scene. It looked like it was time to cut their losses.

Roy and Ray held a brief consultation on what they should do. They decided to kill the engineer and the fireman and run for it. Roy shot the fireman two times with his Colt .45. Ray climbed up into the cab of the engine where Hugh was still guarding the engineer and yelled to Hugh, "Bump him off and let's clear out of here."

Hugh shot Bates in the head with his handgun. Then the three brothers ran off into the forest, leaving behind four dead men and the empty backpacks they had brought to fill with stolen cash.

By now the conductor J. O. Marrett had made his way to the mail car accompanied by a medical student passenger, twenty-three-year-old Lawrence E. C. Joers, who had offered to help with anyone who might have been injured in the explosion. Finding their way to the front of the train through the dense smoke, they discovered the engineer, brakeman, and fireman lying on the ground. Still thinking they were only injured from an accidental explosion, the medical student began to give the engineer artificial respiration. But as he applied pressure to the chest, blood spurted out, revealing gunshot wounds. Now it dawned on them that there had been a robbery and multiple murders. Joers soon found the detonating wires along the track. Marrett ran for an emergency telephone located outside the tunnel and called for help.

Before long another train steamed up the grade carrying a doctor and law enforcement officers who collected evidence. Within hours search parties were combing the area, but no sign of the robbers could be found. Southern Pacific Railroad immediately offered a reward of twenty-five hundred dollars for their capture.

In the wake of the bungled robbery attempt, the three DeAutremont brothers hightailed it to a cache where they had stored some supplies for their escape. They holed up there for nearly two weeks. After what seemed like an adequate period of lying low, Ray borrowed Roy's handgun (Ray had lost his during the robbery) and jumped a train to Medford, intending to continue on to Eugene to retrieve the Nash.

But as Ray walked through town, much to his horror, he spotted a newspaper with pictures of himself and Roy under the caption, "Have you seen the DeAutremont brothers?" There was a fourteen-thousand-four-hundred-dollar reward being offered for them dead or alive. That was enough for Ray, who returned to the hideout to tell Roy and Hugh that the law had identified them as the killers.

Now it was time to run and run hard. The three made their way through the mountains toward the coast. By early November they were on the Klamath River in California where Ray decided to strike out on his own while Hugh and Roy continued moving south to Grenada, California. Here Roy took a job on a farm, and Hugh kept moving.

Unbeknownst to the three brothers, a massive manhunt that included searches on foot, with bloodhounds, and by airplane had been launched. Wanted posters were also being distributed worldwide. Nevertheless, it would be three and a half years before the Tunnel 13 killers would be brought to justice.

The robbery had been such a disaster—the murder of four men and a price on their heads without a penny to show for it. What other mistakes had they made that enabled their names to be connected to the crime so quickly?

The investigating officers found a wealth of evidence at the crime scene and at the cabin on Mount Crest. But two pieces of evidence gave them most of what they wanted. For one thing the serial number of the handgun that had been dropped at the crime scene identified its purchaser as Ray DeAutremont. But the best evidence came in the form of the coveralls that the brothers had used to wrap up the detonator. Authorities bundled it up and sent it to Professor Edward Heinrich of the University of California at Berkeley. He conducted a series of forensic tests on the garment, but his best results came when he simply looked into one of the pencil pockets and found a wadded up piece of paper. He unfolded it carefully. It was a US Postal Service registered mail receipt number 236-L for a letter sent by Roy DeAutremont to his older brother, Verne, who was living in New Mexico.

From those two pieces of evidence, investigators were quickly able to piece together the robbery plot. Hugh was eventually linked as well through handwriting analysis of the aliases he had used at hotels and from the purchases he had made of equipment used in the robbery attempt.

On November 23, 1923, six indictments were issued against the brothers—four counts of murder and one count each for attempted burglary and larceny. More than two million wanted posters were printed and distributed worldwide. The three-year manhunt would cost five hundred thousand dollars.

While on the lam, Ray ended up in Detroit. He was eventually able to contact Roy in California, who joined him there in 1924. They worked their way south, intending to eventually escape the country. Instead they ended up in Ohio where Ray got married and had a baby girl. In early 1927 Roy and Ray went to Steubenville, Ohio, to look for work as coal miners. But the law was closing in. Ray saw a wanted poster of the three of them with Hugh's picture marked as "captured."

After Roy and Hugh had split up in California, Hugh traveled through the Southwest for a while and then journeyed to Chicago. In Chicago he joined the US Army in April 1924 under the name James C. Price. He was assigned to duty in the Philippines.

But the Philippines were not far enough away for Hugh to hide. Before too long the authorities' massive wanted-poster distribution campaign was finally going to pay off. In late 1926 Price's sergeant, Thomas Reynolds, was in San Francisco and saw one of those posters. He immediately recognized Private Price as Hugh DeAutremont. Reynolds took a stroll over to the Southern Pacific Railroad office and told his story.

There had been many false leads and disappointments over the years in the manhunt for the DeAutremonts, but the agents thought this might, finally, be the real thing. They sent one of their men to Manila in February 1927 to check the story out.

By mid-March the agent was back in San Francisco with Hugh DeAutremont in custody. By the end of the month, Hugh DeAutremont was transferred to the custody of Ralph Jennings, sheriff of Jackson County, Oregon, where the crime had taken place.

Three months later an agent from the US Department of Justice arrested Ray at his house in Steubenville. Later that day local police officers nabbed Roy as he was leaving work at a mill.

The two brothers had been fingered by a former coworker who had recognized their pictures from a wanted poster. It was over.

On June 27, 1927, the three brothers were delivered to the Oregon State Penitentiary in Salem to begin serving life sentences. While serving his time, Hugh founded a prison magazine called *Shadows*. Roy worked as a barber, and Ray learned several languages at the prison school and became a modestly talented painter.

Hugh was paroled in early 1958 and moved to San Francisco to work as a printer. Less than three months later, he was diagnosed with stomach cancer and died on March 30, 1959. Roy was diagnosed with schizophrenia, transferred to the Oregon State Hospital, and given a lobotomy. He was eventually paroled and died in 1983 in a nursing home in Salem. Ray was paroled in 1961 and worked part-time as a janitor at the University of Oregon. He died in 1984.

It was years after their robbery attempt that the DeAutremont brothers learned that Train No. 13 carried only its usual cargo of mail on that October day. There was no forty thousand dollars aboard. It was also Oregon's last train robbery.

The three brothers are buried next to their mother at Salem's Belcrest Memorial Cemetery. All three of their names are on a single headstone inscribed side by side, just as they were on those wanted posters so many years ago.

RANGE WARS

Sheep Men Versus Cattle Ranchers

Even for men used to seeing slaughter, this was an appalling sight. Five hundred sheep, belonging to Fred Smith of Paulina, lay dead in the desert near Grindstone. Shot to death, the corpses lay scattered amongst the lava rocks and clumps of sagebrush. Above this grisly scene, the arch of cobalt blue, crystal-clear, high desert sky stretched from horizon to horizon. It was New Year's Day 1905, and it was war.

That afternoon six men on horseback, disguised with masks and blackface, had descended upon the hapless shepherd as he had tended his flock. Surrounding the frightened and unarmed man, the riders leapt from their mounts and dragged him to the ground, holding him immobile as they tied his wrists and ankles and blindfolded his eyes. Now, with the shepherd incapacitated, his sheep were helpless too. The riders remounted their horses and began rounding the animals up, gathering together the herd of about seven hundred. With loud cries and war whoops, they drove them a short distance away from where the shepherd lay and opened fire with rifles, dropping about five hundred sheep on the spot. The survivors ran off into the desert in a panic, destined to be dinner for predators. Their awful task complete, the six riders galloped off. It was not the first such slaughter this lonely country had seen in recent years, and it would not be the last.

During the mid- and late 1800s, cattle ranching was king on Oregon's rolling rangelands and high plains country east of the Cascade Mountains. Stockmen from the Willamette Valley in western Oregon had been bringing their cattle to these parts each spring and summer since the 1860s to take advantage of the lush and nutritious range grass. They also drove their herds of cattle—as many as one hundred thousand head—through the region on their way to help feed gold miners in the rugged mountains of northeastern Oregon. During this period cattle empires, such as the Teal & Coleman Ranch on Trout Creek at Willowdale, were being formed throughout the region, along with countless smaller operations. These cattle barons, great and small, looked upon their empire and saw that it was good—until the sheep men came.

By the 1880s cattlemen and sheep men were sharing the range, and not always amicably. During this period and over following decades, railroad tracks were being laid from the main line along the Columbia River into central Oregon. The town of Shaniko, on the empty plains of Wasco County, was established in 1879 on the route of the Columbia Southern rail line. By 1903 Shaniko was being called the Wool Capital of the World and was the primary distribution center for virtually all the sheep and wool produced across central and eastern Oregon. The railroad provided a more efficient and economical means for cattlemen and sheep men to bring their goods to world markets, encouraging production but also competition for the unregulated open range.

From a stockman's point of view, his cattle were here first and the open range was his. The shepherd and his sheep were interlopers, taking what wasn't theirs. There was a lot about sheep and shepherds the cattlemen didn't like. First, there were just too many sheep. It's estimated that there were about 130,000 sheep grazing in Wasco County between 1885 and 1910. By the early 1900s, perhaps as many as 50,000 cattle and 340,000 sheep shared Crook County's Ochoco and Maury Mountains. Any way a cattleman looked at it, he was outnumbered.

Something else that rankled the rancher was a sheep's eating habits. Cattle ate bunchgrass and other wild, native grasses. Sheep ate those too, but they also grazed on forbs and virtually every other weed and flower out on the range, snipping them off close to the ground. Cattlemen could tell when a herd of sheep had moved through an area because it was stripped of nearly all of its vegetation, leaving a virtual moonscape behind. That didn't sit well with the stockmen.

And finally, it was the very nature of the sheep business that rubbed cattlemen the wrong way. The shepherd usually tended his charges on foot. In cowboy country men rode horses. For that the ranchers looked down upon the shepherd and regarded him as an inferior being.

It was just plain getting harder and harder to be a cattleman. The ranchers let their cattle graze year round on the open range. In the spring they moved their herds into the high country of the Blue Mountains and eastern slopes of the Cascade Mountains where the animals could dine on the nutritious new grass growth. But as more cattle, horses, and sheep came to be grazed in the region, conflicts erupted. The cattlemen raced to get their cows into the mountains first while the sheep men drove their flocks from Morrow, Gilliam, Wasco, Umatilla, Sherman, and Crook Counties with the same idea in mind. At the same time, stockmen from western Oregon were driving increasing numbers of their livestock to graze the Crooked River country, making the situation all the worse. The local cattlemen seethed with resentment. It was only a matter of time before something had to give.

The ranchers out in the Izee and Bear Valley country of Grant County got fed up first. They complained that the sheep men bringing their flocks to the Snow Mountain and Izee country were letting them graze right down to the fenced boundaries of the ranchers' pastures, eating "out their door yards." That was too much. Something needed to be done.

So stockmen of the Izee country had a little meeting one day in 1896 and formed a civic organization they called the Izee Sheep Shooters. Their new organization would discourage the sheep men through the persuasive methods of such famous western diplomats as Colt, Winchester, and Smith & Wesson.

Whenever a flock of sheep came too close to a cattleman's ranch, the Izee Sheep Shooters would ride out to explain to the shepherd the error of his ways. They would hold him and his camp tender at gunpoint while they shot as many of the offending sheep as possible. It wasn't long before word got out among cattlemen about what a fine job the Izee Sheep Shooters were doing, removing those hoofed locusts from Grant County.

It just so happened that the ranchers to the west in Paulina were having the same problem, with sheep men from Wasco County and the lower John Day River area bringing their sheep onto Crook County rangeland and crowding the Paulina ranchers' cattle. The Paulina ranchers invited a representative from the Izee Sheep Shooters to come talk to them about forming a similar organization of their own. Out of neighborly civic duty, Izee cattleman Henry Snodgrass volunteered to speak to the group.

The meeting was held in late July 1898 under a ponderosa pine tree somewhere along Wolf Creek in Crook County. An hour before midnight, nearly forty men gathered around a roaring campfire, listening to Snodgrass describe how the Izee Sheep Shooters operated and what its mission was. Secrecy and, above all, loyalty were imperative to success and for evading the law. The leader of the Izee Sheep Shooters, his weathered face alternating between light and shadow as the flames of the bonfire shot embers toward the black sky, leaned forward and declared that if any man did not want to join the brotherhood of sheep haters and was unwilling to do what was necessary to drive the sheep out of the country, he should leave now and go home to bed.

The rules of the game were so serious that an oath had to be taken by each man who wished to be a member. If while they were engaged in killing sheep it became necessary to kill a shepherd or camp tender, the victim would be buried on the spot. If one of their members were killed in the course of a sheep-shooting operation, his body would be brought home for burial with no word made of the cause or circumstances of his demise. And if any of their company were apprehended by the law and made to stand trial, his fellow vigilantes were obligated to lie under oath to protect him.

Snodgrass went around the campfire, man by man, and made each swear to the conditions he had just set forth. For three of the attending ranchers, it was too much to ask. Fred Powell, Billie Congleton, and Sam Courtney got up and rode off home to bed. The others stayed behind and the Inland Sheep Shooters were born. Other sheep shooters sprang up locally, here and there, on the Oregon rangelands. This vigilante movement spread from Bear Valley to Paulina in 1898, to Camp Creek in 1902, and to Silver Lake in 1903. Many of these were rather loose and informal affairs with a few ranchers occasionally saddling up to "touch up" a herd of sheep, as one stockman put it. But the Inland Sheep Shooters would become the largest and most effective of the bunch. Between 1898 and 1906 the Paulina ranchers who had sworn a blood oath that dark night by the bonfire would destroy thousands of sheep and murder one man.

The first thing the Paulina stockmen did was to establish a boundary, which they called a "deadline," over which they would let no sheep pass. That deadline started on the summit of Wolf Mountain across and over Paulina Butte, then down the Crooked River to the Paulina ranches. They marked this boundary with blazed trees and sent a warning to the sheep men that any sheep that crossed south of that line would be killed. A shepherd caught in the forbidden zone would risk the same fate.

By the time the nineteenth century had turned into the twentieth, the Inland Sheep Shooters had become bolder, progressing well beyond "touching up" a few flocks of sheep here and there. The biggest sheep slaughter the Paulina stockmen ever pulled off was at Benjamin Lake near the Crook-Lake County line on April 28, 1903. That spring three different sheep men from Summer Lake had brought their sheep to Benjamin Lake, making for a combined flock of about 2,700. The sheep men and the camp tenders were armed and had let word go around that they didn't hold much truck with the cattlemen's threats to stay out of "their territory."

But the Inland Sheep Shooters would tolerate no defiance of their orders. Arriving at camp and wearing masks, a posse of sheep shooters jumped the herder on duty, put a sack over his head, and left one of their own to guard him. Then they went looking for the tender, whom they found about a mile away. Slipping a sack over his head, too, they returned him to camp and placed him under guard as well. The sheep shooters swung back on their mounts and casually rode out of camp and into the immense flock of sheep. Calmly, and with grim calculation, they began firing. When they were done, their rifle barrels red-hot and the smoke from their rounds filling the air (along with the bleatings of stricken sheep), only 300 of the original 2,700 animals remained alive.

The sheep killings continued. In February 1904 five masked and armed men attacked a camp containing three thousand head of sheep near Silver Lake. They shot and clubbed the animals, destroying a substantial number before escaping into the desert. Four months later ten masked men killed more than two thousand sheep owned by sheep men Grube and Parker forty miles south of Silver Lake. More than a thousand sheep died in a raid on Little Summit Prairie in the Ochoco Mountains in July of the same year. The toll on the sheep and sheep men was mounting.

While direct defiance by sheep men of the sheep shooters' directive to stay north of their deadline brought deadly retribution, even minor transgressions were dealt with swiftly and decisively. If a shepherd tried sneaking over the line to let his flock feed a little on the cow side of the deadline and then slipped back to the sheep side, the sheep shooters crossed over to pay him a visit. One story tells of a big, red-bearded sheep man from Tennessee who liked to make regular quick trips south of the deadline to let his sheep graze, and then ease the flock back north. With a .45 caliber Colt revolver and .45-60 Winchester rifle at his side, he laughed at any suggestion that the cattlemen could cause him trouble.

But one afternoon, while taking a nap on "his side" of the deadline, he awoke to the sight of a Smith & Wesson revolver stuffed against his face. Then came a crack of thunder as a slug took a piece of skin off his nose and nearly shot out one of his eyes. The masked men took his boots and guns and disappeared. When the shepherd hobbled barefooted into his camp an hour later, he found a note signed by the Inland Sheep Shooters telling him where he could find his boots and gun and advising him that he was now shy five hundred sheep. When the Tennessean rushed to check his flock, he found he was missing 550.

The sheep shooters didn't just limit their works to fighting sheep men and their flocks. They also killed Indians when the opportunity presented itself. Although it had been nearly forty years since the Paiute Indian wars had ended in the region, there were plenty of ranchers who were old enough to remember those days of terror and did not look kindly upon the remaining Native Americans.

In one well-known incident, rancher John Hyde of Izee was riding through Bear Valley in Grant County in October 1898 when he happened upon a band of Indians camped along Deer Creek. The Indians accused the rancher of stealing some horses and tried to work their way behind him. Hyde managed to break away and galloped home to mobilize the Izee Sheep Shooters.

The next morning a heavily armed committee of sheep shooters was hot on the Indians' trail. The sheep shooters caught up with them a ways downstream. Shooting broke out almost immediately. The headman, Chief Albert, died when fourteen slugs slammed into his body. Sheep shooter George Cutting fell dead from Indian fire. The Indians broke and ran, but the sheep shooters caught up to them, dispatching the Indian who killed Cutting. They shot a few of the Indians' ponies for good measure, and then reined their own toward home, fully satisfied with the morning's work.

The local newspaper, the *Prineville Review,* as well as newspapers throughout the state, had been writing a stream of editorials condemning the sheep killings and the perpetrators. On December 29, 1904, the "Corresponding Secretary of Crook County's Sheep-Shooting Association of Eastern Oregon" actually wrote a letter to the *Morning Oregonian* in Portland providing an annual report of eight thousand to ten thousand sheep slaughtered during the last "shooting season." He also suggested that the governor and state government butt out of their business. The letter sparked statewide outrage among decent citizens.

The sheep men had tried to work out their differences with the stockmen. In late June 1904 the Central Oregon Wool Growers Association held a meeting in Antelope to discuss the range war that was clearly getting out of hand, noting that sheep killings had begun earlier than usual that year. The association offered a fifteen-hundred-dollar reward for information about the sheep shooters and appointed several emissaries to meet with the cattlemen to discuss a truce. But it was no go. The sheep killings continued, and the sheep men's sheds and haystacks were burned on a regular basis.

Perhaps the most horrific crime against the sheep men and their sheep happened in April 1904. A shepherd who had recently emigrated from Ireland to find himself overseeing a herd of sheep near Fort Rock was paid a visit by a group of masked men one day. They warned him to remove his flock from the area. He paid them no heed. A couple of weeks later, they returned, riding into the flock of more than two thousand sheep. Their shouting and yelling panicked the animals and they began to run, stampeding blindly before the masked horsemen. They had no clue they were being herded toward a nearby cliff until they began plunging over the edge in waves.

It was not as if there wasn't any law in these parts. But for the few sheriffs and their deputies who patrolled this country, the task of catching a sheep shooter was formidable. The vigilantes usually traveled at night and were heavily armed. Any lawman who rode off into the mountains in the dark to pursue these outlaws would probably not come back. Although the Inland Sheep Shooters were made up of local ranchers, only they knew the identities of their members, and they would never tell.

But when prominent Prineville merchant J. C. Conn disappeared one day, the law had to do something. Conn, who was a known opponent of the sheep shooters, had grabbed his rifle on the morning of March 4, 1904, and headed out into the wilderness to do some hunting. He was never seen alive again.

When he didn't return home as scheduled, his friends became concerned and launched a search that finally yielded Conn's body about a mile west of Silver Lake on April 21. A revolver with one discharged shell lay alongside. At first it appeared to be a suicide, but further investigation showed it to be murder. It appeared that his killers had searched Conn's body for what was believed to be evidence identifying members of the Inland Sheep Shooters and their crimes. An arrest was made, but no one was ever convicted.

Ironically, the range war that probably killed at least ten thousand sheep and one man was ended not by lawmen but by the stroke of the pen. In 1902 the federal government withdrew much of the public lands in the Blue Mountains from public domain, establishing the Blue Mountains Forest Reserve, which would eventually become a national forest. In the fall of 1906, the federal government divided those lands into grazing allotments for both cattlemen and sheep men, guaranteeing them places to graze their herds. Since they no longer were in direct competition for grazing grounds, the threat the two groups once posed to each other vanished, and the range war ended.

No one was ever prosecuted for the years of sheep killing, property destruction, and murder. True to the blood oath those thirty-five or so stockmen took around the bonfire that late July night in 1898, the members of the Inland Sheep Shooters took the knowledge of their comrades' identities with them to the grave.

SOUTH DAKOTA OUTLAWS

CHIEF TWO STICKS

The Disenchanted Rebel

On a gray midwinter morning just three days removed from Christmas 1894, a crowd gathered round the hastily built gallows in Deadwood Gulch, not to greet the new year or join in good cheer but to witness the end of a once proud life made miserable. On that December day happy holiday hymns were replaced by the woeful death-song wail of a lonely Lakota leader facing the end of his trail. Then, with a hood over his head and a new noose encircling his neck, Chief Cha Nopa Uhah, also known as Two Sticks, stepped onto a small, square trapdoor and dropped seven feet four inches into history.

For the elderly Chief Two Sticks, the previous decades must have seemed as a whirlwind on the prairie, a twister that left no Native American, and perhaps no blade of grass on the Great Plains, unscathed. Two Sticks had witnessed much of what had gone right and so much that had gone wrong for his brethren. Before his death at the end of a white man's rope, he had been first triumphant, then disillusioned, and finally, irrevocably, defeated. That he had walked into old age at all seemed surprising.

For Two Sticks had been at the Greasy Grass with Sitting Bull and Crazy Horse, a day when the clearing of a cloud of smoke and dust coupled with the circling of turkey vultures had signaled the end for Yellow Hair and his band of bluecoats, cut down on the rolling banks of the Little Bighorn. In the years after the battle, he watched with despair as an increasing number of his comrades resigned themselves to a fate dictated by the Great White Father in Washington, reluctantly allowing themselves to be assigned to reservations where Indian agents sparingly doled out foodstuffs and government blankets.

One of those Lakota leaders who had never sought surrender was Sitting Bull, with whom Two Sticks had fought at the Little Bighorn. Following the annihilation of Col. George A. Custer and his Seventh Cavalry, Sitting Bull and his followers had fled to Canada. Several years later, hungry and cold, Sitting Bull, his family, and a few remaining warriors surrendered at Fort Buford, North Dakota. Fearing Sitting Bull's influence among his people, the army imprisoned him for two years before allowing him to return to his reservation and people.

The Wounded Knee massacre in December 1890 occurred on the coldest of winter days and left several hundred of his tribe—dozens of unarmed elders, women and children mixed in among them—dead in the snows of a Dakota prairie, shot down by the remnants of the Seventh Cavalry. As the new moons came and went, the loss of his revered friend Sitting Bull and the one-sided "battle" at Wounded Knee still brought a bitter bile to the back of the throat of Chief Two Sticks. The lingering resentment would one day prompt a violent attack on those he viewed as his aggressors that would eventually lead to Two Sticks's death.

For Two Sticks and the remaining rebels of his tribe, and indeed for much of the world, the 1890s were a time of incredible change and challenge. Many whites and Native Americans felt a keen sense of desperation brought on by events they could do little to control. A wave of immigrants had sailed prairie schooners across a sea of grass to settle in the Lakota hunting grounds. In their wake came towns and telegraphs and railroads. In the burgeoning cities and financial centers of the United States, the Panic of 1893 wrought the most serious economic crisis the nation had yet known. Major railroads went bankrupt, followed by a series of bank failures. The National Cordage Company, then the most actively traded stock in the country, went into receivership. At the panic's peak, as much as 18 percent of the US workforce would find themselves unemployed.

The world stage was at least as volatile. On February 15, 1894, French anarchist Martial Bourdin attempted to destroy London's Royal Greenwich Observatory with a bomb, and a month later fellow anarchist Jean Pauwels died in a Paris church when the bomb he was carrying exploded in his pocket. That summer French President Sadi Carnot was assassinated by a twenty-one-year-old Italian anarchist who would himself be executed by guillotine less than two months later.

Rebellion was in the air. On March 25 Coxey's Army, the first major American protest march, departed Massillon, Ohio, for Washington, DC, to bring the plight of the unemployed to national attention. On May 1, as the jobless rioted in Cleveland, some five hundred of populist Jacob Coxey's followers arrived in DC, where the leaders of the march were promptly arrested for walking on the grass of the US Capitol.

But Two Sticks would have known little of what occurred beyond his personal horizon. His needs were more immediate. His was an existence that required attention to his daily subsistence. With a disdain for reservations and given the virtual extermination of game on the prairies, simply living was his primary focus.

The winter of 1893 found Two Sticks traveling with his two sons, Uses a Fight (or Fights With) and First Eagle, as well as a nephew, Kills the Two, and three more men, No Waters, Hollow Wood, and Whiteface Horses. Together, Chief Two Sticks's band roamed the breaks country of southwestern South Dakota, raiding ranches and stealing cattle.

Known to Indian agents as well as their reservation-bound tribal members, Two Sticks and his band were described by a February 11, 1893, story in the

Black Hills Daily Times as "Uncompapas," an unflattering term that implied sneakiness and an underhanded approach to their pursuits. The article claimed that Uncompapas were the type of Native Americans who, when in council with other Plains Indians, always positioned themselves near the exit of the circle so they could flee at the first sign of danger. They were, said the newspaper, still nomadic and had remained as uncivilized as they were a quarter of a century earlier.

In early February, under the cover of darkness, Two Sticks and his small party carried out a raid on a herd of cattle belonging to the Humphrey's cattle ranch, located on the White River, a day's ride west of the Pine Ridge Agency. Contracted to raise beef for the growing agency, the cattlemen sent word of the raid to Capt. George L. Brown, the acting Indian agent at Pine Ridge. In turn Brown quickly telegraphed soldiers at Fort Meade, near present-day Sturgis, advising them to remain on alert for further criminal activity. The Eleventh Infantry captain then dispatched half a dozen tribal police officers to apprehend the culprits.

When the tribal officers finally found Two Sticks's encampment, they quickly moved in to make arrests. Two Sticks and his band opened fire. When the dust had settled, five tribal police were dead and the sixth was wounded. Unlike his compatriot Sitting Bull, who had been killed by Indian police, Two Sticks escaped unscathed and invigorated by the brief battle.

The chief and his followers returned to the scene of their earlier crime—the Humphrey ranch—and killed four of the ranchers, later identified as R. Royce, John Bennett, thirteen-year-old Charles Bacon, and sixteen-year-old William Kelly. By some accounts these four might have been the first white men killed on a reservation since 1876. Two Sticks and his band also exhibited their thirst for revenge by shooting thirty cows and three horses.

Fearing that a full-fledged revolt was in progress, as soon as Captain Brown was informed of the killings, he sent a party of twenty-five Indians commanded by tribal policeman Joe Bush after the murderers. Reports had Two Sticks and his followers holed up at the camp of Young Man Afraid of His Horses. Nineteen years earlier it had been Young Man Afraid of His Horses who had helped negotiate a treaty that allowed white men to mine for gold in the sacred Black Hills. Although opposed by many of the youngest braves, the treaty undoubtedly ended a bitter debate and curtailed a bloody outbreak of fighting with the whites. His levelheadedness would once again be needed.

While at the camp, Two Sticks purportedly told an Indian man named Crow that the hearts of his young followers were bad, and that during their Ghost Dances, the Great Spirit had advised them to kill the whites for all they had done to exterminate the buffalo and steal that which belonged to the Indians.

When Bush and his tribal troops arrived at the camp of Chief No Waters and Young Man Afraid of His Horses, Two Sticks and his band of warriors refused to surrender and a bloody battle commenced. First Eagle, Kills the Two, and Whiteface Horses were seriously wounded in the initial volley. First Eagle died immediately while Two Sticks was seriously wounded and the others were injured.

As the rebel leader lay bleeding on the ground, Chief No Waters worked his camp followers into a frenzy until they were ready to attack the tribal police. But Young Man Afraid of His Horses intervened, and in an effort to prevent further bloodshed, the peacemaker and his faithful followers positioned themselves between No Waters and his people and the tribal lawmen. When Young Man Afraid of His Horses told No Waters that harming the Indian police in support of murderers would result in all of their deaths, No Waters backed down.

But for Captain Brown the confrontation at No Waters's camp was further evidence that additional bloodshed was probable. Afraid the fight over the apprehension of Two Sticks would incite more violence, Brown gathered more than fifty chiefs at Pine Ridge on February 6, 1893, to discuss the murders and the capture of Two Sticks. During the two-hour meeting, most chiefs agreed that Two Sticks was a troublemaker who was prone to be the first to join insurrectionists. Several chiefs confirmed to Brown that they wanted no part in the hostilities and represented friendly tribes.

Two Sticks's shoulder wound was so serious that reservation officials agreed to hold him at the agency until he was sufficiently recovered to travel to Deadwood for trial. Weeks later, when a US marshal arrived to take Two Sticks to justice, the chief refused to cooperate and encouraged No Waters to protect him. The move gave Two Sticks a one-month reprieve, but when No Waters was arrested, Two Sticks had no recourse but to accompany the marshal to the Black Hills. When he was finally placed in a Deadwood jail, Two Sticks suffered a relapse and remained in guarded condition for several months.

"Two Sticks is wounded in the shoulder, Whiteface Horses in the lower limbs," one observer commented. "Their conditions are loathsome in the extreme. They will not allow a white physician to go near them and their condition can be imagined. Whiteface Horses' legs are gangrened to his knees and his demise is looked for anytime. Two Sticks will probably pull through with the loss of his arm."

Whiteface Horses did later succumb to his wounds. After standing trial on charges of instigating and conspiring to commit murder and resisting arrest, Hollow Wood, No Waters, and Kills the Two were sentenced to five years in jail. Hollow Wood and No Waters would die there, but Kills the Two would serve out his term.

As the leader of the rebel band, Two Sticks would face a different and decidedly more severe penalty. He would be hanged by the neck until dead.

On April 11, 1893, shortly after Two Sticks had been transported to Deadwood, the *Black Hills Daily Times* carried the once-proud Lakota leader's purported confession. It was filled with regrets for the actions of his boys, still maintained his innocence, and showed a measurable amount of remorse that, even at the end, Two Sticks hoped would save him from the gallows.

> *My friend I have not much to say for my part. I had nothing to do with the killing of the white men. My son that was killed by the Indian police was the cause of all the trouble. I cannot lie, my boy that is dead killed three of the white men and Whiteface Horses killed the other one. I am going to move away. . . . My boy [Uses a Fight] that is in jail at Deadwood did not have a gun. He had a bow and arrows. He is only eighteen years old and is a coward. My son that is dead had a rifle. Whiteface Horses had a Winchester. The reason we killed them white men did not treat us right. My son said that he wanted to die and be hung.*

As he recuperated from his bullet wound, Two Sticks might have wondered at each passing day why a benevolent government would help him heal just so it could put him to death.

At Christmastime Two Sticks was adjudged to be well enough to be executed and preparations began in earnest. On December 28 all was in readiness and a crowd of curious residents began lurking around the Lawrence County jail yard at 8:00 a.m. By 9:30 those with admission passes were permitted inside an enclosure that consisted of a sixteen-foot-tall solid board fence that spanned the perimeter of the courtyard. At its center stood a solid gallows. By 10:15 two hundred people were packed into the enclosure.

Inside the jail Two Sticks had consumed a last meal of steak grilled over live coals, several slices of bread, and two cups of strong, black coffee. Jailers reported to the assembling press that he had spent his last night sleeping, singing, talking, and walking the floor of his cell. After Two Sticks had finished his meal, Father Florentine Digmann—called "Black Bear" by the Lakota—and W. L. McLaughlin, the condemned's attorney, joined the aging Indian and gently told him that President Cleveland had refused to pardon him for his crimes and that only the gallows and the promise of everlasting life awaited him.

A short time later, a US marshal named Peemiller and a swarm of local dignitaries and reporters walked down the corridor to Two Sticks's cell and the death warrant was read aloud. At first the chief merely grunted. But when asked if he had any reason why the sentence should not be carried out, Two Sticks turned to the marshal and gave it one last try, saying in a clear voice:

> *My heart is not bad. I did not kill the cowboys; the Indian boys killed them. I have killed many Indians, but never killed a white man; I never pulled a gun on a white man. The great father and the men under him should talk to me and I would show them I am innocent. The white men are going to kill me for something I haven't done. I am a great chief myself. I have always been a friend of the white man. The white men will find out sometime that I am innocent and then they will be sorry they killed me. The great father will be sorry, too, and he will be ashamed. My people will be ashamed, too. My heart is straight and I like everybody. God made all hearts the same. My heart is the same as the white man's. If I had not been innocent I would not have come up here so good when they wanted me. They know I am innocent or they would not let me go around here. My heart knows I am not guilty and I am happy. I am not afraid to die. I was taught that if I raised my hands to God and told a lie that God would kill me that day. I never told a lie in my life.*

Raising both his hands to the heavens, Two Sticks then began his death song. In it he proclaimed that his heart was good and that God must accept him into his fold when he died. After the chief had gone on for several minutes and had become increasingly emotional, Father Digmann finally quieted him. Two Sticks turned to the clergyman, grasped his hands, and told him he was a good man. His attorney and the marshal also received his favorable attention.

By some accounts Two Sticks was then allowed to meet with his wife, a Chinese woman called China Mary.

"I'm going to die and go to heaven," Two Sticks sadly told her. She replied, "You go to heaven. I'll go to China."

The callousness of his wife's remark may have been too much. According to witnesses, Two Sticks grabbed a leather strap from a nearby chair, slipped it around his neck, handed one end to another Indian in the adjacent cell, and began violently jerking against it. Eventually subdued by his white jailers and chastised by Father Digmann, Two Sticks was finally resigned to his fate. He said that he was only trying to ensure that if he died, he did so by the hand of his own people, not the white man's. He then grew calm.

Marshals tied his hands behind his back and the slow march to the gallows began. Two Sticks walked with a firm resolve. As he left the jail and entered the courtyard, he caught his first glimpse of the gallows and the curious onlookers gathered in their death vigil.

Led up steps to the platform, the chief was placed atop a three-foot-square trapdoor. He bowed as the clergyman read a short prayer; then as a hush fell over the courtyard, Chief Two Sticks, who had survived seventy-one winters on the plains, raised his head to the heavens and sang his death song once again. Those present were awed by his steady nerves, even as his executioners placed a noose around his neck and a black hood was pulled over his head.

As time stood still and a lifetime of hunts and heroes undoubtedly passed through Two Sticks's mind, the metallic thump of the trapdoor's mechanism heralded his plunge to death. As the floor fell away, Two Sticks plummeted seven feet four inches until the stout rope reached its end, broke his neck, and killed him instantly. He was left to hang unwavering for fifteen minutes before being declared dead by a quartet of local doctors. Without ceremony the remains of Chief Two Sticks were placed in a coffin and hauled to the local undertaker for burial in an unmarked grave.

Thus ended the long life of a Lakota, caught in a sea of change that he could not navigate.

MARTIN COUK

The Curious Case of Minnie Callison's Murder

In its infancy Deadwood was a dangerous place.

A simple slight could get a man shot. An argument over the boundaries of a mining claim was most often settled with a six-gun, a shovel, and a quiet burial beneath the ponderosa pines of the Black Hills. There was no law in any official sense for months after a wave of would-be rich men descended on the gold-filled gulch in 1875.

That gold would fuel the local economy for the next century, bringing with it sheriffs, social refinements, gaslights, and telephones long before those amenities followed the plow across the prairies to the vast American West. But in those early days of Deadwood, in a muddy, bloody town governed only by the limits of its residents' faith and allegiance to accepted social standards, there was a death a day.

For the fledgling *Black Hills Daily Times*—whose editor worked to fill pages with arrivals and departures of well-heeled residents by stage, rail, and horse; skirmishes between cavalry troops and renegade Indians; and what new merchandise had been delivered to the local mercantile—murders, mayhem, and miscreants were as commonplace as a new business opening or a weather report.

But in the early morning hours of August 17, 1878, the community of Deadwood was shocked by the murder of the town's first school teacher, the demure Mrs. Minnie Callison, found bludgeoned to death in her own bed while her husband, John, was out of town tending to his mining claim.

The murder, coming just two years and two weeks after Wild Bill Hickok had been cut down by an assassin's bullet in a local saloon, would later be described by the *Times* as "the most cruel cold blooded tragedy that ever occurred in the Hills."

It was on that cool August morning that Doctor Combs had been summoned to an upper Sherman Street house near the South Deadwood Corral. The frontier doctor knew right where the home was. Everyone knew where Mrs. Callison lived, because everyone knew Mrs. Callison.

A small crowd greeted the doctor on his arrival, where he found Noah Siever acting as an investigator while trying to keep curious onlookers from trampling the crime scene. The doctor would later testify that he found the 5-foot-4, black-eyed, black-haired school teacher lying in a pool of her own blood on her bed.

His initial examination found that Mrs. Callison had been struck eight to ten times in the forehead with a blunt instrument, likely a hammer or hatchet.

"Mrs. John Callison Found Dead in Her Bed This Morning with Her Head Bashed In," screamed the headline in the *Times*. The story provided grisly details of the murder.

> *Another murder was committed last night. The deed was committed some time last night after her retirement to bed, and was evidently done while she was asleep. She was found on her bed with her head partially turned toward the wall. There were no signs of struggle and it is probable she never stirred after receiving the first blow, as the bedding was in good order, and no blood marks were found excepting on the pillow and a few drops which splattered on the wall.*
>
> *The horrible crime was first discovered by Mr. Cal Wilson who was passing the place at the time above stated, and seeing some of the neighborhood women in front of the house talking of Mrs. Callison's strange seclusion, raised the window, and seizing hold on the woman's foot which was exposed to view, and finding it cold pronounced her dead, when the front door was forced open and she [was] found as described, with her head resting on the pillow in clotted blood—a ghastly spectacle.*

The newspaper said that no one had yet been identified as a likely suspect, but it did not hold back from speculating about the motive behind the crime or besmirching the character of the deceased.

"The matter is shrouded in mystery," the *Times* reported. "Plunder could not have been the object of the murder as her impecuniosity was notorious. The only logical conclusion in the premises is that jealousy was the motive which impelled the villain to the commission of the awful deed, for it is whispered that she had a number of admirers in this camp."

In fact, Minnie Callison had arrived in Deadwood with her husband in 1876, not long after Wild Bill Hickok, Calamity Jane, and Colorado Charlie Utter had shown up. Townspeople eager for some semblance of normality learned that Mrs. Callison had been a teacher prior to marriage, and they successfully lobbied her to establish Deadwood's first school. By February 1877 Minnie was teaching twenty-seven frontier scholars.

Within hours of the discovery of Mrs. Callison's body, a coroner's court had convened and was accepting testimony. The doctor gave minute details of the wounds of the deceased, noting she probably had died with the first blow. Mrs. Mary Boughton disclosed that three weeks earlier she had been at the house of Mrs. Callison, who had introduced her to "Professor Sander" and another gentleman.

After the couple had left the Callison home, Mrs. Callison explained to Mrs. Boughton that she did not want to participate in "spiritualistic circles," as it might injure her already fragile health. Mrs. Boughton also testified that she had again visited the Callison home the night before the murder and had met a Mr. Martin L. Couk and Mr. William Taylor. When she left, Mrs. Boughton said she had glanced back and witnessed the two men still milling about outside the Callison house.

Hauled into court, Couk swore he had visited the Callison home between nine and ten o'clock the previous evening, had stayed thirty to forty-five minutes, and had departed with Mrs. Callison in fine health and good spirits at the prospect of visiting her husband at Rockerville. Taylor's testimony was not as certain and he immediately became a suspect, the *Times* reported on August 20.

> *Taylor's evidence was given in a hesitating, reluctant and contradictory manner. About his calling last evening, the conversation that transpired, how long he was there, where he stopped and how long, the witness seemed either indisposed or unable to give any clear, direct and satisfactory account. . . .*
> *At the time we go to press the examination of Taylor was still going on. The evidence thus far is sufficient to create a suspicion against the darky Fields and Taylor.*

The next day the newspaper backtracked, noting it had "done an injustice to this gentleman" known as W. H. Taylor, a well-respected conductor for the Union Pacific Railroad, by questioning his character and suggesting his involvement in the murder of Minnie Callison.

"There is no such impression existing now in the minds of any one [*sic*] in this community of any suspicion against Mr. Taylor," the newspaper admitted. "He is esteemed and respected by all who know him, and his life and character are beyond reproach."

But the newspaper did not apologize for publishing rumors or shy away from taking a potshot at its competition. To the end the *Times* also never questioned whether Gen. Samuel Fields, known as the "Nigger General," was somehow involved in a conspiracy to commit Mrs. Callison's murder because, after all, he was black.

> *Now a word to those sensitive gentlemen who were so highly incensed and indignant by our report. It was street talk yesterday that Mr. Taylor was suspected and was in a tight*

place. The first of this talk that we heard was in conversation between Whitton of the Pioneer, Tyler of the post office news stand and Dolph Edwards. As these gentlemen seemed to understand what they were talking about, whatever street circulation the rumor got, they and such as they are primarily responsible for.

On August 23 the *Times* reported on the return of John Callison, who had come back to Deadwood to make arrangements for his wife's funeral.

"Mr. John Callison arrived here from Rockville [*sic*] last evening, but nothing new regarding the mysterious murder of his wife has been developed," it reported. "He is of the opinion that the darky, Gen. Fields, committed the crime."

Meanwhile, rumors spread through town, all of them breathlessly recounted by the *Times.* "Why wasn't the man who passed in front of Minnie's house between nine and ten o'clock the night before the murder called in to testify at the coroner's jury?" it asked readers. "And what about the lady living on Sherman Street who was asked for directions to Minnie's by a stranger? Then also there is a certain lady who lives behind the Masonic Temple, she was heard weeping loudly at midnight that night and had exclaimed that she knew Mrs. Callison had been murdered."

Nearly two weeks passed between the crime and the first arrests in the Callison case. On September 9 the *Times* gushed at having known all along that Couk and Mrs. Boughton would eventually be arrested for the murder. Their arrests the previous Saturday night "created but little surprise" and had already been predicted by "the knowing ones" in town, it stated. The only surprise, the newspaper said, was that Couk had not been arrested earlier.

Couk was thrown in the primitive county jail, unable to oversee his Lincoln Lode, his half-interest in the Golden Prospect Mine, and his sole ownership of the Monte Verde Saloon on Main Street. After arriving with the first wave of miners in 1876, Couk had built a successful, diversified empire. At one point, according to historian Jerry L. Bryant, the entrepreneur had purchased the Whale Lode in Gold Run for one thousand dollars, then immediately resold it for five times that, big money on the western frontier.

By the time of the trial, Couk had used some of his wealth to hire his own private detective to investigate the case.

Meanwhile, Boughton was confined to her house under guard. It must have been an imposition for the thirty-seven-year-old Boughton, not being able to oversee her downtown restaurant, The Parlor, where she offered a popular fifty-cent special consisting of baked pork and beans.

On September 11, less than a month after the murder, with Couk and Boughton in custody, the preliminary examination of evidence began with Judge

Hill of Lead City presiding. Sheriff Manning testified that Couk had asserted his innocence and sought a fair trial. The second witness, E. Hurlburt, swore he had sold a bottle of chloroform to Couk about a week before the murder.

But Mary Boughton's husband, Mark, was the first to create an uproar in the court's galleries. He related several conversations with the accused, including one during which Couk seemed to insinuate that the relationship between Mark and Mrs. Callison strayed beyond friendship. It's unclear why Mark would have volunteered information that could very well incriminate his wife by creating a possible motive for her to murder her friend.

When questioned about a conversation Mary Boughton had allegedly had with the deceased the evening of the murder, defense attorney William Soery reportedly leapt to his feet and screamed, "In the name of the people, in the name of God, in the name of religion and all that is great and good, that dreadful deed should be searched to its very bottom, even to the most extraneous circumstances bearing on this case, to prove whether the accused is innocent or guilty."

The crowd assembled for the hearing stood and applauded, much to the consternation of Judge Hill, who recessed the court until later that evening. When the court reconvened, Mark Boughton further testified that at about the time of the murder, he had heard a rumor that his wife and Couk were going to leave the country together.

When the preliminary hearing was done, Judge Hill told Couk the evidence against him warranted him being held without bail until a district court trial could be conducted.

Stunned, Martin Couk then rose from his chair at the defense table and said, "I bow meekly to the ruling and decision of the court, but declare that I am as innocent of the crime as when I left my mother's breast."

Nearly a month later, on November 6, 1878, newspaper accounts reveal that Couk was indicted for murder and Mrs. Boughton was indicted for aiding, abetting, inciting, and advising the commission of a felony. The accused were given three days to enter pleas and Boughton was thrown in jail, but she was soon released after her husband and eight friends posted a ten-thousand-dollar bail.

Three days before trial, the *Times* visited Couk in his jail cell, where they said he was in good health and fine spirits, confident in his innocence even after more than two months' imprisonment.

"He is the most hopeful person we ever saw, and we sincerely hope the truth of this great mystery will come out, that innocent parties may not suffer," the newspaper stated.

On November 22 Territorial Assistant District Prosecutor Hastie presented the case against Couk before Judge G. C. Moody. One of the most damning testimonies came from Couk's landlady, Mrs. A. E. Simmons, who said she learned of the murder shortly after the body was found, then returned to her home to awaken Couk.

"When I came back I awakened Mr. Couk, who was asleep upon my bed," Simmons testified. "He started up [and] says, 'Great God, Anna! Have they found her so soon?'"

Simmons also testified that the morning following the murder she found a blood-soaked handkerchief and a towel in Couk's overcoat, as well as a half-full bottle of chloroform. Although the defense tried to discredit Simmons, soliciting testimony indicating she was a spurned lover of Couk's, Simmons was allowed to testify that she had overheard Couk, Mrs. Boughton, and Mrs. Callison planning to leave the country together and willing to kill Mr. Boughton if he interceded.

Two days later the jury found Couk guilty of murder. Uncharacteristically, the *Times* declined to say whether Couk was guilty or innocent, simply reporting that he "now stands before the world with the crime of murderer fastened to him."

By the last day of the month, a worn-looking Couk, "suffering both mind and body," was escorted back into court. Disheveled and obviously disturbed, Couk was given a blanket and allowed to lie down on the floor of the sheriff's office. Meanwhile, his attorney, Judge Brearley, made an impassioned plea. Judge Morgan, representing Dakota Territory, countered by arguing that Couk either murdered Minnie Callison or knew who did.

The final argument held sway. Judge Moody summarily dismissed the request for a retrial and sentenced Couk to be hanged by the neck until dead on January 28, 1879.

In its December 12, 1878, edition, the *Times* reflected on the guilt of Martin Couk and on the court's decision, which it labeled "an occasion of thrilling interest such as has never been witnessed in the Hills before and the like of which will not be likely to occur very soon again." The newspaper further stated that the public would be favorably inclined to have the governor commute Couk's sentence to life imprisonment if he would only reveal all he knew about the death of Minnie Callison. Couk's dedicated attorney headed to the territorial capital of Yankton to request a commuted sentence, even as his client was spewing comments critical of his legal representation. Just two weeks before his scheduled hanging, Couk was granted a writ of error, and his imminent death was postponed while the courts determined if he was due a new trial. The judge said he would not consider resentencing Couk until Mrs. Boughton's trial was finished.

In February 1880 the court reconvened to try its case against Mary Boughton. On Valentine's Day Mrs. Simmons once again testified about the bloody handkerchief and coat, as well as the chloroform. The defense called a string of witnesses in an attempt to impeach her testimony, with some effect. On February 18 virtually the entire town showed up to hear closing arguments, packing the courtroom, the platform, and even the stairs to the point that Judge Moody had to call for order.

After the judge declined to dismiss the case, the assistant prosecutor explored the scope of evidence in the Callison murder "in a very forcible, plain, and at times eloquent manner," the *Times* reported. "His theory was that Mrs. Callison had been chloroformed while asleep, and whilst in that condition murdered."

After four weeks of delays and testimony by seventy-five witnesses, the jury was out for only minutes when it returned with a verdict: not guilty.

"Mary E. Boughton was returned to her husband and the world fully exonerated from any complicity in the terrible murder she was suspected of having been connected with," the *Times* said.

Martin Couk was not as lucky. Moments after Boughton was released, Couk was hauled before Judge Moody who, after expressing his sincere reluctance in doing so, set Couk's hanging for April 16.

The *Times* was incensed that Couk was sentenced to hang while Boughton was set free. By the end of November, the Boughtons had left Deadwood forever, divorced and looking for a place where no one knew them.

As Couk passed a year and a half in a lonely jail cell, his friends began circulating a petition to the governor of Dakota Territory calling for the commutation of his death sentence. The *Times* told it all, and captured its stance on the issue in a March 26, 1880, report.

"Yesterday one of the largest and most numerously signed petitions and the signatures represented the names of the most respectable and business portion of Deadwood inhabitants was forwarded to Gov. Howard asking for commutation of sentence in the Couk case to life imprisonment," the *Times* reported. The petition was accompanied by a letter from Judge Moody urging the same action:

> *To our mind, capital punishment should never be inflicted unless the evidence is positive, and when the evidence as in this case, is purely circumstantial, imprisonment for life, with the chance of executive clemency, if per chance evidence of the prisoner's innocence should come to light, is the more humane way of dealing with criminals. The citizens of the Black Hills are too humane and enlightened to require this blood atonement. It is one of the relics of barbarism that finds no lodgment in the minds of the cultivated people of this territory, and in this particular instance we say let the sentence be commuted to imprisonment for life.*

As Couk's date with destiny approached, efforts for the commutation of his sentence intensified. But on the other side of the territory in Yankton, Governor William A. Howard was battling for his life. On April 10, 1880, Howard died, and on April 15, just a day before he was scheduled to be hanged, Couk was given a reprieve until July 24, allowing time for a hearing before the Territorial Supreme Court. That court subsequently upheld the verdict but reduced Couk's sentence from hanging to life imprisonment. In May, Couk's positive reputation was enhanced when Sheriff Manning reported that during a jail break, Couk had declined to run and had even helped law enforcement officers prevent the escape of several other inmates. The *Times* reported:

> *We learn from Sheriff Manning that evening before last was the fourth opportunity that M. L. Couk has had to escape from our county jail, and that he had not only refused to escape, but has been invaluable to both the sheriff and the community in preventing these jail deliveries. It seems to us, were the time of an execution flying towards us with the wings of lightning, the horrible glare of the gibbet upon our imagination would tempt us successfully to fly from confinement, and if necessary take the chances to die by the officer's bullet rather than be the chief attraction in the public death of a felon.*
>
> *In this land of gold and the excitement of a mining country, our good people should stop and think deeply, lest an innocent man be sacrificed upon the altar of perjury. There is not a vast deal to life at best, and it is not much to stop the ebb and flow long enough to see that justice is done a fellow. It is true that a jury found Couk guilty of murder, but it must be remembered that Couk was not defended as any conscientious lawyer would defend a fellowman [sic] on trial for his life.*

On August 9, 1880, Sheriff Manning set out on the Sidney stage with Couk in tow, intent on delivering the man, at long last, to the Detroit penitentiary where Couk would spend the rest of his life. The *Times* noted that upon his departure, Couk occupied a prominent place in the front of the stage, where young female admirers had presented him with two large bouquets of flowers.

Upon his arrival at Michigan's federal prison, Couk granted an interview with the *Detroit Free Press* in which he expressed his confidence in one day gaining his liberty.

"My only hope is that a bill will be passed by Congress making it possible for my case to go before the United States Supreme Court, and if it goes there I am sure of acquittal for I am innocent," the prisoner told the *Free Press*. "Why, if there could have been such a thing, and, of course, there could not, as to submit my case to a vote of the citizens of Deadwood, I would have had my liberty the day of my conviction."

It would be more than a year before a newspaper again mentioned Martin Couk's name. On November 28, 1881, the *Times* noted that Couk's sister was in Deadwood working to generate support for a gubernatorial pardon. The newspaper reminded its readers of the man's imprisonment for life, "and since that time Martin L. Couk has been in a reformatory at Detroit, as much forgotten by the community in which he lived, was tried and sentenced as though he were dead, until quite recently his sister, a most estimable lady, came amongst us for the purpose of procuring his pardon."

When Miss Couk left Deadwood for Yankton a few days before Christmas 1881, the newspaper reported that she had made many friends who would be supporting her efforts to solicit a pardon from the governor.

Two months later, on Valentine's Day 1882, the *Times* reported on Miss Couk's efforts: "The many friends of Martin Couk, now serving a life sentence for complicity in the Callison murder, will be pleased to hear that their efforts for his pardon are soon to be crowned with success. The pardon is all made out and signed, and only awaits the settlement of some financial matters before it will be issued."

In June Martin Couk was pardoned by newly appointed Governor Nehemiah D. Ordway. In November the *Times* reported that he was visiting Denver after brief stops the previous month in Rapid City and the southern Black Hills, and had plans to soon visit his favored haunts in Deadwood. His name didn't surface again in the newspapers until fifteen years later.

Then on June 1, 1897, the *Daily Pioneer Times* briefly reported on the final fate of the man convicted then pardoned for killing Minnie Callison, Deadwood's first schoolmarm:

> It is reported that Martin L. Couk, who was sent to the pen for life for the killing of Minnie Callison, in Deadwood, in 1878, and who was pardoned about two years ago, was recently hanged in Oklahoma for committing murder. On the scaffold Couk said he had killed seven persons during his life time [sic] but that he did not regret any of his crimes except the one at Deadwood.

STELLA AND BENNIE DICKSON

South Dakota's Own Bonnie and Clyde

For her sixteenth birthday Stella Dickson robbed a bank. For her seventeenth birthday she was sent to a federal prison.

Little Stella Redenbaugh fell for the older, tousle-headed Bennie Dickson during the worst of the Great Depression. He was a promising boxer and former Boy Scout who one day hoped to be a lawyer. In 1918 he and his brother, Spencer, had even rescued a woman when she attempted to drown herself in a local pond. The heroic act led the Kansas governor to propose the boys, who lived in Kansas at the time, for the Carnegie Medal. But somewhere along his life's journey, those who knew him said Bennie had proceeded down a wayward path.

When Bennie married Stella, Stella wasn't yet sixteen. Money was scarce, jobs were nonexistent, and very few in the Midwest had an easy go of it. Undeterred by conventional wisdom, the starry-eyed couple vacationed at a family cabin on Lake Preston in eastern South Dakota. As Stella's special birthday approached, they apparently didn't think much about cake and candles. They thought about cash.

At about 2:30 p.m. on August 25, 1938—just a half hour before the Elkton Corn Exchange Bank's scheduled summer closing—Bennie marched into the foyer and saw the bank's two employees on duty, cashier R. F. Petschow and bookkeeper Elaine Lovley, engaged at the main business counter. Bennie approached, leveled his revolver at the pair, and calmly said, "This is a holdup. Do exactly as I say and there will be no trouble and nobody hurt."

Should a patron enter the bank, Bennie instructed Petschow to lead him or her to the floor behind the counter. When informed by the cashier that the delayed time lock to the bank's vault would not open until 3:00 p.m., the composed criminal said he'd wait, which he did—for thirty-five minutes.

During the period no fewer than twenty individuals entered the bank, including the institution's president, L. C. Foreman. All were scrutinized and quietly led to their holding place on the floor behind the teller's counter. As each customer entered the bank, "the bandit had them hand over their currency, but with an apparent desire not to take money from private individuals, except in instances where indications were that the loss could be well afforded, [and] he had Mr. Petschow look up the balances of each individual customer, to whom in most instances he casually returned their money," the *Elkton Record* reported a week later.

"Mrs. Koehn in the excitement incident to the proceedings dropped a twenty dollar bill for which she had come in to get change, and the robber in a gentlemanly manner picked it up and handed it back to her," the newspaper added. "Roy Kramer had $240 in currency, and after ascertaining that this was his private money and not the property of the Standard Oil Co., and the records showing only a small credit balance, this currency was returned to him."

When Bennie had acquired sufficient resources with which to secure a birthday present for his newlywed wife as well as finance his imminent departure, he herded the bank officials and their customers into the vault, closed the heavy door, and made his getaway. A short time later, the bankers flipped an emergency switch within the vault intended for just such a purpose. The switch activated a warning light in Elkton's Dressel Store, and the captives were soon released.

Within minutes bank officials telephoned news of the brazen daylight robbery to Sioux Falls, and within two hours of the holdup, investigators with the state and federal departments of justice were on the scene. Bennie had been wearing gloves, so efforts to find his fingerprints proved futile. But officials were aware that Bennie had an accomplice, even though they didn't have a clue who either of them was or where they had gone.

With the help of Sheriff Hank Claussen, law enforcement authorities spent the next few days securing evidence they hoped would lead to the apprehension of the desperados. The *Elkton Record* pronounced, "One fact which may be of value in tracing the pair by checking the circulation of the stolen money is that a shipment of new currency had been received on the day of the holdup, and the serial numbers of these bills will be a matter of record."

A week after the crime, Bennie and Stella were leading a life on the lam with as much as twenty-five hundred dollars in cash. But after lying low for two months, their financial reserves began to dwindle. It was time to hit another bank. On the eve of Halloween, they arrived in Brookings, a modest college town in extreme eastern South Dakota that was just recovering from its annual hell-raising Hobo Day. Bennie and Stella would bring life back to the party.

When officials of Northwestern Security National Bank opened the doors for business at 8:30 a.m. on Monday, October 31, they were greeted by a handsome young couple equipped with a machine gun and a sawed-off shotgun. The dynamic duo calmly waited for the delayed time lock to open at 11:00 a.m.

The previous Saturday's celebration of Hobo Day had ensured a brisk Monday morning business at the bank, the *Elkton Record* reported three days after the robbery, in a story adjacent to the newspaper's near-breathless announcement that *Boys Town* starring Spencer Tracy would soon come to the Elks Theatre. When Bennie and Stella arrived in Brookings, a tree-lined bastion of academia, they may have sensed easy pickings. In the two and one-half hours that the heavily armed pair stood vigil, more than one hundred people walked in and out of the bank, making their weekend deposits and loan payments, getting change, and conducting other transactions. None of them was ever aware that they stood one misstep from two desperate fugitives in the midst of pulling off a most daring raid.

At 11:00 a.m. the time lock opened, allowing access to the vault. Bennie and Stella quickly stuffed as much of the available cash as they could into bank bags and chose Northwestern Security officials R. M. DePuy and Jon Torsey as hostages. Coolly, the four left the institution unnoticed and began their getaway. Bennie and Stella got in the front seat of their black Buick while DePuy and Torsey were instructed to stand on the running boards on the outside of the vehicle. Then the car bolted forward. A few blocks later, when it appeared they had not been pursued, "Bennie slowed the sedan and his petite blond-haired accomplice dismissed the bankers with a smile and a good-bye."

A short time later, authorities received reports of the vehicle traveling at a high rate of speed southwest of Elkton. Officials quickly responded but were unable to apprehend the pair.

As they sped down gravel back roads in a cloud of dust, the Depression-era outlaws must have thought themselves another Bonnie and Clyde. Just four years earlier, Bonnie Parker and Clyde Barrow had terrorized the Midwest with a series of bold bank heists and epic gun battles with authorities. After four years of outrunning law officers and capturing the imagination of an entire nation, Bonnie and Clyde died on May 23, 1934, in a hail of gunfire near their Bienville Parish, Louisiana, hideout, struck down by a posse of heavily armed Texas and Louisiana lawmen.

As immortal as only youth can imagine themselves to be, Bennie and Stella didn't likely dwell on Bonnie and Clyde's tragic fate. In their black Buick the newlyweds carried $47,233 in cash and bonds from the Halloween holdup at the Brookings bank, and they were intent on putting as much ground between themselves and pursuing posses as they could.

But the police had all the time in the world. When they eventually tracked Bennie and Stella to a tourist campground in Topeka, Kansas, on November 24, authorities closed in on the pair. After a brief gunfight Bennie and Stella separated, both making good their escape. Bennie fled in his Buick to South Clinton, Iowa, stole another vehicle, and then doubled back to Topeka to retrieve his bride at a prearranged rendezvous point one day after the shootout.

As the couple traveled to Michigan, authorities made several attempts to capture the fugitives. In one incident, while being pursued by a patrol car, Stella grabbed a gun and shot out the cruiser's tires, earning her the nickname, "Sure Shot" Stella. During the shootout a cop's bullet grazed Stella's forehead, leaving a scar she would carry for a lifetime. In a series of confrontations, the bank robbers took three men hostage, stole getaway cars in Michigan and Indiana, and eluded lawmen on country back roads.

Now far from home and aggressively pursued by lawmen from several states, the young couple reached St. Louis and tried to blend in. When Bennie was lured to a hamburger stand by a female informant on April 6, 1939, he discovered too late that the FBI was closing in. As he attempted to flee, a young federal agent put at least four holes in Bennie's back, creating a sixteen-year-old widow and putting an end to Bennie's short lifetime of regrets.

Apparently alerted to her husband's death, Stella fled 250 miles west to Kansas City. When authorities caught up with her the next day, she was unarmed, carried seventy dollars, and was wearing three rings, including the wedding set with seven diamonds that Bennie had provided. With the fight knocked out of her and the romance gone, little Stella Dickson was apprehended without any resistance. When arrested, she also possessed a key to a New Orleans apartment and a poem Bennie had penned. It read, "In the eyes of men I am not just/But in your eyes, O life, I see justification/You have taught me that my path is right if I am true to you."

Returned to South Dakota for trial on bank robbery charges in federal district court in Deadwood, Stella reportedly listened to the proceedings while clutching a doll in her arms. Whether she did so to emphasize her youth to the jury or merely because the doll gave her comfort was never determined. The *Mitchell Daily Republic* claimed she looked "more like a schoolgirl than a gun moll awaiting the proceedings of the court on charges of bank robbery including the taking of hostages, a possible capital offense."

But Judge Lee A. Wyman did determine that Stella was guilty of taking other people's money at gunpoint. Citing her youth and the corrupting influence of her older, now-dead husband, the judge sentenced Stella to two ten-year sentences to be served concurrently. On the day she walked into the West Virginia federal prison for women, she turned seventeen.

While the shock of confinement and the loss of Bennie must have case-hardened her heart, Stella spent her time in prison taking vocational technical courses and thinking about freedom. When she was paroled in 1946, she was just twenty-four years old.

Following her release, she served a stint as a flight attendant, fixed her own plumbing and built her own fence, cared for her disabled brother, and had a lengthy career as a clerk at Kmart. She remarried twice over the course of years, but later in life admitted to a Kansas City neighbor that she had only ever truly loved one man.

As she aged, Stella became increasingly reclusive, adopting more than a half-dozen pets from the animal shelter at which she volunteered. She led a quiet life with few friends save the furry ones she rescued from a hell she had personally known. Her austere lifestyle eventually earned her a pardon for her youthful crimes from President Nixon, but few who knew her in the last decades of her life remotely suspected that little Stella had ever been in trouble with the law.

When she died on September 10, 1995, following an extended illness, no obituary marked the passing of Sure Shot Stella, one of the youngest and prettiest outlaws to ever plague the plains.

TEXAS OUTLAWS

SOSTENES L'ARCHÉVÈQUE

Misdirected Vengeance from "Those Californians"

"When I grow up," Sostenes L'Archévèque vowed, "I'll kill every white man I can." He had a Mexican-Indian mother, and he had seen his French father slain by an American at Sapello in eastern New Mexico. His intense hatred increased as he grew to maturity. At six feet, four inches, he moved like a panther, but his hooded eyes observed white men like a cobra.

L'Archévèque inherited his love of violence from his great grandfather's great grandfather, Jean L'Archévèque, who was thirteen in 1684 when he left France with one hundred explorers commanded by Robert de la Salle. They searched for the mouth of the Mississippi River, and three years later had still not found it. Then, on the Trinity River in Texas, the sixteen-year-old Jean diverted La Salle's attention while others in the party murdered their leader. The assassins argued, separating into two groups. Eventually the one headed by Hiens, an old German pirate, killed some of the other group. They wanted to kill Jean L'Archévèque, but he was away hunting at the time.

Only six of La Salle's one hundred men survived the journey to the New World, but they included Jean, who eventually reached New Mexico and served in the army at the Presidio of Santa Fe. He joined the ill-fated Pedro de Villasur expedition of 1720, which reached further into the interior of North America than any other Spanish expedition. Pawnees killed most of the expedition, including Jean, when it reached the Platte River.

In the 1870s L'Archévèque's operating grounds were around Old Tascosa in the Canadian River valley of the Texas Panhandle. He shared this territory with a more publicized outlaw from New Mexico, Billy the Kid. Most of the law-abiding folks thought Billy the Kid an amateur compared to L'Archévèque. This judgment was not based on the number of notches in their guns—each would have from twenty to twenty-five by the time he was killed—but on their motivation.

Brooklyn-born Billy the Kid wanted to avenge the murder of the only man who had ever treated him decently. He became a hero to many Westerners. L'Archévèque was a hero to no one; he just wanted to kill all the Anglos he could. The way that he killed three sheep men in 1876 should hold the record for perfidy and villainy in the Old West. Out of disgust, his own brother-in-law finally killed him to protect the community.

John Casner and his three sons had hit it rich in the California gold rush. John and his son Lew moved on to Silver City, New Mexico, to prospect. The other brothers took their share, had a thousand twenty-dollar gold pieces minted at Carson City, and invested the rest in 1,600 sheep. Their search for good sheep country brought them and their flock to the Texas Panhandle.

While Miguel García herded three thousand sheep near the place where Wildorado Creek flowed out of high mountains toward the Canadian River that summer of 1876, he saw the Casner flock in the distance. The Casner brothers, with a Navajo Indian boy employed as herder, were slowly moving their sheep toward the free grass of the Palo Duro country.

Miguel welcomed the Casner brothers and told them that they were only about thirty miles from their destination. He admired their sheep and equipment and thought they might be rich. Soon other men met the new sheep men, slowly herding their way through. They referred to them as "Those Californians."

Colás Martínez, boss of the Canadian River country, had been an Indian fighter and a store operator; now he had the largest flock of sheep in the area. He, too, welcomed the Casner brothers and told them they would find good grazing land a week or so on ahead. That very spring Charles Goodnight, Texas's leading cattleman, had ridden into the Palo Duro country seeking cattle range, and Colás had helped him look the country over and pick out the place for his ranch headquarters.

The one bane of Colás's life was the outlaw L'Archévèque, who had married his sister. The señoritas thought L'Archévèque, a tall, lithe blond, was handsome, but what an accumulation of pure hate to have marry into one's family! Goodnight would become the most powerful force for law and order in the Panhandle, and he discussed L'Archévèque and his reputation with Colás.

"Don't worry, Colonel," Colás said. "I will kill him myself if he makes more trouble."

L'Archévèque persuaded a Mexican boy, Ysabel Gurules, to go with him on a hunting trip. Instead, he led the way directly to the Casner brothers' sheep camp. Only one of the brothers was present. L'Archévèque talked to the man long enough to learn that the other brother and their Indian herder were away with the sheep. Then L'Archévèque shot him dead.

Ysabel cried and begged L'Archévèque to let him ride away. L'Archévèque slapped the boy until he agreed to hide while L'Archévèque waited for the second brother to return to camp.

When the second brother arrived, L'Archévèque shot him as he rode up to his tent. Then L'Archévèque ordered Ysabel to find the Indian herder and kill him. Shaking with fear, the boy started crying again, and L'Archévèque beat him. The boy ran, jumped on the faster of their two horses, and galloped away. He was out of gun range when L'Archévèque realized that he was going home instead of

301

following instructions; but the old nag left by the boy was too slow to catch the faster horse.

L'Archévèque decided that it was best that Ysabel had gone. He had only found a few gold pieces on the bodies of the two brothers he had killed. He would have to force the Indian to talk before he killed him. He did not want Ysabel there when he collected the rest of the gold.

The Indian herder, with the sheepdogs, was moving the flock toward the camp when L'Archévèque rode out to meet him. The herder, though frightened, refused to reveal any information. L'Archévèque shoved his pistol into the boy's stomach.

"You tell me where the gold is hidden or you'll die right here and right quick," he snarled.

One of the dogs attacked, knocking L'Archévèque off balance. He recovered, shot the dog, and again demanded that the Indian boy tell him where the gold was.

The boy told him where part of the treasure was hidden, but he did not know about the rest. "They put it in lots of places," the boy stammered. "I only know of the one."

Convinced that the boy told the truth and that no more information could be had, L'Archévèque clubbed him to death with his pistol. While he did this, the other dog attacked. He shot that one to death. The first dog was still unconscious.

L'Archévèque left the bloody scene and returned to the camp, where he found one leather bag full of gold pieces near a spring. Then L'Archévèque roped one of the two dead bodies in the camp and dragged it to the edge of a rock cliff, where he kicked it off, watching it roll and bounce to some bushes below. He took one of the Casner pistols and rode back to Tascosa. When L'Archévèque learned that Ysabel had told others of L'Archévèque's plan to kill the Californians, he decided to hide out a while.

Colás Martínez intended to keep his promise to Colonel Goodnight. He called a meeting of the men in the community, and they agreed that L'Archévèque should be killed. They set a trap by sending word to L'Archévèque that he could find food if he came to the house of Felix Gurules, Ysabel's uncle.

When L'Archévèque crept into the Gurules adobe that evening, Felix Gurules and Miguel García, hiding inside the door, grabbed his arms and stabbed him in the back. Then Colás stepped into the room, cursed L'Archévèque, and shot him twice at point-blank range. Even then the enraged L'Archévèque continued to struggle.

"Pull that knife out of my back, and I'll kill all you bastards," he screamed.

Colás pounded the wounded man's head with his pistol until he slumped into unconsciousness. A few seconds later, L'Archévèque revived. He lunged and struggled, trying to get to his feet. He screamed and cursed, calling down all the evil spirits he could remember to help him attack his enemies.

One of the men tried to choke L'Archévèque; another pounded his head again with the pistol. Barely dazed, L'Archévèque still fought and cursed. Then the third man saw a gold chain around L'Archévèque's neck with something like a cross on it. He ripped it off, and L'Archévèque dropped into unconsciousness. He died the next morning. Besides the three men who attacked L'Archévèque, Sacramento Baca, Francisco Nolan, Agapito Gurules, and one Florentine had watched the gruesome battle.

L'Archévèque was buried on the south bank of the Canadian in an unmarked grave. Although the hate-filled killer finally lay dead, the incident had not ended. About a week later, two of Goodnight's cowboys rode into the abandoned sheep camp, where they saw the body of one of the Casner brothers. They also saw the dog that, with one eye shot out, was still faithfully protecting the sheep. The cowboys moved the sheep down the canyon and turned them over to Dave McCormick, who hated sheep and sheepherders. But McCormick loved dogs, and he soon appreciated his new and intelligent friend and helped him herd the sheep.

When Goodnight returned to Pueblo, Colorado, where he was living at the time, he described the property of the Casner brothers, which had been found, and requested that the news of the killings be published in western newspapers. Two Texans prospecting in Silver City, New Mexico, with John and Lew Casner read the account, and the four men went to the Panhandle to investigate. The Casners had no trouble proving their right to the sheep, and they paid Goodnight for their keep, apparently planning to take them away.

Then rumors arose that the surviving Casners, their Texan miners, and other Texan friends planned to drive all Mexicans out of the Canadian River valley. Goodnight warned them that his well-armed cowboys would prevent such wholesale reprisals. The Casners gave up the grandiose plan but decided to kill everyone directly involved in the murder of the brothers.

Deciding that the best way to find their targets was to look for the brothers' gold coins, the Casners challenged all comers to a horse race in Tascosa and bet five hundred dollars on the outcome. Colás Martínez won the race, but the Casners identified some of the money put up by his backers as coins minted by the brothers. They hired Colás and Felix Gurules to guide them into a canyon for a look at the country.

Twelve miles into the canyon, the Casners and their Texan friends suddenly drew their guns and fired, hitting Colás in the hand. Colás shot one of the Texans in the stomach, and Gurules raced away for his life. Then the wounded Texan shot again before he died, this time killing Colás. The Casners watched their wounded friend die and then resolved to go to the place where the brothers had been killed, hoping to intercept the fleeing Felix Gurules there. They did not know that they had already killed the man who had killed the murderer of the brothers.

Felix Gurules reached the camp where his nephew Ysabel was tending other sheep. Before the Guruleses could get away, the pursuing Casners rode up and shot Felix down in a hail of bullets. Ysabel again begged for his life, and eventually one of the Casners persuaded the others that they should not kill a boy.

But the Casners and their vengeance-minded gang still had men to hunt down and kill. The next day they hanged Agapito Nolan and Florentine from a chinaberry tree, unaware that their victims had been present and approving when the murderer of the brothers had been killed.

Another Mexican, who apparently planned to steal the sheep after the brothers were killed, turned himself in at Fort Elliott for protection. The determined Casners hired five off-duty black cavalrymen to capture the man from his military guard. The next morning the man was found hanging from a cottonwood tree.

Then the Casner gang found Colás's sister (L'Archévèque's widow) and took the money her brother had won in the horse race. That money probably included coins that Colás had taken from L'Archévèque when he killed him, money that the Casners thought proved that Colás was involved in stealing their sheep.

For years afterward when Mexican sheep men were asked why they had moved out of the Canadian River valley of the Texas Panhandle to return to northeastern New Mexico, fear would cloud their faces and they would shake their heads and mutter, "Those Californians."

MYRA BELLE SHIRLEY

A Woman Who Saw Much of Life

Myra Belle Shirley, born in the southwest Missouri town of Carthage on February 5, 1848, inherited her love of violence. Her mother was a Hatfield, one of Kentucky's famous feuding families.

As a young girl, Myra was small, pretty, and full of life, but she also displayed a fiery temper. Her parents operated a tavern that became a meeting place for Confederate soldiers, guerrillas, and bushwhackers during the Civil War. It provided a fine background for the development of one of the West's leading woman outlaws.

Myra was also smart. She entered the Carthage Female Academy when it was organized in 1855. One of the first to master the curriculum of reading, spelling, grammar, arithmetic, deportment, Greek, Latin, Hebrew, and music, Myra also learned to play the piano. A fellow student remembered her as intelligent but "of a fierce nature who would fight anyone, boy or girl, whom she quarreled with; otherwise she seemed a nice girl."

Myra loved horses and the outdoors. She became a fine rider and loved to roam the hills with her brother, John Allison (Bud), six years older. Bud Shirley, wild and daring and also an excellent rider, taught his eager sister how to handle a rifle and pistol.

Bud fought with local guerrillas, attacking antislavery neighbors and Union soldiers. He rode with a group of about forty men. Myra spied on Union troops to assist her brother's guerrilla band.

William Quantrill rode into the area with his Border Ruffians, and one of his men met Myra in November 1862. Both fourteen-year-old Myra and sixteen-year-old Jim Reed instantly discovered a soul mate in the other. Reed, handy with fists and guns, had been riding with Quantrill for a year.

In February 1863, when she was fifteen, Myra learned that some neighbors were sheltering Union troops, and she got this information to her brother's guerrilla band. The band attacked the troops and drove them out, killing two or three.

The Confederate defeats at Vicksburg and Gettysburg later in 1863 convinced most that the Confederacy was doomed, but the guerrillas in southwest Missouri kept fighting. By early 1864 Bud Shirley was one of the men most wanted by Union troops in Missouri. Near the end of June, he was killed by men of the Third Wisconsin Cavalry, riding out of Fort Scott, Kansas.

Myra went with her father to claim her brother's body. As her father laid the body in their wagon, a squad of Union soldiers glowered with contempt. Someone laid Bud's cap and ball revolver on the seat next to Myra. The grief-stricken girl picked up her brother's pistol and began handling it.

"Put that gun down, Myra," her father ordered.

Myra glared at the soldiers and snatched the pistol out of its holster. "You damned blue-bellies will pay for this," she screamed.

As the onlookers scattered in panic, her father ran to the front of the wagon. But before he could reach Myra, she had leveled the pistol at the soldiers and was thumbing the hammer as fast as she could.

The weapon only clicked; someone had removed the firing caps. As the wagon moved away, the soldiers laughed and Myra sobbed helplessly.

Impassioned feelings leading to neighbor-on-neighbor violence had often resulted in warnings to the Shirleys to leave the state, but they had held on stubbornly. On September 22, 1864, most of Carthage was burned and abandoned, including the tavern and home of the Shirleys. But the Shirleys had already left. Disheartened by the loss of his son, John Shirley loaded his family into two wagons and they moved to Scyene, Texas, a small village ten miles southeast of Dallas, where a cousin of the family and other Missourians had already settled. Sixteen-year-old Myra drove one of the wagons. Her fury at Yankees still burned like a fever.

The Shirleys started farming about a mile east of Scyene. They got off to a bad start. They lived in a dugout at first, and then built a four-room house. Water had to be hauled in barrels from distant Trinity Creek. Neighbors complained that they took too much water and didn't leave enough for others. Remembering the violence between neighbors in Missouri, the Shirleys kept to themselves. The rough and hearty backslapping Texans thought them unsociable.

Myra attended the one-room community school but very irregularly. She had already mastered the courses at the female academy in Missouri, and she looked down on the other pupils. With her scathing tongue and fiery temper, the others thought her wild. She and fifteen-year-old brother Edwin helped care for the two younger boys. The family changed the name of seven-year-old Cravens to John Allison in memory of Bud. Myra's only entertainment was riding horseback along Mesquite Creek and collecting news from Missouri.

Frank and Jesse James, the Younger Brothers, and others from Quantrill's raiders were now riding as a band of robbers, and Myra followed their news closely. Perhaps she would hear something of Jim Reed. The robbers could not use the gold they stole from railroads and banks because it was not functional in transactions by common people—it just became incriminating evidence. So six of them—including Jesse James and Cole Younger and at least three more Younger brothers—rode three hundred miles to San Antonio to sell their gold to a Mexican broker at a deep discount. On their return ride north in July 1866, they stopped at the Shirleys' for a short visit.

Some speculate that Cole Younger seduced Myra on this trip, but other than the fact that Myra's first child was said by some to be named Pearl Younger, there is no evidence to support the story. Myra Belle did say in an interview in later years that the first man she fell in love with and the first man she married was "a dashing guerrilla."

Belle's dashing guerrilla was Jim Reed. His father died in 1865, and his widowed mother moved with her children, including Jim, to Collin County, Texas, settling near McKinney, where a couple of relatives were living.

The Reeds and the Shirleys renewed old friendships, and love flamed anew in Belle and Jim. They married in Collin County on November 1, 1866. Jim moved in with his in-laws, helping with their farming. He considered buying land of his own, but when that fell through in 1867, he and Belle joined his mother and brothers and they all returned to Missouri to farm there.

Belle had a daughter, Rosie Lee, in September 1868. She idolized the child and called her "my little pearl." From this description by a loving mother has come—from writers more filled with imagination than facts—the story (and a book) that Belle's first child was Pearl Younger, illegitimate daughter of noted outlaw Cole Younger. Belle's parents and her brothers always called the child Rosie Lee.

Soon after the birth of his daughter, Jim Reed killed a man in Arkansas who had just killed Jim's younger brother. Jim fled to Indian Territory because the only lawmen there were United States marshals, and there weren't many of those.

In 1870, not feeling safe even in the Territory, Jim took his family and fled to Los Angeles, California. Jim rode horseback the whole distance, and Belle and Rosie Lee rode a stagecoach.

Belle often described her time in California as the happiest period of their lives. Their son Edward was born there in 1871.

In early 1872 Los Angeles police learned that Jim Reed was wanted in Arkansas. Again he fled, this time at night and again on horseback. Belle and the children traveled around Cape Horn on a sailing ship and took refuge with her parents, who had moved from the farm into Scyene. Jim reached them soon afterward, having ridden through the southwest United States and parts of Mexico.

The two families were crowded in a three-room house, but John Shirley had apparently prospered. He acquired a place in the country for his daughter and her family. Jim and Belle began managing a string of racehorses, and they did a lot of horse trading. Belle took care of the business end of their venture because Jim, with a price on his head, had to keep under cover.

Jim was often mixed up in deals involving stolen cattle and horses, but the community—then in the carpetbagger stage of Texas history—overlooked his faults. They treated him as an ex-soldier, persecuted by Yankees and carpetbaggers.

Once, Jim was thrown into jail in a little town, and Belle refused to leave him. The next day she visited the jail, dressed in a black dress and a heavy black veil. Later the jailer discovered that Jim had walked out, wearing Belle's costume. The "inmate" remaining in the jail was Belle!

"I have committed no crime," Belle told the jailer. "The Bible says that a woman should cleave to her husband, doesn't it? Well, I only did my duty."

Belle was kept in the cell for a few days and then released without charges.

About 1873 a Dallas County sheriff named Nichols put Jim in jail, and Belle threatened to kill the sheriff. The next day Nichols was shot dead in a Dallas street, and Belle was credited with the killing. Many newspapers reported the crime, and the *Kansas City Star* carried a drawing of Belle galloping furiously away from the murder surrounded by a hail of bullets. However, there is no record that Belle was ever charged with the killing. Jim was released soon after Nichols was slain.

Also in 1873 Jim Reed and Belle, dressed as a man, and two other men, all masked, robbed a rich Creek Indian, said to have stolen a large sum from tribal funds. The robbery occurred in the Indian's home in nearby Indian Territory. The four robbers tortured the Indian and his wife by putting ropes around their necks and hoisting them off the floor to make them talk. After the man had been "hanged" seven times and his wife three, they disclosed where thirty thousand dollars in gold was hidden. Soon after the robbery Belle came out with a new string of racehorses, and her horses were accepted into all the big race meets throughout Texas.

Belle often disguised herself as a man. Shortly after the robbery of the Creek Indians, she was in the Riggs Hotel in Bonham, Texas, wearing a young man's clothing while the robbery was being discussed. When the discussion mentioned Belle and Jim, a Dallas lawyer spoke up. He said he knew Belle intimately and she was a "no good" woman. The hotel was crowded, and the lawyer had to share his bed that night with a "young man."

The next morning Belle told her bedmate, "Partner, I'm not a man. You tell your wife that you slept last night with Belle Reed!" One writer added the touch that she struck him with a riding whip as she stormed away contemptuously.

Another popular story about Belle related that during one of Jim's absences she set herself up in an unnamed Texas town as a rich Southern widow. She attended church regularly, patronized the town's leading dressmaker, milliner, and beauty parlor, and was soon accepted by the most respectable people, including a prominent banker. One night the late-working banker let Belle into his office. She drew a pistol, relieved the bank of thirty thousand dollars in greenbacks, and disappeared. Before leaving, she bound and gagged her victim. He had difficulty with explanations to his wife the next morning.

We have no proof of this story, but it sounds just like something Belle would enjoy doing.

We do have details of Belle's involvement in one of Texas's most notorious stage robberies. Sometime in February 1874, she and J. M. Dickson and his wife rented a house in San Antonio to study stage schedules and plan the robbery. On Thursday, April 1, the three moved to San Marcos and camped on the bank of the beautiful San Marcos River, probably at the site of present Aquarena Springs. The next day Jim Reed, the leader, joined them with Cal Carter and John Nelson.

Reed, Carter, and Nelson left the camp on Sunday, purchased some rather poor riding horses, and waited just north of the Blanco River, near present-day Kyle, Texas. On Tuesday evening, April 7, they held up the San Antonio to Austin stage about two miles north of the Blanco station. The nine passengers included the president and teller of the San Antonio National Bank, the president's brother, two other San Antonio businessmen, two discharged soldiers, a lady from St. Paul, Minnesota, a man from Fort Concho, and a young German who had just boarded the stage in San Marcos.

The robbers moved their saddles to the better-quality stage horses and rode east toward Lockhart. Then they doubled back northwest toward Fort Concho, before the trail was lost.

Besides one thousand dollars from the bank president (who hid his watch in the grass), they got smaller amounts of cash and jewelry from all the others. The total of cash was twenty-five hundred dollars, and mail sacks were also taken. The next day the Texas legislature met and authorized a reward of three thousand dollars. Others added to the reward until it reached seven thousand dollars.

When the United States marshal questioned the three campers left behind, Belle gave her name as Rosa McComus. This was the name of an acquaintance of Belle's whom she did not like because of her stuck-up attitude. Belle often used that alias with impish delight.

Belle and the Dicksons were examined by the United States magistrate but released without being charged.

Later in August 1874, Jim Reed was shot to death by John Morris in a Collin County farmhouse. Morris was an acquaintance of Jim, and the two men were traveling together when they stopped at the farmhouse for a meal.

Jim usually carried a repeating carbine as a saddle gun. This time he entered the house unarmed, as it appeared that Morris had persuaded him that the farmer was squeamish about having weapons in his house. So Jim left his pistol belt on his saddle, and he leaned his carbine against the house, just outside the door. Morris also entered unarmed, but then slipped out, got his own pistol, and returned to shoot Jim in the back for the dead-or-alive reward then being offered for the robbery of the stage. Different versions of the killing differ in details, but there is no question that Morris killed Jim for the reward.

Jim Reed's murder was the great sorrow of Belle's life, but she reacted more with rage and a thirst for vengeance than with grief. She certainly got even with John Morris.

Morris could not get the reward without proving that the man he had killed was Jim Reed, so Belle was summoned to identify the body. The weather was hot, no undertakers were available, and Belle knew that Jim would have to be buried soon. She also knew that no one in the community would admit that they knew the notorious outlaw. The identification that Morris needed could only come from her.

She looked at her husband's bullet-riddled body and then at Morris. Her lips curled in cold hate and scorn. "This sonofabitch Morris," she said, "appears to have murdered the wrong man. If anybody gets the reward for killing Jim Reed, they'll have to kill Jim Reed. This isn't him." Belle turned and rode away without another word. Jim Reed was buried in an unmarked grave, and John Morris did not get the reward.

Belle's vengeance even extended to Jim's own family. She always blamed Jim's brother Solly for not hunting Morris down and killing him.

After her husband's death, Belle moved back to Scyene. Her father died shortly after, and her mother moved away. Belle tried to train Rosie Lee as a dancer, and she appeared once on a stage in Dallas when she was fourteen, but the girl had a nervous disorder and fainted easily. Edward, too, was in poor health.

In 1876 Belle was running a livery stable near Dallas. Besides her influential friends in Dallas, she knew many of her husband's outlaw friends. Soon she was dealing in stolen horses and described by Emmett Dalton, Cole Younger's cousin, as a "fence for horse thieves." Belle's granddaughter, Rosie Lee's daughter Flossie Doe, wrote about her grandmother, explaining that "stealing from a damned Yankee or a carpetbagger was different from stealing from a Texan, and Myra Reed never stole a horse from a Texan."

Flossie Doe's middle name was well chosen. Her mother, then known as Pearl Younger, never revealed the name of the girl's father. Perhaps she didn't know.

Belle's neighbors had never paid attention to her long rides on horseback, sometimes for a week at a time. They assumed she was meeting Jim in some secret hideout. But now they began gossiping about Belle's morals. Being faithful to an outlaw husband was one thing; consorting with outlaws to whom she was not married was another. Belle's friends dropped her away, and she was no longer welcome in respectable Dallas homes.

In 1878 Belle was jailed in Dallas for possession of stolen horses. After about a week, a deputy sheriff let her out, and they disappeared together. A month later he was back with his wife. He claimed that Belle had grabbed his pistol and forced him to let her out. Then she kept him busy cutting wood, carrying water, and doing all the camp cooking. He made his escape from her only by great watchfulness and ingenuity. At least that's what he told his wife.

The incident demonstrates Belle Reed's ability to dominate men. From this point on, most of her outlaw career was played out in Kansas and Indian Territory, although she returned to Texas from time to time. She apparently selected and discarded lovers at will, never finding one to replace the outlaw with whom she first fell in love.

Her lovers—a few of them husbands—included Sam Starr, Blue Duck, John Middleton, Jim July, Jack Spaniard, Jim French, and Bruce Younger, Cole Younger's cousin. All were outlaws, and all except Bruce Younger died violent deaths, most shot to death by lawmen.

Since Bruce Younger was one of Belle's husbands, it is possible that Pearl Younger got her name from her stepfather and not from a casual acquaintance between her mother and a famous outlaw.

In 1883 Belle became the first woman tried in the courtroom of Isaac Parker, the celebrated "hanging judge" of Fort Smith, Arkansas. The jury found Belle guilty of two counts of stealing horses. Although the judge had already sent eighty-eight men to the gallows, he was unexpectedly lenient, giving Belle six months in a federal prison.

On February 2, 1889, two days before her forty-first birthday, Belle was shot by a bushwhacker as she rode her horse about a mile from her home in Indian Territory. He shot Belle in the back with a shotgun and then, to make sure she was dead, shot her in the face with a pistol. The crime was never solved.

Rosie Lee had the following carved on her mother's grave marker:

> SHED NOT FOR HER THE BITTER TEAR,
> NOR GIVE THE HEART TO VAIN REGRET.
> 'TIS BUT THE CASKET THAT LIES HERE,
> THE GEM THAT FILLS IT SPARKLES YET.

About a year before, while being interviewed by a newspaper reporter, Belle provided what might have been a better inscription when she said, "I regard myself as a woman who has seen much of life."

JUAN NEPOMUCENO CORTINA

Border Bandits

J. Frank Dobie, Walter Prescott Webb, and other historians estimated that Mexicans stole nine hundred thousand head of Texas cattle during the twenty-five years from 1850 to 1875. *Huero* (red-complexioned Spaniard) Juan Nepomuceno Cortina was supreme chieftain of the hundreds of Mexican cattle thieves during their long scourge on the border. They did, however, leave enough cattle that the region between the Nueces River and the Rio Grande became the incubator for the range cattle industry in America.

Cortina, born May 16, 1824, in Camargo, Tamaulipas, had an uneducated, undistinguished *ranchero* father, but his mother's family was as renowned as any that Spain sent to the New World. Juan, the black sheep of the family, never learned to read and only learned to sign his name after he proclaimed himself governor of Tamaulipas.

As a lieutenant in the Mexican Army, Cortina resisted the American invasion of 1846. After the war the army caught him stealing horses from his own government and discharged him. He took civilian employment and then murdered his employer for some unknown reason.

Cortina's mother owned most of the land surrounding Brownsville and Matamoros on both sides of the Rio Grande. Making his headquarters on the American side, Cortina claimed that all the cattle in the area belonged to him as descendants from his grandmother's original herd. He began paying fifty cents per head for all cattle delivered to him in the free trade zone on the Mexican side of the river. He soon had three thousand men "licensed" to deliver cattle. He warned the men that if they stole on the Mexican side, he would see them hanged; if on the American side, he would see them protected.

Called by some the Red Robber of the Rio Grande, Cortina made an impressive appearance as he rode into Brownsville each morning for coffee. His fair complexion, brown hair, grayish-green eyes, and reddish beard set him apart from his people. He inherited personal charm and excellent manners from his mother, and he had become fearless, self-possessed, and cunning. A strong, muscular man of medium height, he had leadership flair, a gambler's disposition, and a good intuition about the character of his followers.

The simmering difficulties of Texas ranchers over the growing loss of their cattle to Mexico broke into open war on July 3, 1859. That morning, while Cortina drank his coffee, he saw a Brownsville city marshal arrest a drunken Mexican who had formerly worked for Cortina. The marshal's conduct seemed unnecessarily harsh, and Cortina remonstrated, mildly at first. Upset at the interference, the marshal answered with an insult, and Cortina shot him in the shoulder. Then he galloped out of town in grand style, the rescued man seated on his horse behind him.

No one knows exactly where Cortina spent the following two months, but rumors kept circulating about mounted men gathering on both sides of the river for some kind of military action. After all, the nation that a dozen or so years before had, with questionable right, invaded Mexico now had seen one of its own law officers shot while making an arrest in an American city. What would the Yankees do now? Cooler heads tried to get Cortina out of Texas, but they couldn't find him.

Before daylight on September 28, Brownsville residents heard the gallop of horses and shouts in the streets—*Vivan Cortinas! Mueran los Gringos* (Kill the Yankees)! *Viva la República de México!* By dawn Cortina and a hundred men had captured Brownsville. Cortina wanted to kill the sheriff, but the man escaped. Cortina's men did kill three Americans, whom he described as "wicked men." They also broke into the jail, killed the jailer, and freed about a dozen prisoners. Major Samuel P. Heintzelman, who had recently commanded American troops in south Texas, reported to Colonel Robert E. Lee that an American city of almost three thousand people was occupied by armed bandits, a calamity previously unheard of in the United States.

In his first proclamation Cortina said they would not hurt the innocent but would strike for the emancipation of the Mexicans. He added, "our personal enemies shall not possess our land until they have fattened it with their own gore."

Brownsville residents appealed to Mexican soldiers under General Caravajal to protect them. So for a time Mexican soldiers quartered in a US fort—Fort Brown had been evacuated some months before by the United States Army— were protecting Americans on American soil from Mexican bandits under the command of a man who claimed—falsely, as he was born just south of the Rio Grande—that he was an American citizen.

For the next two and a half months, Cortina's men faced both Americans and other Mexicans protecting Americans in skirmishes, most of which the Cortina forces won. By early December Cortina had become a great conqueror, and Texans feared that he might force the international boundary back to the Nueces River, 130 miles to the north. The Mexican flag flew over Cortina's headquarters, and men flocked to join him.

On December 14 regular army troops under Major Heintzelman, assisted by Texas Rangers, engaged the Cortina forces. In a series of skirmishes, the army and Rangers forced Cortina to retreat about a hundred miles up the river to Rio Grande City, where he crossed into Mexico, and the Cortina occupation of south Texas ended.

An occasional cross-border raid into Texas continued to remind ranchers that the bandit Cortina was still alive and well. He was indicted for stealing cattle at least twice by the Cameron County grand jury, but they could never find him to prosecute.

In February 1860 Cortina showed up at La Bolsa, apparently planning to capture the steamboat *Ranchero,* owned by Richard King and Mifflin Kenedy, who were raising cattle on their King Ranch, a hundred miles northeast. John Ford's Texas Rangers crossed the Rio Grande and chased Cortina away.

The next month Colonel Robert E. Lee, then commanding the Eighth Military Department in San Antonio, got orders to demand that Mexico break up Cortina's bands. If the authorities refused, Lee was authorized to pursue Cortina's troops into Mexico. Lee led troops to the lower Rio Grande Valley but could not find Cortina. He did return with the promise of Mexican officials that they would try to find Cortina and arrest him.

In May 1861, when Texas seceded from the Union, Cortina invaded Zapata County and attacked the county seat. Santos Benavides, a captain in the Confederate Army, drove Cortina back into Mexico. Throughout the Civil War, Cortina continued to steal cattle in Texas. When General E. O. C. Ord began investigating lawlessness on the Rio Grande frontier, the Mexican government became concerned and took Cortina into custody in July 1875. He was paroled to Mexico City and never again allowed to hold power in Mexico.

Cortina died on October 30, 1894, and was buried in Mexico City with full military honors.

In July 1875, when the Mexican authorities isolated Cortina in Mexico City, Rosalie Lira Cortina and her husband, Ramón Cortez Garza, had just christened their son, born on June 22, Gregorio Cortez Lira. The parents were transient laborers, then living near Matamoros. We don't know if Gregorio was a grandson of Juan Cortina, but he grew up to take Cortina's place in the legends of border banditry.

Gregorio's parents moved to Manor, just outside Austin, when the boy was twelve. From ages fourteen to twenty-four, Gregorio and his brother Romaldo worked as seasonal farm hands and *vaqueros* in Karnes, Gonzales, and neighboring counties.

Gregorio, standing five feet nine inches tall and weighing 145 pounds, was small but wiry. His shoulders stooped slightly, and his jet-black hair tumbled in heavy curls, partially hiding his long, aquiline face. He talked without affection and took pains to make himself clear, often repeating statements to be sure he was understood.

Gregorio married Leonor Diaz, and their first child was born when Gregorio was sixteen. Gregorio and Romaldo, married but childless, took their families with them as they followed the seasonal work.

In 1900 the Cortez brothers settled down on rented land in Karnes County to farm for themselves. On June 12, 1901, Gregorio and Romaldo had just finished their noon meal and were resting on the front porch of Gregorio's house. Gregorio lay full length on the floor, his head in Leonor's lap. Gregorio's mother and Romaldo and his wife sat nearby. Gregorio's children were inside, eating their meal. The day was hot and clear, and the brothers' tall corn promised a good harvest for their first year as independent farmers.

Thirty-one-year-old W. T. (Brack) Morris, serving his third term as Karnes County sheriff, rode up with one of his deputies, Boone Choate, supposedly an expert in Spanish. Morris was looking for a horse thief wanted in Atascosa County. The only description he had was "a medium-sized Mexican with a big, red, Mexican hat." Morris had talked to Mexicans in Kenedy and learned that one of them had recently acquired a mare in a trade with Gregorio Cortez. Later investigation would reveal that Gregorio had the mare legally, and that the Kenedy informant knew the mare's history when he talked to Morris.

Romaldo greeted the lawmen at the gate and then returned to the house to say to Gregorio, "*Te quieren*," which literally means, "you are wanted," but was a common way of saying, "someone wants to talk to you." Choate thought that both brothers knew that Gregorio was a wanted man, and he probably told that to Morris.

When Gregorio came out to the front fence, Choate asked if he had traded a *caballo* (horse—the correct term in agricultural communities for the male equine) to the informant. Apparently Choate could not think of *yegua,* the word for mare. Gregorio answered truthfully, "No."

Sheriff Morris got out of his buggy and told Choate to tell the brothers that he was going to arrest them. Choate interpreted Gregorio's response as "No white man can arrest me." It appeared later at Gregorio's trial that he had said, "You can't arrest me for nothing." Gregorio had never been in trouble or arrested before. Apparently Choate had misunderstood another Spanish word.

Romaldo, unarmed, stood about twelve feet away, listening and watching. Morris suddenly drew his weapon, shot Romaldo in the face, and fired at Gregorio, but missed. There was evidence at the trial that Romaldo was moving toward Morris when he shot him. Gregorio's return shot mortally wounded the sheriff. Choate ran away as fast as he could.

Morris staggered to the gate and collapsed. Gregorio shot him again as he lay on the ground. The family treated Romaldo's wound, loaded him into the sheriff's buggy, and carried him to his own house, while Morris was wandering away in the chaparral, bleeding to death. Gregorio saddled a small sorrel mare for himself and a horse for his brother, and set out for Kenedy to get medical care for Romaldo.

Riding through the brush was difficult because Romaldo, feverish, kept falling off his horse. Finally Gregorio stopped and laid his dying brother under a tree. From mid-afternoon until dark the two lay in the brush less than five miles from Gregorio's home while a posse of at least fifty searched the area. The posse didn't find Morris's body until they stumbled on it the next morning. The posse did find the Cortez family, and they terrified the children, who cowered under the table while the men were in Romaldo's house.

Gregorio had to abandon both animals and carry Romaldo all five miles into Kenedy. It took him from sunset until one o'clock in the morning. He left his brother with a family that he knew could obtain medical aid, and then disappeared into the darkness.

Knowing that his pursuers would expect him to head south to the border, Gregorio struck out on foot to the north. He hoped to reach Gonzales County, hide for a few days, and then move on north to Austin, where he had relatives. It took him forty hours to travel about eighty miles to Gonzales County. He had to travel slowly to avoid the posses that were looking for him.

At sundown on the fourteenth, after those forty hours, Gregorio reached the Schnabel ranch, where he knew he could hide with a friend, Martín Robledo.

Gregorio's wife, mother, and sister-in-law had all been jailed, and Robert M. Glover, Gonzales County sheriff and a good friend of Sheriff Morris, had talked to them and pressured them to tell him where Gregorio planned to hide.

By the time Gregorio came out on Robledo's porch to rest his feet after his harrowing hike, Glover's posse were in the brush behind the house, planning their attack. Present at the house were Robledo; his wife; their three sons, ages eighteen, sixteen, and thirteen; a visitor, Martín Sandoval; and a half-grown boy, Ramón Rodríguez, who lived with the Robledo family.

Glover had four deputies, ranch owner Henry Schnabel, and one Mexican in his posse. There was evidence that the posse had been drinking on their way to the Robledo house. Glover divided the posse into three groups to surround the house and attack from three sides at once. The first shots were exchanged between Glover and Gregorio, and Glover was killed. After that exchange Robledo, his oldest son, and Sandoval all ran into the brush to hide, as did Gregorio. There was no evidence that any of them, except Gregorio, was armed or fired any shots.

Heavy firing continued, and Henry Schnabel, the rancher, was killed by one of the posse. Mrs. Robledo and the three younger boys, all unarmed, were in the house when the deputies broke in, after the other men had run into the brush.

Mrs. Robledo was shot while shielding her sons, and the Rodríguez boy was also wounded.

The officers initially reported that ten rifles were confiscated in the house. By the time of the trial, the evidence showed that only one rifle was in the house, the normal weaponry in country homes at that time. It had not been fired.

After the posse left with Mrs. Robledo and the younger boys under arrest, Gregorio slipped back into the house and got his shoes. This time he headed straight for the Rio Grande. On Saturday morning he reached the Guadalupe River and the home of another friend, Ceferino Flores. In the two and a half days since he had killed Sheriff Morris, he had walked nearly a hundred miles. Flores took Gregorio's pistol and gave him his own, along with his sorrel mare and saddle.

Riding now on the second small sorrel mare in his memorable flight, Gregorio again struck southwest. A posse followed close behind, and it stopped to give Flores the rope treatment—successive "hangings" until he told what he knew. Flores served two years in prison for helping his friend.

Between Saturday morning and Sunday evening, the little sorrel mare carried Gregorio from the Guadalupe to the San Antonio River. It was only fifty miles on the map, but with posses and bloodhounds looking for him, the doubling back and giving of false leads, and sometimes the shooting, Gregorio rode many more.

Shortly after noon Sunday a fresh posse picked up his trail. For six hours Gregorio galloped, circling and zigzagging, with mounted pursuers sometimes as close as five hundred yards behind. About six o'clock the little mare stopped. She could go no farther. Gregorio barely slipped off her back before she fell over, dead.

He took the saddle and bridle and hid in the brush while the closest posse broke into small groups and continued its search. After dark Gregorio found a little brown mare in a pasture, saddled her, cut the fence, and started on the last segment of his flight.

He passed through Floresville, about a hundred miles from Cotulla. Dodging pursuers constantly, it took him three days and almost three hundred miles of riding to reach Cotulla. The posses had to stop from time to time for fresh horses, and one of them killed at least six horses in the pursuit.

Sometimes Gregorio would collect a small group of cattle and herd them along to hide his tracks. Once, desperate for water, he drove a small group to a water hole and drank in plain sight of armed pursuers, who thought he was a local *vaquero*.

Finally, near Cotulla, the little brown mare could go no farther. Gregorio rode her into a thicket and went ahead on foot. By noon on June 20, the mare had been found and the thicket surrounded. Trying to look like a *vaquero* without a horse,

Gregorio walked on through Cotulla. On the evening of June 20, he reached a water tank where he lay down and slept for two nights and a day. He woke on the morning of June 22, his twenty-sixth birthday. Later that day he surrendered, without resistance, to a small group of Texas Rangers.

In the ten days since he had shot Sheriff Morris, Gregorio had crisscrossed seven counties, traveling hundreds of miles—some on the backs of three small mares and some on foot—as he evaded more than a hundred peace officers and their deputized posses. During this long and deadly manhunt, at least nine Mexicans had been killed, three more wounded, and seven more arrested.

For the next thirty-four months, Gregorio was moved through a succession of county jails as Texas authorities prosecuted him for murdering three persons and stealing a horse. After reversals by the appellate court in Austin, retrials, one hung jury, and one dismissal by a judge, the total number of trials reached eight.

The only defense lawyer who stayed faithful to the end was R. B. Abernathy of Gonzales. It brought him neither money nor popularity, and no one could accuse him of courting Mexican votes. At that time in that part of Texas, Mexicans were not allowed to vote in primaries.

Before Gregorio's first conviction was reversed and while he waited for his second trial, a mob of three hundred to three hundred fifty people tried to take him from the Gonzales County jail and lynch him. Sheriff F. M. Fly, who had succeeded Glover, held the mob off and saved Gregorio's life. Interestingly, the mob did not want him for killing a sheriff (he had already been convicted of one of those crimes), but for killing rancher Schnabel. At that time it was common knowledge that the rancher had been killed by a fellow posseman. Fly said most of the mob was from Karnes County.

Gregorio's long siege of trials ended on January 1, 1905, when he started serving a life sentence for Glover's murder. Abernathy kept working, and twelve years later Governor Oscar B. Colquitt pardoned Gregorio.

When Gregorio walked into freedom at age thirty-eight, he had spent a third of his life in prison, all because he had traded a mare for a stallion and an interpreter didn't know the difference. He died of pneumonia three years later in Anson, Texas, over five hundred miles from the border on which he was born and which he had once tried desperately to reach with the help of three little mares.

UTAH OUTLAWS

THE CASTLE GATE PAYROLL ROBBERY

The Most Technical Robbery Ever Pulled in Utah

The daring and well-planned Castle Gate payroll robbery of 1897 made Butch Cassidy's reputation—on both sides of the law. It was considered a criminal masterpiece, leaving little doubt that Butch Cassidy was one of the greatest criminal strategists the West had ever seen. This job also made him the undisputed leader of the gang known as the Wild Bunch.

Large, rich veins of coal had made Pine Canyon in Carbon County, Utah, an important mining center. The Castle Gate Mine, owned by the Pleasant Valley Coal Company, was the largest mining concern in the area, employing hundreds of men.

It also had a tempting payroll. It didn't take long for such a prize to catch the attention of the Wild Bunch. And the mine, near Price, Utah, was between two famous hideouts—Brown's Hole and Robber's Roost—making a disappearing act after a heist easier.

The Denver and Rio Grande Railroad and the Pleasant Valley Coal Company were understandably nervous about the amount of outlaw activity in the area. To thwart robberies, the payroll trains were well guarded, and paydays and routines were constantly changed. Miners never knew on which day they'd be paid. Even the mine's paymaster didn't know when the money was due to arrive from Salt Lake City.

Butch had carefully studied the scenario and decided that a direct attack on the train would be too risky. He concluded that the best approach would be to rob the paymaster just after he took the money from the train. Since no one knew when the money would show up, the outlaws had to be ready, waiting about inconspicuously until the payroll came in.

The sky was robin's-egg blue and the April sun promised a warm afternoon. E. L. Carpenter, paymaster for the Pleasant Valley Coal Company, had a sore toe, so he hadn't changed out of his bedroom slippers before picking up the payroll from the noon train. He could hear the whistle blast signaling to the miners that later that day they would be paid. Paydays always made him nervous, and he'd be happy when this one was over.

As Carpenter gingerly lifted his sore foot onto the wooden stairs leading up to his office, he caught the subtle glint of light on the barrel of a well-used Colt.

He felt the powerful prod of the .45 in his ribs as the man came in close. In a quiet voice, the smiling cowboy with the big gun said in his right ear, "I'll take them moneybags, sir. Stay calm since I'd hate to shoot a hole in you."

Butch Cassidy had Carpenter by surprise. It seemed impossible to Carpenter that he was being robbed while hundreds of miners milled about, waiting for their pay. But most of the men were foreigners who didn't speak much English. They probably had no idea what was going on. And there was no mistaking that six-gun. Without a fight, he loosened his fingers on the large case and the money sacks. Carpenter's assistant, a man named Lewis, threw down the bag of silver he was carrying and prudently dove into the hardware store when he saw the gun.

Now that he thought of it, Carpenter realized he'd seen this cowboy and one other sitting on the stairs when he'd walked out to the train. In fact, they'd been hanging about for days. He noticed the two unsaddled horses the men rode. They were tied next to his office. One of the men had now mounted and had his hand on his pistol.

Horses were rare in this mining town—that should have been a clue. The canyon was so steep and narrow that there was barely enough room for the train and the buildings that served the miners. It was nearly impossible to bring in a wagon. Saddle horses were discouraged. Besides, the miners weren't stockmen—few, if any, had mounts.

Butch quietly walked to the man on the horse, Elza Lay, and handed him some of the loot. As Butch grabbed the reins of his horse, Carpenter regained some of his lost courage and ran, sore foot and all, up the stairs to his office yelling, "Robbers! Robbers!"

Someone fired a rifle.

The loitering miners pushed in closer to see what was going on. Butch's well-trained horse became nervous. As Cassidy tossed a moneybag near his horse's head, the animal spooked and bolted down the street.

For a moment, Butch looked after his mount. There he was, alone, horseless, stunned, gun holstered, a large bag of Castle Gate gold in one hand. He ran for his frightened mount. Quick-thinking Elza headed off the mare. After several futile tries, he grabbed the reins and brought the gray, named Babe, back to his partner. Butch snatched the reins and, in one jump, managed to get seated on the tall horse while still carrying the gold. Babe reared up several times. Elza spurred his horse, and Babe followed him down the narrow way.

Beyond a section house up the canyon, the robbers stopped and quickly put the money into canvas bags, making transport easier. They had at least seven thousand dollars in twenty-dollar gold pieces, some currency, and silver. They left the silver, which was too heavy to carry, and picked up the saddles they'd hidden.

Since there were few horses in the canyon, the outlaws had pretended to be training their "racehorses"—working them on the steep canyon trails. In that era, it was the custom for racing buffs to condition their animals by riding cross-country without a saddle. Each day after working out their mounts, Butch and Elza hung around the saloon, drinking and loafing. They'd become temporary fixtures at the watering hole, so they hadn't looked out of place in a town with few horses.

Carpenter ran for the telegraph office. The nearest law was in Price, ten miles away. The telegraph man looked up at the frustrated Carpenter and told him the lines had been cut. Thinking clearly, Carpenter hobbled to the train in his bedroom slippers and told the engineer to fire up the engine. There was still a head of steam, so off they went. Carpenter didn't know it, but he passed Butch and Elza, who were behind the section house saddling up.

The train screamed toward Price.

Carpenter had the whistle pulled down, signaling to the town that something was wrong. When the train pulled to a stop, Sheriff Donant was at the platform. Donant wasn't thinking as clearly as Carpenter. It took him several hours to get his posse organized—and then he took off in the wrong direction. In the meantime, Carpenter telegraphed the news about the robbery to all the local towns.

But the third member of the outlaw gang, Joe Walker, had cut the telegraph wires out of the canyon. He was leaving Price when he saw the train come in, whistle blowing. Joe knew the law would be on their trail soon. He'd planned on cutting the line to Emery County, west of Price, but decided he'd better meet up with his partners instead.

They rendezvoused at Desert Lake. Butch and Elza decided to lead the posse on a roundabout route while Joe took the money to Florence Creek and back to the hideout in the Roost. Butch knew where he was going, and he wouldn't have the loot to slow him down. Joe would slip off unseen, and no one would be the wiser.

At the same time, posses were gathering in Castle Gate, Huntington, and Cleveland. Some members of the posse were less than enthusiastic about catching up with the robbers. The leader of the Huntington posse, for example, had loaned his horse, Babe, to Butch for this caper, and the leader had no intentions of catching up with his friend.

Butch knew the Utah backcountry like the sun wrinkles on his face. He had mounts and provisions stashed so he could replenish his supplies. He had spent the winter planning this job and had the contingencies covered. Besides, the locals were more than eager to loan or sell a horse. He'd always treated ranchers and farmers with respect—and paid them well for their services. There was little love lost between the local folks and the mining company. At one ranch, Butch and Elza pulled in about midnight with exhausted mounts. Butch asked if they could exchange their exhausted horses for new horses. Butch picked out two good horses and asked the rancher what price was fair. The rancher said twenty dollars. Butch gave him fifty, generating goodwill among the locals and inspiring a lack of cooperation with the law.

It was a long chase, but Butch and Elza were always in control. In the end, the famous lawman Joe Bush was not far behind. The Bush posse was small but dedicated. It also included Carpenter, who was still wearing his bedroom slippers. He was a determined company man.

In Mexican Hat, a black dog named Sunday had befriended Butch and followed him down the trail. The outlaws were traveling fast, and the black dog was keeping up pretty well. However, after a while it began to lag behind. Looking through his field glasses, Butch noted that the Bush posse had pulled ahead of the faithful canine. In fact they'd passed the dog not knowing it was there. Butch could see his furry friend, tongue out, tired, trying to keep up. Butch had a soft spot for animals, especially a dog this faithful. He had Elza wait in the rocks and fire shots at the posse with his Winchester, pinning them down.

Elza knew he wasn't to hit any of the lawmen. Butch's orders were to shoot but never to kill unless there was no other choice. With his long gun, Elza started lobbing shots at the lawmen, who quickly took cover while Butch slipped around them and rescued the faithful hound. He gave the animal a drink, dropped down the draw, and circled ahead of the posse carrying Sunday on his saddle.

"This dog has stayed with me better than most posses," he said. "I've got to respect that."

Dog and outlaws made it to the Flat Tops and lost themselves in the Roost. Butch had planned well. Along the way, they had horses and supplies—and help from other gang members or ranchers as needed. They had ridden south of Price, west to Cleveland, down Buckhorn Wash to San Rafael, across seventy miles of desert.

They met up with Joe Walker and divided up the gold. The posse gave up. No one is sure what happed to the dog, Sunday, but it is certain Butch found a good home for him.

As a postscript to this caper, which is steeped in folklore, the outlaws holed up for nearly three months. Legend has it there were a couple of women hanging about camp to make life a little more interesting. The boys played poker until they went stir-crazy. About the end of June, the Wild Bunch decided to head back to Brown's Hole, where the action was. They rode hard for five days, crossing the Green River and the Book Cliff Mountains and finally hitting Crouse Creek and friendly faces.

They were loaded from the robbery, so they gathered up some party-starved cowboys (some members of the Wild Bunch riders and anyone else who wanted free drinks) and headed over the state line into Carbon County, Wyoming. Their favorite watering holes were in a couple of one-horse towns called Dixon and Baggs. They came into town with guns blazing.

Local merchants started sharpening pencils—this would be good business. Hopefully no one would accidentally get shot. The Bunch all bought new suits, took baths, and got shaves. Some bought new derby hats. Then they started to party.

To say they shot up the towns might be an understatement. Legend has it that in one saloon alone, there were more than twenty-five bullet holes in the bar (who knows about the roof) before the party ended. It was all in fun—and no innocent bystanders got killed—although one imagines most sensible townsfolk, accustomed to these occasional group forays with the bottle, sent all the respectable women and children to the country. Every bullet hole was gladly paid for (a dollar a hole). Dixon and Baggs had quite a reputation for hosting outlaws. Legend has it that a rustler got sick and needed a doctor from the larger town of Rock Springs. No doctor, however, would risk coming. The lofty sum of two thousand dollars in gold was offered, but the good physician refused to go to the sick man. Lucky for him, he was not taken at gunpoint.

There was a lot of big talk about how well the job had gone, and the money flowed as fast as the whiskey. Rumor has it that Carpenter was the butt of many a toasted glass. One Bunch cowboy even offered to send him a pair of boots since he'd heard that Carpenter was riding with the posse in his bedroom slippers.

ORIN PORTER ROCKWELL

The "Destroying Angel" Gunfighter

Porter Rockwell was a legendary gunfighter from Utah Territory.

His trademark was his long hair, his long beard, and his uncanny skills as a man hunter. Historians still argue whether he was a cold-blooded killer who hid behind his badge, the avenger for the Mormon Church, or a rugged lawman doing his duty in a harsh land.

Rockwell was appointed US deputy marshal in 1849, holding the commission until his death in 1878. His detractors called him the "Angel of Death" or the "Destroying Angel." Most agree Rockwell was one of the best gunfighters in Western history. He may have been in more gunfights than any marshal or sheriff of record. In his day, he was as famous as Brigham Young or Wild Bill Hickok. His career was controversial and long.

What many don't realize is Rockwell was a man of paradoxes. He was a religious man. He was also a bodyguard and personal friend to both Joseph Smith and Brigham Young. He was a successful businessman and rancher. At the time of his death, two of his ranches were worth nearly thirty thousand dollars. In the Great Basin, he was noted for his horses' bloodlines. As a scout and a mountain man, he led dozens of parties across the Great Plains and to California. He was trusted by Brigham Young to collect ten thousand dollars in tithing from Sam Brannon in the California gold country. He was also trusted with large sums of money by freight companies. He was a wagon master, a miner, a temple worker, and a polygamist.

Porter Rockwell was launched into the public eye in Nauvoo, Illinois. The press was fascinated by his long hair and beard, as well as his absolute fidelity to the Prophet Joseph Smith. Rockwell was not only Smith's bodyguard; the two had been best friends since childhood. He was one of the first people baptized into the Mormon faith in 1830. Rockwell had been accused of the attempted murder of Lilburn Boggs, the former governor of Missouri. Boggs helped lead the persecution against the Mormons, so there was little love lost. With a five-thousand-dollar reward on Rockwell's head, Joseph Smith was asked by a reporter if his bodyguard was guilty of the charges filed against him. Smith reportedly laughed and said no. Boggs was still living—Porter would not have missed. When he was taken by authorities in Nauvoo, Rockwell was supposed to have been carrying enough firepower to shoot seventy-one shots without reloading. Certainly this is an overstatement, but the point is Porter was always well armed. Had he known what was in store for him, he might have resisted. He was jailed on trumped-up charges and spent nine months in horrible conditions. He was beaten and nearly starved to death as he was moved from jail to jail. He was told repeatedly by his captors that if he would give up Joe Smith, he would be freed immediately. He replied, "I'll see you all damned first and then I won't."

In 1843 Smith blessed him, saying, "In the name of the Lord . . . so long as you remain loyal and true to the faith, you need fear no enemy. Cut not your hair and no bullet or blade can harm [you]." Throughout his life, Rockwell took Smith's blessing seriously because he felt he was protected. Smith's son once commented, "He was absolutely fearless and cared little about the amenities of society." Simply put, Rockwell felt he had a shield from God and could not be shot or stabbed.

Whatever one thought of Rockwell, no one questioned his skill with fire-arms, his courage, which was often foolhardy, or his tenacity to bring back his man (one way or another). He didn't think twice about charging into a herd of buffalo and selecting the largest bull. He wanted to see if he could kill the beast with a single shot from his pistol. His ball hit the animal squarely in the head but to no effect. The angry bull chased him until he outran it. During the Utah War in 1857, when federal troops marched to Utah Territory to fight the Mormons, Rockwell and six men galloped among the tents of several thousand soldiers, shooting and yelling. On another occasion, there was a two-thousand-dollar reward on Rockwell's head for a man he felt he had killed in self-defense. Plotting with his friend Sheriff Backenstos, he had Backenstos turn him in. The two men split the reward.

The worst day of Rockwell's life was the day the Prophet Joseph Smith was murdered at Carthage, Illinois. Rockwell felt he should have been with his friend to protect him, but Smith had specifically ordered him to stay in Nauvoo. On reporting the news in Nauvoo, a heartbroken Porter Rockwell told a guard at the Nauvoo Temple, "Joseph is killed! They have killed him. They have killed him. God damn them, they have killed him." Shortly thereafter it was learned that a mob of Carthage Greys was approaching the city. Rockwell was asked if he would help hold them off. Stinging from the death of Joseph, he had a score to settle. He happened to have fifty rounds on his person, several repeating rifles, and his handgun(s), so he was ready for action. As the first Carthage man charged, Por-ter aimed at his belt. The slug lifted him off his horse. Porter yelled, "I got him. Thank God!" Rockwell was afraid his shot might have been too far off—after all the horse was galloping. He shot was true and he helped turn the mob.

Porter Rockwell was cool in dangerous situations. A story, spun in the *Salt Lake Tribune* (1924), illustrates his bravado. Rockwell had become so famous that men trying to build their reputations traveled long distances to match their skills. They hoped to carve a big notch on their gun barrels if they could beat him. One aspiring pistolero from a Mexican border town came to Utah County to put Rockwell to the test. In a rather unsportsmanlike fashion, he got the drop on Porter. Of course, his weapon was drawn, cocked, and pointed when he called Rockwell out. The would-be killer taunted the older gunman about his long hair. Knowing he had the drop, he told Rockwell how he was going to kill him. Cool and unassuming, Rockwell looked at the kid and then at the Colt pointed at him. He said something like, "You wouldn't try and shoot a man without a cap on that pistol, would ya, son?" The kid wasn't going to live to see his next birthday. He looked down at his pistol to check his cap. That hesitation was all it took. Rockwell drew his Colt and shot the aspiring pistol fighter dead.

The Eastern reading public had an insatiable appetite for frontier stories—especially if the stories were sensational and the characters were larger than life. To make articles more interesting and ostensibly more balanced, the press determined, almost arbitrarily, what side of the law someone was on. Sometimes a subject was whitewashed, another time vilified. It didn't matter if the text was based on facts as long as it was a good story. Checking sources and thorough reporting wasn't a part of the job description. Often a writer took an article someone else had written and spiced it up. If ten men sounded good, twenty sounded better. Orin Porter Rockwell made good copy. He was the subject of countless newspaper stories and magazine articles. Exaggeration was a journalistic art form. For example, *The Salt Lake Tribune* wrote, "[Rockwell] had participated in at least a hundred murders." Fritz Hugh Ludlow from *Atlantic Monthly* was curious and decided to see for himself. He came to Utah for the express reason to interview Rockwell. He discovered, in spite of what he read, that he liked the man. He might have been the Destroying Angel, but he wasn't the monster from hell who had been so often vilified in the press. "He had the face of bull-dog, courage . . . but good natured . . . I went riding with him [on the Fourth of July, the two rode out to inspect Rockwell's ranch]." The press's attitude was shifting. Richard Burton, the famous journalist and explorer, also visited Utah and wrote about Rockwell. They became good friends.

Careers and lives were made and broken by creative journalism. The press courted the likes of George Armstrong Custer, Calamity Jane, and Buffalo Bill, who were represented as nonpareil. Bill the Kid, on the other hand, wasn't a boy scout, but he wasn't the homicidal murderer with twenty-one notches on his belt as was reported. The Kid's problem was he picked the losing side during the Lincoln County War. Wild Bill Hickok is reported to have killed scores and scores of men in fair fights (not counting Mexicans and Indians). The truth is he may have killed eight or nine men in gunfights, including those he shot by accident (like his deputy). He was a good storyteller and knew how to cultivate the press, but he was mostly a drunk and never able to fill the shoes the press created for him. The Earp brothers, champions of the press, were pimps and brothel owners. They used their badges to further their business interests. They were murderers. They were brave, but as lawmen, like Hickok and Holliday and Masterson, they were hired by business interests to keep the peace and promote the businesses of the men who signed their checks. Such men were powerful and also owned or influenced the press. Whether one was a lawman or outlaw in many cases depended on the printing presses.

Was Porter Rockwell an outlaw? It depends on who you read.

Some of the material written about him was outlandish. Nelson Slater in *Fruits of Mormonism* wrote that Rockwell tracked a man into the brush, killed him, and lopped off his head. Never mind that Rockwell was in California at the time. Another Eastern writer discussed how a man had a difference with Rockwell, and later the fellow was found with a bullet in his head. There were no witnesses, but all were certain it was the Destroying Angel. The legends multiplied, then shifted directions, especially tales about his superhuman powers. James T. Harwood, in his biography *A Basket of Chips,* says he was standing near his father's shop when he overheard Porter and another man arguing. The man was angry and fired his gun at nearly point-blank range, but each time he pulled the trigger, his shots hit all around Rockwell. In another tale, near 7-Mile Pass, an outlaw started shooting at Rockwell. Rounds hit near him but he wasn't hit. Perhaps the most interesting is the report of the lead coming so close to him and yet not killing. When he took his jacket and vest off, the spent bullets fell out of his pockets.

A more realistic Rockwell story might be the following vignette. Overland Stage was bringing a shipment of gold from California. Rockwell was hired to meet the stage not far from his ranch and provide additional security. Official concern was well-founded since the stage was held up coming off Dugway Mountain. The stage drivers said they saw what looked like a body in the road face down. When one of the men rolled the body over, he found he was looking into the bore of a large, cocked revolver. The men were quickly disarmed. The robber shot the lock off the strongbox, loaded the gold, and fled. Rockwell questioned the two men carefully, asking about the highwayman's gun, his clothes, and his horse. The driver later commented that Rockwell asked him a thousand questions. Rockwell was noted for being thorough. He wanted all the information he could get that might prove useful later on. He headed west to Simpson Springs on the Pony Express trail. He quickly ate at the station, loaded some biscuits in his pockets, and headed out on the trail even though it was dark. He found where the robbery occurred and started his manhunt.

He tracked the man to a place called Canyon. He knew the gold had been hidden, and he wanted to wait and see if he could find where it was stashed. His efforts paid off. He followed the outlaw to the canyon and drew down on him. Rockwell had the man at gunpoint and had him hold his hands in the air after disarming him and securing his horse. As Rockwell started to rope the outlaw, the fellow foolishly tried to kick him. Rockwell, not one to put up with nonsense, gave him the side of his pistol barrel. Doing this caused his hat to come off, and the robber saw his hair and recognized who he was up against. He would have been more careful had he known.

Rockwell headed back to his ranch on Government Creek. Not trusting the slippery outlaw, he left his own horse in a far pasture and the outlaw's horse in the barn. Rockwell carefully tied up the robber because he knew how tired he was and he had to sleep. Putting both saddles and bridles under his bed, as well as the outlaw's boots, he slept with the gold and his pistols just to be sure. He had his ranch hand help guard the outlaw, and then he fell into a deep sleep. In the night he heard a horse gallop off.

Somehow his prisoner escaped in the night. He had no boots and no saddle, so Rockwell felt he could find him. However, he felt he needed to turn the gold in to the Overland Stage officials in Salt Lake. Rockwell was surprised there was little enthusiasm at the Overland to get the outlaw and bring him to justice—even though the company had their gold back. They wouldn't authorize Rockwell expense money for the chase. Not one to let a man best him, Rockwell took a month off and followed the robber on his own time. He never found him. Some say this is the only man who ever escaped Marshal Rockwell.

There was, and still is, a lot of hype about the marshal. He did shoot some men in his day—perhaps some outside of his jurisdiction—but he wasn't the vicious, uncontrolled killer with one hundred men to his count. He faced more than his share of murder accusations. In fact, there was an old charge hanging over his head when he died. Rockwell took it in stride. He was brave and fearless, no question of that. He was a colorful character who drew positive and negative press like a lightning rod. He helped tame the Great Basin, he fought in the Utah War, he liked whiskey, he ran taverns, he was a Mormon temple worker, he was bodyguard to the prophets, he was Brigham Young's go-to guy, and he survived a lot of gunfights.

It seems no bullet had his name on it, as Joseph promised. While he never took a slug or a blade, there was one battle the old gunfighter could not win. His heart gave out at age sixty-five. He died at home in his bed, surrounded by his family.

WASHINGTON OUTLAWS

LAWRENCE KELLY

Shrewd Smuggler

In March 1891, Lawrence Kelly snuck onto his four-ton sloop with another illegal batch of opium. The sixty-five half-pound cans he carried would fetch a tidy profit. But only if he was careful. The law had been getting too close to him lately, so he decided to travel a more circuitous route. That day he sailed from Victoria, British Columbia, to Olympia, Washington. From there he walked to the train station at Tenino twenty miles away, carrying the opium in a satchel. At Tenino he boarded a southbound train.

Unfortunately for Kelly, US Customs agent Charles Mulkey of Tacoma boarded the same train. While walking through the smoking car, he spotted the bag Kelly was carrying and immediately became suspicious. He walked over, seized it, and began to search it, despite protests from Kelly. When he found the cans of illegal opium, he arrested Kelly. When the train stopped at Castle Rock, Mulkey took Kelly and a nearby witness off the train and headed back to Tacoma, where Kelly appeared before the US commissioner.

How did Lawrence Kelly become a smuggler of opium? His early life showed no signs of defiance; in fact, it seemed just the opposite. Kelly was born about 1839 in the British Isles. When he was a young man, he joined the British Army and then later became a sailor. His British sloop docked at New Orleans just after the American Civil War broke out, so he deserted the ship and joined the Confederate Army.

Shortly after the end of war, Kelly immigrated west, sailing around South America on the ship *Young America* and ending up in the Pacific Northwest. His life of crime began about 1872, when he was caught smuggling Canadian silks into the United States. He was fined five hundred dollars, but this punishment didn't curb his smuggling. His smuggling operation soon made him enough money to build a nice home on Guemes Island, just across Guemes Channel from Anacortes. His house stood high on a bluff, from which Kelly had an awe-inspiring view of the Guemes Channel, Bellingham Channel, and Rosario Strait.

In 1877 he married Lizzie Coutts, almost twenty years his junior. Shortly after their wedding, he transferred the title of his house to his wife, so that if he was ever arrested, the house could not be seized to pay his fines. This act seems to indicate he never planned to make a living by legitimate means. For a time, he and Lizzie easily lived off the money he made as a smuggler.

At first Kelly used an ordinary fishing sloop to carry illegal goods from Canada to Washington state. His bright red boat was easily visible, but the authorities didn't bother him. He could outrun the law anyway. He knew all the coves and bays like the back of his hand, and his small boat could travel easily in shallow water through which the bigger customs boats couldn't pass. He smeared pot black and tallow on his boat to make it glide more easily through the water. If someone chased him and he couldn't get away, he dumped the smuggled goods overboard so he wouldn't be caught with them.

Smuggling was not an unheard-of crime in the United States in the nineteenth century. During the Civil War, liquor, blankets, and wool were smuggled from Canada into the United States for use by soldiers. Smuggling increased dramatically, however, when the railroads began to import large numbers of Chinese workers as laborers for canneries, hop fields, mines, and public works. Though they caused some difficulties with white workers, Chinese laborers worked hard, took fewer breaks, could be paid less, and did not drink.

Then the Exclusion Act of 1882 prevented Chinese laborers from entering the United States legally. Smugglers saw an opportunity in the Pacific Ocean channels between Washington state and British Columbia. In no time at all, smugglers began to sneak Chinese workers into the United States, and Kelly joined their ranks. The smugglers took Chinese immigrants to places where a large number of Chinese were already living, so they would blend into the population. Sometimes the smugglers hid the immigrants in the smaller San Juan Islands to wait for the perfect opportunity to take them to the United States mainland. Smugglers generally received fifty dollars per person brought into the country, so smuggling was a good moneymaking operation.

Chinese workers used a large amount of opium, and soon the illegal trade of that commodity grew, too. A refinery in Victoria on Vancouver Island manufactured as much opium as the Chinese workers could ever want. Opium could be imported legally, but it was very highly taxed, so the drug was often smuggled into the country to avoid the customs duty.

Whether his cargo was human or other contraband, it made no difference to Kelly. He would smuggle anything. But once his activities were discovered, the law was perpetually at his heels.

Customs agent Thomas Caine noticed that Kelly frequently used the Swinomish Channel, between Fidalgo Island and the mainland, to deliver his stolen goods. On December 21, 1882, Caine hid in the channel, waiting for Kelly to show up. For some reason Kelly suspected he was being watched. As he approached the area where Caine hid, he quietly jumped into the water and swam, pushing his boat in front of him. In spite of Kelly's stealth, Caine could still see the boat when it appeared out of the early morning fog. He waited until the sloop got close, and then ordered Kelly to surrender. Kelly did, without a fight. He was carrying forty cases of Chinese wine and a man from China, both illegal. Fortunately for Kelly, the Chinese man testified at Kelly's hearing that he was not a "coolie," or illegal Chinese immigrant, but a merchant with business in Portland. Kelly was cleared of the smuggling charge but was fined one hundred fifty dollars for the illegal importation of Chinese wine.

The incident did nothing to deter Kelly. In July of 1883, the authorities caught Kelly with illegal goods and fined him three hundred ninety dollars. Four months later, on November 17, he was assessed a fine of twenty dollars. The fines were just minor annoyances to Kelly.

In 1886 he bought some property on Sinclair Island from Thomas P. Hogin, also registering this property in his wife's name. From high on a bluff, the house had a commanding view of the waterways. He could see the Strait of Georgia that ran between Washington state and Vancouver Island. From this vantage point, he could easily watch for customs ships.

By outward appearances, Kelly seemed to be living an ordinary life. He and his wife had six children who attended school on Sinclair Island. At one time, Kelly was a member of the school board. If the townspeople were aware of his occupation, they didn't harass him about it. Perhaps some even sympathized with him. By the late 1880s, he mainly smuggled opium from Victoria. He stashed the opium on Vancouver Island until the weather was favorable and a successful delivery on the mainland was likely. Then he took the opium to Port Townsend, Seattle, or some other Washington port. He made about twelve dollars per pound of the drug.

Not long after moving to Sinclair Island, Kelly had another serious brush with the law. Customs inspectors seized his Whitehall boat on May 16, 1886, in Tacoma. Unfortunately for Kelly, he had just loaded 567 tins of opium, equivalent to 364 pounds. He was held on a bail of three thousand dollars. In the end, Kelly was fined only one hundred dollars, but the seizure of his boat threatened to end his career.

But his luck had not yet run out. In fact, he got right back into the business and seemed to work with impunity. Dozens of his deliveries around the Puget Sound area went undetected, even though the customs boats were getting stronger and faster, and smugglers were getting caught more and more frequently. Kelly and others devised new tricks to keep from getting arrested. Kelly put the opium in a weighted sack, tied the sack to a rope, and tied the rope to a ring bolted into the hull of his boat. The boat dragged the opium along underwater, so that a casual inspection of the ship would detect nothing on deck. Sometimes Kelly tied a sack of opium to a float when customs inspectors came near, and then he would retrieve it when the inspectors were gone.

The smuggling of Chinese immigrants became more dangerous too. To hide them, some smugglers resorted to sewing them into potato sacks, then stashing them in some small cubbyhole of the ship. Anyone who inspected the ship might conclude the ship was transporting a cargo of vegetables. Sometimes the Chinese were left on an uninhabited island or on barren rocks to wait for a boat to take them to the mainland. Supposedly smugglers even tossed the illegal immigrants overboard in order to avoid arrest. Kelly always denied doing that, but he admitted that sometimes he delivered the Chinese back to Vancouver Island and let them believe they were in the United States.

Herbert Foote Beecher, son of the famous evangelist Reverend Henry Ward Beecher, came to Washington in 1883. For two years he plied the waters between Port Townsend and the San Juan Islands in his gospel ship *Evangel*. He heard stories about Kelly and other smugglers, and it wasn't long before the information he obtained led to arrests, larger fines, and confiscation of greater amounts of opium. Kelly was captured several times and paid increasingly higher fines.

Efforts like Beecher's led to Kelly's 1891 arrest by customs agent Mulkey aboard the train. When he appeared before the US commissioner in Tacoma, Kelly denied ownership of the satchel. He claimed that Mulkey planted the opium in his bag while he was in the washroom. The commissioner did not believe him and sentenced him to two years at the McNeil Island Federal Penitentiary. Amazingly, Kelly's neighbors on Sinclair Island did believe him. They tried to petition for Kelly's release, but they were unsuccessful.

Customs officers converged on Kelly's hideout at Sinclair Island. They took his ship *Alert* and sold it for $3,221.83 to pay his fines. They couldn't prove he had transported illegal opium, but they could at least charge him with entering and leaving foreign ports without proper paperwork. They claimed he had been to Victoria and back several times without declaring his manifest.

While he was at McNeil Island, Kelly's fines mounted to the point where he had to sell his island property in order to pay them. To support herself, his wife kept house for a man in Anacortes whose wife was hospitalized. After his release, Kelly went to Anacortes in a drunken rage and threatened his wife with a gun. She alerted the police, but Kelly had disappeared.

In 1896 Kelly stole a box of tools from carpenter D. J. Davis of Anacortes. A man named J. H. Young became suspicious when he saw Kelly and another man sneaking toward the wharf, so Young asked Davis to check on his tools. They were missing, so Young, Davis, and J. A. Crookham formed a search party. Marshal Stevenson, J. W. Bird, H. H. Soufle, R. McCormick, and George Layton formed another.

At first neither search party could find the two men, but then Young spotted Kelly in a boat off Guemes Island. The marshal's party followed the Fidalgo Island shore and circled around Burrows Bay. Young's party sailed across the bay to Cypress Island, where they found two men and their camp but no boat or tool chest. Somehow Kelly slipped away again. The next day the marshal went back to the island to resume the search. He found a cabin and a dog. Stevenson, Bird, and Soufle snuck up to the cabin and peered inside. There they found Kelly asleep, so they pounded on the door and demanded entrance. Kelly opened the door, and he was immediately arrested. He resisted briefly, but when he tried to get to his rifle, Stevenson knocked him down and handcuffed him.

The posse returned to Anacortes. While their boat docked, Kelly jumped overboard and disappeared into the water. He somehow swam away, even though he was handcuffed. A week later a man named Ipsen spotted two men and a boat on the beach near Deception Pass between Fidalgo Island and Whidbey Island. He watched them for a short time and became convinced they were smugglers. He disguised himself as a settler and approached their camp. By the time he arrived, the men were gone, but a search of their tent yielded about five thousand dollars' worth of opium. Ipsen suspected the stash belonged to Lawrence Kelly, but others didn't think so. They figured that Kelly knew the Puget Sound area too well to let himself be trapped on an island by a high tide.

The next day one hundred feet of cable was stolen from a local sloop, five boxes of codfish were taken from Matheson's wharf, and a rowboat was stolen from W. Mathews's landing on Guemes Island. Because Kelly was known to be in debt due to his fines, he was suspected of the thefts, but no proof of his guilt ever surfaced.

In 1901 Kelly was captured in Seattle. He had just arrived from Vancouver Island and had booked a room at the Granville Hotel. He left two suitcases full of opium in his room while he went out for the evening. Unfortunately he got drunk that night and was picked up by the police. While he was in jail, the Seattle police received a tip from Vancouver Island police. They sent an investigator to Kelly's hotel room, where they found the opium. Amazingly, he paid only a five-dollar fine, and the opium was not even confiscated.

The next day a Seattle policeman followed Kelly when he left for New Westminster on Vancouver Island. Kelly checked in at the Fraser House, went out for dinner and a stroll, and then returned to the hotel. Once Kelly returned to the hotel, the officer decided he could probably take a break. But that was just what Kelly was counting on. That night he snuck out and crossed back into Washington. A few months later, as he debarked a steamer in Portland, he was arrested for possession of eight hundred dollars' worth of opium. He spent several months in the Multnomah County jail in Oregon.

Kelly appeared in the news again in January 1904, when customs agent Fred F. Strickling heard that Kelly was going to try to smuggle opium by train. He boarded the train at its northern-most stop in Washington at Sumas, near the Canadian border. He figured he would have no trouble intercepting Kelly.

At each train stop, he asked the conductor if anyone had boarded. Finally, the conductor answered in the affirmative: A man boarded the train at Nooksack.

Strickling strode down the aisle until he found the man the conductor had described. He approached the man and told him he needed to look inside his valise. Kelly was defiant and refused. When Strickling insisted, Kelly shoved him out of the way and fled down the aisle. Before Strickling could react, Kelly jumped off the train. Strickling pulled the emergency cord, and the train stopped. Inside Kelly's luggage were sixty-five tins of opium. Strickling ordered the engineer to back up the train to the place at which Kelly had jumped off.

Luckily for Strickling, Kelly knocked himself out when he jumped. Strickling quickly handcuffed him, confiscated his gun, and took him on the train to Deming. Kelly's face and shoulders were cut up from his rough landing in the cinders along the track, so the Deming station agent asked a local doctor to patch up the prisoner. Shortly afterward Strickling escorted Kelly to Sumas and on to Bellingham, where he was arraigned before US Commissioner H. B. Williams. He was released for one thousand dollars in bail, after which posting, he promptly skipped town.

He was at large for over a year, until Fred E. King and Fred C. Dean captured Kelly on July 18, 1905, near Anderson Island. They had disguised themselves as fishermen trolling the areas of Puget Sound that Kelly was known to haunt. They pretended to be just passing by, when they approached Kelly and pulled out their badges. He surrendered without a fight. He was carrying sixty pounds of opium at the time. He received a two-year sentence at McNeil Island but was released early for good behavior. The moment he was released, a US marshal hauled him straight back to jail in Seattle for the earlier offense on which he had jumped bail. In May 1909, Kelly was sent back to McNeil Island for a one-year sentence.

After his release, Kelly found that going straight meant hard times. He retired from his life of crime in 1911, when he was about seventy years old. He contacted the Daughters of the Confederacy and was admitted to a Confederate soldiers' home in Louisiana, where he died. So ended the twenty-five-year career of one of the most notorious smugglers on the Pacific Coast.

MAX LEVY

King of the Shaghaiers

The 1890s were a wild time for Port Townsend, Washington. The town was the port of entry for goods and immigrants coming into the United States from Canada. It was a busy port that shipped timber and the local fish harvest far and wide. After a long day's work, sailors trudged into the nearest saloon to whet their whistles. Trouble was brewing between the union and non-union sailors, and they kept a wary eye on each other as they drank. On August 11, 1893, the uneasy truce came to an end.

About 8:00 p.m., someone assaulted a non-union sailor. A few minutes later he escaped, but he was in bad condition when he reached the Latona Saloon. The Latona, owned by Max Levy, was the headquarters of the non-union sailors. Whether the sailor's non-union status was the cause of the beating is not known. But it would soon become an excuse for an all-out brawl.

Some union sailors followed the man to the Latona. Someone sent word to the union headquarters, and a large union force converged on the saloon. At first the two groups just taunted each other from either side of the street. Then one of the union men tried to enter the Latona for a drink. Levy stopped him at the door. Two of his employees, Charles Gunderson and barkeeper Robert Kirk, picked up their weapons and prepared to do battle. The three men warned the union man that he better stay away or there would be trouble.

The union men ignored the warning and swarmed the saloon. No one knows who fired the first shot or threw the first punch. Union sailor James Connor was shot twice, in the right shoulder and in the right hip. Otto Anderson, a waiter who had nothing to do with the dispute, was slightly wounded in the stomach from a stray bullet. Ricardo Gueraro was hit in the right leg. He was not part of the dispute, but had just come into town and had been drawn to the altercation by the noise. Union sailor Joseph Dixon attempted to smash the window of the Latona but badly cut his arm on the glass. Someone also tried to hit Levy's wife, who was watching from the second-story window, with a rock. Fortunately, he missed his target.

The fight went on for some time before the police could get it under control. Officer Brophy escorted Levy, Gunderson, and Kirk to the jail to protect them from the mob. The crowd was in an ugly mood and wanted to lynch the men. As it was, every ground-floor window of the Latona Saloon was broken. The inside looked like a hurricane hit it.

Early the next morning, the saloon district showed signs of resuming the argument of the previous night. About 10:00 a.m., an argument broke out between the union and non-union sailors. But this time, officers were ready. They broke it up before it got too far. One shot was fired, but no one was hurt. Several others were arrested and charged with inciting a riot and for property damage to the Latona Saloon. They were held in a different part of the jail from where Levy and Gunderson were staying.

By that time, Levy was known as the king of the shanghaiers. The practice of shanghaiing, forcing a man to sail on a ship against his will, had been around for hundreds of years. But it wasn't until the 1850s that it became known as shanghaiing at San Francisco's Barbary Coast. Being "sent to Shanghai" was what happened when a man was knocked out and placed on a ship on its way to the Orient. The men who engaged in this practice became known as "crimpers."

Levy was born in San Francisco so he was well familiar with the practice. He prospected for a short time in the Klondike before coming to Port Townsend in 1889. He became part owner of the Chicago Clothing Company with a man named Thomas Newman. A short time later, he married Lucy Hogg, daughter of a local sea captain. They would have one son, named James Maxwell Levy.

Soon after his arrival in Port Townsend, Levy met a man named Ed Sims. Sims was a respectable businessman and in fact was a deputy US shipping commissioner. His position suited Levy just fine. Since 1895 a man was required to sign on a ship before the consul of the country that owned the ship or before a US shipping commissioner. The sailor was supposed to be fully aware of what he was doing (i.e., not intoxicated) before he would be accepted or he would be denied passage. With Sims as commissioner, it was easy for Levy to get away with certain business arrangements.

Sims's financial backing also allowed Levy to purchase a share in a sailors' boardinghouse and saloon. The boardinghouse was located on the waterfront, just across the street from the City Hall. The rear of the building opened on the dock. It was a handsome brick structure that got the attention of sailors just coming into port. Many chose it as a place to stay. But many sailors did not have the money to pay for the lodging, so Levy would lend them enough to pay for their room and board.

When a ship came into port, it often needed extra hands. The captain would call upon Levy to supply some men. For each man supplied, Levy received some money from the ship's captain. This included a "finder's fee" for Levy and an advance on the sailor's wages, which paid off the money the sailor owed to Levy for staying at his boardinghouse. This arrangement made the sailor indebted to the ship's owner and earned a fat profit for Levy.

The problem was, some sailors weren't amenable to going out to sea at that particular time. Maybe they were waiting for a particular ship to come in. Maybe they were too sick to go to sea. Some of the men the boardinghouse owners signed up weren't even sailors. But it didn't matter. Levy wasn't too picky when it came to giving the ship's captain what he wanted.

Levy wasn't one to get his hands dirty either. He just gave the orders to his "runners" and then stood back to collect the money. These runners didn't hesitate to use force whenever necessary to get their quota of sailors. They waited until a man passed out when he had too much to drink. Sometimes they didn't have time to wait, so they put "knock-out drops" in a man's drink. Once the man was out cold, they would dump him in a skiff and row him out to the waiting ship. Sometimes they used the town's soiled doves to help them separate the sailor from his valuables before they left him onboard. By the time the man woke up the next day, he was far out to sea.

Levy chose his victims carefully. He never shanghaied an Indian. By that time, most Indians were under the jurisdiction of the US Bureau of Indian Affairs. So if there was a complaint, the federal government would soon come poking around. Levy wanted no part of that. He also avoided taking local residents. If his runners couldn't find any professional sailors, they took farmhands or loggers or soldiers or even vagrants. For the most part, a man's race didn't matter one iota.

Levy's most notorious runner was a man named Gunderson. He used any method to do Levy's bidding, including beating people into insensibility. One time Gunderson and fellow runner Chilean Pete snuck aboard a British ship to convince the sailors to desert. The runners would pay them to desert, but they would get double their money back when the ship's captain went to Levy to hire another crew. Unfortunately, this particular time they were caught in the act. They quickly jumped off the ship and frantically rowed toward Levy's boardinghouse.

The ship's mate and boatswain gave chase in a small rowboat. When they caught up with the shanghaiers, Gunderson tried to knock them out with an oar. The ship's mate fired his gun, fatally wounding Chilean Pete and wounding Gunderson in the shoulder. A trial followed the shooting, but the jury found the mate not guilty since Chilean Pete had been engaged in piracy. Gunderson was charged, too, but escaped conviction by claiming he had not boarded the ship and that he was there at the invitation of the sailors.

Levy's favorite tactic was to dispose of one crew so that he could be paid to supply another. He lured them with promises of better conditions that he knew about on another ship. Of course, the conditions really were no better and were sometimes worse. But the sailors didn't know any better when they did what he wanted. On one occasion, he succeeded in convincing three different crews to abandon the ship *America* before the ship was finally able to sail with a full crew.

One man who had been shanghaied on a ship to Hong Kong swore he would get even. It took two years before he finally got back to Port Townsend, and he headed straight for Levy's office. When he found him, two of his runners were talking to him. Though outnumbered, he jumped on them anyway. It wasn't long before he lay unconscious on the ground.

Eventually Gunderson shanghaied one victim too many. He was trying to get a man drunk, but it was taking too long. So he finally knocked him down with a bar stool and then kicked him in the face. The man fought back, but Gunderson was just too powerful. He dragged him aboard a ship bound for Australia. As soon as he could, the sailor came back to Port Townsend. He went straight to Levy's boardinghouse. There he accosted Gunderson and stabbed him seven times. Gunderson survived, but tendons in his neck and arms were severely damaged. He ended his relationship with Levy and lived out the rest of his days as a fisherman.

When he was arrested for the altercation at his saloon in 1893, Levy went to trial for assault. Levy was defended by A. R. Coleman, from the shipowner's association of San Francisco. Coleman explained how Gunderson had only fired warning shots into the floor. But when the union men ignored it and lunged toward them, Levy and Gunderson were just defending themselves. Two non-union sailors named Ralston and Lanstrum testified that Levy had not been armed and that he had only come out from behind the bar to try to settle things down.

Of course, the union men had a different story. Their attorneys, James Hamilton Lewis and E. S. Lyons, claimed Levy had kicked and beat up the victim without provocation. Union agents McGlynn and Benedikton also claimed that the fight had not been a union versus non-union issue. They said a man had gone into the saloon because he had lost a ring there two weeks ago. He had simply gone in to demand the return of his ring. The fight started when he was kicked out of the saloon.

The first trial ended with a hung jury. The second jury acquitted Levy, even though there had been witnesses to the event. The others charged with inciting a riot were also acquitted. Shortly afterward some of the union issues were settled. The union agreed to a five-dollar-per-month salary reduction on deep-sea vessels. Other salary reductions were made.

Levy went right back to his old tricks, shanghaiing sailors and relieving them of their money. Levy and his runners once beat up a ship captain and one of his sailors because they dared to hire a sailor without Levy's consent. He still engaged in his favorite trick, which was to run off a crew so that a ship's captain would have to pay him to assemble a new one.

Levy also cut corners whenever he could. He generally received about ninety dollars a man and about twenty dollars to pay for clothes and other things the sailor would need while he was at sea. One time Levy supplied about twenty sailors for a British ship. But before the ship could sail, the sailors threatened to mutiny. The ship's captain called Levy about the problem. Levy called the British consul to help. For once Levy's plan backfired.

After talking to each sailor, the consul discovered that the clothing supplied was woefully inadequate. In fact, some of it looked like it could have been taken out of trash dumpsters or off corpses. Some of it was even women's clothing! The consul discovered what Levy had done and told him he would have to supply appropriate clothing. Levy grudgingly did what he had to, but it was one of the few times he didn't get away with it.

Early in 1896, Levy was again in trouble with the law. He shanghaied two men for a British ship that was in port. He and one of his runners, Thomas Newman, rowed them out to the ship and left them there. As he was rowing away, one of the shanghaied men jumped overboard, trying to escape. Thomas Breen saw him jump and went to rescue him. Levy beat up the man for his trouble. Levy was charged with assault with a deadly weapon, but the case was dismissed.

In May 1896, Levy and Newman were charged with stealing some baggage belonging to a sailor named Alex Von Hagen. The charge was brought before Commissioner James G. Swan. Newman had stored Von Hagen's baggage onboard his ship. Then he asked Von Hagen to sign a promissory note for fifty dollars that he supposedly owed Levy for his room and board. Von Hagen refused because he thought the bill was much too high. Newman refused to give Von Hagen his luggage until he paid.

Levy told a slightly different story. He admitted that they took the luggage. He said that he would have gladly given it to anybody who had come after it; all they had to do was ask. Swan dismissed the case after ordering an assistant to escort Levy and Von Hagen to get the missing baggage.

The incident must have left Levy in a foul mood. Just a few days later, he was involved in an altercation that would land him back in jail. A sailor named Charles M. Carlson was leaning on a railing outside the Red Front Clothing House when Levy approached him. He threw a rock at Carlson and injured his eye.

Levy was charged with assault and battery. Ex-judge Morris B. Sachs defended Levy. Originally the case was slated to be heard by City Magistrate Jones, but Sachs asked for a change of venue to Judge Woods's court. Rather than place his case in the hands of one man, the prosecuting attorney moved for a jury trial. It took some time before the case was placed on the docket. Finally Carlson got his day in court.

Carlson testified that the assault was totally uncalled for and unprovoked. Three other men, William Debbert, Eugene Thurlow, and Charles Webber, were in the street nearby, and all saw Levy hit Carlson. They could not say what provoked the assault or if it was justified, but could verify that Levy did strike Carlson. None of them saw Carlson strike back.

Levy testified in his own defense. He said that Carlson was interfering with his boardinghouse business. He said Carlson was trying to entice men away. The night he hit him, he saw Carlson standing in front of the Red Front store and decided to talk to him about what he was doing. While talking, he said Carlson kicked him in the stomach. He was only defending himself when he hit Carlson back.

Two other witnesses said they saw Carlson strike first. Webber and Debbert said they did not see Carlson kick Levy. Carlson also denied that he had struck Levy. Due to the conflicting testimony, the jury could not reach a decision. Contemporary papers suggested that many people sympathized with the crimpers.

In 1906 shanghaiing was brought to an abrupt halt. New laws prohibited any runner, shipping concern, or steamship agency from hiring a sailor who was drunk. The law also stated that once a sailor was onboard, he could leave for just cause by bringing it before the board of commissioners. Steep fines were imposed against those who failed to obey the law, anywhere from two hundred to five hundred dollars for each occurrence.

This law made it difficult for Levy to continue on as he had before. He kept his hand in the business for a little while though, taking care to keep a very low profile. His business was damaged further when steamships started rapidly replacing sailing vessels. Fewer hands were needed to man the new ships, which further eroded his boardinghouse business. Unions were also doing a better job of protecting sailors' rights. By 1910 Levy gave it up. In 1912 he moved his family to San Francisco. He died there in 1931.

His financial partner, Sims, remained in Port Townsend. He earned a handsome profit from the two canneries he owned in Blaine and Port Townsend. He also dabbled in mining, logging, and oil, and eventually became a state legislator. He died in September 1945.

WYOMING OUTLAWS

THE ASA MOORE GANG

Lynched by Vigilantes

When the Union Pacific Railroad left Omaha to lay tracks westward, a makeshift town was assembled at each significant "end-of-track." Each town created by the U.P.'s advance was preceded by another unofficial town consisting of gamblers, saloonkeepers, and soiled doves who preyed upon the railroad workers. These unofficial towns often preceded U.P. towns by months, each resident trying to reserve the best location for his or her operation before the railroad's surveyor arrived to make the town official.

The town of Laramie had been platted by the railroad's chief surveyor, Sam Reed, in February 1867 on land just north of Fort Sanders, which had been established only two years earlier. By the time the first railroad men arrived in Laramie, a tent city had already been set up for two months. Among the first of its three hundred citizens were businessmen planning on establishing legitimate enterprises. The new residents also included the outlaw element, including several men who would become minor players in Asa Moore's gang in Laramie.

The town of Laramie formed a new government on May 1 and the following day elected Melville C. Brown mayor. Brown could do nothing to govern the town because of the rowdy outlaw element, already well entrenched, so the entire slate resigned in three weeks.

As soon as Laramie's elected government collapsed, Asa "Ace" Moore declared himself mayor and appointed O. S. Duggan town marshal. Duggan in turn hired Con Weiger, Edward "Big Ed" Bernard, and "Heartless Ed" Franklin as his deputies. These four men with Moore were known as the "five bosses." To round out the slate, Moore appointed "Long" Steve Young as justice of the peace. Moore was also the proprietor of two saloons in Laramie—the Diana and the Belle of the West. The latter was used as his base of operations for criminal activity.

The five bosses used their authority to recover money from those who won on their gaming tables—not a frequent occurrence. They also arrested other innocent people with money on some pretext. The five bosses would take them into the back rooms of the Belle of the West saloon, conduct a mock trial, pick them clean, and, if they seemed no threat, turn them loose. If the five sensed trouble from their mark, they would murder him. The bodies of their victims would be buried in unmarked graves on the prairie or dumped in a boxcar to be found later at some distant location.

In August 1868 Duggan, who was embroiled in the controversial shooting of eighteen-year-old Robert Reed, lost his job and was nearly lynched by a mob led by the murdered boy's father. That's when things began to unravel for the Moore gang.

In late September the good citizens of Laramie began organizing a large vigilante committee. The leaders were Tom Sears, an army veteran and legitimate saloon owner; John Wright, a saddle maker; and Nathaniel K. Boswell, a member of the Rocky Mountain Detective Agency. They were determined to rid their town of the unwanted element. They held a people's court with the defendants in absentia, and then planned an organized strike for October 18, 1868, to arrest the guilty parties. The committee had compiled a list of more than fifty undesirable individuals, and among them were six men marked for execution. Moore's gang, the most prominent among the outlaw element in Laramie, was included on the list; and Moore, Weiger, Bernard, and Young dominated the execution list of six desperate men.

At 8:00 p.m. on October 18, 1868, five hundred men gathered on the far side of the tracks behind the railroad repair shops. From there groups of men deployed to prearranged locations. At the sound of a gunshot fired by Sears, they were to move in and capture their assigned men from the list. Then the plan was to sort them out, hang the six condemned men, and put the rest of the undesirable men and women on a special train out of Laramie—under threat of death should they return.

However, a shot was prematurely fired, unrelated to the plan, and only the party assigned to the Belle of the West saloon was in position. They made their move. The targeted men in the Belle of the West met the attack with gunfire, and the battle lasted fifteen minutes. Con Weiger and Ed Bernard were badly wounded; henchman Charles Barton, a coronet player, was killed; William Willie, a fireman on Union Pacific's engine 69, was shot through the bowels and expected to die; and William McPherson was shot through the leg but was expected to recover. Many others among the undesirables were wounded, and some may have died later on the train or thereafter.

Weiger and Bernard were taken to an unfinished shed behind the Frontier Hotel, where preparations were made to hang them. Asa Moore, uncertain of his status after the melee, went to the shed and ordered the vigilantes to release Weiger and Bernard. Instead, one of the men stepped up, put his shotgun into Moore's belly, and announced that Moore's name was on the list of six and that he would join Weiger and Bernard. The three men had their hands tied behind them, had nooses placed around their necks, and were hoisted up. It was reported that before they were strangled to death, their bodies were riddled with bullets. The bodies were left hanging throughout the night and well into the next morning.

Long Steve Young was captured at Lawson's ranch nine miles from Laramie. He was brought to town and told of the hangings. The committee seemed satisfied that they had hanged enough outlaws for one day, so they ordered Young to leave the city by 7:30 a.m., as he had missed the special train. According to the original plan, he was also ordered not to return to Laramie under threat of death. Stupidly, Young disobeyed his orders and went to the scene of the hangings. When he saw the bodies of his friends still suspended, he declared that "no strangling sons of b—s" could drive him out of town and challenged anyone to molest him. Half a dozen committee members then stepped out from the crowd and warned him to leave or they would "shoot his brains out on the spot." Young promised that he would leave, but threatened to return with his friends and exact revenge upon the vigilantes. Young, however, reneged on his promise and did not leave town as ordered.

Young was followed around town until 10:00 a.m. and once again was told to leave within the hour, but he again defied and challenged the vigilantes. The vigilantes then seized Young and dragged him to the main railroad crossing at the foot of B Street near the depot, selected a telegraph pole, tied his hands behind his back, put a noose over his head, and pushed him up a ladder. When lynching was imminent Young begged for a chance to leave town, but it was too late. In the presence of hundreds of spectators, without ceremony or delay, the vigilantes pulled the rope taut, tied off the loose end, and jerked the ladder out from under Young's feet. One of the vigilantes thought Young was taking too long to die and pulled down on Young's legs, which snapped the rope. Young's body fell. While he lay on the ground senseless, one of his victims rushed forward from the crowd and kicked and stomped his head. The vigilantes pulled the angry man away, tied a new noose around Young's neck, and pulled him up once more. It took but a short time for Young to finish strangling to death.

The committee secured a job wagon and went to the shed to collect the bodies of Moore, Bernard, and Weiger. When Young was declared dead, they cut down his body. The remains of the four men were driven to a place three-quarters of a mile from the city and buried in a single wide, deep grave. En route the "women" of the dead men tried several times to pull their men off the wagon, but the vigilantes would not allow it, nor would they allow any kind of marker to be placed over their grave.

Duggan fled from Laramie after he was nearly lynched, and Franklin, who was not on the execution list, was placed on the train and threatened with death if he returned. Moore, Bernard, and Weiger had pushed their luck too far, fleeced too many innocents, and murdered too many good men, but they finally got what they deserved—an ignominious death at the end of a rope. Young, a party to all of Moore's outlaw antics, was given a second chance but failed to heed the warnings, and he joined the others, dangling at the end of a rope from a telegraph pole and then buried in an unmarked grave on the prairie, like so many others he helped put there.

BUTCH CASSIDY AND THE SUNDANCE KID

Those Elusive "Wild Bunch" Boys

Robert Leroy Parker, best known as Butch Cassidy during the heyday of his criminal career, is among the half-dozen most elusive outlaws of the Old West—even in death. His only capture and imprisonment was in 1894 for a crime that he probably didn't commit, but by then Cassidy was already a confirmed desperado.

His first reported death occurred about May 14, 1898, near Price, Utah. On July 24, 1898, the *Salt Lake Tribune* reported: "The supply of Butch Cassidays [*sic*] seems inexhaustible. You will find him in every county of the state . . . several of him have been killed." By 1903 Cassidy had been killed more than a dozen times. According to the *Vernal Times,* "He must have more lives than a whole family of cats." Cassidy continued to die over and over on three continents during the next forty-five years.

The most likely spot for the demise of Butch Cassidy, and his sidekick the Sundance Kid, was in San Vicente, Bolivia, in 1908, though the date varies and is often reported as 1909 or 1911. Their death scene in San Vicente was made popular by the blockbuster movie titled with their aliases. Cassidy also died at least seven times in Argentina between 1904 and 1935, twice in Honduras, once each in Ecuador and Uruguay, and several times in Venezuela during the early 1900s. He only died twice in Europe, once of old age in Ireland and once murdered in Paris, France, about 1906.

In the United States there were many reports of Cassidy's death as well. Those reports include: eight deaths in various Nevada towns; six deaths in Utah; several deaths in Washington State, Oregon, and California; a death in Wyoming and one in Colorado after the turn of the twentieth century; and in the East one death in New York City and one somewhere in Georgia.

Harry A. "Sundance Kid" Longabaugh "died" only a few times in the United States, but he outlived his partner in crime. His death, after expiring with Cassidy all over South America, was reported first in Fort Worth, Texas, in 1954. Then he was reported dead in a Utah prison in 1955, in Oregon in 1956, in Montana in 1957, and finally in Wyoming in 1967.

The deaths of popular outlaws are often disputed, even when there is indisputable evidence, so it is no surprise that the reported deaths of Butch Cassidy and the Sundance Kid are controversial and numerous. However, the lives and criminal careers of most of Wyoming's "Wild Bunch" outlaws have been well documented, making Cassidy and Sundance the notable exceptions to the rule.

The Wild Bunch was aptly named. They were certainly wild by any standard, and they were also more of an assorted "bunch" than a "gang." The Wild Bunch was a coalition of individual desperados and small gangs that hid out at the Hole-in-the-Wall, which was located in a desolate part of Johnson County, Wyoming, where a wall of parallel hills ran for fifty miles. There was a gap, or "hole," on the east, which could be defended by a few men. No hideout would be safe without a "back door," and to the west of the Hole-in-the-Wall, there were numerous trails out of the area providing the men an avenue for escape.

On any illegal outing the participants could include a number of different men from the Wild Bunch, and this may have been intentional as lawmen often had to guess which members of the bunch had participated in a particular crime. At times there were one hundred to one hundred and fifty wanted men hiding at Hole-in-the-Wall, and any of them could be recruited for a particular job. Those "jobs" took them to various parts of the Southwest, including Colorado, Montana, Arizona, and Nevada, where the Wild Bunch engaged in rustling horses and cattle, robbing banks, and holding up stagecoaches and trains.

Robert Leroy Parker, one of the most famous gang members, was born in Beaver, Utah, in 1866. He was still quite young when he left home after a minor skirmish with the law, more of a misunderstanding than a crime. He soon met Mike Cassidy, whose last name he would later adopt as his alias, and the two engaged in cattle rustling. In 1884 altered brands were discovered and the cattle were traced back to Parker. He fled, and to ensure that his family would not be shamed by his criminal activities, it was then he adopted the alias Butch Cassidy and went to Telluride, Colorado. He tried to follow the honest path of a teamster, but he was too restless to settle down. After a few months in Colorado, he moved on to Wyoming.

Cassidy befriended others interested in making quick, easy money, and in 1889 he and a small party rode to Telluride and robbed the San Miguel Bank. Cassidy laid low for several years after the Colorado bank robbery, but in 1894 he was arrested for stealing horses. He was tried, convicted, and sentenced to a two-year term at the prison near Laramie. Prison hardened Cassidy and there he became convinced that he needed to form a gang. After his release on January 19, 1896, he met Harry Longabaugh and, seeing no reason for delay, formed the Wild Bunch. They robbed a bank in Utah and then in August robbed another bank in Montpelier, Idaho.

After the Idaho robbery, Sundance and Cassidy parted ways for awhile. During that time Sundance was involved in a number of train robberies. When Sundance and Cassidy reunited at the Hole-in-the-Wall in late 1898, Sundance shared his train robbery experiences with Cassidy. The men immediately began to plan an assault on a train. Cassidy recruited a dozen men into a gang that came to be called the "Train Robber's Syndicate," virtually a gang within a gang. Their first train-robbing excursion was thwarted by an undercover lawman. Cassidy would next plan to rob a train at Wilcox, Wyoming.

Cassidy, in planning the Wilcox train robbery, knew that posses would be on their trail quickly, so he developed a system of horse relays so that his men would always have fresh horses for their getaway. For days before a robbery, Cassidy would scout the region for good horseflesh, building a string that was bred for endurance and very fast over short distances. He would place the horses at the place of the robbery and along the escape route. When in place, Cassidy would see to it that all the horses were pampered for days before the robbery took place.

At 2:00 a.m. on June 2, 1899, two men waving lanterns on the tracks motioned the Union Pacific train No. 1 to stop at milepost 609, one mile west of Wilcox, Wyoming. There was a small wooden bridge up ahead and engineer W. R. Jones thought it might have washed out. An engineer could not jeopardize his train by ignoring an emergency signal, so Jones brought his train to a halt.

Two men, masked and armed, boarded the engine. Next they gained entrance to the express car and blasted open the safe. The contents were quickly removed and the robbers disappeared into the darkness. Later their trail revealed that they had horses tied a short distance away and rode north toward Casper. The trainmen could not identify any of the robbers, but deduced that Cassidy, Harvey "Kid Curry" Logan, and "Flatnose" George Curry were involved along with other members of the Wild Bunch. It was supposed that the men got very little, as there was not much in the safe. Rewards of three thousand dollars per man ensured that there would be many large posses in the field, and it was estimated that nearly four hundred men participated in the pursuit at different times and places. However, the robbers were never captured for the robbery.

As anticipated by Cassidy, posses took to the field in great strength and with all due speed. The day following the robbery, a Union Pacific special train arrived at Casper with Converse County Sheriff Josiah Hazen, fresh horses, and men. A local rancher, Al Hudspeth, reported that three fugitives were camped at Casper Creek six miles northwest of town, and they had run him off at gunpoint when he stopped to visit. When he described the men, the lawmen knew they were Harvey Logan, George Curry, and Elza Lay. Inquiries were made and it was determined that the three men had stopped in Casper to buy supplies. Hazen called for reinforcements, and a posse of twenty men set out to capture the three train robbers.

The posse took the field Monday and from Casper Creek followed the trail to within five miles of the horse ranch at Salt Creek. They had proceeded only a few hundred yards past that point when Curry shot and killed posse man Tom McDonald. Oscar Heistant, sheriff of Natrona County, had his horse shot from under him by one of the robbers during a withering fusillade, so Heistant was sent afoot to the nearest ranch with orders to bring back more men.

The three fugitives and the reinforced posse continued a running gun battle throughout the day, but the fugitives managed to escape. On Tuesday Sheriff Hazen and Dr. J. F. Leeper came to a draw and dismounted to look for a trail. Just as Hazen called to Leeper that he had found the tracks, Harvey Logan stood up from his hiding place behind a boulder, took careful aim, and shot the sheriff in the stomach. The three fugitives kept up the fire for a short time, but when the rest of the posse came up, they mounted and fled again. Hazen was taken back to Casper and then by special train to Douglas, where he died at 5:00 a.m. on Tuesday.

The killing of Hazen outraged Wyoming's citizens, and a hundred trackers were dispatched to look for a trail. The US marshal organized a posse of fifteen handpicked deputies, and bloodhounds were put on the scent. The governor mobilized the state militia, and more than a hundred men volunteered for posse service. Even with all this effort and large rewards, the three train robbers managed to elude capture and escaped the region.

The Wild Bunch took fourteen months off before returning to Wyoming, waiting for interest in the huge rewards to wane. Finally on August 29, 1900, they were ready to rob another train. One of the robbers slipped aboard the blind baggage of Union Pacific's train No. 3 as it pulled out of Tipton, Wyoming, located midway between Rawlins and Rock Springs in Sweetwater County. The robber climbed over the tender and took the engineer and fireman hostage at gunpoint. When the train was two and a half miles west of Tipton, he ordered the train to stop, and three other robbers appeared from the shadows. They began shooting their pistols along the sides of the passenger cars to prevent any interference, and when they felt secure, they went to the express car and forced their way in by threatening to dynamite the car. E. C. Woodcock, the same messenger they had robbed at Wilcox, opened the door and gave no resistance.

As soon as they were inside, they placed a large charge of Kepauno Chemical Company's Giant Powder on the through safe and blew it apart, along with most of the express car. The amount taken was later disputed. The Pacific Express Company reported a loss of $50.40, but Woodcock said he carried fifty-five thousand dollars, and Cassidy later said they had taken forty-five thousand dollars. There was three thousand dollars' worth of damage done to the express car.

On the run the gang buried the treasure, believing for some reason that it could be traced to them. Then the group rode to Huntington, Nevada. The railroad and the express company offered a reward of one thousand dollars for each man for a total of eight thousand dollars, but the robbers again eluded lawmen.

The Tipton robbery convinced the railroad that they needed to do something to stop the robberies of their trains in Wyoming. Recognizing the efficient getaway method that Cassidy developed using relays of fresh horses, the railroad started dispatching special horse car trains to the scene as soon as a robbery was reported. One month after robbing the train near Tipton, the men who had fled into Nevada robbed the bank at Winnemucca. Then, once again, the Wild Bunch laid low until interest cooled. In late June 1901 three men, Cassidy, Logan, and Ben Kilpatrick, and Laura Bullion went to Wagner, Montana, to rob a train. Wagner and the Great Northern Railroad had been chosen because the Union Pacific was then using those special horse cars and posses for speedy pursuits in Wyoming.

This was to be Cassidy's final robbery in North America, and he planned to flee to South America with a big haul. There he planned to rendezvous with Sundance, who was already aboard a ship bound for Argentina in the company of Etta Place. They recruited O. C. "Deaf Charley" Hanks, a Montana train robber, and on July 3, 1901, Kilpatrick boarded as a passenger in Malta while Logan slipped onto the blind baggage. When the train neared Exeter Switch, three miles east of Wagner, Logan climbed over the tender and captured engineer Tom Jones and his fireman at gunpoint. The other two robbers were waiting on the tracks and waved a flag to signal the place to stop the train. The two outside men fired their pistols along the sides of the cars to keep the passengers from interfering, but several shots were too close and ricocheted into the cars, causing several minor wounds.

The robbers broke into the express car and blew open the safe, which contained forty thousand dollars in bank notes sent to the Montana National Bank in Helena. The plunder was loaded onto horses, and the four robbers rode south across the Milk River and turned east. After four days following their trail, lawmen said they believed that the fugitives were better mounted than any of the posses and were probably somewhere between the Missouri River and the Hole-in-the-Wall. The Great Northern Express Company offered a five-thousand-dollar reward for their arrest and five hundred dollars for each conviction. The company circulated descriptions, and all but Cassidy were captured, convicted, and sentenced to prison terms.

As planned, Cassidy booked passage to South America and joined Sundance. There he tried to live an honest life as a rancher. It was generally believed that he later returned to a life of crime, which led to his death in that San Vicente cantina, or perhaps he returned to the United States or Europe under an alias and lived out his life in relative obscurity—"dying a thousand deaths" here and there.

Of all the outlaws in Wyoming's rich criminal history, Butch Cassidy and the Sundance Kid are its best-known habitual criminals—outlaws in every respect. They were wild, but also careful planners, and committed more than a dozen successful robberies of banks and trains after they graduated from petty thievery and rustling. Cassidy had been arrested a half-dozen times during his early career but was only convicted twice before maturing into an armed robber. Sundance was convicted only once, surprisingly spending his time in a local jail for a serious offense. Where and when these elusive outlaws died will probably never be determined, but even if the law never expiated their crimes, time eventually overtakes everyone.

THE LAST SHEEP CAMP RAID

After the Union Pacific Railroad tracks crossed the southern edge of Wyoming in 1868, herds of cattle and flocks of sheep began to grow. In 1870 a tally showed that there were just eight thousand cattle and fewer than sixty-five hundred sheep in the territory, but ten years later the sheep population had grown to over half a million and was growing rapidly, and in 1885 cattle tallied at 1.5 million head. It was clear that livestock would be a primary industry in Wyoming, prompting the establishment in 1873 of the Laramie County Stock Grower's Association to protect both sheep and cattle. However, conflicts between the cattlemen and the sheep men had already begun in other parts of the West. On February 7, 1874, the *Cheyenne Leader* newspaper reported:

> *A bitter feud has for a long time past existed between the cattle and sheep ranchers in the southern portion of the Territory, resulting in the frequent driving away and killing of sheep. The evil having become so great and the civil authorities unable to cope with it, the employment of the military was at one time contemplated to take offenders into custody. One of those, an extensive and wealthy cattle herder named Montgomery, living about thirty miles south of Pueblo [Colorado], having been identified as one of a party of raiders who drove away and killed a large number of sheep has been sentenced to two years' imprisonment.*

In 1879 the Wyoming organization, which was controlled by the cattlemen, changed its name to the Wyoming Stock Grower's Association as conflicts were already heating up between cattlemen and sheep men in Wyoming. When the conflicts turned violent, the Wyoming Wool Grower's Association was formed as an adversary to the politically influential cattlemen. Conflicts were over the use of and access to grass and water, as it was believed that cattle could not survive on ground where sheep had grazed. There were private lands, but the majority of the available pasturage consisted of large tracts of open range and government land—and the government only grudgingly allowed grazing on its lands. The cattlemen claimed certain lands as "theirs by prior use" and established enforced dead lines—boundary lines beyond which any stray sheep could be shot or clubbed to death. While cattle generally could roam free on whatever range they were placed and were gathered up only during roundup seasons, sheep had to be herded. The life of a herder was lonely and difficult, as described by Episcopalian Bishop Ethelbert Talbot (October 9, 1848–February 27, 1928) in his 1906 book *My People of the Plains:*

> *Perhaps one of the most profitable industries in that western land in 1887 was sheep-growing. The high plateaus, foot-hills, and mountain lands, where the grass is very nutritious, furnished excellent pasturage for sheep, which, by instinct, can dig down through the snow and get their food, and thus survive the winter. One man often owns a herd numbering many thousand. . . . The life of a sheep-herder is a peculiarly lonely one. Often months pass without giving him the opportunity of seeing a human being. His faithful dog is his only companion. He generally has a team and a covered wagon in which he sleeps at night during the winter, and wherein he stores the necessary provisions for his daily food. It is his duty to seek the best available pasturage, and, when the grass in one neighborhood has been exhausted, to drive the flock to a new and fresh supply. . . . Their condition is often rendered more pitiable from the fact that between the cattle and sheep men a most bitter antagonism exists. This has been caused by dissensions arising from the occupation of pasture-land. Where a flock of sheep has long run no food is left for cattle, for they eat the grass so closely and trample the ground in such a manner as to destroy it for other stock. Where the land all belongs to the government, one has, technically, as much right as another. The advent of a large flock of sheep is always resented by the cow-boy, and many have been the deadly feuds that have arisen. In the interests of peace, a sort of distribution is sometimes made, allotting large areas to the sheep men with the understanding that they do not invade the territory reserved for other stock.*

In 1886 and 1888 Wyoming's cattle herds were decimated by a devastating winter—after an early thaw, a long-term freeze left a layer of thick ice over the grass, which the cattle could not penetrate. Sheep by instinct would dig down to their food so, though the weather took a toll, the two harsh winters were not nearly as devastating to the sheep men. Struggling to survive in the cattle business, the cattlemen became desperate, and after the turn of the century, violence erupted in Wyoming. The killing of sheep and sheep men became almost commonplace, their relative isolation leaving them particularly vulnerable to such attacks. The methods used to slaughter sheep included shooting, clubbing, spreading poison where the sheep grazed, and driving them over cliffs. In July 1902 cattlemen raided a sheep camp near Thermopolis and killed a flock master, and later that year raiders slaughtered two thousand sheep and killed the herders. In 1904 bushwhackers murdered a sheepherder near Kirby Creek, in present-day Hot Springs County.

On August 23, 1905, a raiding party of ten masked men rode into the White Springs sheep camp of Louis A. Gantz, captured the herders, and forced them at gunpoint to leave. The raiders then tried to drive the flock over a cliff, but most of the sheep turned away and scattered, forcing the men to shoot into the uncooperative flock, killing about five hundred in all. They then tied a fine team of horses to one of the wagons and shot them, and finished by setting three sheep wagons on fire. The total loss was valued at over forty thousand dollars, but the raiders remained unidentified and thus eluded arrest.

On Wednesday, January 10, 1906, Utah sheepherders A. N. Garsite and Robert Allen, who had driven their sheep onto a disputed range near Burnt Fork, Wyoming, were attacked and shot to death by twenty raiders, their sheep were clubbed to death, and their wagons and outfits were burned. In yet another attack, on April 29, 1907, raiders used dynamite to destroy the Trapper Creek camp of John Linn (aka Lynn). The raiders captured the herder and bound him, then proceeded to dynamite the camp wagons and slaughter the sheep with dynamite, killing over seven hundred head. This raid occurred near the same place in Big Horn County where an attack had occurred in 1905.

In late March 1909, Joseph Allemand and Joseph Emge, Frenchmen who jointly owned two flocks of sheep each numbering twenty-five hundred, began a journey that ended with their deaths, in the last reported armed raid by cattlemen on a sheep camp in the West. The Frenchmen had decided to drive their flocks twenty-five miles from Worland to their ranch on Spring Creek in Nowood Valley, seven miles southeast of Ten Sleep and thirty-five miles from the nearest railroad. Although they would be driving their sheep over government land, where grazing of any stock—sheep or cattle—was legally permitted, this was an area claimed by the cattlemen through "prior use." Allemand's and Emge's presence at Spring Creek caused great concern for the cattle ranchers, who were determined to see the sheep men off the land. In fact, Allemand had previously been warned to keep his sheep out of Nowood Valley, but he insisted he had the right to be there and would not be humiliated by being driven off. On April 2, before reaching their destination, Allemand telephoned his wife to say he would not be able to return home that night as he had intended, since they would arrive at their camp at a late hour. He set up camp at one wagon with Emge and Jules Lazier, Allemand's French nephew and one of his herders, while sixteen-year-old Charles "Bounce" Helmer and Pierre "Pete" Cafferal, also Frenchmen, used the other. Helmer and Cafferal set up their wagon some distance from the Emge wagon near the junction of the streams at the county road, while Emge and Lazier positioned their wagon on a branch of Spring Creek, because each pair of herders was responsible for one flock and they were determined to keep their sheep from mingling.

At ten o'clock that evening, Emge, Lazier, and Allemand were asleep in their wagon when a masked party of seven prominent Big Horn Basin cattlemen rode up and commanded, "Strike a light and step out of your wagon!" The party was led by thirty-five-year-old George Saban and included thirty-five-year-old Thomas Dixon, fifty-four-year-old Edward Eaton, twenty-nine-year-old Herbert L. Brink (who was a Colorado fugitive), forty-nine-year-old Milton A. Alexander, Charles Farris, and William Keyes. However, as soon as the order was given, the seven men opened fire and riddled the wagon with rifle bullets. Emge and Lazier were killed, or at least mortally wounded, in the first fire and Allemand was seriously wounded. Brink, Dixon, and Eaton again ordered the men to strike a light and come out of the wagon while Saban, Alexander, Farris, and Keyes began shooting and clubbing the sheep near the wagon. Allemand was the only one able to walk, but because of his wound he could not strike a light. He stepped onto the wagon tongue and pleaded, "My God, boys, please don't kill my sheep." Brink then fired a single rifle shot, which killed Allemand. After the Frenchman collapsed, Brink dismounted, took the camp shovel, and struck a heavy blow to his neck to be sure he was dead. Dixon and Eaton then poured coal oil on the wagon and set it afire, and the bodies of Emge and Lazier were incinerated beyond recognition.

The party next rode to the wagon of Helmer and Cafferal, pulled them out, and took the two men away some distance without giving them a chance to see the murder scene. Afraid that the light from the burning wagon would make it possible for the surviving shepherds to identify them, the cattlemen warned Helmer and Cafferal to leave the region and never return. The raiders had only killed twenty-five head of sheep before deciding to run off Helmer and Cafferal, but they returned to the flocks and scattered them so that the coyotes and wolves could take their toll. They next threw their guns into the mud of Spring Creek, as it was known that modern ballistics testing could identify the murder weapons, and then rode off.

However, unbeknownst to the cattlemen, Cafferal had recognized Eaton. The herders brought news of the atrocity to Ten Sleep, but the telephone wires had been cut by the raiders before they had attacked the camp, so word did not reach Sheriff Felix Alston until the following day. Sheriff Alston, County District

Attorney Percy Metz, and Deputy Sheriff Joe Cusack left immediately for the scene. When they arrived they found clear tracks of the raiders, but they could only follow a short distance because six inches of snow had fallen and covered the trail. The guns were found in the creek and recovered, and the scattered sheep were gathered and put under the care of a herder until an administrator of the estates of Allemand and Emge could be appointed.

The Wyoming Wool Grower's Association had previously instituted a standing reward of one thousand dollars for the identification, arrest, and conviction of raiders. They assigned their own detective—Joe Lafors, of Tom Horn fame—to the case, and the Big Horn County Wool Grower's Association added another thousand dollars to the reward for the arrest and conviction of the murderers. It was anticipated that the reward could grow as high as five thousand dollars for the arrest of the raiders once the county and state added to the amount. However, similar raids had been going on for several years in different parts of Wyoming and not once had a reward been paid for an arrest, prompting Governor Bryant Brooks to call for action. Additionally, the citizens of Big Horn Basin were outraged by the brutality of the murders, as it could not be proven that Emge and Lazier were dead before their wagon was set on fire.

Following the murders, Sheriff Felix Alston and detective Lafors conducted a more in-depth investigation. They were able to identify boot tracks at the scene as those of Brink, as well as determine ownership of the guns that had been recovered from the mud of the creek. On April 15 the grand jury convened to hear the evidence offered by Sheriff Alston and detective Lafors, and to hear testimony from Farris and Keyes, who had turned state's evidence, as well as from William Goodrich and William Garrison. On May 3 indictments were returned against all the defendants, and they were arrested. When it appeared that Garrison might be called again to testify against his friends, he put all of his important paperwork in order, and then wrote a note to Sheriff Alston telling him where the papers were located and describing his preferences for the disposition of his remains. He then walked out on the prairie and shot himself through the head.

Brink's trial began on November 7, after a charge of jury tampering was resolved in late October; after testimony concluded, the case went to the jury at 6:00 p.m. on November 11. Brink was found guilty of first-degree murder and sentenced to hang, but immediately negotiations began regarding the other four defendants. Saban, on behalf of Alexander, Dixon, and Eaton, had insisted, "If you cannot save the life of Brink we will all hang from the same tree." It was then agreed that Brink would get a new trial, plead guilty to second-degree murder, and receive a life sentence. However, before any action could be taken to schedule a new trial, Governor Brooks commuted Brink's sentence to life in prison on the first-degree murder charge. On November 13, 1909, Saban and Alexander were given sentences of twenty to twenty-six years for second-degree murder, and Dixon and Eaton were given sentences of three to five years for arson; all five convicted criminals were delivered to the prison at Rawlins. Charles Farris and William Keyes, members of the raiders' party who turned state's evidence and testified against their fellow raiders, were branded traitors and had to dispose of their Wyoming property; for their safety they and their families were escorted out of the state. On November 17 William Goodrich, the other witness against the raiding party, received word that his Ten Sleep property had been burned to the ground.

In 1911 Felix Alston, the sheriff who investigated the raid, was appointed warden at the Rawlins prison. Not long afterward Eaton and Saban appeared on summer road crews working in the Big Horn Basin area. Assignment to road crews was reserved for prisoners expecting to be pardoned or released the following fall, but both men still had years to serve on their sentences. In late May Eaton contracted spotted fever from a tick bite and died on June 1, 1912. Meanwhile, Saban seemed to have so much freedom to roam over the Big Horn Basin countryside that some may have thought he was a free man. In December 1913 Saban was assigned to the road crew (which usually was returned to the prison in November) that was sent to Worland to work on the new industrial institute. As Christmas neared, Warden Alston dispatched prison guard D. O. Johnson to Worland to bring Saban back to the prison, but the convict convinced his guard to stop over in Basin so he could draw money from the bank. They arrived on Wednesday, December 17, and Saban withdrew his money, but it was too late to start for Rawlins, so they took rooms at the Anters Hotel. Johnson lost track of his prisoner at 7:00 p.m. but was not concerned as Saban had trusty status, and he expected his prisoner to return that evening. At eleven the next morning, when Saban could not be found in Basin, Johnson sounded the alarm. During the investigation that followed, it was determined that Saban had been driven to Montana by Ora Allen, and he was thought to be in the Bridger area, where his mother and sister lived. Allen was arrested on December 29 but released two days later, and no charges were filed. Montana officers agreed to assist in finding and arresting Saban, but when the Wyoming authorities showed no interest, Sheriff J. C. Orrick of Billings dropped the investigation and Saban was never returned to prison.

Thomas Dixon had his sentence commuted and was released from prison on November 1, 1912. Milton Alexander was paroled, and on February 13, 1917, he was granted a full pardon by Governor John Kendrick. Brink was released from prison on November 2, 1943, after serving thirty-four years of his life sentence.

Index

Bibliography

Alaska Outlaws

Klutuk

Bell, Tom. "Memories of a Murder," *Alaska Magazine,* October 1991.
Ferrell, Ed. *Frontier Justice,* 98–102.
Hatfield, Fred. *North of the Sun: A Memoir of the Alaskan Wilderness.* New York: Birch Lane Press Book, 1990.
———. "Of Traps and Treasures—Klutuk," *Alaska Magazine,* September 1984.

Nellie "Black Bear" Bates and William Schermeyer

Butler, Anne M. *Daughters of Joy, Sisters of Misery: Prostitutes in the American West, 1865–90.* Champaign: University of Illinois Press, 1987.
Hunt, William R. *Distant Justice.*
Murphy, Claire Rudolf, and Jane G. Haigh. *Gold Rush Women.* Anchorage: Alaska Northwest Books, 2003.

Jefferson Randolph "Soapy" Smith

Berton, Pierre. *Klondike.*

Arizona Outlaws

Augustine Chacón

Edwards, Harold L. "This is the Greatest Day of My Life: The Hanging of Augustin Chacón." *True West,* November 1995: 14–21.
Burgess, Glenn, ed. *Mount Graham Profiles, Volume 2, Ryder Ridgeway Collection.* Safford, AZ: Graham County Historical Society, 1988.
Rickards, Colin. "The Hairy One—Arizona's Deadly Bandit." *The West: True Stories of the Old West* 14, no. 1 (December 1970): 30–31, 56–64.

James Fleming Parker

Allen, Paul L., and Peter M. Pegnam. *Arizona Territory: Baptism in Blood.* Tucson: Tucson Citizen Publishing Company, 1990.
Miller, Joseph, ed. *The Arizona Story.* New York: Hastings House, 1952.

Trimble, Marshall. *Arizona: A Cavalcade of History*. Tucson: Treasure Chest Publications, 1989.

———. *Arizona Highways: The Law of the Gun*. Phoenix: Arizona Department of Transportation, State of Arizona, 1997.

Way, Thomas E. *The Parker Story*. Prescott, AZ: Prescott Graphics, 1981.

Weiner, Melissa Ruffner. *Prescott Yesteryears: Life in Arizona's First Territorial Capital*. Prescott, AZ: Primrose Press, 1979.

Wilson, R. Michael. *Crime & Punishment in Early Arizona*. Las Vegas: Stagecoach Books, 2004.

Albert Wright "Burt" Alvord

Block, Eugene B. *Great Train Robberies of the West*. New York: Coward-McCann, Inc., 1959.

Bond, Ervin. *Percy Bowden: Born to be a Frontier Lawman*. Douglas, AZ: Bond, 1976.

Chaput, Don. *The Odyssey of Burt Alvord: Lawman, Train Robber, Fugitive*. Tucson, AZ: Westernlore Press, 2000.

Coolidge, Dane. *Fighting Men of the West*. New York: E. P. Dutton & Co., Inc., 1932.

Haley, J. Evetts. *Jeff Milton: A Good Man with a Gun*. Norman, Okla.: University of Oklahoma Press, 1948.

Hendricks, George D. *The Bad Man of the West*. San Antonio, Texas: The Naylor Company, 1942.

Patterson, Richard. *The Train Robbery Era: An Encyclopedic History*. Boulder, Colo.: Pruett Publishing Company, 1991.

Ringgold, Jennie Parks. *Frontier Days in the Southwest*. San Antonio, Texas: The Naylor Company, 1952.

Theobald, John and Lillian. *Wells Fargo in Arizona Territory*. Tempe: Arizona Historical Foundation, 1978.

White, Scott, as told to John Edwin Hogg. "Bad Men's Nemesis: The adventures and experiences of an Arizona sheriff, in a land and a time when a man often wore a moustache, but always wore a gun." *Touring Topics,* April 1931: 25–26.

California Outlaws

Tiburcio Vasquez

Chronicles of the Old West 4, no. 6 (May 2004).

Henshall, John A. "Tales of the Early California Bandits," *Overland Monthly* (1909).

John Allen

Birmingham, Stephen. *California Rich.* New York: Simon & Schuster, 1980.

Borthwick, John D. *The Gold Hunters.* Wales: MacMillan Publishing, 1917.

Brock, M. J., and W. B. Lardner. *History of Placer & Nevada Counties.* Los Angeles: Historic Record Company, 1924.

Carson, James H. *Recollections of California Mines.* Oakland, Cal.: Biobooks, 1950.

Haslam, Gerald W. *Coming of Age in California.* Walnut Creek, Cal.: Devil Mountain Books, 2000.

Horan, James D. *The Authentic Wild West.* New York: Crown Publishers, 1977.

Houston, James. *Californians: Searching for the Golden State.* New York: Knopf Publishing, 1992.

Jackson, Joseph H. *Bad Company.* New York: Harcourt, Brace, 1946.

Jones, Thomas. *You Bet: How the California Miners Did It.* New York: New Publishing Company, 1936.

Loya, Joe. *The Man Who Outgrew His Prison Cell.* New York: Rayo Publishing, 2004.

Nash, Jay R. *Encyclopedia of Western Lawmen & Outlaws.* New York: Paragon House, 1989.

National Police Gazette XL, no. 239 (April 22, 1882).

Oppel, Frank. *Tales of California.* San Francisco: Castle Books, 1989.

Real West Magazine VIII, no. 42 (July 1965).

Real West Magazine VIII, no. 43 (September 1965).

Sann, Paul, and James Horan. *Pictorial History of the Wild West.* New York: Bonanza Books, 1965.

Secrest, William B. *Perilous Trails, Dangerous Men: Early California Stagecoach Robbers and Their Desperate Careers.* Clovis, Cal.: Word Dancer Press, 2002.

Thurston, Clarke. *California Fault.* New York: Ballantine Books, 1996.

Juan Flores

Cox, Bill. "Back-Country Bad Man," *High Country Magazine* (June 1968).

Colorado Outlaws

The Musgrove Gang

Collier, William Ross, and Edwin Victor Westrate. *Dave Cook of the Rockies.* New York: Rufus Rockwell Wilson, 1936.

Jessen, Kenneth. *Colorado Gunsmoke.* Boulder, Colorado: Pruett Publishing Company, 1986.

Smiley, Jerome C. *History of Denver*. Denver: Old Americana Publishing Co., 1901.

Watrous, Ansel. *History of Larimer County*. Fort Collins, Colorado: Courier Printing and Publishing Company, 1911.

Pug Ryan

The Summit County Journal, 1908.
Summit Historical Society.
Gilliland, Mary Ellen. *Colorado Rascals, Scoundrels, and No Goods of Breckenridge, Frisco, Dillon, Keyston, and Silverthorne*. Silverthorne, Colorado: Alpenrose Press, 2005.

Lou Blonger

Parkhill, Forbes B. *The Wildest of the West*. Denver: Sage Books, 1957.
Van Cise, Philip S. *Fighting the Underworld*. Boston: Houghton Mifflin Co., 1936.

Idaho Outlaws

The Eddys and the Splawns

Conley, Cort. *Idaho for the Curious*. Cambridge, ID: Backeddy Books, 1982.
Elsensohn, Sister M. Alfreda. *Pioneer Days in Idaho County*. Caldwell, ID: Caxton Press, 1951.
Idaho County Free Press. "Counterfeiting case verdict," June 4, 1897.
Moscow Mirror articles. May 1897.

Diamondfield Jack

Conley, Cort. *Idaho for the Curious*. Cambridge, ID: Backeddy Books, 1982.
Grover, Davis. *Diamondfield Jack: A Study in Frontier Justice*. Norman: University of Oklahoma Press, 1986.
Idaho State Historical Society. "Jackson Lee Davis AKA Diamondfield Jack, Inmate #820," undated article on website of the Idaho State Historical Society, www.idahohistory.net/OldPenDiamondfield.pdf, accessed August 10, 2006.

Lyda Lewis

Anderson, William C. *Lady Bluebeard: The True Story of Love and Marriage, Death and Flypaper*. Boulder, CO: Fred Pruett Books, 1994.

Arentz, Bob. *Murder in Idaho: A Compilation of Famous Idaho Crimes.* Idaho State Historical Society files, 1946.

Argosy magazine. "Lady Bluebeard," April 1957.

Rhodenbaugh, Edward F. *Toxicological Investigation in the Case of William Gordon McHaffie, Deceased, of Twin Falls, Idaho.* Submitted September 8, 1921. Copies available in the Anderson collection at the Albertson Library at Boise State University, Boise, ID, and elsewhere.

Kansas Outlaws

Kate Bender

Nash, Jay Robert. *The Great Pictorial History of World Crime.* Lanham, MD: The Scarecrow Press, 2004.

The New York Times. "The Bender Family: A New Theory in Explanation of the Sudden Disappearance of the Murderous Family," November 30, 1876.

The New York Times. "The Benders in Custody," July 31, 1880.

The New York Times. "The Alleged Benders Held," November 21, 1889.

The New York Times. "Says They're Not the Benders," January 12, 1890.

The New York Times. "Said to Be the Benders," July 24, 1901.

The New York Times. "Dying Man Clears the Bender Mystery," July 12, 1908.

The New York Times. "Kate Bender Dead," May 6, 1910.

Wood, Fern M. *The Benders: Keepers of the Devil's Inn.* Fern M. Wood, 1992.

Young, Richard, and Judy Dockrey. *Outlaw Tales: Legends, Myths, and Folklore from America's Middle Border.* Atlanta: August House, 1992.

Henry Brown

Coke, Tom S. *Old West Justice in Belle Plaine, Kansas.* Bowie, MD: Heritage Books, 2002.

O'Neal, Bill. *Encyclopedia of Western Gunfighters.* Norman, OK: University of Oklahoma Press, 1991.

George "Bitter Creek" Newcomb

O'Neal, Bill. *Encyclopedia of Western Gunfighters.* Norman, OK: University of Oklahoma Press, 1991.

Rutter, Michael. *Bedside Book of Bad Girls: Outlaw Women of the American West.* Helena, MT: Farcountry Press, 2008.

Shirley, Glenn. *West of Hell's Fringe.* Norman, OK: University of Oklahoma Press, 1990.

Missouri Outlaws

The Slicker War

Lay, James H. *A Sketch of the History of Benton County, Missouri.* Hannibal, MO: The Winchell & Ebert Printing and Lithographing Company, 1876.

St. Louis Globe Democrat, July 12, 1896.

Synhorst, Curtis H. "Antebellum Vigilantes: The Slicker War in Missouri." *Gateway Heritage* 3, no. 1 (Summer 1982): 34–48.

Thomas, Clarke, and Jack Glendenning. *The Slicker War.* Aldrich, MO: Bona Publishing Company, 1984.

Vincent, J. W. "The 'Slicker War' and Its Consequences." *Missouri Historical Review* VII, no. 3 (April 1913): 138–45.

Frank and Jesse James

Beights, Ronald. *Jesse James and the First Missouri Train Robbery.* Gretna, LA: Pelican Publishing, 2002.

Brownlee, Richard S. *Gray Ghosts of the Confederacy: Guerrilla Warfare in the West, 1861–1865.* Baton Rouge: Louisiana State University Press, 1984.

Christensen, Lawrence, et al. *Dictionary of Missouri Biography.* Columbia: University of Missouri Press, 1999.

Croy, Homer. *Last of the Great Outlaws: The Story of Cole Younger.* New York: Duell, Sloan and Pearce, 1956.

Kansas City Times, September 27 and 29, 1872, and October 15 and 20, 1872.

Koblas, John. *The Great Cole Younger and Frank James Historical Wild West Show.* St. Cloud, MN: North Star Press of St. Cloud, 2002.

Parrish, William. *A History of Missouri. Volume III: 1860 to 1875.* Columbia: University of Missouri Press, 1973.

Settle, William A. *Jesse James Was His Name.* Columbia: University of Missouri Press, 1966.

Stiles, T. J. *Jesse James: Last Rebel of the Civil War.* London: Vintage Books, 2002.

Yeatman, Ted. *Frank and Jesse James: The Story Behind the Legend.* Nashville, TN: Cumberland House, 2000.

The Pendergasts

Christensen, Lawrence, et al. *Dictionary of Missouri Biography.* Columbia: University of Missouri Press, 1999.

Dorsett, Lyle. *The Pendergast Machine.* Lincoln: University of Nebraska Press, 1968.

Larsen, Lawrence, and Nancy Hulston. *Pendergast!* Columbia: University of Missouri Press, 1997.

McLear, Patrick. "'Gentlemen, Reach for All': Toppling the Pendergast Machine, 1936–1940." *Missouri Historical Review* XCV, no. 1 (October 2000): 46–67.

Reddig, William. *Tom's Town: Kansas City and the Pendergast Legend.* Columbia: University of Missouri Press, 1986.

Montana Outlaws

Con Murphy and George "Big Nose" Parrott

Aasheim, Magnus, ed. *Sheridan's Daybreak, Sheridan County, Montana.* Plentywood, Mont.: Sheridan County Historical Society and Sheridan County Homemakers, 1970.

Abbott, E. C., and Helena Huntington Smith. *We Pointed Them North: Recollections of a Cowpuncher.* Reprint. Norman: University of Oklahoma Press, 1971.

Adams, Ramon. *Burs Under the Saddle: A Second Look at Books and Histories of the West.* Norman: University of Oklahoma Press, 1964.

———. *More Burs Under the Saddle: Books and Histories of the West.* Norman: University of Oklahoma Press, 1979.

———. *Six-Guns and Saddle Leather: A Bibliography of Books and Pamphlets on Western Outlaws and Gunmen.* Rev. ed. Norman: University of Oklahoma Press, 1969.

Allison, Janet S. *Trial and Triumph: 101 Years in North Central Montana.* Chinook: North Central Montana Cow Belles, 1968.

Alvin, John. *Eastern Montana, a Portrait of Its Land and People.* Helena: Montana Magazine, 1982.

Anderson, Norman, and Fern Wallen, eds. *Crosby Diamond Jubilee, 1904–1979.* Crosby, N.D.: Historical Committee, 1979.

Archer, John. *Saskatchewan, a History.* Saskatoon, Saskatchewan: Western Producers Prairie Books, 1980.

Baker, Pearl. *The Wild Bunch at Robbers' Roost.* Reprint, Lincoln: University of Nebraska Press Bison Books, 1989.

Bartholomew, Ed. *Black Jack Ketchem, Last of the Holdup Kings.* Houston: Frontier Press, 1955.

———. *Biographical Album of Western Gunfighters.* Houston: Frontier Press, 1958.

Bennett, Estelle. *Old Deadwood Days.* New York: J. W. Sears and Co., 1928.

Bertino, Belvino. *The Scissorbills.* New York: Vantage Press, 1976.

Bertins, Belle. *Culbertson Diamond Jubilee Book.* Culbertson, Mont.: Searchlight Publishing, 1962.

Betenson, Lulu, as told to Dora Flack. *Butch Cassidy, My Brother.* Reprint. New York: Penguin Books, 1976.

Billington, Ray. *Westward to the Pacific: An Overview of America's Westward Expansion.* St. Louis: Jefferson National Expansion Historical Association, 1979.

Breihan, Carl. *The Day Jesse James Was Killed.* New York: Bonanza Books, 1962.

Breihan, Carl, and Charles Rosamond. *The Bandit Belle.* Seattle: Superior Press, 1970.

Breitmeir, Stella, ed. *Thunderstorms and Tumbleweeds: East Blaine County, Montana, 1887–1987.* Harlem, Mont.: Centennial Book Committee, 1986.

Brekke, Alan. *Kid Curry, Train Robber.* Chinook, Mont.: Privately printed, 1989.

Brown, Mark. *Plainsmen of the Yellowstone: A History of the Yellowstone Basin.* New York: G. P. Putnam's Sons, 1961.

Brown, Mark, and W. R. Felton. *Before Barbed Wire: The Frontier Years.* New York: Henry Holt and Co., 1955.

Burlingame, Merrill, and K. Ross Toole. *A History of Montana.* 3 vols. New York: Lewis Publishing Co., 1957.

Centennial Book Committee. *Thunderstorms and Tumbleweeds 1887–1987,* ed. by Stella Breitmeir. East Blaine County. Harlem, 1989.

Cheney, Roberta. *Names on the Face of Montana.* Rev. ed. Missoula, Mont.: Mountain Press, 1984.

Cheney, Truman, and Roberta Cheney. *So Long, Cowboys of the Open Range.* Helena, Mont.: Privately printed, 1990.

Coburn, Walt. *Pioneer Cattleman in Montana: The Story of the Circle C Ranch.* Norman: University of Oklahoma Press, 1972.

Costello, Gladys, and Dorothy Whitcomb Klimper. *Top o' the Mountain: Charley Whitcomb, Mining Man in Zortman.* Great Falls, Mont.: Privately printed, 1976.

Cunningham, Eugene. *Triggernometry.* Reprint. Caldwell, Idaho: Caxton Printers, 1971.

David, Robert. *Malcolm Campbell, Sheriff.* Casper, Wyo.: S. E. Boyer and Co., 1932.

Davis, Jean. *Shallow Diggin's.* Caldwell, Idaho: Caxton Printers, 1962.

Dawson County Bicentennial Committee. *Montana Stockgrowers 1900 Directory of Marks and Brands.* Reprint. Glendive, Mont.: Dawson County Bicentennial Committee, 1974.

Dempsey, Hugh A. *Big Bear: The End of Freedom.* Lincoln, Nebr.: Bison Books, 1984.

Didier, Hazel, ed. *The Yesteryears*. Malta, Mont.: Phillips County Historical Society, 1978.

Drago, Harry. *Great American Cattle Trails*. New York: Bramhill House, 1965.

Duvall, Walter, with Helen Duvall-Arthur. *Memories of a Filly Chaser*. Great Falls, Mont.: Privately printed, 1992.

Eide, Marlene, ed. *The Wonder of Williams County, North Dakota*. 2 vols. Williston, N.D.: Williams County Historical Society, 1975.

Engbretson, Dave. *Forgotten Names, Empty Saddles: Outlaws of the Black Hills and Wyoming*. Aberdeen, S.D.: North Plains Press, 1982.

Ernst, Donna. *Sundance, My Uncle*. College Station, Tex.: Creative Publishing Co., 1992.

Federal Writers' Project, Works Progress Administration. *Colorado*. The American Guide Series. Reprint. New York: Hastings House, 1946.

———. *Idaho*. The American Guide Series. Reprint. New York: Oxford University Press, 1960.

———. *Montana*. The American Guide Series. Reprint. New York: Hastings House, 1946.

———. *North Dakota*. The American Guide Series. Reprint. New York: Oxford University Press, 1950.

———. *Oklahoma*. The American Guide Series. Reprint. Norman: University of Oklahoma Press, 1941.

———. *South Dakota*. The American Guide Series. Reprint. New York: Hastings House, 1952.

———. *Texas*. The American Guide Series. Reprint. New York: Hastings House, 1940.

———. *Wyoming*. The American Guide Series. Reprint. Lincoln, Nebr.: Bison Books, 1981.

Fletcher, Robert. *Free Grass to Fences*. New York: University Publishers, 1960.

Franzen, Doris, ed. *Footprints of the Valley*. 3 vols. Glasgow, Mont.: History Committee, 1991.

French, William. *Some Recollections of a Western Ranchman*. New York: Argosy-Antiquarian, 1965.

Friesen, Gerald. *The Canadian Prairie, a History*. Toronto: University of Toronto Press, 1984.

Garcia, Andrew. *Tough Trip through Paradise, 1878–1879, [the autobiography of] Andrew Garcia*. Edited by Bennett H. Stein. Reprint. Sausalito, Calif.: Comstock Editions, 1986.

Giebel, Doug, ed. *In Print: Havre, Montana*. Vol. 1. Big Sandy, Mont.: Privately printed, 1987.

Hegne, Barbara. *Border Outlaws of Montana, North Dakota and Canada*. Eagle Point, Ore.: Privately printed, 1993.

Horan, James. *The Gunfighters: The Authentic Wild West.* New York: Crown Publishers, 1976.

———. *Desperate Men: The Rise, Reign, and Fall of the West's Most Notorious Outlaws.* Rev. ed. New York: Ballantine Books, 1974.

———. *The Wild Bunch.* New York: Signet Books, 1958.

Horan, James, and Paul Sann. *Pictorial History of the Wild West.* New York: Crown Publishers, 1954.

Howard, Joseph Kinsey. *Montana: High, Wide, and Handsome.* New Haven, Conn.: Yale University Press, 1974.

Jordan, Arthur. *Jordan.* Missoula, Mont.: Mountain Press, 1984.

Kelley, Charles. *The Outlaw Trail: A History of Butch Cassidy and His Wild Bunch.* Rev. ed. New York: Bonanza Books, 1959.

Kennedy, Michael, ed. *Cowboys and Cattlemen, a Roundup from Montana, The Magazine of Western History.* New York: Hastings House, 1964.

Kenworth, Jesse. *Storms of Life: The Outlaw Trail and Kid Curry.* Bozeman, Mont.: Quarter Circle Enterprises, 1990.

Kirby, Edward. *The Rise and Fall of the Sundance Kid.* Iola, Wis.: Western Publishers, 1983.

Kuykendall, W. L. *Frontier Days.* Cheyenne, Wyo.: Privately printed, 1917.

Lamb, F. Bruce. *Kid Curry: The Life and Times of Harvey Logan and the Wild Bunch.* Boulder, Colo.: Johnson Books, 1991.

Lamb, Frank. *The Wild Bunch.* Edited by Alan Swallow. Denver: Sage Books, 1966.

Lefors, Joe. *Wyoming Peace Officer.* Laramie, Wyo.: Powder River Publishers, 1953.

Lenz, Louis. *The N.P.R. Data Tables.* Walla Walla, Wash.: Privately printed, 1978.

Long, Phillip. *Forty Years a Cowboy.* Billings, Mont.: Cypress Press, 1976.

Loomis, John A. *Texas Ranchman: The Memories of John A. Loomis.* Edited by Herman Viola and Sarah Loomis Wilson. Chadron, Nebr.: Fur Press, 1982.

Malone, Michael, and Richard Roeder. *Montana, a History of Two Centuries.* Seattle: University of Washington Press, 1976.

Martin, Albro. *James J. Hill & The Opening of the Northwest.* New York: Oxford University Press, 1976.

McAuliffe, Eugene. *Early Coal Mining in the West.* Omaha: Newcomen Society, 1948.

Meloy, Mark. *Islands on the Prairie.* Helena: Montana Magazine, 1986.

Mercer, A. S. *The Banditti of the Plains.* Reprint. Norman: University of Oklahoma Press, 1987.

Merriam, H. G. *Way Out West.* Norman: University of Oklahoma Press, 1969.

Miller, Nyle, and Joseph Snell. *Great Gunfighters of the Kansas Towns, 1867–1886.* Lincoln: University of Nebraska Press, 1963.

Mokler, Alfred. *The History of Natrona County [Wyo.].* Chicago: R. R. Donnelly and Sons, 1923.

Montana Writers Project. Montana Writers Project Inventory: Livestock History for Daniels, Sheridan, and Valley Counties, Circa 1939. In Montana Historical Society Archives, Helena.

Murray, Erlene Durrant. *Lest We Forget: A Short History of Early Grand Valley, Colorado, Originally Called Parachute, Colorado.* Grand Junction, Colo.: Quahada, 1973.

Noyes, Alfred. *In the Land of Chinook, or, The History of Blaine County.* Helena, Mont.: State Publishing Co., 1917.

O'Neal, Bill. *Encyclopedia of Western Gunfighters.* Norman: University of Oklahoma Press, 1979.

Overholser, Joel. *Fort Benton, World's Innermost Port.* Fort Benton, Mont.: Privately printed, 1989.

Paladin, Vivian, ed. *From Buffalo Bones to Sonic Boom: Seventy-fifth Anniversary Souvenir.* Glasgow, Mont.: Jubilee Committee, 1962.

Parker, Watson. *Deadwood. The Golden Years.* Lincoln: University of Nebraska Press Bison Books, 1981.

Patterson, Richard. *Historical Atlas of the Outlaw West.* Boulder, Colo.: Johnson Books, 1985.

Phillips County Jubilee Committee. *Railroads to Rockets, 1887–1962: The Diamond Jubilee of Phillips County, Montana.* Malta, Mont.: Phillips County Jubilee Committee, 1962.

Pointer, Larry. *In Search of Butch Cassidy.* Norman: University of Oklahoma Press, 1977.

Progressive Men of Montana. Chicago: A. W. Brown and Co., 1901.

Rankin, M. Wilson. *Reminiscences of Frontier Days.* Denver: Privately printed, 1935.

Ranstrom, Barbara, and Dan Friede, eds. *Chinook: The First 100 Years.* Chinook, Mont.: Centennial '89ers, 1989.

Redford, Robert. *The Outlaw Trail. A Journey Through Time.* New York: Grosset and Dunlap, 1981.

Robbins, Vista, ed. *A Local Community History of Valley County.* Glasgow, Mont.: Montana Federation of Women's Clubs, 1925.

Rue, L. E., ed. *Plentywood's Golden Years, 1912–1962.* Plentywood, Mont.: Golden Anniversary Committee, 1962.

Russell, Charles M. *Good Medicine: The Illustrated Letters of Charles M. Russell.* Garden City, N.J.: Doubleday, 1930.

———. *Trails Plowed Under.* New York: Doubleday, 1927.

Sandoz, Mari. *The Cattlemen.* Reprint. Lincoln: University of Nebraska Press, 1978.

Santee, Ross. *Lost Pony Tracks.* New York: Bantam Books, 1956.

Sedlacek, Signe, ed. *Grit, Guts and Gusto: A History of Hill County.* Havre: The Hill County Bicentennial Commission, 1976.

Segars, Lorretta, ed. *One Hundred Years in Culbertson, 1887–1987.* Culbertson, Mont.: Steering Committee, 1986.

Selcer, Richard. *Hell's Half Acre.* Fort Worth: Texas Christian University Press, 1991.

Sharp, Paul. *Whoop-Up Country: The Canadian-American West, 1865–1885.* Norman: University of Oklahoma Press, 1973.

Shirley, Glenn. *Henry Starr, Last of the Real Badmen.* New York: David McKay, 1965.

———. *Law West of Fort Smith.* Reprint. Lincoln, Nebr.: Bison Books, 1968.

———. *West of Hell's Fringe: Crime, Criminals, and Federal Police Officers in Oklahoma Territory, 1889–1907.* Norman: University of Oklahoma Press, 1978.

Siringo, Charles. *A Cowboy Detective: A True Story of Twenty-two Years with a World Famous Detective Agency.* Reprint. Lincoln: University of Nebraska Press, 1981.

———. *A Lonestar Cowboy.* Cleveland: The Arthur Clark Co., 1919.

Smith, Helena Huntington. *The War on Powder River: The History of an Insurrection.* Reprint. Lincoln: University of Nebraska Press Bison Books, 1967.

Stone, Elizabeth. *Uinta, Its Place in History.* Laramie, Wyo.: Privately published, 1924.

Syverad, Edgar. *Historic Sheridan County.* Plentywood, Mont.: Privately printed, 1939.

Thiessen, Nancy. *Empty Boots, Dusty Corrals.* Salt Lake City: Sterling Press, 1986.

Thomas, Lewis, ed. *The Prairie West to 1905: A Canadian Sourcebook.* Toronto: Oxford University Press, 1975.

Turner, Peter. *North-West Mounted Police.* 2 vols. Ottawa: King's Printer and Controller of Stationery, 1950.

Walker, Don. *Cleo's Cowboys.* Lincoln: University of Nebraska Press, 1981.

Walker, Tacetta. *Stories of Early Days in Wyoming, Big Horn Basin.* Casper, Wyo.: Prairie Publishing Co., 1936.

Waller, Brown. *Last of the Great Western Train Robbers.* New York: A. S. Barnes, 1968.

Warner, Matt, as told to Murray King. *Last of the Bandit Riders.* New York: Bonanza Books, 1938.

Watts, Peter. *A Dictionary of the Old West.* New York: Promontory Press, 1987.

Webb, Walter Prescott. *The Great Plains*. Reprint. New York: Grosset and Dunlap, 1972.

———. *The Texas Rangers*. Boston: Houghton-Mifflin, 1935.

Wellman, Paul. *A Dynasty of Outlaws*. Lincoln: University of Nebraska Press Bison Books, 1986.

Willard, John. *Adventure Trails in Montana*. Helena, Mont.: State Publishing Co., 1964.

———. *Honky-Tonk Town: Havre, Montana's Lawless Eva*. Guilford, Conn.: TwoDot imprint, Globe Pequot Press, 2006.

———. *"Long George" Francis: Gentleman Outlaw of Montana*. Guilford, Conn.: TwoDot Imprint, Globe Pequot Press, 2005.

Wolle, Muriel Sibell. *Montana Pay Dirt*. Denver: Sage Books, 1982.

Young, Paul. *Back Trail of an Old Cowboy*. Lincoln: University of Nebraska Press, 1983.

Articles

"Beaver Creek Originally Part of Military Post," *Great Falls Tribune*, June 6, 1943.

Breihan, Carl. "Big Nose George Parrott," *The Branding Iron* [newsletter of the Los Angeles Corral of the Westerners], September 1955.

Brekke, Al. "The Currys Were a Wild Bunch, Harlem to Hole-in-the-Wall," parts 1 and 2 in *Chinook Opinion,* June 29, 1988; July 6, 1988.

Buck, Dan, and Anne Meadows. "The Wild Bunch in South America," parts 1–4 in *The Journal* [of the Western Outlaw-Lawman History Association], 1991–1992.

———. "Where Lies Butch Cassidy?" *Old West,* Fall 1991.

Coburn, Walt. "The Night 'Dutch Henry' Played Santa Claus," *True West,* September–October 1969.

Cochran, Keith. "A Bisley with a History," *Gun Report,* September 1966.

Costello, Gladys. "A Frontier Marshall Turns in His Star," *Great Falls Tribune,* November 4, 1954.

———. "Former Stagecoach Driver [Ruel Horner] Recalls Little Rockies Boom," *Great Falls Tribune,* November 22, 1959.

———. "Malta Cattle Country," *Montana Magazine,* Spring 1977.

DeMattos, Jack. "Gunfighters of the Real West," *Real West,* October 1983.

Donovan, Roberta. "Ghost Towns Haunted by Feel of Montana's Past," *Great Falls Tribune,* June 18, 1978.

Dullenty, Jim. "He Saw Kid Curry Rob Great Northern Train," Quarterly of the National Association and Center for Outlaw and Lawman History, 1985.

Dullenty, Jim, and Ben Garthofner, with Robbie Lucke. "New Gold Rush in the Little Rockies," *True West,* March 1984.

Ferris, Robert, ed. "Prospector, Cowhand, and Sodbuster," in *National Survey of Historic Sites and Buildings,* Vol. 11. Washington, D.C.: National Park Service, 1967.

Fletcher, Bob. "Smoke Signals," *Montana the Magazine of Western History,* April 1952.

Gilette, F B. "Many Notorious Badmen Were at Saco," *Nashua Independent,* March 23, 1931.

Gunderson, Carl. "The High Line," in *A History of Montana, Burlingame and Toole.* New York: Lewis Historical Publishing, 1957.

Johnson, Dorothy M. "Durable Desperado Kid Curry," *Montana the Magazine of Western History,* April 1956.

Kindred, Wayne. "Harvey Logan's Secret Letters," *True West,* October 1994.

Lamb, John A. "Harvey Logan's Lost Journal," *True West,* October 1994.

Larson, Kim. "Ursulines Return to Roots for 100th Anniversary: Early Days Come Alive," *Billings Gazette,* November 13, 1983.

Mann, Robert. "Outlaws of the Big Muddy: The North End of the Outlaw Trail," *The Journal* [of the Western Outlaw-Lawman History Association], Spring–Summer 1992.

Miller, Robert. "Kid Curry, Montana Outlaw," *Montana Magazine,* Spring 1976.

Morin, Marvin. "Two Graves in Montana, Mute Evidence of Frontier Violence," *True West,* March 1984.

Powers, Jacob Mathew. "Montana Episodes: Tracking Con Murphy," *Montana the Magazine of Western History,* Autumn 1980.

Ritch, John. "Two Two-Gun Gunners of the Ranges Were Real: He-Men of the Golden West," *Miles City Star,* Golden Jubilee issue, May 24, 1934.

Saindon, Bob. "Stealing of Coat Finally Led to Man's Hanging by Mob," *Glasgow Courier,* Diamond Jubilee issue, October 9, 1962.

———. "The Shooting of Long Henry," *Glasgow Courier,* Diamond Jubilee issue, October 9, 1962.

Steckmesser, Kent. "Lawmen and Outlaws," in *A Literary History of the American West.* n.p.: 1987.

"Where Was Loney Curry at Train Robbery Holdup?" *Great Falls Tribune,* Montana Parade section, November 17, 1957.

White, Richard. "Outlaw Gangs of the Middle Border: America's Social Bandits," *Western Historical Quarterly,* October 1981.

Wilson, Gary A. "Con Murphy, Montana's Last Vigilante Hanging," *Great Falls Tribune,* September 23, 1984.

Newspapers

Chinook Opinion
Fort Benton River Press
Great Falls Tribune
Harlem News
Havre Advocate
Havre Herald Plaindealer
Havre Plaindealer
Havre Promoter
Malta Enterprise
Seattle Times
Spokane Spokesman Review

Nebraska Outlaws

Blackbird

Sheldon, Addison Erwin. *History and Stories of Nebraska*. Chicago, IL: The University Publishing Co., 1914.

Flatnose Currie and the Wild Bunch

Ernst, Donna B. *The Sundance Kid: The Life of Harry Alonzo Longabaugh*. Norman, OK: University of Oklahoma Press, 2009.
Nash, Jay Robert. *Encyclopedia of Western Lawmen & Outlaws*. New York: Marlowe & Co., 1992.
"Wild Bunch," *Britannica Student Encyclopedia*.

Annie Cook

Lears, Jackson. *Rebirth of a Nation: The Making of Modern America, 1877–1920*. New York: HarperCollins Publishers, 2009.
Sehnert, Walt. "Annie Cook and Her Evil Obsession," *McCook Daily Gazette* (McCook, Nebraska), April 27, 2009.
Yost, Nellie Snyder. *Evil Obsession: The Annie Cook Story*. Lincoln, NE: Dageforde Publishing, Inc., 1991.

Nevada Outlaws

Andrew Jackson "Big Jack" Davis

Eureka Daily Sentinel, September 5, 6, 7, 9, 1877.
Virginia City Territorial Enterprise, November 1, 1866; December 16, 1870; September 5, 9, 1877.

Nicanor Rodrigues

Block, Eugene B. *Great Stagecoach Robbers of the West.* Garden City: Doubleday & Co., 1962.

Drury, Wells. *An Editor on the Comstock Lode.* Palo Alto: Pacific Books, 1936.

Sacramento Daily Union, April 24, 1856.

William Thorington

Bancroft, Hubert Howe. *The Works of Hubert Howe Bancroft,* vol. 36. San Francisco: The History Company, 1887.

Ellison, Robert W. *Territorial Lawmen of Nevada,* vol. 1. Minden, NV: Hot Springs Mountain Press, 1999.

Fairfield, Asa. *Fairfield's Pioneer History of Lassen County, California.* San Francisco: H. S. Crocker, 1916.

Makley, Michael J. *The Hanging of Lucky Bill.* Woodfords, CA: Eastern Sierra Press, 1993.

Thompson & West. *History of Nevada.* Berkeley: Howell-North, 1881 (reproduction 1958).

New Mexico Outlaws

Vincent Silva

Bryan, Howard. *Wildest of the Wild West: True Tales of a Frontier Town on the Santa Fe Trail.* Santa Fe: Clear Light Publishers, 1988.

De Baca, Carlos. C., *Vincent Silva: New Mexico's Vice King of the Nineties.* Las Vegas: Smith-Hursch, 1938.

L'Aloge, Bob. *The Code of the West.* Las Cruces: Yucca Tree Press, 1992.

McGrath, Tom. *Vincent Silva and His Forty Thieves.* Las Vegas: Fray Angélico Chávez History Library, 1960.

Simmons, Marc. *When Six-Guns Ruled.* Santa Fe: Ancient City Press, 1990.

Stanley, F. *Desperados of New Mexico.* Denver: World Press, 1953.

Therp, N. Howard. *Bandits of New Mexico.* Santa Fe: Fray Angélico Chávez History Library.

"The Worst Outlaw." *Santa Fe Reporter,* August 13, 1981, p. 19.

Pancho Villa

Askins, Charles. *Gunfighters.* Washington, DC: National Rifle Association of America, 1981.

Dean, Richard R. *The Columbus Story.* Columbus, NM: Friends of Pancho Villa State Park, 1991.

"Pancho Villa's Columbus Raid." Oral history videotape, Pancho Villa State Park, Columbus, NM.

"Prisoners Here from Columbus." *The Deming Headlight,* March 17, 1916.

Wallace, Andrew. "The Sabre Retires: Pershing's Cavalry Campaign in Mexico, 1916." Tucson, *The Smoke Signal, Tucson Corral of the Westerners,* Spring 1964, no. 9.

Yockelson, Mitchell. *The United States Armed Forces and the Mexican Punitive Expedition: Part 1 & 2.* Washington, DC: The US National Archives & Records Administration, September 2, 2006.

Hoodoo Brown and the Dodge City Gang

Hertzog, Peter, *Outlaws of New Mexico,* Santa Fe, NM: Sunstone Press, 1984.

Nash, Jay Robert. *Encyclopedia of Western Lawmen & Outlaws.* New York, NY: Da Capo Press, 1994.

http://blog.gratefulweb.net/2010/09/old-west-hoodoo-brown.html.

http://en.wikipedia.org/wiki/dodge_city_gang.

http://en.wikipedia.org/wiki/hoodoo_brown.

www.edge.net/~dphillip/Outlaw.html.

www.farwest.it/?p=339.

www.legendsofamerica.com/we_dodgecitygang.html.

Oklahoma Outlaws

Ned Christie

Harmon, S. W. *Hell on the Border: He Hanged Eighty-Eight Men.* Muskogee, Okla.: Indian Heritage Association, 1971.

Shirley, Glenn. *Heck Thomas, Frontier Marshal.* Norman: University of Oklahoma Press, 1981.

Speer, Bonnie Stahlman. *The Killing of Ned Christie.* Norman, Okla.: Reliance Press, 1990.

Steele, Phillip. *The Last Cherokee Warriors.* Gretna, La.: Pelican Publishing Company, 1974.

Henry Starr

Harmon, S. W. *Hell on the Border: He Hanged Eighty-Eight Men.* Muskogee, Okla.: Indian Heritage Association, 1971.

Nix, Evett Dumas. *Oklahombres: Particularly the Wilder Ones.* Lincoln: University of Nebraska Press, 1993.

Shirley, Glenn. *Last of the Real Badmen: Henry Starr.* Lincoln: University of Nebraska Press, 1976.

George Birdwell

Smith, Robert Barr. *Tough Towns: True Tales from the Gritty Streets of the Old West.* Guilford, Conn.: Globe Pequot Press, 2007.

Oregon Outlaws

The DeAutremont Brothers and Range Wars

Alexander, Doug. "Secret Deal." *The Beaver,* Canada's National History Society, December/January 2006, pp. 22–27.

Atwood, Kay, and Dennis Gray. *As Long as the World Goes On: The Land and People of Southwestern Oregon.* Portland: The Oregon History Project, Oregon Historical Society, 2005.

Bartlett, Grace. *From the Wallowas.* Enterprise, OR: Pika Press, 1992.

Blakely, James, and Herbert Lundy. "When the Juniper Trees Bore Fruit." *Portland Oregonian,* March 12, 19, and 26, 1939.

Braly, David. *Juniper Empire: Early Days in Eastern and Central Oregon.* Prineville, OR: American Media Co., 1976.

Brogan, Phil. *East of the Cascades.* Portland, OR: Binford & Mort, 1971.

Capi, Lynn. "1923 Botched Train Holdup Nears Anniversary." *Statesman-Journal,* October 7, 2003.

Chipman, Art. *Tunnel 13.* Medford, OR: Pine Cone Publishers, 1977.

Crook County Historical Society. "Reign of the Vigilantes." Pamphlets #44 and #58, Bowman Museum, Prineville, OR.

Crook County Historical Society. "Sheep and Cattle Wars." Pamphlets #57 and #141, Bowman Museum, Prineville, OR.

DeAutremont, Ray. "Ray DeAutremont's Confession." June 23, 1927.

Finn, John D. "Bandits' Stolen Gold Still Missing." *News-Register,* McMinnville, OR, July 6, 2011.

Highberger, Mark. *Snake River Massacre.* Wallowa, Ore.: Bear Creek Press, 2000.

Horner, John Harley. "The Horner Papers." Wallowa County Historical Society.

Joers, Lawrence E. C. "Passenger on Number 13." *Oregon,* January 1980, pp. 125–30.

Kramer, George. "Mining in Southwestern Oregon: A Historic Context Statement." Eugene, OR: Heritage Research Associates Report No. 234, December 1999.

McArthur, Lewis A. *Oregon Geographic Names.* Portland: Oregon Historical Society Press, 1982.

McArthur, Lewis A., and Lewis L. McArthur. *Oregon Geographic Names.* Portland: Oregon Historical Society Press, 2003.

McCarthy, Linda. *A History of Oregon Sheriffs, 1841–1991*. Portland: Oregon Sheriffs Association, Taylor Publishing Company, 1992.

Meier, Gary and Gloria. *Oregon Outlaws*. Boise, Idaho: Tamarack Books, 1996.

Oregon Sheriff's Archives, Benton County.

Oregon Sheriff's Archives, Grant County.

Oregon Sheriff's Archives, Harney County.

Oregon Sheriff's Archives, Jackson County.

Oregon Sheriff's Archives, Malheur County.

Oregon Sheriff's Archives, Marion County.

Oregon Sheriff's Archives, Umatilla County.

Oregon State Archives. "Oregon Blue Book." Salem, OR, 2011.

Personal communication, Gary Dielman, curator, Baker County Library, Baker County Historical Society, Baker City, OR.

Peterson del Mar, David. *The World Rushed In: Northeastern Oregon*. Portland: The Oregon History Project, Oregon Historical Society, 2005.

Salem Public Library. "Salem Online History."

Warren, Larry. "Oregon's Legendary Sheriff." *Frontier Times,* October–November 1973, pp. 6–9.

Washington Sheriff's Archives, King County.

Webber, Bert. *Oregon's Great Train Holdup*. Fairfield, WA: Ye Galleon Press, 1973.

Wells, Fargo. "Wells, Fargo Since 1952." Wells, Fargo Museum.

South Dakota Outlaws

Chief Two Sticks

Brown, Dee. *Bury My Heart at Wounded Knee: An Indian History of the American West*. New York: Henry Holt and Company, 1970.

Carr, G. Sam. "Sioux Chief Two Sticks." *Wild West* (June 2001).

Newson, T. M. *Thrilling Scenes among the Indians. With a Graphic Description of Custer's Last Fight with Sitting Bull*. Chicago and New York: Belford, Clarke and Company, 1884. http://digital.library.wisc.edu/1711.dl/ History.

Reno, Marcus A. *The Official Record of a Court of Inquiry Convened at Chicago, Illinois, January 13, 1879, by the President of the United States upon the Request of Major Marcus A. Reno, 7th U.S. Cavalry, to Investigate His Conduct at the Battle of the Little Big Horn, June 25–26, 1876*. Pacific Palisades, Calif.: U.S. Government, 1951. http://digital.library.wisc .edu/1711.dl/History.Reno.

Utley, Robert M. *The Lance and the Shield: The Life and Times of Sitting Bull*. New York: Henry Holt and Company, 1993.

Martin Couk

Bennett, Estelline. *Old Deadwood Days*. Lincoln, Neb.: University of Nebraska Press, 1982.

Black Hills Daily Times, November 3, 1877; August 20, 21, 23,1878; September 9, 11, 1878; November 6, 19, 22, 23, 25, 30, 1878; December 2, 1878; January 24, 1879; February 3, 12, 14, 15, 17, 18, 19, 1880; March 6, 13, 16, 26, 1880; April 2, 15, 1880; May 20, 25, 1880; June 17, 1880; August 10, 28, 1880; October 12, 1881; November 28, 1881; December 21, 1881; February 14, 1882; November 2, 1883.

Bryant, Jerry L. "Deadwood's First Schoolteacher." Deadwood, S.Dak., research for Adams Museum; unpublished. October 2003.

Deadwood Daily Pioneer Times, June 1, 1887.

Parker, Watson. *Deadwood: The Golden Years*. Lincoln, Neb.: University of Nebraska Press, 1981.

Stella and Bennie Dickson

Cecil, Charles F. *Remember the Time*. Brookings, S.Dak.: Charles Cecil Publishing, 2002.

Elkton Record, September 1, November 3, 1938.

Interview. Dr. Matthew Cecil, professor of journalism, South Dakota State University, Brookings, South Dakota, April 2007.

Newton, Michael. *Encyclopedia of Robbers, Heists, and Capers*. New York: Facts on File, 2002.

Texas Outlaws

Sostenes L'Archévèque

Haley, J. Evetts. "L'Archévèque, the Outlaw." *The Shamrock Magazine,* Fall 1958.

McCarty, John L. *Maverick Town: The Story of Old Tascosa*. Norman: University of Oklahoma Press, 1946.

Parkman, Francis. *La Salle and the Discovery of the Great West*. Boston: Little, Brown, and Co., 1880.

Turner, George. "A Killer's Legacy of Terror." *Amarillo Sunday News Globe,* September 25, 1966.

Myra Belle Shirley

Austin Daily Statesman, April 9 and April 17, 1874.

Marriage record of James C. Reed and Myra Belle Shirley, recorded November 11, 1866, in Volume 3, Page 49, Marriage Records of Collin County, Texas.

Rascoe, Burton. *Belle Starr, the Bandit Queen.* New York: Random House, 1941.

Shackleford, William Yancey. *Belle Starr, the Bandit Queen.* Girard, Kansas: Haldeman-Julius, 1943.

Shirley, Glenn. *Belle Starr and Her Times.* Norman: University of Oklahoma Press, 1982.

West Texas Free Press, April 11, 18, and 25; May 2; August 15; and September 5, 1874.

Juan Nepomuceno Cortina

Dobie, J. Frank. *A Vaquero of the Brush Country.* London: Hammond, Hammond & Co., 1949.

Paredes, Américo. *With His Pistol in His Hand: A Border Ballad and Its Hero.* Austin: University of Texas Press, 1958.

Stuart, Ben C. "The Rio Grande Raiders." *The Texas Magazine,* March 1910, 46–50.

Thompson, Jerry D. *Juan Cortina and the Texas–Mexico Frontier.* El Paso: Texas Western Press, 1994.

US Congress. House. *Texas Border Troubles.* 45th Cong., 1st sess., serial 1820. H. Misc. Doc. 64.

———. *Troubles on the Texas Frontier.* 36th Cong., 1st sess., serial 1056. H. Exec. Doc. 81.

Utah Outlaws

The Castle Gate Payroll Robbery and Orin Porter Rockwell

Baker, Pearl. *The Wild Bunch at Robbers Roost.* New York: Abelard-Schuman, 1971. Reprint. Lincoln: University of Nebraska Press, 1989.

Betenson, Bill. "Lula Parker Betenson." *Outlaw Trail Journal,* Winter 1995.

Betenson, Lula, and Dora Flack. *Butch Cassidy, My Brother.* Provo, Utah: Brigham Young University Press, 1975.

Achilles [Sirine, Samuel D.]. *The Destroying Angels of Mormondom; or a Sketch of the Life of Orrin Porter Rockwell, the Late Danite Chief.* San Francisco, 1878.

Arrington, Leonard J. *Brigham Young: American Moses.* New York: Alfred A. Knopf, 1985.

Bagley, Will. *Blood of the Prophets: Brigham Young and the Massacre at Mountain Meadows.* Norman: University of Oklahoma Press, 2002.

Beadle, J. H. *Western Wilds, and the Men Who Redeem Them.* Cincinnati: Jones Brothers, 1878.

Brown, Dee. *The American West.* New York: Charles Scribner's Sons, 1994.

Buck, Daniel, and Anne Meadows. "Showdown at San Vincente." *True West,* February 1993.

———. "Where Lies Butch Cassidy?" *Old West,* Fall 1991.

Burroughs, John Rolfe. *Where the Old West Stayed Young.* New York: William Morrow and Company, 1962.

Burton, Sir Richard Francis. *The City of the Saints and Across the Rocky Mountains to California.* London, 1861; New York, 1862.

Dewey, Richard Lloyd. *Porter Rockwell: A Biography.* New York: Paramount Books, 2006.

Dullenty, Jim. *The Butch Cassidy Collection.* Hamilton, Mont.: Rocky Mountain House Press, 1986.

Ernst, Donna B. "Black Gold and the Wild Bunch." *Quarterly of the National Association and Center for Outlaw and Lawmen History,* March 1994.

———. "Friends of the Pinkertons." *Quarterly of the National Association and Center for Outlaw and Lawmen History,* June 1995.

———. "The Sundance Kid: Wyoming Cowboy." *Western Outlaw-Lawman History Association Journal,* Spring 1992.

Hayden, Willard C. "Butch Cassidy and the Great Montpelier Bank Robbery." *Idaho Yesterdays,* Spring 1971.

Horan, James. *The Wild Bunch.* New York: Signet Books, 1958.

Jenson, Andrew. *Latter-day Saint Biographical Encyclopedia,* 4 vols. Salt Lake City: Andrew Jenson History Company, 1901–36.

Larson, T. A. *History of Wyoming.* Lincoln: University of Nebraska Press, 1965.

Meadows, Anne. *Digging Up Butch and Sundance.* New York: St. Martin's Press, 1994.

Morn, Frank. *The Eye That Never Sleeps: A History of the Pinkertons National Detective Agency.* Bloomington: Indiana University Press, 1982.

Patterson, Richard. *Butch Cassidy: A Biography.* Lincoln: University of Nebraska Press, 1998.

———. "Did the Sundance Kid Take Part in the Telluride Robbery?" *Western Outlaw-Lawman History Association Journal,* Summer 1994.

———. *Historical Atlas of the Outlaw West.* Boulder: Johnson Books, 1985.

Pointer, Larry. *In Search of Butch Cassidy.* Norman: University of Oklahoma Press, 1977.

Redford, Robert. *The Outlaw Trail: A Journey Through Time.* New York: Grosset & Dunlap, 1976.

Schindler, Harold. *Orrin Porter Rockwell: Man of God/Son of Thunder.* Salt Lake City: University of Utah Press, 1993.

Slatta, Richard W. "The Legendary Butch and Sundance." *The Mythical West: An Encyclopedia of Legend, Lore, and Popular Culture.* Santa Barbara, Calif.: ABC–CLIO, 2001.

Stegner, Wallace. *Mormon Country.* New York: Hawthorne Books, 1942.

Van Alfen, Nicholas. "Porter Rockwell and the Mormon Frontier, A Thesis Submitted to the Department of History of Brigham Young University in Partial Fulfillment of the Requirements for the Degree of Master of Fine Arts." Provo, 1938.

Walker, Herb. *Butch Cassidy.* Amarillo: Baxter Lane Company, 1975.

Washington Outlaws

Lawrence Kelly

New York Times. "A Smuggler Captured; Taken with Sixty-Five Cans of Opium in His Possession," March 15, 1891.

Seattle Post-Intelligencer, May 15, 1909.

Clark, Cecil. *The Daily Colonist,* April 8, 1962.

Cummings, Jo Bailey, and Al Cummings. *San Juan: The Powder Keg Island.* Friday Harbor, WA: Beach Combers, 1987.

Davenport, Marge. *Afloat and Awash in the Old Northwest.* Tigard, OR: Paddlewheel Press, 1988.

Dirks, Farmer. "Ship Owned by Pirate Kelly Discovered Here." *American Bulletin.* Anacortes, WA, September 2, 1955.

———. "Case of Missing Tools When Kelly Was Alive." *American Bulletin.* Anacortes, WA, September 9, 1955.

———. "Smuggler Kelly a Bad One, But Paid His Debts." *American Bulletin.* Anacortes, WA, September 12, 1955.

Jones, Roy Franklin. *Boundary Town: Early Days in a Northwest Boundary Town.* Vancouver: Fleet Printing Company, 1958.

McCurdy, James G. "Criss-Cross Over the Boundary: The Romance of Smuggling across the Northwest Frontier." Portland, OR, *The Pacific Monthly,* Volume XXIII, January to June 1910.

McDonald, Lucille S. "Kelly, the King of the Smugglers: Guemes, Sinclair Islands Were Headquarters of Notorious Operator in Years Long Past." *Seattle Times,* March 29, 1959.

———. *Making History: The People Who Shaped the San Juan Islands.* Friday Harbor, WA: Harbor Press, 1990.

———. "Old Records Tell How Puget Sound Customs Men Went About Tracking the Smugglers." *Seattle Times,* July 27, 1952.

Richardson, David. *Pig War Islands.* Eastsound, WA: Orcas Publishing Company, 1971.

Short, E. T. "The End of Lawrence Kelly." *Tacoma Times.*

Telephone interview with Pat Nelson, great-granddaughter of Lawrence Kelly, August 18, 2000.

Max Levy

Port Townsend Daily Leader, August 12, 1893.
Port Townsend Daily Leader, August 13, 1893.
Port Townsend Daily Leader, August 15, 1893.
Port Townsend Daily Leader, August 16, 1893.
Port Townsend Daily Leader, August 24, 1893.
Port Townsend Daily Leader, September 13, 1893.
Port Townsend Daily Leader, September 24, 1893.
Port Townsend Daily Leader, November 15, 1893.
Port Townsend Daily Leader, November 16, 1893.
Port Townsend Morning Leader, May 19, 1896.
Port Townsend Morning Leader, May 21, 1896.
Port Townsend Morning Leader, May 23, 1896.
Port Townsend Morning Leader, April 6, 1906.
Port Townsend Leader, August 28, 1996.
Seattle Times, September 9, 1962.
Canfield, Thomas W. *Port Townsend: An Illustrated History of Shanghaiing, Shipwrecks, Soiled Doves, and Sundry Souls.* Port Townsend, WA: Ah Tom Publishing, Inc., 2000.
Dillon, Richard H. *Shanghaiing Days.* New York: Coward-McCann, Inc., 1962.
Newell, Gordon. "Maritime Events of 1903." *H.W. McCurdy Marine History of the Pacific Northwest.* Seattle: Superior Publishing Company, 1966.
Newell, Gordon. *Sea Rogue's Gallery.* Seattle: Superior Publishing Company, 1971.
Simpson, Peter. *City of Dreams: A Guide to Port Townsend.* Port Townsend: The Bay Press, 1986.

Wyoming Outlaws

The Asa Moore Gang

Carroll, Murray L. "Judge Lynch Rides the Rails Bringing the Law to Laramie." *True West,* October 1995, p. 12.
Cheyenne (WY) *Daily Leader:* January 22, 1868; May 6, 1868; October 19–22, 1868.
Engebretson, Doug. *Empty Saddles, Forgotten Names: Outlaws of the Black Hills and Wyoming.* Aberdeen, SD: North Plains Press, 1984.
Gorzalka, Ann. *Wyoming's Territorial Sheriffs.* Glendo, WY: High Plains Press, 1998.

Butch Cassidy and the Sundance Kid

Baker, Pearl. *Utah 1890–1910: The Wild Bunch at Robbers' Roost*. New York: Ballantine Books, 1965.

Buck, Daniel, and Anne Meadows. "Butch & Sundance: Still Dead?" *NOLA Quarterly*, April–June 2006, p. 40.

Dullenty, Jim. "Wagner Train Robbery." *Old West*, Spring 1982, p. 40.

Ernst, Donna B. "Robbery Along the Great Northern." *True West*, June 1998, p. 46.

———. "The Wilcox Train Robbery." *Wild West*, June 1999, p. 34.

Horan, James D. *The Wild Bunch*. New York: Signet Books, 1958.

New York Times: July 3, 1901; July 6, 1901; July 8, 1901; October 16, 1901.

Overstreet, Charles. "A Train Robbery Turned Bad." *Old West*, Winter 1998, p. 49.

St. Louis Globe Democrat: November 29, 1892.

The Last Sheep Camp Raid

Basin (WY) *Republican*: August 31, 1905.

Buffalo (WY) *Voice*: September 2, 1906.

Carbon County Journal (Rawlins, WY): January 2, 1914; January 16, 1914; January 23, 1914.

Cheyenne (WY) *Leader*: February 7, 1874.

Gazette (Billings, MT): November 7, 1909.

Nevada State Journal (Reno, NV): November 7, 1909.

Rawlins (WY) *Republican*: November 2–13, 1909; November 20, 1909; December 25, 1913; January 8, 1914.

Reno (NV) *Evening Gazette*: April 30, 1907.

Schillinger, Duane. *In Wyoming's Prison, Hungry Men May Become Vicious Men, 1901–1981*. Bloomington, IN: Author House, 2004.

Sioux County (IA) *Herald*: January 17, 1906; April 17, 1909.

Talbot, Ethelbert P. *My People of the Plains*. New York, NY: Harper & Brothers, 1906.

Waterloo (IA) *Evening Courier*: November 17, 1909.

Sources

Outlaw Tales of Alaska, 2nd edition, John W. Heaton
    Klutuk
    Nellie "Black Bear" Bates and William Schermeyer
    Jefferson Randolph "Soapy" Smith

Outlaw Tales of Arizona, 2nd edition, Jan Cleere
    Augustine Chacón
    James Fleming Parker
    Albert Wright "Burt" Alvord

Outlaw Tales of California, 2nd edition, Chris Enss
    Tiburcio Vasquez
    John Allen
    Juan Flores

Outlaw Tales of Colorado, 2nd edition, Jan Murphy
    The Musgrove Gang
    Pug Ryan
    Lou Blonger

Outlaw Tales of Idaho, 2nd edition, Randy Stapilus
    The Eddys and the Splawns
    Diamondfield Jack
    Lyda Lewis

Outlaw Tales of Kansas, Sarah Smarsh
    Kate Bender
    Henry Brown
    George "Bitter Creek" Newcomb

Outlaw Tales of Missouri, 2nd edition, Sean Mclachlan
    The Slicker War
    Frank and Jesse James
    The Pendergasts

Outlaw Tales of Montana, 3rd edition, Gary A. Wilson
    Con Murphy
    George "Big Nose" Parrott

Outlaw Tales of Nebraska, T. D. Griffith
    Blackbird
    Flatnose Currie and the Wild Bunch
    Annie Cook

Outlaw Tales of Nevada, 2nd edition, Charles L. Convis
    Andrew Jackson "Big Jack" Davis
    Nicanor Rodrigues
    William Thorington
Outlaw Tales of New Mexico, 2nd edition, Barbara Marriott
    Vincent Silva
    Pancho Villa
    Hoodoo Brown and the Dodge City Gang
Outlaw Tales of Oklahoma, 2nd edition, Robert Barr Smith
    Ned Christie
    Henry Starr
    George Birdwell
Outlaw Tales of Oregon, 2nd edition, Jim Yuskavitch
    The DeAutremont Brothers
    Range Wars
Outlaw Tales of South Dakota, 2nd edition, T. D. Griffith
    Chief Two Sticks
    Martin Couk
    Stella and Bennie Dickson
Outlaw Tales of Texas, 2nd edition, Charles Convis
    Sostenes L'Archévèque
    Myra Belle Shirley
    Juan Nepomuceno Cortina
Outlaw Tales of Utah, 2nd edition, Michael Rutter
    The Castle Gate Payroll Robbery
    Orin Porter Rockwell
Outlaw Tales of Washington, 2nd edition, Elizabeth Gibson
    Lawrence Kelly
    Max Levy
Outlaw Tales of Wyoming, 2nd edition, R. Michael Wilson
    The Asa Moore Gang
    Butch Cassidy and the Sundance Kid
    The Last Sheep Camp Raid